From Gorky to Pasternak
SIX WRITERS IN SOVIET RUSSIA

FROM GORKY
TO PASTERNAK

Six Writers in Soviet Russia

HELEN MUCHNIC

Random House
New York

ACKNOWLEDGMENTS

Parts of these chapters, in somewhat different form, appeared as follows:
"Gorky"—in *Comparative Literature,* ed. Chandler B. Beall, University of Oregon, Eugene, Oregon
"Blok," "Mayakovsky," "Leonov," "Sholokhov"—in *The Russian Review,* ed. Dimitri von Mohrenschildt, 235 Baker Library, Hanover, N.H.
"Pasternak"—in *The Slavic and East European Journal,* ed. J. T. Shaw, Indiana University, Bloomington, Indiana

Acknowledgments are due for permission to quote, as follows:
The Oxford University Press, New York, for passages from Aylmer Maude's *Life of Tolstoy*
Crown Publishers, New York, for passages from *Soviet Literature, an Anthology,* edited and translated by George Reavey and Marc Slonim (Copyright 1934 Covici, Friede, Inc., and used by permission of Crown Publishers, Inc.)
Russell & Russell, for a passage from Leon Trotsky's *Literature and Revolution* (New York, 1957)
The Viking Press, Inc., for passages from the Compass edition of Gorky's *Reminiscences of Tolstoy, Chekhov, and Andreyev,* translated by S. S. Koteliansky and Leonard Woolf (New York, 1959)
Macmillan & Co., Ltd., for Sir Maurice Bowra's translation of Blok's "I Have Forebodings of Thee" in *A Book of Russian Verse* (London, 1947)
The Macmillan Company, for Avrahm Yarmolinsky's translation of Lermontov's "Gratitude" and Blok's "To Sin, Unshamed" in *A Treasury of Russian Verse* (Copyright 1949 The Macmillan Company, New York, and used by permission)
Simon & Schuster, for passages from Aylmer and Louise Maude's translation of Tolstoy's *War and Peace* (Copyright 1942 Simon and Schuster, Inc., New York, and used by permission)
New Directions, for passages from Boris Pasternak's *Safe Conduct: Selected Writings of Boris Pasternak,* translated by Beatrice Scott (Copyright © 1958 New Directions, New York; reprinted by permission of New Directions, Publishers)
Pantheon Books, Inc., New York (1959), and Collins Publishers, London, for passages from Boris Pasternak's *I Remember, Sketch for an Autobiography,* translated by David Magarshack

CONTENTS

From Gorky to Pasternak
SIX WRITERS IN SOVIET RUSSIA

INTRODUCTION

I

Toward the end of 1901 three great Russian writers met at Yalta. Each was there for reasons of health, and their meeting had not been prearranged. But in retrospect this meeting seems an epitome of changes that were taking place in the thought of the country, of major trends in its intellectual history. It was a little drama of Russian letters at the turn of the century. The three were Tolstoy, who was seventy-four years old; Chekhov, who was forty-two; and Gorky, thirty-three. In them three epochs met, three modes of thought, three classes of society: Tolstoy the landed aristocrat and enlightened individualist of the nineteenth century; Chekhov the middle-class intellectual of a transitional period, respectful of science, impatient with philosophical abstractions, troubled by his inability to integrate his fragmentary observations; and Gorky the proletarian revolutionist, very sure of his goals and his knowledge. The younger men looked upon Tolstoy with both veneration and distrust: he was a sage, a god, a magician, but his wisdom belonged to an age that had passed; the present was erecting new temples to other deities. Chekhov had long since admitted that Tolstoy, who once "filled his soul," had "departed" from it, leaving "the house empty," and Gorky's attitude was a complex mixture of resentment and awe. They admired, that is, the timeless qualities of the great old man —his artistic genius and moral stature—but disapproved of what seemed to them an outmoded social philosophy. Tolstoy was isolated, they thought, out of touch with Russia; the bold theories he was evolving could have no fruitful application and only gave scope to fanatics, opinionated, mealy-mouthed "Tolstoyans," who were retarding the progress of the country. Their age of industrial development, official repression, social stagnation, and growing proletarian discontent was not a time to be preaching nonresistance to evil by force, abstinence, asceticism, individual salvation, return to the land.

These practical objections involved less tangible, and more fundamental differences: attitudes to society, the mind, and the self, the elements that had shaped the main, that is, the "realistic" tradition of Russian literature. The work of the great Russian realists, while extremely varied, had always had this in common, that, rooted in the immediate life of the senses, it grew and developed in the broader reaches of idealism; remaining faithful, that is, to lived experience, it interpreted this experience in terms of ideals, and belonged as much to the life of reason as to that of the senses. That is why, although strongly national in outlook, inspired by the specific interests of a given place and a given moment, it has always had something to say to men of other nations and other times. Of this tradition, Tolstoy and Chekhov were essential parts; but if their art was an art of reason, reason itself played very different roles in their work. The whole of Tolstoy's creation was formed in a conflict between the ways of thought and the ways of feeling. His understanding of men took rise in the unhappy consciousness that rational processes prevented knowledge, that if anything could be known outside one's self, such knowledge must come intuitively. His entire philosophy (ethics, aesthetics, theory of history) proceeded, therefore, from the belief that simplicity, direct apprehension, a sense of the moment were the only means of grasping the meaning of an event, and of distinguishing right from wrong whether in morality or in art. Reflectiveness, analysis, attempted reconstruction of the past vitiated truth. It troubled Tolstoy that he and the world were not the same, and his great novels were a supreme effort to bridge the enormous gap between himself and all that lay beyond himself. His success is the special mark of his achievement: an imaginative identification with people, animals, and things so extraordinary as to endow whatever he writes about with a unique completeness and thence, however trivial to the world at large, with the importance of authentic being. But though he distrusted the mind, he was the most rational of anti-intellectualists, following the mind as far as it would go before acknowledging its inadequacy.

Chekhov's realism was not so inward nor so complex. His was the scientist's position that took empiric reality for granted. The world lay open to examination, and the observer's role was not unnatural. Chekhov looked on with a wry sympathy. Sometimes he diagnosed his nation's ills, but, unlike Tolstoy, he was chary of prescribing remedies. Suspicious of generalizations, he saw only how the mind was used or misused on specific occasions.

Gorky, in almost superstitious reverence, worshiped the mind, convinced of its omnipotence. But, as he himself acknowledged, he did not know how to think. At the time of the Yalta meeting, he was as yet unsure of his method and, except in a very general way, of his purpose. Three years earlier, his first collection of stories had brought him sudden fame in Russia, and he took his role as artist very seriously; seriously, that is, in its public capacity as a moral and educational influence. Now, talking eagerly with Tolstoy and

Chekhov, he jotted down comments on them which, as it turned out, contained some of the best pages he was ever to write: shrewd, rapid observations, very different from the analytic profundity of the one and the poetic grace of the other; and, although he himself was not aware of this, much better than the rhetorical play, *The Lower Depths,* on which he was at work, and which within a year was to make him as famous abroad as at home. His head was full of projects, and with all his admiration of Chekhov and his awe of Tolstoy, he knew that his writing would not be at all like theirs. His background was different from theirs, his knowledge and understanding of Russia were different, he addressed himself to another audience and was infinitely more concerned than they with the reactions of his readers.

The great change in Russian literature from the nineteenth century to the present has been largely due to altered relations between the writer and his audience, and the process of this change is already evident in the three friends at Yalta. Tolstoy's independence was absolute; he stood in calm defiance of the world, and whether others chose to follow or denounce him could not ruffle his composure. Chekhov was equally indifferent to public opinion, but, objectively concerned with what men were, rather than with what they should be, he was, paradoxically perhaps, closer to them than the all-encompassing Tolstoy, who demanded as much of all human beings as he asked of himself. Gorky, on the other hand, was completely involved in the lives and opinions of others; he was entirely dependent on his position in society. For unlike Tolstoy, the clear-headed rationalist and Romantic egotist who understood others as an extension of himself, and unlike Chekhov, in his scientific detachment, Gorky could be himself only as a member of some social or doctrinaire group of men. Tolstoy and Chekhov were too individualist to be partisan. Tolstoy might be the chosen legislator and prophet of a sect, Chekhov could be generally recognized as the most truthful chronicler of his epoch; neither achieved eminence by joining any clan or allying himself with any school of thought. They were originators, not followers. But Gorky had to follow before he could lead.

You must produce and express what has ripened in your soul [Tolstoy had written his friend, the artist Nikolay Nikolaevich Gué, in 1889], for it is something no one but you will ever express. . . .

Yes! As you know, what matters is not that Nikolay Nikolaevich be praised, but to feel that you are saying something new and important and something people need. And when one feels this and works for this—as you, I hope, are now working—it is the greatest happiness on earth. One is even ashamed of the privilege.

But is the artist always a good judge of people's needs and even of his own ripeness? In Tolstoy's case, were the "ripened" thought, the "needed" sermonizing of his old age as necessary to people as the wonderful, dramatic insights of his earlier years? Gorky certainly subscribed to the utilitarian view of art, but his idea of what was "needed" was not the same as Tolstoy's. And as for the process of "ripening in the soul," what seemed ripe to him, Tolstoy was likely to consider quite raw.

In the last two decades of the nineteenth century and the beginning of the twentieth, the nature of art and the artist's function called for redefinition. Tolstoy was the sole survivor of that Golden Age of Russian literature which had both flourished and declined under the aegis of utility. Now, reacting against this attitude, poets were insisting on the values of formal elements and of subjectivity, and engaging in a variety of artistic experiments. At the same time, civic-minded liberals braved imprisonment and exile, and wrote works of radical social protest. In art, that is, as in the thought of the time, there was a vast abundance of opinions, attitudes, and theories. Merezhkovsky and Vladimir Soloviëv were elaborating their several theologies; the anarchist Kropotkin and the terrorist Stepniak abroad, and the liberal Korolenko at home advocated political reform or revolution. Russian literature had once seemed homogeneous, rooted, as it were, in the same subsoil of basic attitudes and philosophic questions. Now it was breaking up, no longer the voice of a nation but of antagonistic coteries. Like religious and political thinkers, artists were becoming either more partisan than ever, or trying to free themselves altogether from the yoke of doctrines. There was a critical division between the "inward" and the "outward" school, which was by no means confined to Russia; in France, for example, it was equally sharp. Tolstoy, aware of both tendencies, sympathized with neither; and set forth his objections in *What Is Art?*, that notorious treatise on aesthetics on which he worked for fifteen years, before publishing it in 1898. Modern art was to him a logical consequence of the unfortunate splitting up of society, which ever since the Renaissance had divided men into groups of special interests and made artistic communication impossible. Emotions, he held, were the province of art as ideas were of speech; an artist "infected" others with his feelings, and the greater his work, the more universal were the emotions it communicated. But art could no longer express, as it had in the Middle Ages, a simple human experience that was the property of an entire people; it was no longer simple nor universally intelligible, now that it had become the plaything of coteries, the instrument of cliques, and increasingly the vehicle of inartistic concerns. One school, like Zola's, substituted for emotion the spurious values of factual curiosity; another, that of Gautier, Baudelaire, Verlaine, Mallarmé, made a cult of obscurity. And Tolstoy quoted passages from these writers which, he said, conveyed nothing to him. The polarities of Naturalism and Symbolism, which he condemned here in French literature, were complicated in Russia by the urgency of political issues; and indeed Russian literature in the twentieth century may be seen, in general outline, as a tragic contest between the two schools Tolstoy condemned, involving, like all great tragedy, the minds, the hearts, and the lives of men.

Russian Symbolism, like Russian Realism of the nineteenth century, paralleled, but did not imitate the French, differing from it in that it sought to be a way of life rather than a literary method. "The Symbolists did not wish to distinguish the writer from the man, the literary biography from the personal one," the poet and critic Vladislav Khodasevich wrote of them in a penetrating analysis.

Symbolism did not wish to be only a school of art, a literary trend [he wrote]. It was always straining to become a method of creativity and living, and in this lay its deepest, perhaps unrealizable, reality; but, in truth, its entire history was passed in the constant pursuit of this reality. It was a series of attempts, sometimes truly heroic, to fuse life and creation, to find a kind of philosopher's stone of art.

Of course, Khodasevich remarks, this attempted fusion did not belong to the Symbolists exclusively; it was only "most deeply and vividly experienced" by them, and was the source of their "gravest error," of their "mortal sin." The sin consisted in this, that having proclaimed the cult of individuality, Symbolism failed to provide it with any aim other than that of "self-development." It demanded "development," but "how, in whose name and in what direction," it "neither wished nor could" point out. "All paths were open and there was but one duty—to go as fast as possible and as far as possible." All that was required was that one be "completely possessed" by no matter what, whether by God or the devil. And so, there was a feverish pursuit of emotions and "experiences," regardless of consequences. Acting became life itself. The world was literally a stage, and the "beet juice" that oozed out of a puppet might well be the life blood of a living man. The central "experience" was love, which was required to be absolute, passionate, perfect. It was an "all or nothing" philosophy, a self-dramatization, an extravagant fantastication of emotions that wrecked happiness and led to suicide. Some of Russia's finest writers were involved in these tragic absurdities.

But the identification of art with life had always been more or less characteristic of Russian letters. Pushkin, Turgenev, Chekhov were unusual in their sophisticated detachment; that "poetic distance" which is the usual assumption of Western artists was, and still is, exceptional among the Russians. So that, as an attitude to life, the primary significance of the Symbolist school was not so much its metaphysics or aesthetics as its individualism, its insistence that individual experience, however eccentric or extreme, was an ultimate value. This individualist attitude, variously manifested, not only in Symbolism itself but in its several offshoots—Acmeism, Futurism, Formalism, as well as in the entirely personal nightmares of such writers as Leonid Andreyev—was to clash most sharply with the dogma of Soviet art.

II

The year 1905 is the watershed between the old Russia and the new. Chekhov did not live to see it, he died in 1904. Tolstoy, faithful to his views of nonresistance, remained in harried but uncompromising aloofness at Yasnaya Polyana.

I have lately returned from Yasnaya [his daughter Mary wrote his friend and biographer Aylmer Maude on January 22], where I spent two months. My father was well, but he is tormented by demands made on him to take part in current events. The Liberals want to draw him into their camp, the Conservatives into theirs, and the Revolutionists into theirs, and he does not belong to any one of them and only asks to be left in peace. People do not understand or admit his point of view, and think that in consequence of what is happening in Russia, he must come down from his Christian standpoint and say something new, and something they want him to say.

In general the war and all that is now happening in Russia is depressing, and weighs like a heavy burden on us all.

In February the London *Times* printed an article by Tolstoy written in answer to innumerable questions addressed to him from abroad about his views on what was taking place in Russia. His opinion was that the events were retarding progress, and that the only means of counteracting evil was through the moral perfectibility of individuals. News of the article appeared in the Russian press on the second of March, and three days later Gorky penned a vitriolic "open letter" to Tolstoy, which, however, he did not publish, having decided that the mass of protests it had already elicited made his own unnecessary. It has come out in the recent, complete edition of his works.

"Count Lev Nikolaevich!" he wrote, "great is the charm of your name; the literate people of the whole world harken to your words," and it was for this reason, because the whole world believed him, that he must be answered, Gorky went on. For what Tolstoy had said about the events that were taking place in Russia was untrue and misleading.

This is what I want to say to you, Count [he continued]. You no longer know what the plain people of our country live by; you do not know their spiritual world. You cannot speak of their desires; that right you relinquished the moment you stopped listening to the voice of the people. That is so, Count!

He himself had often seen with what "impatience and irritation" Tolstoy would "push aside" the opinions of the peasants and workers who came to see him, when "these opinions did not harmonize with the ideas to which [he had] surrendered [his] once independent soul." Resting on the summit of his belief in "individual perfectibility," he had lost sight of the people he kept at a distance and refused to know, and did not see how far they had gone "on the road to the realization of their human rights."

You have called untimely and unwise the actions of those to whom it is unbearably painful to see Russians going hungry, deprived of rights, crushed by the weight of oppression; to see how, through ignorance and fear, they are capable, for a glass of vodka, of beating and murdering anyone who is pointed out to them, even children.

That is an error, Count.

"You have called unwise" the work of those who want to establish the kind of order in Russia in which men might be

able to speak freely and entertain what faith they choose
without fear of being sent to jail or hard labor, like the
Dukhobors and thousands of other Russians who are

exiled, crippled, broken by our ruling class, which has grown savage in its efforts to maintain its power over the nation.

That is unjust, Count.

Count Lev Nikolaevich! The name you have earned as the
greatest of contemporary literary artists does not give you the
right to be unjust to men who love their people unselfishly and
sincerely, and work for them no less than you do.

More than you . . .

For these people are enduring the kind of suffering which
Tolstoy himself had once said he would want to undergo
for the sake of his beliefs.

These unknown, modest men suffer silently and manfully; in
hundreds of thousands they perish in the struggle for the liberation of their people, because they are ashamed of spiritual enslavement. You have the right to disagree with them, but you have
no right not to respect them, Count!

You are wrong in saying that land is all the peasant needs. In
this you contradict the Gospels, which you consider one of the
sources of pure wisdom. "Man lives not by bread alone," it is said
in them, and you yourself know that the Russian people, in addition to ownership of land, want also freedom of thought and faith,
and you know that for this they are sent to Siberia, driven out of
Russia.

In days when blood is shed in the streets of Russian cities,
when children are beaten up by the police, when after men
and women are shot down, the wounded are not permitted
to be moved away for a certain length of time, at a moment
when there are men who can "be hired for fifty kopeks a
day to cut down the intelligentsia, the purest and most un-
selfish section of the Russian nation," when in a senseless,
unnecessary and ruinous war that so fills newspapers with
"accounts of the sufferings of soldiers" that the sheets seem
"red and damp with human blood and the imagination pictures fields strewn with the corpses of peasants who have

been forcibly dressed in soldiers' coats," at a time of such barbarity as this, how is it possible "to think of peace and the peace of one's soul . . . to be concerned with one's own moral perfectibility?"

Finally, Tolstoy's letter to the *Times,* in addition to being callous, untruthful, and unjust, was also harmful, Gorky said, for it played into the hands of "vultures and parasites" who, in the interests of a tyrannical power, "defend injustice . . . preach nasty lies, and in every way corrupt Russian society." Gorky could see them "grinning" and "throwing in the face of the honest, manly men of Russia, the oppressive, insulting, triumphant and malicious words: 'Lev Tolstoy is not with you!' "

Thus Gorky inveighed against Tolstoy with fierce moral indignation reminiscent of Zola's celebrated *J'Accuse!* The scornfully repeated "Count!" was a pointed accusation of snobbery. Tolstoy was the irresponsible aristocrat, out of touch with the masses of his countrymen. His egotism shut him away from their needs and hopes, their sufferings and their heroism. He neither understood men nor cared for them, and in a period of national catastrophe and a bitter struggle for human rights, remained in the callous aloofness of his social and literary eminence. He had long since forfeited the right to be the spokesman of the Russian people; he who had once been independent was now a creature of tyranny.

It is hardly surprising that in a period of war and revolution, Tolstoy's severe morality could seem immoral, his exacting sense of individual responsibility, capricious and irresponsible, and his broad view of human ethics, an inhuman injustice to living men. Such judgments are habitual when public disasters engage all sympathies and cause any universal contemplation of human affairs to appear brutal and selfish. But in the history of Russian thought these wartime attitudes have been always prevalent; the year 1905 brought to a focus issues that had been long debated, and which were presently to come into even sharper conflict—the essence of the argument, with all its ramifications, being social as against individualist ethics, a man's

responsibility to others as against his responsibility to himself, the rights and duties of public and private interests.
This was the substance of Gorky's quarrel with Tolstoy,
which, although not primarily concerned with art, had a
bearing on aesthetics. The artist's status, Gorky implied,
was by no means autonomous; even the greatest artist of
the age had no right to an ethical position that disregarded
the actual, the immediate, the practical distress of his society. There could be no question as to the primacy of the
outer over the inner world. It was the empiric realm beyond himself that dictated the good man's, and the responsible artist's, thoughts and attitudes. By contrast to the
Symbolists, who shaped reality to their imaginations and
rubbed out the distinction between life and art by seeing
life as art, Gorky, and others like him, achieved the same
obliteration by the reverse process of seeing art as life. For
the moment, the intelligentsia were inclined to be with him.
That was why, although he was soon to change his mind,
he now thought them "disinterested" and "pure." In vary-
ing degrees, the principal writers of the day—Merezhkovsky and his wife Zinaïda Hippius, Balmont, Sologub,
Vyacheslav Ivanov, Bely, Blok—objected to the war and
favored the revolution. Then the war was lost, and the revolution was put down.

The failure of the revolution was a shock to the intelligentsia, and just as serfdom had given rise to the Repentant Nobleman, so 1905 engendered the Repentant Intellectual. In 1909 a collection of essays was published in an
attempt to reappraise the intellectual's credo, a *mea culpa*
of the Russian intelligentsia who, knowing themselves responsible for the revolution, were now impelled to examine
the reasons for its failure. It was called *Landmarks* (*Vekhi*),
and it became the center of a furious debate. Lenin called
it "an encyclopedia of perfidy"; and in his vocabulary, and
in that of other revolutionists, Gorky among them, the ap-
pellation "Vekhovtsi," given to its contributors and their
sympathizers, became a term of opprobrium. The contributors were men of widely divergent interests; they differed greatly in their "practical desires," as the editor,

M. O. Gershensohn, explained in the preface, but held a
basic principle in common: that "the inner life of the individual was the only creative force of human existence
. . . the only sound basis for any social structure." It was a
position that had been long out of favor with radical thinkers, the one for which Gorky had denounced Tolstoy in his
Open Letter: the principle of the primacy of the individual's inward life over general public concerns, the "life of
the spirit" over the life of politics and sociology. To the
Vekhovtski, contemporary events were an occasion for re-
viewing and analyzing the whole course of Russian intellectual history; and however varied their approach—theological, sociological, cultural, political—the central argument
was not that the failure of the revolution was due to some
tactical error, but that the idea of revolution itself was
wrong. For too long, ever since the westernizing reforms of
Peter the Great, Russia had lived on borrowed thought,
grasping alien notions without assimilating them, failing to
develop organically, mistaking momentary issues for basic
values, jumping at palliatives instead of focusing on essential reforms. "The Russian intellectual," wrote Gershensohn,
supplying an essay entitled "Creative Consciousness," is a
man who "in the literal meaning of the word, lives *outside
himself;* that is, recognizing as the only object worthy of his
interest and concern something that lies beyond his personality—the people, society, government"—so much so that he
is considered "egoistic and indecent" if he ever thinks about
himself. This extraverted attitude, forced on Russians by the
despotism of public opinion, operates in all spheres of
thought, not only in politics and sociology, but in metaphysics, theology, ethics, education, jurisprudence. In every
one of them reason is subjected to the criterion of public
good, a worship of "the people," to such a degree that, as
Berdyaev pointed out in his contribution, "Philosophic
Verity and the Intellectuals' Truth," preoccupation with
philosophy has for a long while been considered "immoral"
in Russia, a sign of "indifference to the needs of peasants and
workers"—a tendency intensified by the rise of Marxism,
which had caused the intelligentsia to be increasingly inter-

ested not in truth as such, not in "metaphysical verities, but only in whether metaphysics . . . will serve the interests of the proletariat." It was a state of mind in which "love of egalitarian justice, public good, the well being of the people, [had] all but destroyed concern for truth"; the attitude of the intelligentsia, said Berdyaev, might be formulated as follows: "may truth vanish without a trace, if through its destruction people's lives will become happier."

A similar chaotic utilitarianism reigned in Russian jurisprudence, wrote Kistyakovsky ("In Defense of Law"). "The Russian intelligentsia has never respected the law," he said. And there was nothing in Russian literature comparable to Montesquieu's *L'Esprit des Lois,* Rousseau's *Contrat Social,* Hobbes's *Leviathan,* Locke's *Of Government,* or Milton's discourses on freedom of speech and the press. Although "from time immemorial" Russians had recognized that "social development [depended] on the situation of the individual," the idea of "legal individuality" was foreign to them. Never had they seen that individual rights could be protected only by constitutional government. So unaccustomed indeed to the notion of these rights were even the most liberal members of the intelligentsia, that they were perfectly ready to abandon them for the sake of "momentary benefits." The clearest evidence of this lack of understanding was the nature of Russian social organizations: they were formed on purely external regulations, on rules, not on convictions of what was legal, so that the intelligentsia's concept of law was "at a stage of development corresponding to the forms of police government." Nowhere in the world was there so much talk of "party discipline," and this was not entirely due to the novelty of public organizations in Russia. A much better reason was that the intelligentsia were "not familiar with convictions about legality which might impose an inward discipline. We require outward discipline because we have no inner discipline."

Similar remarks were made by A. S. Izgoyev, who wrote on education; by Peter Struve, who discussed the revolutionary concepts of the intelligentsia; by S. N. Bulgakov, who considered its heroic ideal; by S. L. Frank, who wrote

on the ethics of nihilism. All found fault with the enslavement of Russian intellectuals to public opinion, with their
lack of mental independence, the mechanical schemes and
utilitarian goals of their thinking, with the erroneous and
superficial assumptions on which even their noblest hopes
were based. All demanded a change of spirit through deeper
self-awareness, a realization that "man cannot live perpetually outside himself," and that only the one who knows
himself can have strong and clear desires, and is thence capable of effective public action. The crippled, restless, dissatisfied members of the intelligentsia must stop blaming others
for their failure, must heal the self-inflicted rupture between
their personalities and their professed beliefs, and be impelled to public interests by inward necessity, not by external pressure, their natures no longer split between the
demands of "the *I*" and the interests of "the we." "We
shall free ourselves from outward oppression only when
we free ourselves from inward slavery; that is, when we assume responsibility and stop blaming outside forces for
everything," concluded Berdyaev; Kistyakovsky believed
that a genuine understanding of law could come only after
the intelligentsia had "looked into" the inner world; Struve,
that society was ideally an educator, not as an "organization" but as a stimulus to creativity, to "the positive work
of a man on himself, in his struggle within himself for the
sake of creative tasks"; Izgoyev, that the average Russian
must be taught to relinquish his yearning for self-sacrifice, which was tantamount to a love of death, and learn to
love life and have faith in the value of his work; and Bulgakov, that he must give up the idea of social miracles and
upheavals, and "re-educate" himself "gradually and labori-
ously," without "leaps," without "cataclysms," but only
with "persistent self-discipline." The great Russian writers
alone, said these contributors, had been capable of retaining
their independence under stress of social demands.

The years that followed "1905," the notorious era of
Pobedonostev, were a period of political repression, of the
development of a strong underground revolutionary movement, and, despite a prevailing pessimism, of lively ex-

perimentation in art. Realism was no longer the dominant
literary school. Its chief representatives, Kuprin, Bunin,
and Andreyev, were developing in new directions. The main
trends were theological, metaphysical, and symbolic. Between 1905 and 1914 some of the most notable works of the
Symbolists were written, and new literary theories were formulated and propounded. The October Revolution led to
an artists' exodus. Kuprin, Bunin, Andreyev, the Merezhkovskys, Balmont—all left Russia. Rozanov retreated to a monastery. Vyacheslav Ivanov stayed on for several years, but
left in 1924. Some individualist, nonpolitical writers, however, would not depart; and it was possible for them at first,
in spite of extreme physical hardship, to continue their
highly original work. After all, they thought, "revolution"
meant novelty, new beginnings in thought and art, as well
as in politics. The Revolution itself and the civil war, the so-
called period of Militant Communism, were heroic: the violence was elemental, a great purifying storm from which a
new society would emerge, "new men" with a stauncher,
nobler philosophy than any in the past. These were the
hard years of 1918 to 1922, when the main problem of the
Bolsheviks was to win the fight without destroying the land,
to stem destruction, and to make power-drunk proletarians
realize that overthrowing the bourgeois regime need not involve destroying its works of art, that the cultural heritage,
however vile its class origins, was national and must be
preserved. The period of reconstruction called for reappraisals and redefinitions: writers felt obliged to formulate
what they conceived to be their function in society, and the
years from 1923 to 1932, when the Union of Soviet Writers
was established by official decree, were rich in manifestoes
and programs—proclamations that exhibit an increasingly
bitter conflict between the two opposing attitudes which the
Vekhovtsi had pointed out as characteristic of Russian
thought: the individual's ascetic submission to the interests
of society, on the one hand, and on the other, his insistence
on the absolute value of his independent personality. The
debate grew sharper, as an uncompromising dictatorship
defined Marxism more and more narrowly and realized

how useful art could be as a means of propaganda; presently, when art was made a branch of politics and aesthetic beliefs were looked upon as signs of loyalty or treachery, views on art became quite literally a matter of life and death.

The individualists, always on the defensive, were in the beginning at liberty to voice their credos. Thus in 1922 a group of writers, announcing their absolute freedom from politics, called themselves "The Serapion Brothers," after a novel of E. T. A. Hoffmann, and declared:

We are no school; no direction; no band of Hoffmann imitators. . . .
We called ourselves the Serapion Brothers because we object to compulsion and boredom, and because we object to everybody writing the same way. . . .
Each one of us has his own distinct physiognomy and outlook upon literature. Each one of us exhibits the traces of the most varied literary influences. "Each of us has his own drum." . . .
In February 1921, at a time of widespread regimentation, registration, and barrack-room regulations, when but a single iron and boring statute was made applicable to all, we decided to foregather without statutes or chairmen, without elections or voting . . . and we took an oath to remain true to the very end to the statute of the anchorite Serapion. . . .
We think that present-day Russian literature is amazingly decorous, conceited, and monotonous. We are allowed to write stories, novels, and compulsory dramas in both the old and new styles, but only provided that they are social and inevitably upon contemporary themes.
We demand but one thing: that a work of art be organic and real, and that it live its own peculiar life.

Then there was the Society for the Study of Poetical Speech, OPOYAZ, whose members produced some of the most remarkable works of criticism in the Russian language: Zhirmunsky on Pushkin, Eichenbaum on Gogol and Tolstoy, Tinyanov, Shklovsky, Tomashevsky on the theory of literature. They called themselves Formalists, holding that a piece of writing can be understood only through a study of its structural elements. They proclaimed:

OPOYAZ assumes that there are neither *poets* nor *writers,* but only *poetry* and *literature.* All that a poet writes is significant only as part of his work, and is absolutely worthless as the expression of his "ego." Once a poetical work is regarded as a "human document" or as a jotting from a diary, it may interest the author, his wife, relations, acquaintances, and the type of maniac who passionately pursues the question "Did Pushkin smoke?"—and nobody else. *The poet is a master of his craft. And no more. But to be a good master necessitates a knowledge of the requirements of those for whom the work is intended, and it necessitates, moreover, a participation in their life. Otherwise the work will not go forward or answer any need.*

The poet's social role cannot be understood from an analysis of his individual qualities and habits. *A general investigation into the devices of the poetic craft is essential,* and so is their distinction from the intertwining spheres of human endeavor and that of the laws of historical development. Pushkin was not the founder, but only the chief of a school. Had there been no Pushkin, *Evgenyi Onegin* would still have been written. America would have been discovered without Columbus. . . .

Poets do not invent themes, they take them ready-made from their environment.

The poet's work begins with the working out of the theme, with the discovery of a corresponding literary form. To study poetry is to investigate the laws of this literary process. *The history of poetry is the history of the development of the devices constituting its literary formation. . . .*

This view of the poet's social role and of his given theme is Marxist in essence, but the Formalists soon became anathema to the Soviet regime.

OPOYAZ [the manifesto continued] *"is the best educator of the Proletarian literary youth.*

Proletarian poets still suffer from the thirst for "self-expression." They are all the time breaking away from their class. They are not satisfied to remain simply Proletarian poets. They look for "cosmic," "planetary," or "profound" themes. They seem to think that, thematically, a poet must break away from his environment, and only then will he be able to create something "eternal."

OPOYAZ will demonstrate to them that all greatness comes

from answering the problems of the day, that the "eternal" is now and was once "actual," and that a great poet does not express himself, but merely executes a social command.

OPOYAZ *will help its comrades, the Proletarian poets, to overcome the traditions of bourgeois literature by a scientific demonstration of the moribund and counterrevolutionary elements in their work.*

OPOYAZ will help Proletarian creation, not by vague discussions about the "Proletarian spirit" and "Communist consciousness," but by a precise and technical demonstration of the devices underlying contemporary poetical creation.

OPOYAZ *is the gravedigger of poetical idealization.* Opposition to it is futile. Especially for Marxists.

But the proletarian youth could not understand this scientific approach to literature, nor were they in a mood to accept bourgeois leadership. All over the country they had formed their own cultural organizations, dedicated to the proposition that only proletarians by origin could create a proletarian art. "Bourgeois culture," they announced, "is decomposing like a corpse. . . . The great artist—the proletariat—is creating a new culture." Members in the "proletcult" groups were drawn from the working class exclusively, and the movement became sufficiently important to be recognized by the central government, which, in April 1918, established a "section of independent cultural-educational organizations—'Proletcult'" within the Commissariat of Public Education. Bourgeois culture, Proletcult announced, was "based on slavery, property, and robbery," and the artist of the new society could have no truck with it. Proletcult, however, lasted but a very few years, reaching its apogee in 1920, then going into a rapid decline and being replaced during the NEP period by a more formidable organization, which demanded not only autonomy, but control, of art. This new organization assumed the function of watchdog over art, called itself "On Guard," and attacked the Serapion Brothers, the Formalists, and other writers of "bourgeois" tendencies. "The most inexcusable muddle reigns in our own ranks upon all questions of literature," it declared in a manifesto of 1923:

This must come to an end. We must stand for a firm and consistent Proletarian line in literature. The old battle flags must be once more proudly and unconquerably raised before the face of reviving bourgeois literature and the wavering Fellow-Travelers. . . .

Nobody would undertake now to deny the existence of Proletarian literature. Proletarian literature has acquired a definite social significance which was particularly manifest in the years of civil war, when the old writers either escaped abroad or entrenched themselves in pure art or middle-class niceties, while the younger bourgeois attempted various formal subtleties. . . .

Standing *On Guard* over our fundamental problem—the widening and deepening of the content, and the working out of a new synthetic form of Proletarian literature—we shall engage in merciless battle against both stagnation and self-repetition of *several groups of Proletarian writers and the excessive pursuit of form* and its various elements.

While engaged in this work we shall stand firmly *on guard over a firm and clear Communist ideology* in Proletarian literature. In view of the revival, ever since the beginning of NEP, of the activity of bourgeois literary groups, all *ideological doubts* are absolutely *inadmissible,* and we shall make a point of bringing them to light.

We shall stand *on guard over the organizational structure* of the All-Russian Association of Proletarian Writers, and we shall fight for its consolidation.

We shall fight those Manilovs [the reference here is to the sugary character of Gogol's *Dead Souls*], who distort and slander our revolution by the attention they pay to the rotten fabric of the Fellow-Travelers' literary creation, in their *attempt to build* an aesthetic *bridge between the past and the present.*

We *shall fight* those *diehards* who have, without sufficient criteria, congealed in ecstatic pose in front of the granite monument of *old bourgeois-gentry literature,* and who do not wish to emancipate the working-class of its oppressive *ideological burden.*

We *shall fight* those *desperate* people who, in search of the new, support all the acrobatics of literary juggling and propound theories of "the future," forgetting the present and sinking into the slime of flowery phrases.

And finally, as a public group in Proletarian literature, *we count it our duty to fight not only against manifest white-guard and finally discredited literary tendencies, but also against those writ-*

ers' groups which disguise themselves with the false mask of revolution, but which are, in reality, reactionary and counterrevolutionary.

A clear, firm, and severely consistent Communist policy in art and literature will be the leading principle of our review. . . .

We count upon the support and active collaboration of all proletarian writers, of all comrade Communists and workers, working in the sphere of the artistic word or interested in it, and *we call upon them to join in a communal and united effort to build up proletarian literature and Communist solidarity, and to wage an unflagging struggle upon the ideological front.*

On Guard succeeded in its efforts at consolidation; and the All-Russian Association of Proletarian Writers, RAPP, became, until it was disbanded by decree of the Communist Party in 1932, an absolute dictator in the realm of literature.

It is hard to tell how much of this pugnacious squabbling was inspiried by genuine convictions. The times demanded partisanship. There was no common ground for debate, no meeting of argument with argument when the very assumptions of discourse were radically antagonistic; arrogance was fashionable, since discussion was impossible. Those who had always believed in artistic autonomy found themselves beleaguered and obliged to defend their independence with the very weapons used against them: intransigent, peremptory declarations of faith. The besiegers were too fanatical to be scrupulous, and in all this vituperative bickering one voice only appeared to speak of the new Marxist aesthetic with critical authority. This was the pungent voice of Leon Trotsky, whose *Literature and Revolution* came out in 1923. Flamboyant and perceptive, maliciously flippant about individual writers, it was serious in the realm of theory, and sparkling in diction. But its outstanding merit was the ability (which in the heat of partisanship seemed to have been all but lost) to see the moment in historical perspective. While various factions were proclaiming themselves to be true oracles and seers of the future, Trotsky pointed out that their age was an indeterminate period between two epochs, and that all its writers were figures of transition. There was always a lag between event and idea, he said. The Russian intelligentsia used to think that "mind and critical reason moved the world," but they were wrong. "As a matter of fact, all through history, mind limps after reality," and "the place of art is in the rear of the historic advance." As for the "reality" of revolutionary Russia, it was so complex, so drastically novel that it would take a long while for its meaning to be fully assimilated. In time, of course, a new art would come into being to express this new reality, but this would not be a Proletarian, but a Socialist art, and the two should not be confused. The Proletarian State was but a steppingstone to the Socialist; its "historic significance" and "moral grandeur" lay precisely in that its purpose was to obliterate itself; and since its function was to "lay the foundation" of a culture that would be "above classes," *proletarian art* was a contradiction in terms. "Literary works of talented and gifted proletarians" were already in existence, but they did not constitute a "proletarian literature." They were a beginning only, the source from which Socialist literature would develop. They expressed

. . . in writing the molecular process of the cultural rise of the proletariat. . . . The letters of the workers, the local poets, the complainants, are carrying on a great cultural work, breaking up the ground and preparing it for future sowing. But a cultural and artistic harvest of full value will be, happily! Socialist and not "proletarian."

Culture was an evolutionary, an organic process. One could not create it "by laboratory methods. . . . Our epoch," said Trotsky, "is not yet an epoch of new culture, but only the entrance to it," and although he had a clear idea of what this culture would be like, he had no illusions about the rapidity of its development, nor did he exaggerate the role which the Party was to play in bringing it about:

Art must make its own way and by its own means. The Marxian methods are not the same as the artistic. The Party leads the proletariat but not the historic processes of history. There are do-

mains in which the Party leads, directly, and imperatively. There
are domains in which it only cooperates. There are, finally, domains in which it only orientates itself. The domain of art is not
one in which the Party is called upon to command. It can and
must protect and help it, but it can only lead it indirectly. . . . At
any rate, the Party cannot and will not take the position of a literary circle which is struggling and merely competing with other
literary circles. The Party stands guard over the historic interests
of the working class in its entirety. Because it prepares consciously and step by step the ground for a new culture and therefore for a new art, it regards the literary fellow-travelers not as
the competitors of the writers of the working class, but as the real
or potential helpers of the working class in the big work of reconstruction. The Party understands the episodic character of the
literary groups of a transition period and estimates them, not from
the point of view of the place which these groups occupy and can
occupy in preparing a Socialist culture. If it is not possible to determine the place of any given group today, then the Party as a
Party will wait patiently and gracefully.

But the official doctrine, which evolved in the following decade and has continued to this day, was based on a different
concept of the relation between art and life and between
the Party and art. Shaped by Gorky on the basis of Lenin's
theories, and called by a phrase of Stalin's coinage, "Socialist
Realism," it is proclaimed by orthodox Soviet critics to
be a true reflection of a new society, that of the People's
Democracy, in which Party interests and those of ordinary
citizens are identical—a unity of thoughts and aims that is
a measure of the superiority of the Communist State over
the bourgeois, where the artist is alienated from both his
government and his fellow citizens. Even the name of the
new doctrine was chosen by way of contrast to the dominant
school of nineteenth-century art, when artists, who were not
an integral part of their society, could do no more than
stand aside and criticize their age. Their method was now
called "Critical Realism." Socialist Realism differed from it
in being a cultural force: it not only mirrored and evaluated
society but helped to build it. In another phrase of Stalin's,
artists were "engineers of souls."

The development of this doctrine has been traced by
Soviet authors to its origins in the views of the enormously
influential Vissarion Belinsky, who in the nineteenth century steered Russian literature in the direction of social
commentary—from him, through Marx and Engels, to a
famous article of 1905 in which Lenin declared that Socialist literature must be Party literature, that "The socialist proletariat must advance the principle of Party literature, develop this principle, and introduce it into life in as full and
entire a form as possible," and thence, in the evolution of
Gorky's theories, to its final formulation. This could not
have happened, they insist, had not life itself been so radically changed as to obliterate the distinction between
Romanticism and Realism and make heroism, once the
property of legends only, a part of daily life. Gorky had
seen his nation attain this happy state, had found that in
order to embody his ideals, he no longer needed to invent
admirable men: he could see them in the flesh, for they
were all around him, the ordinary workers of Russia. Nor was
it difficult now, as it had been formerly, to distinguish between faith and knowledge. The problem no longer existed,
since men's ideals had been realized and what they believed
had become reality; now faith and knowledge were one.
No longer was it necessary to think of the good in terms of
divinity, not even of a man-created, humanistic God. For
man himself embodied all ideals; his life on earth embraced
all miracles of faith and legend. Gorky believed indeed
that a new life had come to be, and with it a new art; and
in 1928, only five years after Trotsky's essay, he was announcing that it was wrong to speak of a "proletariat" in
Russia. "I see no proletarians here; I see real masters, in
whose hands are factories and mills, in whose hands is
political power. . . . There are no longer any proletarians,
there are only the actual masters of the land." Naturally,
without proletarians there could be no proletarian art; there
was only the art of a Socialist Russia. "Comrade Stalin," proclaimed Comrade Zhdanov, Secretary of the Central Committee of the C.P.S.U., in opening the First All-Union
Congress of Soviet Writers in 1934 (as quoted in *Problems*

of Soviet Literature, published by International Publishers,
New York), "has called our writers engineers of human souls.
What does this mean? What duties does the title confer upon
you?

In the first place, it means knowing life so as to be able to depict it truthfully in works of art, not to depict it in a dead, scho-
lastic way, not simply as "objective reality," but to depict reality
in its revolutionary development.

In addition to this, the truthfulness and historical concreteness
of the artistic portrayal should be combined with the ideological
remolding and education of the toiling people in the spirit of socialism. This method in *belles lettres* and literary criticism is what
we call the method of socialist realism.

Our Soviet literature is not afraid of the charge of being "tendencious." Yes, Soviet literature is tendencious, for in an epoch of
class struggle there is not and cannot be a literature which is not
class literature, not tendencious, allegedly nonpolitical.

It is in such terms as these, in tones of flaming enthusiasm,
that Socialist Realism has usually been expounded. As another example, one may cite an article on Gorky contributed
by the critic B. Byalik to a collection of 1948, entitled *Problems of Socialist Realism.*

It is a great happiness [he writes] to feel that the surrounding
world is your world, to see in your native land the embodiment of
your ideal, to have the right to present actual reality as a daydream that has been fulfilled. Such a right and such happiness
writers of the past did not possess, nor do the writers of contemporary foreign lands. Such a right has been granted only to our
Soviet writers. But this right is inextricably bound up with great
responsibility: to be an active participator in the building of the
new life, to devote to it all one's thoughts and ideas, all one's
aspirations and hopes, to love it with an active, creative love, and
just as actively to hate its enemies—in a word, to be true to the
Leninist principle of the party-mindedness [partiynost'] of literature . . .

A reader of Soviet literature grows accustomed to such
tirades as these. Their sincerity need not be questioned, but

neither can one escape the realization that on the grounds of
this sincerity, some of the finest poets of Russia, of the
Western world indeed, have been unmercifully silenced.
Their martyrology is well known, and I shall not review it.
Mine is another task: to trace the life and work of six outstanding authors, each of whom is interesting and important
in himself, as well as for his contribution to Russian letters.
As personalities they are extremely varied, and also as artists, so much so that each of them might be studied as
the center of a distinct school of writing. As a group they
are, as it were, a microcosm of Russian literature in the
twentieth century, an age of such rapid change as to make its
several years appear to be not twelvemonths, but epochs.
And so, although they are contemporaries, their dates of
birth, the periods in which their minds were formed, have
set them apart from one another. In the crucial year of 1905,
Gorky was already a leader of the revolutionary movement
and a well-known writer, Blok had published his first volume of poems and was still a university student, Pasternak
and Mayakovsky were in school, Leonov was six years old,
Sholokhov was born that year. All have been involved in
the momentous events that have tried the mettle of their
countrymen and have, at times, driven their consciences to
tragic wanderings along devious and unaccustomed ways.

1

MAXIM GORKY

(1868-1936)

I

His name was Alexey Maximovich Peshkov, but he called himself Gorky; that is, "The Bitter." "Today for the first time," he said in a letter of February 19, 1933, "I wrote on an envelope, instead of N.-Novgorod, Gorky. That is very embarrassing and unpleasant." Nizhni-Novgorod, the ancient town on the Volga, was his birthplace and his home, if "home" it can be called, during the greater part of his childhood and youth; and in 1932 it was renamed by the pseudonym he had adopted just forty years earlier, when his first short story was published. Such honors are not usually accorded artists, not even in the U.S.S.R. Pushkino, the former Tsarskoe Selo, is not a great city; Yasnaya Polyana is a national shrine; but there is no "Tolstoy" on the

map of Russia, nor is there a "Lermontov," a "Dostoevsky,"
a "Nekrasov." There are only Leningrad and Stalingrad and
Gorky. This is because Gorky, along with Lenin and Stalin,
shaped and disseminated the country's official philosophy.
The Soviet Encyclopedia calls him "the father of Soviet
literature . . . the founder of the literature of Socialist Realism," and mentions hundreds of Soviet enterprises that
are also named for him: theaters, five universities, smaller
educational organizations, literary and scientific institutes,
an outstanding publishing house, kolkhozes, factories, etc.
This is a tribute to his influence and his prodigious labors,
political, social, educational, as well as literary. So numerous
were they, that Gorky gives the impression of having been
not just a man, but a whole institution in himself.

He was already well known before the Bolshevik Revolution. In 1898 his first book, a two-volume collection of stories, was a resounding success. Four years later, at the age of
thirty-four, he was the youngest member ever to have been
elected to the Imperial Academy of Science; and when the
Czar revoked this honor on the ground that it could not be
conferred on an enemy of the state who had already served
several sentences in jail, Chekhov and Korolenko sent in
their resignations. At the close of the same year, in December 1902, *The Lower Depths* brought him European fame.
During the revolution of 1905 he played a prominent role,
was one of the delegation of writers who, in an attempt to
avert disaster, called on Count Serge Witte on the eve of
what came to be known as Bloody Sunday, witnessed the
bloodshed in the streets of St. Petersburg, harbored the priest
Gapon, who had led the fateful procession to the Winter
Palace, and wrote the first of his many descriptions of the
occasion in an excited letter to his wife, while Gapon was
sleeping in his rooms:

And so [he summarized] the Russian Revolution has begun, my
friend, on which I congratulate you solemnly and sincerely. The
dead—they are not disturbing: only with blood is history re-
painted in new colors.

A few days later he was arrested and imprisoned in the Peter and Paul Fortress. There was a rumor that he would be hanged, and liberals all over the world, among them such renowned men as Anatole France, Rodin, Poincaré, Swinburne, Meredith, and Hardy cried out in protest. Within a month he was freed, but banished from St. Petersburg, pending his trial, which was to take place in the spring. He was eager for it, he wrote his friend and publisher, K. P. Piatnitsky, and would insist on it, so he might "shame the family of the Romanovs and their ilk." Were he condemned, he would have "a superb opportunity to explain to Europe just why [he was] a 'revolutionary' and what were the motives of [his] 'crime against the existing order' which massacred the peaceful and unarmed inhabitants of Russia, including even children." But the trial was several times postponed, then called off, in view, no doubt, of the clamor which the affair aroused, and the following year Gorky went to an eagerly sympathetic United States to raise funds for a new revolution.

That trip began with an ovation, but turned into an outrageously comic scandal (there is a lively account of it, *L'Affaire Gorky,* by M. R. Werner, in the *New Yorker* for April 30, 1949). Large crowds greeted him when he arrived, he was fêted at dinners and receptions, Mark Twain and William Dean Howells called on him. But four days after his triumphal entry the scandal broke. Inspired by the Imperial Embassy in Washington, fanned by the *New York World,* whose editors were piqued because he had given exclusive publication rights to the *American,* it concerned Gorky's relations with the woman who was accompanying him as Mme. Gorky. The information was spread over the front pages of newspapers that she was actually Mme. Andreyeva, a well-known actress of the Moscow Art Theater, who was not legally married to him, and that he had been separated from his real wife for several years. It did not signify that the separation had been amicable, that friendly relations continued between husband and wife, and that, after all, this was an entirely private affair: he was accused of immorality and turned out of hotels and apartments; there were demands that he be deported for bigamy; parties that had been planned in his honor were cancelled. The *Sun* declared that "the purity of our inns was threatened"; Senator Knute Nelson of Minnesota pronounced Maxim Gorky a "horrible creature . . . about as immoral as a man can be"; Mark Twain refused to preside at a large literary banquet, which in consequence did not take place; and one newsman advocated that the man be returned to Russia "to be knouted, as he deserves." He was not "returned," thanks to a civilized couple, Mr. and Mrs. John Martin, who persuaded him and Mme. Andreyeva to stay with them in their home on Staten Island and in the Adirondacks during the summer. The literary fruits of this visit to America were a humorless invective, *The City of the Yellow Devil,* and one of Gorky's worst and most influential novels, the propagandist *Mother,* which he wrote in Upstate New York.

In October he settled in Capri, and stayed there until 1913. His Italian villa was a meeting place for Russian artists, writers, politicians; Leonid Andreyev, Brodsky, Chaliapin, Lunacharsky, Lenin visited him there. He was enormously busy: codirector with Piatnitsky of the publishing house Znanie (Knowledge); editor of the legal Marxist journal, *Novaya Zhizn'* (*New Life*); contributor to Lenin's newspapers, the *Proletarian* and the *Star;* and in 1912 literary editor of *Pravda.* In 1907 he went to London as delegate to the Fifth Congress of the Social-Democratic Party; in 1908 he delivered a course of lectures on Russian literature in a school for workingmen on Capri, which he and Lunacharsky had organized; his correspondence was vast and his writing copious. Between 1907 and 1913 he published, apart from articles and essays, seven plays, *The Barbarians, The Last, The Eccentrics, Children of the Sun, False Money, Vassa Zheleznova,* and *The Zykovs;* four novels, *Confession, Summer, Okurov Town,* and the lengthy *The Life of Matvey Kozhemyakin;* two books of sketches, *Tales of Italy* and *Russian Tales;* and *Childhood,* the first part of his autobiography. In all of these he sought to counteract the pessimism which prevailed in Russian literature during these years, to inject into it a note of hope and energy.

Bunin alone is true to himself [he wrote in a letter of 1907]. The others have all reached a kind of wild frenzy and are not aware, apparently, of their own acts. One senses something alien —a malicious, harmful influence that disfigures human beings. . . . Literature is being assailed by a variety of paranoiacs, sadists, pederasts, and different kinds of psychopathological personalities. . . . One senses spiritual chaos, confusion of thought, a sickly, neurotic hastiness. Simplicity of language is disappearing and with it, its strength. Beauty, at best, is exchanged for prettiness, instead of silver—tinfoil. It is all understandable, and—offensive.

And again:

There are many Russian writers here . . . gloomy people. They sit frowning and meditate in silence on the vanity of all that's earthly and the insignificance of man; and they talk of the dead, of graveyards, toothache, head colds, of the tactlessness of socialists, and other such matters that lower the temperature of air, body, and soul. Flowers wither, flies give up the ghost, fish die, and stones grimace as if they were about to vomit. Ah, me!

In 1913, when a general amnesty was extended to political offenders, Lenin persuaded him to return to Russia. He was enthusiastically welcomed by the proletariat: "Moscow alone sent me over seventy greetings . . . bakers, and stocking makers, plumbers. . . . I am greatly touched"; but the intelligentsia were not so cordial. In their sharp glances Gorky seemed to detect the question: "What are you thinking of doing now, you devil?" And, all in all, he found his country strange:

My impressions? . . . I don't understand a thing! Everything is so mixed up, everyone is so crumpled, so devoid of any divine likeness, that, really, you look at something that stands before you and try to figure out: what being is that creature imitating? . . . Joking aside, I have not yet got used to my fatherland; every now and then, I suddenly find myself astonished: everyone is speaking

Russian! Not very well, tiresomely, but still—it's Russian! And even certain literary men sting each other verbally on paper with Russian words, though they construe them in a way that is heterodox and foreign. Really!

At the outbreak of the First World War, Gorky was in Finland, but he soon returned to Petrograd and did all he could in opposition to that hideous contrivance of imperialists, as he saw it, that meaningless and bestial massacre:

All in all, the atmosphere is stifling [he wrote a friend who was exiled in Siberia]. Never before have I felt myself so necessary to the life of Russia and haven't for a long time sensed such energy in me, but, dear comrade, I confess that now and then, one grows limp and everything turns black before one's eyes. It's very hard. Especially is one irritated by the intelligentsia; they're so apathetic, so lazy, careless, inefficient—it's hopeless!

Just the same, in some matters one succeeds. One succeeds, principally, because the Petersburg proletariat has reared some very fine men.

The Russian proletariat is faced with problems of a scope the West has no idea of. . . . We live in desperate contradictions.

Men are becoming more and more brutalized and insane [he wrote in the fall of 1915], in terror of the war which they initiated. . . . The old world is strong even in its death throes—strong! There is a lot of poison in it.

Men live in terror, but even terror does not prevent cheats from cheating. The bourgeoisie is consolidating, becoming stronger and, of course, is robbing the country, robbing—as it has never robbed before! . . . The government is not yielding to the pressure of the bourgeoisie, opposing it through inertia, mechanically.

Between these two powers is democracy, the proletariat. Both powers are afraid of it, no less than of the Germans, are afraid and threaten each other: unrest among the people will soon begin. . . .

The people carry on the war, the most terrible of all those that have ever been. The people labor, but there is nothing to eat. Petersburg is short of bread; there is no wood, no sugar, etc. Of course, the country has both bread and sugar, and everything that's needed, but most of all it has swindlers. Thence, the high cost of living.

That winter he wrote George Bernard Shaw:

The happy rumor has reached me that you stand above the chaos of passions, roused by the senseless war, which is destroying millions of those of our planet's population who are most active, most gifted in creative work.

And at the end of 1916 to H. G. Wells:

I have just finished correcting the proofs of the Russian translation of your latest book, *Mr. Britling*, and want to express my admiration, for you have written a splendid book! It is, without question, the best, the boldest, the truest and the most humanistic of all the books written in Europe during this accursed war. I am certain that in future, when we shall have become more humane again, England will be proud that the first voice of protest—and of such vigorous protest—against the cruelty of war was heard in England, and all honest and cultured people will speak your name in gratitude.

He founded a new publishing house, Parus (The Sail), and a review, *Letopis'* (*Annals*), in which he wanted to combat the unenlightened prejudices of the war years:

Those who are undertaking the journal [he wrote the eminent physiologist and botanist, K. A. Timiryazev] would like to restore to the memories of men terrified by events, the universal significance of West European culture at its roots, and especially of its essential foundation, science.

He also planned a series of *Lives of Great Men* for young people, to which, among others, he asked Romain Rolland, H. G. Wells, and Nansen to contribute:

Let us remind our children [he wrote Rolland, asking him for a biography of Beethoven] that men were not always so weak and bad as, alas, we are now; let us remind them that all peoples have had, and still have, great men, honorable hearts! It is essential to do this precisely in these days of triumphant cruelty and beastliness. . . .
You are one of those rare men whose soul has remained un-

clouded by the madness of this war, and it is a great happiness to know that you have retained in your noble heart the best principles of humanity.

This was at the end of 1916. When in 1917 the February Revolution let loose in Russia wild masses of vengeful men, Gorky attempted to arrest their destructiveness by founding a committee for the protection of works of art and issuing such appeals as the following:

Citizens, the old masters are gone, leaving behind them an enormous inheritance. It now belongs to the whole nation.

Citizens, guard this inheritance, guard the palaces; they will become palaces of your national art; guard the pictures, statues, buildings—these are the embodiment of your spiritual power and of that of your ancestors.

Art consists of those fine things which gifted men have created even under the oppression of despotism, and which testify to the power and the beauty of the human mind.

Citizens, do not touch a single stone; guard your monuments, buildings, old objects, documents—all these are your history, your pride. Remember that this is the soil from which your new national art will grow.

After the Bolshevik Revolution, he organized numbers of enterprises to protect and save scholars and writers. "The debt of Russian culture to him," wrote D. S. Mirsky, who was presently himself to benefit by his protection, "was very great. Everything that was done between 1918 and 1921 to save the writers and other higher intellectuals from starvation was due to Gorky."

His health had not been good ever since, in an attempted suicide, he had injured his left lung at the age of seventeen; and now, having overtaxed his strength, and also finding himself at odds with such powerful Bolsheviks as Zinoviev, he left Russia for a number of years. From 1921 to 1923 he lived in Germany, then in Sorrento, with trips to the U.S.S.R. in 1928, 1929, and 1932, returning there in 1933 to remain the last three years of his life. But these years were almost as strenuous as those of the war and revolution. He estab-

lished several more publishing enterprises: in 1921, with
Vladislav Khodasevich, a journal called *Beseda* (*Colloquy*)
—"strictly literary and scientific; it will not publish political articles . . . its contributors, principally foreigners"—
which, because of the interference of Soviet censors, was
obliged to suspend publication after seven issues; in 1928
another one, *Our Achievements,* intended as a tribune for
all the workers of the nation; and still another, called
Abroad. He inaugurated several multivolume publications,
*A History of the Civil War, A History of Factories, A His-
tory of a Young Man of the Nineteenth Century, The
Building of the U.S.S.R.;* and wrote five more plays, *The
Old Man, The Talkative Worker, Somov and Others, Yegor Bulychev and Others,* and a new version of *Vassa Zheleznova;* several volumes of sketches and reminiscences; the
last two parts of his autobiography; a novel, *The Artomonov
Business;* and a prose epic, *The Life of Klim Samghin*
(translated into English as four separate novels: *Bystander,
The Magnet, Other Fires,* and *The Specter*), which was left
unfinished at his death. His already voluminous correspondence grew even larger; he gave advice and encouragement
to scores of writers and would-be writers, to Leonid Leonov,
Valentin Katayev, Olga Forsh, Vsevolod Ivanov, Gladkov,
Fedin, Tikhonov, Alexey Tolstoy, Sergeyev-Chensky, among
those who became known in Soviet literature, and to numbers of workers who had but recently learned to read and
were just beginning to write.

You ask about my health [he wrote from Sorrento on January
12, 1929, to V. S. Dovgalëvskiy, Soviet envoy to France]. Thank
you! I shall answer thus: I am able to work, I work no less than
twelve hours a day. Unfortunately, I am tormented by insomnia
and, thence, headaches; these I am experiencing for the first time
in my life.

But the work is amazingly interesting. *Our Achievements* has
added greatly to my number of correspondents, and every day,
from all parts of the Soviet Union, twenty-five to thirty persons
send me all manner of instructions, good wishes, advice, curses,
etc. . . .

And two years later, on January 3, 1931, to a worker who was urging him to come back to Russia, he gave his reasons for staying away:

Of course, there are places in the Soviet Union that are no worse than Sorrento, but if I lived in the Union, I would live in Moscow, for to live on the Black Sea, for example, would make no sense: it's almost as far from Moscow as Italy. But in Moscow I would be kept from working by various meetings, visits, etc. Here I live in complete isolation, in solitude, and this permits me to work quietly from ten to twelve hours a day. In Moscow I would be tempted by the theaters, by trips here and there; here I do not go to the theater and in two months haven't been in the city— which is three kilometers from my apartment.

In the spring of 1928 he went to Russia, and exhausted himself in traveling and making speeches; in 1929 he was elected to the Executive Committee of the Fifth Congress of the Soviet Union; in 1933 he helped found an institute for experimental medicine; in 1934 he organized the First Soviet Writers' Congress and was made president of the Writers' Union, and in December was elected by the writers as their deputy to the Moscow Soviet. In 1935 he became director of the Institute of Literature of the Academy of Sciences and was named delegate to the Congress for the Defense of Culture in Paris, which he was unable to attend for reasons of health. He died, working to the end, on June 18, 1936. At the Moscow Trials the following year, Trotskyites were charged with responsibility for his death, but this charge has not been substantiated and the circumstances in which he died remain unclear. His ashes are sealed in the wall of the Kremlin.

II

"I know Russian life and Russian literature pretty well," Gorky wrote in the spring of 1910, "and I can say, not without regret: no one invents less than I do. Some day I will write my autobiography and justify in it, in documentary fashion, citing individuals and places, all the events and states of soul that sometimes seem improbable in my stories." He was referring to the dark picture of Russia which for twelve years he had been presenting in plays, novels, stories; and three years later, in August 1913, the first installment of his autobiography appeared in *Russkoye Slovo* (*The Russian Word*).

On the floor, under the window, in a half dark, crowded room, lies my father, dressed in white and uncommonly long; the toes of his bare feet are strangely wide apart, the fingers of his gentle hands, lying peacefully on his chest, are also crooked; his gray eyes are tightly shut by the black circles of copper coins, his kind face is dark and frightens me by its wickedly bared teeth.

My mother, half naked, in a red skirt, is on her knees, combing back my father's long, soft hair from the forehead to the nape, with the black comb that I used to saw watermelon rinds with; my mother keeps saying something without stopping in a thick, harsh voice; her gray eyes are swollen and seem to be melting, running out in large teardrops.

My grandmother holds me by the hand—round, large-headed, with enormous eyes and a funny, crumbly nose; she is all black, soft, and extraordinarily interesting; she is crying too, accompanying my mother in a special, good kind of way; all of her is trembling and she jerks me, pushing me toward my father. I resist and hide behind her. I am frightened and uncomfortable.

I have never before seen grown-up people cry, and I do not understand the words my grandmother keeps repeating:

"Say goodbye to daddy; you will never see him again. He has died, my pigeon, before his time, before his hour!"

I had been very ill—had just got up; during my illness—that I remember well—my father used to care for me gaily; then suddenly he vanished and his place was taken by my grandmother, a queer person.

"Where have you come from?" I asked her. She answered, "From up above, from Nizhni, and I didn't come, but rode! One doesn't walk on water! . . ."

That was funny and ununderstandable: up above, in the house, lived bearded, painted Persians, and in the basement, an old, yellow Kalmuk sold lambskins. One could ride down the stairs on the banisters or, if one fell, one could roll down head over heels— that I knew well. But what had water to do with it? It was all wrong and amusingly mixed up. . . .

She spoke tenderly, gaily, smoothly. I made friends with her from the very first day, and now I wanted her to go away with me quickly out of this room.

My mother depresses me; her tears and wailing have roused a new, anxious feeling in me. It is the first time I have seen her like this. She is always strict, talks little. She is clean, smooth, and big, like a horse; she has a hard body and very strong arms. But now, somehow, she has become all unpleasantly bloated and dishevelled; everything she has on is torn; her hair, which always lies neatly on her head like a big, light hat, has spread over a naked shoulder, fallen over her face, and half of it, plaited in a braid, hangs down, brushing my father's sleeping face. I've been standing a long time in the room, but she hasn't glanced at me once. She keeps combing my father's hair and howling, gulping tears.

Some dark peasants and a sentinel-soldier look in at the door. He shouts angrily: "Take him away—quick!"

The window is hung with a black shawl; it billows like a sail. Once my father took me out riding in a boat with a sail. Suddenly there was a clap of thunder. My father laughed, pressed me close between his knees and shouted: "Don't be afraid of anything, Lex!"

Suddenly my mother sweeps up heavily from the floor, sinks down again straightway, falls on her back, her hair spreads over the floor; her blind, white face turns blue, and baring her teeth like my father, she says in a terrible voice: "Shut the door . . . Alexey, get out!" Pushing me aside, my grandmother rushes to the door and shouts: "My dears, never mind, don't touch, go away for Christ's sake! It's not cholera. It's birth pangs. Please, good men!"

I conceal myself in a dark corner behind a trunk and see from there how my mother writhes on the floor, sighing and gnashing her teeth, and how my grandmother crawls around her and says tenderly and joyfully: "In the name of the Father and the Son! Have patience, Varyushka! . . . Most holy Mother of God, who intercedes. . . ."

I am frightened; they are busy on the floor by my father, brushing against him; they moan and shout, but he is motionless and seems to be laughing. This lasts a long while, this business on the floor; more than once my mother gets up and falls again, my grandmother rolls out of the room like a big, soft, black ball; then, suddenly, in the darkness, a child cries. "Praise be to God!" says my grandmother, "It's a boy!" And lights a candle.

I must have fallen asleep in the corner. I remember nothing more.

This is the opening of Gorky's autobiography. The event takes place in 1872 in Astrakhan, to which the boy had been brought in infancy; he is now four years old. Unintentionally, the episode is symbolic. The corpse, the uncontrolled, dishevelled grief, the sudden birthpangs, the crude intrusion of officialdom, the writhing on the floor of a dark little room with a black shawl flapping at the window, and the child forgotten in a corner—it is all an image of the squalor, pain, and harshness that is the core of Gorky's life and the theme of all his work. At the age of four a father's gaiety and affection are already only memories to him; the pleasant outing in a sailboat will not be repeated; and for a long time to come he will stand in a dark corner, gazing in tense and troubled incomprehension on the tragically sordid scene that unfolds before him. But the grandmother will also be there to hold him by the hand; big, soft, efficient, strong, she will offset an infinitude of cruelty, give him courage, and teach him tolerance and appreciation.

The boy's mother had married a tradesman whom she loved, defying her father, Basil Kashirin, who wanted her to marry into the nobility. This father had once been a Volga boatman, but had risen from poverty and grown prosperous as a dyer in Nizhni-Novgorod, where he was so much esteemed that he was thrice elected elder of his guild. Now his shop was failing, thanks to the cloth factories that were springing up in Russia and cutting into the business of dyers; and his two sons were battling over their sister's dowry. It was into this embittered household that grandmother Kashirina brought the child and his mother; the newborn infant died on board ship on their way up.

For the next six years Alexey Peshkov lived in his grandfather's house, the witness and the victim of senselessly cruel stupidity. The sadistic old man delighted in beating his grandsons in a kind of ritual punishment, which he administered publicly at the end of every week; and although at first Alexey was protected by his special position in the family, by his mother who inspired something like awe, and by his grandmother, who took his part, he too was birched before long, and the first time to within an inch of his life. Once his grandfather, in a fit of violence, laid about his grandmother's head with his bony fists, and the boy helped her pull out the bent hairpins that had been driven into her scalp. His uncles and cousins, accustomed to such behavior and brutalized by it, drank, quarreled, lied, cheated, played mean pranks on defenseless persons, tormented animals. Uncle Yasha had tortured his wife to death and to ease his conscience resolved to raise a cross on her grave. Tsiganok, the gypsy foundling who had been taken in by the Kashirins and kept as a servant all his life, was made to carry the massive object up a steep hill to the graveyard; it crushed him when in a moment of danger the uncles dropped their end and jumped out of harm's way. He had been a strong, agile, gay fellow, a wonderful dancer, and very kind: at the time of Alexey's terrible beating, he had stuck his arm under the rod to save the child what blows he could. The boy loved him, and now he saw him bleed to death and heard his uncles, without a trace of sorrow or remorse, thank their stars for having themselves escaped his fate. Uncle Misha made drunken raids on the house, and one day set it on fire. Grandpa turned out old Gregory when his eyesight failed him, the faithful old Gregory who had once been his partner; and now the boy would meet him begging in the streets. His mother had married again, and once Alexey opened the door to see her kneeling on the floor to which she had fallen; her head thrown back, she grasped the chair on which she was leaning, while his stepfather, stretching his long leg, kicked her breasts with the pointed toe of his boot. The child rushed at him with a knife, but the mother pushed her husband aside, and the knife only ripped his coat and grazed his skin.

With complete sincerity and fully aware of what I was saying [Gorky concluded this chapter of his life], I told her that I would murder my stepfather and then kill myself. I think I might have done so; at any rate, I might have tried. Even now I see that long, vile leg in its brightly braided trousers; I see it swinging in the air and kicking a woman's breast.

Remembering these leaden abominations of our savage Russian life, I sometimes ask myself: are they really worth talking about? And with renewed assuredness, I answer myself: yes, they are, because this living, foul truth is not yet dead. It is this truth that must become known in its very roots, so as to be eradicated from man's memory, from his soul, from this whole dismal, shameful life of ours.

And there is another, more positive reason which impels me to paint these abominations. Although they are revolting, although they oppress us, crushing to death many fine souls, yet so sound and young in spirit is the Russian man that he is surmounting, and will surmount, them.

Our life is amazing not only because the layer of beastly filth in it is so fat and fruitful, but because through this layer there sprouts, nonetheless, that which is clear-colored, sound, and crea- tive; the good emerges, the humane, rousing invincible hope in our regeneration into a bright, a human life.

In its earnestness and optimism, its plain speaking and blunt encouragement, this passage is characteristic of Gorky. And what he says in it is what, with a variety of illustrations, he is always saying. Weighed down by a mass of harsh experi- ence, he wrote not so much to unburden himself as to pass on to others the lessons he extracted from his dreadful knowledge, to make men look straight upon the "beastli- ness" of Russia and labor to exterminate it. Show man what he is and what he can become, he thought, teach him and give him a chance to work, and he will build a good world. Without illusions about innate goodness nor any sanctimoniousness, he liked to discover fine qualities in bad men, even in his grandfather, whom he permitted to be- friend him in the course of the illness that followed his brutal beating. As for good people, they drew him to themselves like magnets. Their mere existence engendered faith in hu- manity: men like the one they nicknamed Good Idea, who

rented a small outhouse in the grandfather's garden, living
there in seclusion, busy with books and scientific experiments, and who was driven out because he was suspiciously
different from everybody else; or the Bishop Khrisanph, who
once visited Alexey's school and treated the boys with a humane understanding which was quite new to them; and
always, and above all, like the grandmother Akulina
Kashirina.

"She is something like a saint," old Gregory said of her,
"even though she drinks and takes snuff." Grandma "cooked,
sewed, dug in the garden, spun around all day like an
enormous top driven by an invisible whip, took snuff,
sneezed with relish, and would say, wiping her perspiring
face: 'Greetings, lovely world, forever and ever! . . . Praise
to thee, Queen of Heaven, how good everything has become!'" In times of crisis, it was on her that everyone re-
lied. She was the one to care for the sick, deliver children,
make peace in the warring household, and take command
when the house was set on fire. She loved animals and they
obeyed her. "What is it, little one? What is it, kitten? Want
to play a while?" she would say to the enormous horse,
Sharap, who would playfully nip her shoulder, pull the silk
kerchief off her head, peer into her face and neigh softly, as
she patted him and gave him sugar. At the time of the fire,
he ran wild and wanted to throw his rider:

Grandpa let go the halter and jumped off, shouting, "Mother,
hold him!" She sprang toward the legs of the rearing beast, stood
before it, her arms spread out; the horse neighed pitifully and
stretched toward her, looking askance at the flames. "Now don't
you be afraid!" said grandma in a bass voice, patting his neck and
taking up the halter. "Why, would I leave you in this horror, oh
you little mouse! . . ." The little mouse, three times her size, followed her humbly to the gates, snorting, examining her red face.

She rescued a starling from a cat's claws, mended its broken
wing, made it a wooden leg, and having cured the bird,
taught it to speak: it learned to ask for *kasha* and uttered
something like a greeting when she came into the room.
"Look," she would say, gazing at the sky at night, "a star

has fallen! It's some pure soul that's pining, thinking of mother earth! It means—a good man has just been born somewhere." The world was dear to her. " 'My God, my God! How good everything is!' . . . That was the cry of her heart, the watchword of her entire life." And when her grandson once asked her why his uncles were so vicious, "They are not vicious," she said quietly, taking snuff, "they are simply—stupid!"

She was pious in a homely way, praying to a kindly God in whom she confided:

Grandma tells God in detail everything that has happened in the house . . .

"Lord, thou thyself knowest—everyone wants the best for himself. Michael is the elder; he ought to stay in the city, it would be insulting to him to have to go beyond the river, and the job there is new, untried; what might happen, no one knows. But father, he loves Jacob best. Is that good, not to love one's children equally? He's stubborn, the old man; if only, O Lord, thou wouldst put some sense into him!"

Looking on the dark icons with her large, luminous eyes, she advises her God: "Bring him a good dream, O Lord, so he may understand how to divide the property between them." She crosses herself, bows down to the ground, striking her large forehead on the floor, and straightening up again, says insinuatingly: "If Thou wouldst smile on Barbara with some kind of gladness! How has she angered Thee, how is she more wicked than the others? How is this: a healthy young woman, but living in sorrow. And be mindful of Gregory, O Lord! His eyes are getting worse and worse. If he grows blind, he will go begging through the world. That's not good! He's spent his whole strength on grandpa, but will grandpa help! Oh, my Lord, my Lord . . ."

The boy likes grandma's God. "Her God was with her all day long; she spoke even to animals about Him." And when she was made fun of for this, "You think beasts don't understand God?" she would cry. "Every creature understands Him as much as you do . . ." Her God was "equally kind, equally close" to everything on earth; He was understandable and not frightening, but "it was impossible to lie before Him, shameful." She even pitied her dear God. " 'He gazes, gazes from His heaven down upon the earth, on all of us, and how He weeps at certain times, how He sobs: "Oh, people, you, my people, my dear people! Oh, how I pity you!"' And she herself weeps, and without wiping her wet cheeks, goes into the corner to pray." Grandfather prayed differently to a different God. He would wash and dress himself, comb his hair, smooth out his beard, look himself over in the mirror, and then "carefully, as it were, sneakingly," would approach the icon.

For a minute he stands silently, his head lowered, his arms down at his sides, like a soldier. Then, thin and straight, he says imposingly: "In the name of the Father, and the Son, and the Holy Ghost!" It seemed to me that after these words, a special silence fell upon the room, even the flies buzzed more cautiously.

Grandpa's is a just, cruel, and fearsome God. But the boy, finding it hard to believe in God's cruelty, suspects "that grandfather invents all this on purpose to inspire me with fear, not of God but of himself."

Grandma is bigger and stronger than grandpa. Why does she let him beat her? Because, she says, he is older, and besides, he is her husband. "God will demand of him an accounting for me, but I am ordered to endure." The story of her life is of a kind habitual in the annals of the Russian peasantry, and she herself is a familiar type, one of those greathearted, uncomplicated souls who make brilliant their humdrum existences through a fine, innate sense of beauty and of right. Her mother, a serf lacemaker, was granted freedom when she crippled her right arm in jumping out the window to escape the amorous advances of her master. With her baby daughter she went begging from city to city, and when the child was nine, taught her her craft. Akulina, who became very skillful and was in great demand, was spotted by Kashirin's mother as a suitable wife for her son:

"She saw I was a hard worker, a beggar's daughter, therefore, I'd be pliant—so-o. . . . She herself was a baker and a mean-minded woman, may it be forgiven her. . . . Dear me, why should we remember the wicked? The Lord sees them Himself;

He sees them, but the devil loves them." And she laughs a hearty laugh; her nose shakes in a comical way, but her eyes, shining thoughtfully, caress me, speaking of everything even more intelligibly than her words.

And here is grandma dancing:

Everyone began to beg her; and suddenly she stood up youthfully, smoothed out her skirt, straightened herself, throwing back her head, and walked around the kitchen . . .

Uncle shook and stretched himself, closed his eyes and began to play more slowly. Tsiganok stopped a minute; then, springing up to her, began to dance around grandma, bending his knees, throwing out his legs, while she swam noiselessly along the floor as if on air, moving out her arms, lifting her eyebrows, her dark eyes gazing somewhere into the distance . . .

Grandmother is not dancing, she seems to be narrating something. Now she walks quietly, reflectively, swaying, peering around from under her hand, and her whole large body oscillates uncertainly, her feet touch the ground cautiously. She stops, suddenly frightened by something, her face twitches, frowns, and immediately lights up in a kind, welcoming smile. She steps aside, letting someone pass by, putting somebody off with her arm; hanging her head, she has grown still, listening, smiling more and more gaily —and all at once, she is torn from the spot, spun in a whirl; all of her has grown straighter, taller, and it is now impossible to take one's eyes off her, so wildly beautiful and charming has she become in these moments of a magical return to youth!

Her dignity, grace, and intelligence are the endowment of a born artist. She has a feeling for poetic values, a superb memory, and a narrator's gift. She is like Pushkin's famous nurse, an illiterate peasant artist, a *skazitel'nitza* (or "teller of tales"), one of those who from early times have been much prized by Russian writers and have had a profound influence on Russian literature. Like Pushkin's Arina Rodionovna, Akulina Kashirina holds her place in Russian letters; and there is no one whom Gorky has drawn with so much care and so much love. She is his masterpiece. No one in the whole enormous corpus of his productions is so fully alive as this large, shapeless woman, speaking in her deep, mel-

low voice, in her forceful, spirited, peasant speech, rolling
in and out of rooms, dignified and humble, affectionate and
wise. The boy could not have enough of her recitations:
fairy tales, saints' legends, stories about men and women she
herself had known, or long poems of folk heroes which she
recited in the singsong form of ancient tradition. It was
mostly from her that he imbibed the imagery, structure,
and cadence of that native Russian speech which formed
his own literary language, for unlike Pushkin, he did not
transform folk art, he adopted it. It was by her that his
taste and his ethical standards were shaped, for although
he did not accept her humility and superstition, he never
forgot them nor lost his appreciation of the qualities they
represented. She dominated his childhood; her influence
was lasting; and he might well have entitled the first part
of his autobiography *Grandmother,* as he once intended to
do. And this beloved, gifted woman was to perish in the
morass of Russian savagery like the best men Peshkov was
to meet as he knocked about his country. She died a beggar,
and no doubt it was partly in tribute to her and to others
like her, and in anger at their fate, that he called himself
"The Bitter."

Soon after the time he wanted to kill his stepfather,
Alexey's mother died, and a few days after her funeral his
grandfather said to him: "Well, 'Lexis, you're not a medal.
Your place is not around my neck. Get out into the world."
This is the end of *Childhood.* The boy was ten years old.

Perforce one thinks of that other famous narrative of a
Russian boy's life, Tolstoy's, which was also called *Childhood,* not *My Childhood,* for like Gorky's, it was intended
to be the history of all children, not of just one individual
child. Indeed, Tolstoy, insisting that his story was not autobiography at all, invented a name for his little boy. But although he called him Nicholas Irtenyev and made several
important circumstances and events of his life different
from his own, so obviously does his creation resemble himself that one cannot see it as other than a slightly modified
self-portrait. Tolstoy's purpose, however, was very different from Gorky's. His theme was a child's, any child's, men-

tal and emotional development. Gorky's theme was Russia. "It is not about myself I am speaking," Gorky explained, "but about that narrow, stifling circle of terrifying impressions in which the Russian man used to, and indeed still does, live, even to this day." Tolstoy's interest was psychological; Gorky's social. And that is why everything in Tolstoy's story is centered on the little boy, every small occurrence has its importance only in the effect it has on him, whereas Gorky's child is not the focus of attention at all, but an instrument used to record the habits of brutal people in a barbarous society. That is also why Tolstoy's work is remarkable for the way it captures fleeting emotions or embryonic thoughts, for the exquisite distinctions it draws between the true and the false within the minds of men, why it is made up of such events as that final one, when Nicholas Irtenyev, left by his mother's coffin, experiences in the few minutes he is alone, unaffected by others' opinions and expectations of him, his one and only instant of genuine, self-forgetful grief; why, on the other hand, in Gorky's story there is very little about what the child feels or thinks, but a great deal about what he sees and hears. Tolstoy's fine points of emotion and morality are not for Gorky, who must deal with cruder men and more primitive modes of behavior—theft, murder, cheating—that leave no room for introspection. Alexey Peshkov takes for granted what Nicholas Irtenyev discovers bit by bit, and he must doubt everything that Nicholas takes for granted. Indeed, the subjects of these works are incommensurable: the life of a little nobleman in his pleasant, comfortable home, and that of the browbeaten urchin in the dingy quarters of an impoverished tradesman. Both childhoods end with the deaths of the boys' mothers. To Nicholas the event marks a stage in self-awareness; as a result of it, he becomes conscious of himself as a separate being, a member of society, differentiated from his family as he has not been hitherto. To Alexey it means only that he must set forth to earn his living, his childhood ends at the age at which the other's started. To Nicholas the world has always been a secure place of love and ease, of education, books, and music; what he must now learn is how to conduct himself in a familiar and, on the whole, satisfactory community. To Alexey the world is harsh and alien; it has given him neither the time nor the need for self-examination. And it is this world, against which he has been so roughly thrown, that he is obliged to question; himself he must accept, whatever he may be. The contrast between the circumstances of Tolstoy's early life and Gorky's must account, as much as temperamental differences, for the wide divergence of the realistic methods which they developed. Tolstoy's formidable personality always dominates his world. One cannot read anything he writes without being aware of him in every episode, every description. But Gorky is effaced in his crowded scenes; to write about himself he draws pictures of others, and it is in these portraits that he is exceptionally strong. Even his grandmother, with all her influence on him, all the charm she exerts, stands out independently in her own right; her grandson has not permitted himself to step into the foreground to obscure her. It is, after all, the massive spectacle of Russia and her people that is important to him, not himself, nor any individual, except in so far as he may be typical of some aspect of the nation.

I I I

Gorky never wrote anything better than *Childhood*. The second and third parts of his autobiography, *In the World* and *My Universities*, which came out in 1915 and 1923, are prolix and monotonous by comparison. Doubtless the absorbing public activity in the years of war and revolution—the debates, the letters, the meetings—made concentration difficult. Besides, in these stages of his life, there was no majestic grandmother to fill the central place. And so the later reminiscences are a picture gallery, loosely assembled and chronologically arranged.

I think of myself [said Gorky in *Childhood*] as a hive to which various gray, simple persons, like bees, brought the honey of their knowledge and their thoughts about life, generally enriching my soul, each as best he could. The honey was often dirty and bitter, but all knowledge is honey just the same.

Knowledge is Gorky's passion, to know and understand, his consuming interest. He paints his portraits in the light of it, and is expert in bringing out the grayness of his "simple persons" and in suggesting the bitterness of the honey they bring him. The hive itself, however, remains shadowy, its depth and inward structure problematical.

After leaving his grandfather's home, the child held a series of jobs: he was errand boy in a shoe store, dishwasher on a Volga steamer, general helper in a draftsman's establishment, kitchen boy on another ship, assistant in an icon maker's shop, supervisor on construction projects at the great yearly fair of Nizhni-Novgorod—all this before the fall of 1884 when, at the age of sixteen, he made his way to Kazan in the hope of entering the university there. It is a somber record, lightened by one bright word that recurs in it time and again, "interesting": "Everything was terribly interesting; everything held me tense, and from everything there seeped into the heart a kind of quiet, untiring sadness." And always, in each phase of his career, some one person stands out.

In *Childhood*, in addition to Akulina Kashirina, there had been Good Idea, who, deeply moved by the grandmother's tales, told the boy he must preserve them; when the tearful child asked "Why is it they don't any of them like you?" he explained, "Because I am a stranger. Understand?" He was, in Gorky's experience, "the first of an endless series of strangers in their own land—her best people." Now there was Smoury, the chef on his first steamer—enormous, gruff, sardonic, and kind, with little use for human beings but a great reverence for books. "The difference between people," he instructed, "is their stupidity: one is smarter, another less smart, a third—an utter fool. And to become brighter one must read the right books, black magic and what have you. You must read all the books so you'll find the right ones." Alexey read out loud to him from the miscellany the strange man had stored away in his trunk: *The Teachings of Omir; Memoirs of an Artilleryman; The Letters of Lord Sedengali; Concerning the Bedbug, A Harmful Insect, and also Concerning the Extermination of the Same, with a Supplement of Advice against Those that are Attendant upon It;* but also some of Gogol's stories, and *Ivanhoe,* and *Tom Jones.* "You—read!" Smoury would say. "If you don't understand a book, read it seven times, if you don't understand it seven, read it twelve times." And when they were parting: "Farewell. Read books, that's the best there is!"

He took me under the arms, lifted me up, kissed me, and set me firmly down on the harbor deck. I was sorry both for him and for myself; I almost started to bawl as I saw him going back to the ship, pushing the stevedores aside, large, heavy, solitary. . . . How many was I later to meet such as he—kind, solitary men, broken off from life!

At a later stage, there was the widow of some fairly prominent political personage who moved into the neighborhood, beautiful, worldly, different from anyone Alexy had ever known. She rode horseback and received visitors, one of whom performed so wonderfully on the violin that when the windows were open, passers-by stopped on the sidewalk to listen to him. She herself played the piano, and young Gorky would stand outside, entranced: "That music intoxicated me. I could see nothing but the window, and back of it, in yellow lamplight, a woman's shapely figure, her proud profile and white hands flying like birds over the keyboard." (One thinks, by contrast, of little Nicholas Irteneyev blissfully dozing off in a big armchair to the sound of his mother's playing a Field concerto.) To himself he called her Queen Margot, and he daydreamed of finding a treasure which he would give her to make her rich. She introduced him to the great Russian writers of an earlier day—Pushkin, Turgenev, Aksakov, Tyutchev—and she would often say "thoughtfully and with annoyance: 'you ought to be

studying, studying, and I keep forgetting this! Oh, Lord.
. . .'" She too soon went away. Then there was the stoker
on his second ship, a man who looked everyone straight in
the eye, held himself to be anybody's equal, and was too
self-reliant ever to feel himself insulted. "Have you ever
been insulted?" the boy once asked. "Why, who'd ever insult me? I am strong. I'd give it him!" "I don't mean beat-
ings; has your soul been insulted?" "The soul can't be insulted, the soul won't admit insults. Nothing can touch the
human soul in any way," he said. Alexey saw in him something that was "alien to everybody, as there had been in
Good Idea," and thought that he was himself "aware of his
uniqueness, of men's inability to understand him. . . . He
had been everywhere, had sinned with every woman who
crossed his path; he talked of everything good-naturedly,
calmly, as if he had never in all his life experienced either
insult or abuse." He was a puzzle, a locked trunk, to which
the boy tried to find the key, immensely drawn to him and
yet put off by what seemed to be his indifference to human
beings. And the riddle still unsolved, he too dropped out of
sight, having been suddenly persuaded by a stranger, a
eunuch who had come on board, to accompany him to his
sect in Siberia. "Why did the man go he knew not where?
And what kind of man was Jacob Shoumoff?" What kind of
man was Peter Vassilich, the expert in ancient icons, who
drove a hard bargain with the owner of the icon shop and
helped him cheat his customers? A strong, sinewy old man,
who appeared to know everything, "the city's whole life, all
the secrets of the merchants, the clerks, the priests, the petty
tradesmen." He too was mysterious, as if "engulfed in a bottomless emptiness" into which one might fall if one came
too close to him. In this he was somewhat similar to the
stoker Shoumoff, but he was like Grandpa in the stories he
told; they were never fanciful and had the same meaning
as his: "wealth was always obtained by sinning against
men and God. Peter Vassilich did not pity men, but of God
he spoke with warm feeling, sighing and shutting his eyes."
He was attractive because he knew so much about mysterious human life and because of "his ability to talk vividly

and interestingly. It sometimes occurred to me that just such was the prophet Elijah as he went through the world, solitary and vengeful."

His last two summers in Nizhni, Alexey was required to keep an eye on the workers hired by his employer for construction projects at the fair. These men were much older and more experienced than he; it was awkward for him to treat them as potential thieves. Besides, he liked them, especially the carpenter Ossip, who filled his horizon as Jacob Shoumoff had filled it, and who reminded him also of Smoury and Peter Vassilich. It was impossible to tell what this man's attitude to men might be. He seemed always to be making fun of them a little, and also to understand them thoroughly. He reversed Alexey's impressions of those who were in his charge, and left him dumfounded by his wisdom. "He seemed to me much wiser than all the people I had ever met; I walked around him in the same mood as around the stoker Jacob, wanting to know, to understand the man," but he was unseizable; he "wriggled and slipped" away. In his staunchness he was like Peter Vassilich, but "different . . . pleasanter," and suddenly, with all his cleanliness and neatness, he would "resemble the stoker Jacob, indifferent to everything." In fact, he was in one way or another like all the old men Alexey had ever seen, including grandpa. "All of them were extraordinarily interesting old men, but I felt that to live among them was impossible—it was painful and disgusting. They seemed, as it were, to corrode one's soul; their wise speeches covered one's heart with reddish rust. Was Ossip kind? No. Mean? Also no." His wisdom, however remarkable, was nevertheless deadening, "and at last I began to feel that he was in every way inimical to me."

By the age of fifteen Alexey had grown depressed: his work was meaningless, this raising of structures that were invariably destroyed by spring floods, which no one did anything to control; the sordid life about him, so stupidly brutal, so mean and loathsome that as he recalled it he wondered how it was he did not lose his mind at the time or kill someone. The reading he had done showed him the possibility of a more generous, more intelligent life. But how

was one to find it or build it in this land of self-satisfied ignorance, depravity, and ill will? He thought: "All men are
strangers to one another, in spite of kind words and smiles;
and indeed all are strangers on earth; no one, it seems, is
bound by strong feelings of love. Only grandmother loves
to live and loves everything. Grandmother and the magnificent Queen Margot." The only way out of the slough was
learning; and Gorky's struggle for an education seems almost as difficult and his determination to get it as great as
that of men born deaf and blind. His grandfather had
taught him the Church Slavonic alphabet and made him
spell out words in the Bible; his mother coached him in secular texts and tried to make him memorize verses. Of formal
schooling he had had less than a year, and a very unhappy
year, at that: the teachers disliked his impudence, and the
boys, who knew that he was trying to earn a little money as
a ragpicker, complained that he smelled of garbage—quite
meanly and unfairly, for he always washed himself and
changed his clothes after his scavenging expeditions; and
only Khrisanph, the visiting priest, was kind to him. Nevertheless, he had been given a prize at the end of the term—a
certificate of merit, of which his grandfather was very proud,
and some books, which he promptly sold for fifty-five kopeks
to help out his grandmother, who was sick. This was in the
spring of 1878; that fall he went out "into the world." The
people he was now living with were afraid of books. They
were written by "fools and heretics" said the draftsman's
mother-in-law; and her daughter declared solemnly: "It is
very harmful to read books, especially in one's youthful
years." Even the priest at confession, to which Alexey was
once made to go and for which he prepared himself with
fearsome searchings of soul, had no interest in the sins he recited and only wanted to know if he ever read "forbidden
books." When, by the merest chance, he got hold of books
again, he had to read them secretly, in the shed where he
chopped wood, or standing by the window of the attic
where he slept. He saved candle drippings, and with a piece
of twisted thread for wick would make himself a miserable,
smoky light that hurt his eyes. He read whatever came to

hand. It was mostly trash, but in the midst of it he stumbled
upon Edmond de Goncourt's *Les Frères Zemganno* and
Balzac's *Eugénie Grandet*. They were a revelation. They
showed him that one could deal gently and calmly with the
kind of truth with which he was familiar. "There were no
villains" here, nor any "good souls. There were simply men,
wonderfully alive; they made it impossible to doubt that everything they said and did had been said and done precisely
so and could not have been done otherwise." In addition,
old numbers of an illustrated journal, which he found
stored away under a bed, gave him glimpses of other parts
of the world, unlike the dreary Russia he knew. Then came
Queen Margot, and with her—Pushkin, Heine, Béranger.

The rest was bigotry, gossip, drunkenness, cynicism, cruelty, and crime. The word "dreary," declined in all its cases
and formed into every conceivable part of speech, sighs like
a bleak refrain throughout the pages of the autobiography.

Across the Volga, cloud shadows drag themselves slowly; falling
over into meadows, they grow lighter, just as if they had washed
themselves in the water of the river. Everything around is half
asleep, everything is so deadened, everything moves so unwill-
ingly, of sad necessity, not through burning love of motion, of life.
And one wants so much to give the whole earth and one's self a
good shove, so that all things, myself included, might spin in a
joyous whirl, a festive dance of people in love with one another
and with life, which was intended to be a different kind of life,
beautiful, cheerful, honest. . . .

He must, he decides, do something with himself or perish.
And encouraged by a nineteen-year-old student, Evreinov,
who assures him that he is cut out to be a learned man, that
universities are in need of such as he, that he can live with
his own family, prepare for entrance examinations in the
fall and winter, and in some five years become a scholar—so
encouraged, Gorky goes to Kazan. Grandma sees him off:

I stand in the ship's stern and see how, at the edge of the pier,
she crosses herself with one hand and with the other wipes her

face on the corner of an old shawl, her eyes filled with the light of an unquenchable love of people.

Suddenly and painfully he realizes that never again will he meet anyone "so tightly, so warmly close" to him; and this is his last glimpse of her.

In Kazan, which is the setting of the third part of the autobiography, ironically entitled *My Universities,* he soon discovers that Evreinov's widowed mother has all she can do to keep herself and her two sons alive on a beggarly pension. Ashamed to be eating her bread, he gets himself odd jobs on the wharves, enjoying the men he meets there, "nakedly greedy, coarse-grained," with angry, scornful views on life and a carefree attitude toward themselves. At first he envies these thieves and vagabonds, until he discovers that when they get together at night to talk, smoke, and reflect on life, they hardly listen to one another; each man talks about himself; and everything they say is in the past tense, as if everything has happened already and nothing else will ever happen again. They, too, are unsatisfactory, not like people in good books. The university, meanwhile, has refused him: he is too young and too ill prepared. In the cellar of a burned-out house, a refuge in bad weather, he comes across university men, makes friends with one of them, Guriy Pletnev, and moves in with him into a crowded tenement, peopled by students, prostitutes, and half-crazy dreamers. Among them Pletnev, gay, agile, witty, with a gift for music and a mellow, thrilling voice, is like "a good spirit in tales of magic." He earns his living, eleven kopeks a night, as proofreader on the night shift of a newspaper and, "like nearly all gifted Russians . . . lives on the means with which nature has endowed him, without trying to strengthen and develop them."

From now on Gorky's canvas becomes more crowded than ever. Vignettes of men and women, appreciative, humorous, indignant, fill his pages. Quite understandably, this part of his autobiography became some of Lenin's favorite reading, for it tells the story of how a revolutionist is made.

The youth now meets men who hold secret meetings, discuss forbidden books, establish an underground press, get arrested and sent to jail or to Siberia; factory workers, two of whom become his special friends: a consumptive young atheist, Jacob Shaposhnikov, who spits out his lungs as he reviles God, and the wise old Nicholas Rubzov; there are theological students who organize loathsome orgies in houses of prostitution; there is a Tolstoyan who propounds with overbearing hatred the doctrine of humility and love, and a meek little man who knows all the prayers to the Virgin by heart, flogs his small children, and is brought to court for torturing his wife. In the illegal library of the baker for whom he works, Peshkov reads works of social philosophy and popular science: Adam Smith, Chernishevsky, Lavrov, Pisarev, Tolstoy, Plekhanov.

Then an illiterate letter from Nizhni brings news of grandma's death. And Jacob Shaposhnikov dies, and Rubzov is hauled off to jail; and a police inspector tries to make an informer of Alexey. All these impressions and experiences are a disordered chaos; and suddenly—or perhaps not so suddenly as it appears—Alexey Peshkov realizes that he cannot go on living. One October day in a drenching rain he sees a prostitute dragging a drunkard up the street, "holding him under the arm, pushing him, while he mumbles something and snivels. The woman says wearily in a muffled voice: 'Such is your fate.'" And Peshkov thinks: "I too am dragged and shoved into wretched corners, that show me dirt, misery, and a strange motley of human beings. I am tired of it all." He feels helpless, and since he has always despised helplessness, begins to look on himself "coldly, with alien, hostile eyes," sensing in himself the contradictions he detects in every man, "not only of words and deeds but also of feelings."

I was being drawn in all directions, toward women and books, toward workers and the gay world of students, but I was getting nowhere and lived "neither here nor there," spinning like a top, while someone's unseen but mighty hand kept whipping me on with an invisible, scorching lash.

In December 1887 he tries to kill himself: he buys a revolver, and intending to put a bullet through his heart, succeeds only in damaging his left lung, which gives him trouble for the rest of his life.

The incident lowers him further in his own eyes, but he is saved from a more serious depression by a man who unexpectedly befriends him. This is Michael Antonovich Romass, a political offender recently returned from imprisonment in Siberia. Alexey used to see him, silent and observant, at discussion meetings; and now, feeling that at long last a chance to do something worth while has been given him, he agrees to help him with the shop which he keeps in a nearby village on the Volga as a means of carrying on propaganda among the peasantry. With great tact, Romass restores his self-esteem and helps him straighten out his chaotic impressions:

"You must study [he says], yes, but in such a way as not to have books shut people off from you. . . . Those students of yours gabble a lot about loving the people. But I tell them: it's impossible to love the people. . . . To love means to agree with, to indulge, to overlook, to forgive. That is the way to deal with women. But is it possible to overlook the people's ignorance, to agree with the delusions of their minds, to indulge their every villainy, to forgive their beastliness? No? . . . Well, you see, what you should impress upon the peasant is this: 'Though you're not bad in yourself, brother, you live badly and can do nothing to lighten your life, to make it better. Even the beast, I'd say, lives better than you do, cares for himself more rationally than you, defends himself better. And yet it is from you, the peasant, that everything has grown, the nobility, the priesthood, the scholars, the czars, all of them were peasants once. See? Understand? Well, learn to live so they don't muzzle you.'"

He gives him Hobbes's *Leviathan* to read, Machiavelli's *Prince*, and other classics. This is the teaching the youth needs to find his way through all he has seen, the people he has known, and the theories he has heard, those of the Populists, the Tolstoyans, the Marxists. But the happy interlude with Romass is of brief duration. In August 1888 the rich, resentful peasants of the village burn down his house. Romass decides to set up shop elsewhere, and Alexey, with a peasant friend of his, travels down the Volga to the Caspian Sea, as stowaway, or doing odd jobs. Toward the end of their voyage, as they are unceremoniously taken off their barge, his pal philosophizes:

"You've got to choose the truth that suits you! There, the other side of the gully, there's a flock grazing, a dog running, a shepherd walking. Well, what of it? What good will our souls, yours and mine, get out of that? Look at things simply, my dear fellow: man is evil, that's the truth, and the good man—where is he? The good one, he's not been invented yet, and that's a fact!"

So ends the autobiography, a story of how Gorky tried to find "the truth that suited him," through the examples of many evil men and the precepts of the few good ones who now and then emerged miraculously through the darkness of a dreary world. What followed is recorded in other writings and the annals of Russian history.

For another year he continued with a variety of miscellaneous jobs, made a pilgrimage to Moscow in the vain hope of seeing Tolstoy, returned to Nizhni, where he worked at first in a warehouse, rolling kegs of beer, and then as clerk in a lawyer's office. Because of his bad lung, he was rejected by the army. Then, at the end of 1889 he ventured to show his first ambitious piece of writing to Vladimir Korolenko, whom Romass had known in exile and who was now living in Nizhni. He was proud of this piece, "The Song of the Ancient Oak," a "philosophic poem" in prose and verse. It was the distillate of all his thinking, and he was sure it would set the world on fire. But Korolenko, leafing through it and speaking kindly, was so devastating in his criticism, which the young author recognized as astute and perfectly just, that he wanted "to run away in shame." He consigned his work as a "sacrifice to the all-cleansing fire," and for almost two years wrote nothing more. One night he came upon Korolenko in the street and put to him a ques-

tion that had long bothered him: "How is it you are so
calm?" "I know what I have to do," said Korolenko, "and
am convinced of the usefulness of what I am doing."

In quest of conviction and usefulness, Peshkov left Nizhni
in April 1891 to wander over Russia. He went to Bessarabia,
to Odessa, to Tiflis, and after two years was "exhausted," as
he recalled much later, by the "variety and weight" of the
impressions he had gathered, feeling himself "a rich man
who does not know what to do with his accumulations and
spends his treasure senselessly, scattering all he has for anyone who cares to pick up what he has thrown away." But
in Tiflis he met someone who appreciated his gift, took him
seriously, and made him write. This was also a political
exile, Alexander Mefodeevich Kaliuzhnyi.

You were the first [Gorky wrote him thirty-four years later] to
look upon me not only as a fellow with a strange biography, a
shiftless vagabond, something amusing but dubious. I remember
your eyes as you listened to my stories about what I had seen and
about myself. I straightway understood that before you one could
not brag about anything, and it seems to me that it is thanks to
you that I have never bragged about myself nor the sorrows with
which life has so generously supplied me.

You were the first, I say, who made me look seriously upon myself. I owe it to the thrust you gave me that for over thirty years
now I have been honestly serving Russian art.

It was in Kaliuzhnyi's apartment that Peshkov wrote his first
published story, "Makar Chudra"; and it was Kaliuzhnyi who
arranged for its publication in the local newspaper, *Caucasus*. There it appeared in September 1892, signed by the
pseudonym, "M. Gorky," which had occurred to the author
in the publisher's office. In October he returned to Nizhni;
Korolenko now helped him publish his short stories and
sketches, and two years later persuaded him to become a
reporter on a paper in Samara. In 1896 he took on the same
kind of work back in Nizhni, and in 1898 came the triumphant publication of his collected stories. Fifty years later,
when the Soviet Academy brought out his complete works,
the edition comprised thirty volumes.

IV

Gorky early discovered "the truth that suited him," a broad, general truth that he spent his life explaining and describing; the illustrations changed as Russia changed, but the truth remained the same. In 1928, in answer to letters he was receiving daily about his literary beginnings, he addressed a long article to workers and soldiers, entitled "How I Learned to Write." Two reasons, he said, had impelled him: "the pressure of an exhaustingly barren life" and such an abundance of impressions that "not to write was impossible." The former caused him to produce romantic fables, like "The Song of the Falcon" and "The Song of the Stormy Petrel," in an attempt to bring color to drabness, enthusiasm to dullness; the latter, to write realistic tales and sketches of that drabness and that dullness, which, as one knows from his autobiography, he had experienced abundantly. He did not, like Zola, for example, decide to seek out the mean side of life for scientific and humanitarian purposes; he was born into it, and his journalistic work added to his store of gruesome documents. His most telling reports for the Samara and Nizhni papers were eyewitness accounts of savage incidents, such as the one of a young woman who, tied naked to a cart, was dragged through the village streets and horsewhipped by her husband in punishment for adultery, while the villagers looked on in sadistic delight, a sketch that ends: "And thus I saw that all this is possible among illiterate, shameless people, grown wild in wolvish lives of envy and greed." (Gorky had taken the woman's part on this occasion, and was beaten for his pains.)

But the early stories, those that appeared in the *Tales and Sketches* of 1898 or a few years later, were mostly a determined transmutation of "shameless, wolvish" existence, a paean of praise to human possibilities, a Hymn to Man. The sea and the steppe are their usual setting:

The immense sea, lazily breathing by the shore, has gone to sleep and is motionless in the distance, bathed in the light blue brilliance of the moon. Soft and silvery, it has mingled there with the blue southern sky and is sound asleep, reflecting the transparent web of feathery clouds, which, motionless, do not conceal the golden pattern of the stars. It is as if the sky were bending closer and closer to the sea, wishing to understand what the restless waves were whispering as they crept sleepily upon the shore.

So begins "The Song of the Falcon," a distant echo of Gogol's large rhythms and his anthropomorphic imagery; but commonplace by comparison, the words not so subtly chosen, the sounds not so exquisite, for this is not a fragment of a subjective lyric but the prepared backdrop for a rationally contrived parable. And "Makar Chudra":

A cold, damp wind blew from the sea, carrying over the steppe the pensive melody of splashing waves.

And "Chelkash":

Darkened by dust, the light blue, southern sky is misty; the hot sun looks into the greenish sea, as through a thin gray veil.

And "Mal'va":

The sea was laughing. Beneath the light breath of a sultry wind, it quivered, and mantling itself in fine ripples that reflected the sun with blinding clarity, smiled to the light blue sky in a thousand silver smiles.

Against this background of a resplendent Nature, heroic deeds are sung, and crimes are committed. There is the story of the falcon and the snake. The falcon, wounded in battle, has fallen into a crevice, where the snake, creeping up, addresses him:

"What, are you dying?"
"Yes, I am dying!" answered the falcon, sighing deeply, "But well have I lived! Joy have I known! I have fought bravely. I have

seen heaven. You'll never see it so close as I have. Oh, you poor creature!"

"What of it—heaven?—an empty place. Why should I crawl there? I am well off here; it's damp and warm."

After all, thinks the snake, what does it matter whether one creeps or flies? Everyone comes to the same end, and returns to dust. And if the falcon wants so much to see the sky again, why doesn't he come to the edge and try his wings, perhaps they will lift him. With a last effort, the falcon drags himself up to the brink of the ravine, straightens his wings, and falls into the sea. The snake, meditating on his death and on his passion for the sky, forgetting that he who is born to crawl cannot fly, coils himself up and leaps into the air. He falls on the crags, but is not hurt, and laughs:

So that's the pleasure in flying skyward! It is in falling. Oh, funny birds! The earth unknowing and bored upon it, they strain up skyward and search for life in a torrid desert . . . I have seen heaven, I've flown up to it, and having fallen, have more faith in myself . . . I know the truth. To their appeals I will give no credence. Of earth created, by earth I live.

Meanwhile the waves, bearing the falcon's corpse, sing of the meaning of life: "The brave man's folly—that is life's wisdom! . . . To brave men's folly we sing our song." So sings the Crimean shepherd to the author by the softly splashing sea and the "grandly thoughtful" mountains.

Another time, the wise old gypsy, Makar Chudra, by a campfire on a windy autumn night, tells him a story of gypsy love—of the gifted and irresistibly handsome Loiko Zobar, who, overwhelmed with love for the proud beauty Radda, chooses to murder her rather than submit to the condition she sets as the price of her surrender: that he bow publicly at her feet and kiss her right hand. "You keep [this story] in mind," says the old gypsy, "and once you do, you'll be free as a bird your whole life long." "Chelkash" is concerned with a similar kind of freedom, the freedom of adventurous, lawless, great-souled independence by contrast to the conventional servility of money-grubbing; and

"The Old Woman Izergil" is another instructive legend, recited, this time, by an ancient Moldavian woman. It is about Danko the brave, who, chosen by his people to lead them out of the poisonous forest into which they have been driven by their enemies, tears his heart out and holds it up flaming to light their way, dying when he has brought them to the land of freedom. When the story is finished, Gorky, listening to the sad rumbling of the sea, meditates on "the strength of the bold Danko, who burned his heart for the sake of men, and died without asking anything of them in return," and on "the fantasy of men which has created so many beautiful, powerful legends."

These heroic fables embodied revolutionary aspirations; and the most famous of them, "The Song of the Stormy Petrel," was a transparently symbolic prose poem which prophesied a political storm and welcomed it. Written in 1901, its publication was forbidden by the censor, but it circulated in thousands of manuscript, typewritten, and hectographed copies, and became the battle song of revolutionary groups. Presently the young Mayakovsky was to be inspired by it and by the story of the brave Danko.

V

In 1898 Chekhov was living in Yalta; and Gorky, hearing that V. S. Mirolyubov, the editor of a literary journal whom he had recently met, was on his way there, asked him to pay his respects to the author whose "talent he esteemed highly and from whom he expected soul-shaking productions of supreme beauty and power." Chekhov replied cordially that he would be glad to see his books, and Gorky sent him his newly published volumes with the following "declaration of love":

. . . I am sending them, and am taking this opportunity to write you, Anton Pavlovich. As a matter of fact, I want to make you a declaration of the sincerest, warmest love, which I have nurtured timidly for you since the days of my early youth. I would like to express my rapture before your astonishing talent—melancholy and breathtaking, tragic and tender, always so beautiful, so fine. Ah, the devil, I clasp your hand, the hand of an artist and a warmhearted, a sad man probably—yes?

May God grant you long life to the glory of Russian literature. May God grant you health and patience—good spirits, may God grant you!

How many wonderful minutes have I had with your books, how often have I wept over them and raged, like a wolf in a trap, and laughed long and sadly.

Perhaps you too will laugh at my letter, for I feel I am writing nonsense, something incoherent and rapturous; but, you see, it's all so stupid because it comes straight from the heart, and everything that comes straight from the heart is, alas, stupid, even if it's great. You yourself know that.

Once again I clasp your hand. Your talent is a pure, clear spirit, enmeshed, however, in earthy bonds, the vile bonds of daily living—thence, its melancholy. Let it sob! Even in sobbing, a cry to heaven is clearly heard.

This rhapsody was the beginning of a warm friendship that lasted until Chekhov's death, and of a delightful correspondence. Chekhov became fond of Gorky and thought him highly gifted, shaped, as he wrote a friend of his, of "the kind of dough out of which real artists are made," although there were serious faults in his writing. In answer to Gorky's request for his opinion of his stories, he wrote:

My opinion? An unquestionable talent, and what is more, a genuine, a big talent. In the story "In the Steppe," for example, it manifests itself with unusual power; and I even became envious that it was not I who had written it. You are an artist, a wise man. You feel superbly. You are plastic, that is, when you portray a thing, you see it and handle it! That is real art. There now is my opinion, and I am very glad I can tell you of it. Very glad, I repeat, and if we were to become acquainted and could chat together an hour or so, you would be convinced of how highly I esteem you and of what hopes I rest in your gift.

Shall I now speak of defects? That is not easy. To speak of the defects of a talented man is just like speaking of the defects of a big tree that grows in the garden; for it is not for the most part a question here of the tree itself, but of the tastes of the one who is looking at the tree. Isn't that so?

I will begin by saying that, in my opinion, you have no restraint. You are like the spectator in the theater who expresses his raptures so unreservedly that he keeps both himself and others from listening.

Specifically, Chekhov found fault with Gorky's descriptions of nature, his portrayal of women, his love scenes, and with his choice of words that were inappropriate to the kind of story he was writing. The descriptions of nature should be briefer and simpler:

The frequent mention of languor, whispers, velvetiness, etc. makes these descriptions somewhat rhetorical, monotonous, and chills, almost tires, one.

And words like "accompaniment, disc, harmony—such words interfere."

How old are you? [Chekhov asked] I don't know you, don't know who you are or where you're from; but it seems to me that while you're still young, you should leave Nizhni and live for two or three years rubbing yourself against literature and literary people, so to speak . . . that you might climb into literature definitively, head and all . . .

To this Gorky replied:

You wrote me nicely, Anton Pavlovich; and what you said about pretentious words was neatly, justly put. I can't for the life of me drive them out of my vocabulary, and what hinders me further is my fear of being coarse. And then, I am always hurrying somewhere. I am not good at polishing things, but worst of all, I live exclusively on my literary earnings. There is nothing else I know how to do.

I am self-taught, thirty years old. I don't think I will ever be better than I am, and may God grant me to keep a hold on the rung to which I have stepped: it is not high, but for me—sufficient. And, all in all, I am not a very interesting figure . . .

Chekhov, apparently afraid that he had hurt the young man's feelings, wrote back:

It seems you have misunderstood me somewhat. I did not write you of coarseness but only of the awkwardness of foreign words, words not of Russian extraction, words seldom used. In other writers such words, for example, as "fatalistically" pass unnoticed, but your things are musical, well shaped, every little rough stroke in them cries out to high heaven. Of course, it's a matter of taste, and it may be that my views express the excessive irritability or conservatism of a man who has long since adopted definite habits . . .

You are self-taught? In your stories you are altogether an artist and moreover, a really cultured one. It is precisely that coarseness is least characteristic of you. You are wise, and your feelings are fine and elegant. Your best things are "In the Steppe" and "On the Raft"—have I written you about that? These are splendid things, models; one senses in them an artist trained in a good school. I don't think I am mistaken. The only fault: there is no restraint, no grace. When on any given occasion, a man expends the least possible number of movements, that is grace. But in your expenditure, one feels excess.

This praise evoked a rare bit of self-revelation on Gorky's part:

You said I misunderstood your words about coarseness—maybe! Maybe I am elegant and talented, and may the devil take me! In my elegance and talentedness I won't believe, even if you talk to me about it again, twice or ten times over. You said I was wise. Here I laughed. It made me at once gay and bitter. I am as stupid as a steam engine. From the age of ten I've stood on my own feet, I've had no time to study, I've swallowed life, I've worked, and life has warmed me with the blows of its fists and, nourishing me on all that is good and evil, has finally warmed me up and set me going, and so, here I fly. But there are no rails under me. I feel things freshly and not feebly, but I don't know how to think. A wreck awaits me. The comparison is really not bad!

There is probably no better commentary on Gorky's work than this exchange of letters. What Gorky says about himself explains and corroborates the impression created by his writings; and Chekhov's criticism holds good not only for the early, but for all his work. Gorky is usually perceptive, but seldom profound, often monotonous, often tiresome, nearly always faulty; and one notes sadly how, despite his remarkable achievement, a man so gifted, and so successful, could have failed so much. What Chekhov called *excess* a harsher critic might have termed *inflation, magniloquence, turgidity,* to describe that strident rhetoric which is characteristic of Gorky, that loud anxiety of his to make a point, to stamp in an idea immediately and unmistakably.

There are not many stories like those which Chekhov singled out for special praise, in which men's passions are not utilized as texts for sermons, and so are not reduced to formulas. "On the Raft," indeed, in its ironic reversal of habitual notions of morality and in its balanced, indeterminate mood is not unlike Chekhov's own work. Here is the "good," weak, reflective Mitya, whose very earthy wife is seduced by his own life-loving, vigorous father. Their robust animal happiness disgusts him:

"I will go away . . . As fast as I can, away from you, you soulless, godless people! Why are you alive? Where is your God? I will go away. I will leave you, you senseless wolves. You feed on one another's flesh. Curses on you!"

But Serge, his companion, comments in a way with which we are made to sympathize:

"Thinking! Is that an occupation for an ordinary man? There, look, your father doesn't try to be clever—he simply lives. He's good to your wife, and with her makes fun of you, you wise fool."

"In the Steppe" is a tale of treachery and murder, which concludes with the following brief exchange between author and narrator:

"Do you sometimes think of the carpenter [that is, of the murdered man]?" I asked.
"As you see, or as you've heard. . . ."
"And—nothing?"

He laughed. "And what am I supposed to feel? . . . I am not guilty of what happened to him, as you are not guilty of what happened to me. And no one is guilty of anything, for we are all of us equally—swine."

In Chekhov's manner, the story depends on understatement for its effect of wry irony, of the logic of crime when extreme want has destroyed elementary concepts of decency and ethics, and is dominated by a quiet sense of an inevitably paltry, brutal, pitiful humanity. And yet, unlike Chekhov's, its effect is merely chilling: our pity is not roused, we are not made to care for the starving vagabonds involved in the plot, and the grand, calm setting in which the action takes place, dissipates, instead of intensifying, our sense of terror:

The steppe, silent and empty, all bathed in the bright morning sun, unfolded around us, united with the sky at the horizon in such a clear, tender, generous light that every black and unjust business seemed impossible within the mighty reaches of this free plain, covered by the light dome of heaven.

In 1899, Gorky wrote a supremely good story called "Twenty-six and One." The scene is a bakery, where from six in the morning until ten at night, twenty-six men work in a small, low-ceilinged, black cellar that never gets a ray of light: its windows have been covered with thick iron netting to keep the men from giving bread to passing beggars. They are a sick and brutal lot, and their one distraction is the daily visit of a sixteen-year-old servant girl who lives upstairs. Each morning her gay, blue eyes peer in at the little window of the hallway door and her clear, sweet voice calls out: "Little prisoners, give me a bun!" They let her in and fill her apron with their rosiest and freshest buns. Her presence transforms them:

Dirty, dark, hideous men, we look up at her—the door's threshold is four steps above the floor—we look at her, tilting our heads, and wish her good morning, and use special words in speaking to her, words which we have only for her.

And when she has gone, they talk of her without the disgusting crudeness with which they speak of other women:

Perhaps this was because she never stayed long with us; she'd flash before us like a star falling from heaven, and would vanish; but also, perhaps, because she was little and very pretty;

and finally because, although their convicts' labor reduced them to beastliness, they nevertheless "remained men, and like all men, could not live without worshipping something." At any rate, their gift of buns becomes almost a sacred ritual, "a daily offering to an idol." They are protective to her; they tell her "to dress more warmly, not to run fast up and down stairs, not to carry heavy loads of wood." She is to them a symbol of purity, they think of her as their own, they love her. And if one of them asks occasionally why they spoil the girl, he is quickly silenced:

We had to have something to love; we had found this, and what the twenty-six of us loved must for every one of us remain unshakable, our Holy of Holies, and anyone who opposes us in this is our enemy.

Along comes a young soldier who boasts that no woman can resist him. The bakers taunt him with their Tanya. "It's easy enough to cut down saplings," one of them mumbles, "you try a real pine." He takes up the dare, and Tanya falls. When they have proof of this, the men surround her in the muddy courtyard of their bakery, and abuse her in vile language. She stands astonished, then slowly raising her arms to tidy her hair, says calmly, loudly: "Oh, you miserable prisoners!" and walks in their direction as if they were not there. They give way before her. "You beasts," she says. "You vermin!" And goes away, "straight, beautiful, proud."

But we remained in the middle of the yard, in the dirt, in the rain, beneath the gray sunless sky. . . . And then we too went silently away to our damp pit of stone. As formerly, the sun never looked in at our windows, and Tanya never came again.

This little tragedy of an idol broken by its worshipers, not in malice or anger, but through their very adoration; of a deity toppled by those who, now that it is gone, have nothing to live for; of a faith that has been lost, a source of light that has been put out, is, like nothing else in Gorky, full of sympathy with man's tragic inclination to destroy himself unwittingly, setting traps for what he loves and lives by. There is the pathos also of the fall itself. The little deity has been cheated, the child-goddess has lost her innocence and the respect of men. But she is in love, and free, and her pathos is not comparable to the tragedy of the creatures who have lost her, the miserable bakers once more abandoned to their jail and their diseases. The final exchange of insults implies that there is no common ground between the healthy and the sick, the captive and the free. If Gorky seldom attained such powerful effects as this, it was because he himself did not appreciate them. To "Twenty-six and One," he preferred "The Old Woman Izergil," of which he wrote Chekhov that he would "probably never again write anything so straight and beautiful," and florid, grandiloquent pieces, like "Birth of a Man," which expounded the "Truth" that "suited him."

This "truth" was that "man is the axle of the world," but in Russia men do not respect themselves and do not know how to live; that an unenlightened government keeps them ignorant and encourages them to be lazy and grasping; that official tyranny and obscurantism make social outcasts of good men, and that for this reason, vagabonds who cannot tolerate the narrow life, the unimaginative minds of petty tradesmen, are better than respected citizens. Bourgeois comfort is not for them, because they feel at home only where nothing ties them down, and where the horizons are as boundless as the questions they put to life. If they steal, drink, kill, it is that their society does not give their large natures scope enough. Some of them, like the baker Konovalov, are artists in their work, but, because their lives are aimless, they are lost as men. They wander and philosophize by the "laughing" sea and on the vast reaches of the steppes.

"You're wandering?" [says the old gypsy to the author]. "That's good. . . . That's right. . . . and when you've looked your fill, lie down and die. That's all there is to it!

"Life? Other people? . . . What do you care? You yourself are life—aren't you? . . . Do you suppose you're wanted by anyone? You're neither bread, nor a staff, and nobody needs you. . . .

"Who can say why he lives? No one can say, my falcon. One needn't even ask oneself. . . . Live, and that's all there is to it."

When Chelkash was on the sea,

. . . a broad, warm feeling always arose in him. It took hold of his entire soul and cleansed it somewhat of the nastiness of daily living. He valued this, and liked to see himself better here, in the midst of air and water, where thoughts about life always lose their sharpness and life itself its price. At night the soft sound of its sleepy breathing floats smoothly over the sea. This limitless sound pours calm into the soul of man and, tenderly taming its savage impulses, gives birth in it to mighty dreams.

A man must understand freedom and experience grandeur and must have something to worship. A man must dream, and that is why so many men cherish illusions and tell lies about themselves. "You don't believe?" asks a drunkard, having just spun a fantastic yarn about himself.

"I do believe [replies Konovalov]. How can one not believe a man! Even if you see he's lying, believe him, listen to him, and try to understand why he is lying. Sometimes lying explains a man better than the truth. And, after all, what kind of truth can any of us tell about himself? Only the filthiest. . . . But a lie, one can make beautiful. Right?"

Konovalov (who, incidentally, was drawn from life) is here voicing Gorky's own views:

Really [he wrote Chekhov in 1900], our day is in need of the heroic: everybody wants something rousing, bright, the kind of thing, you know, that does not resemble life but is higher than life, better, more beautiful. It is absolutely essential that present-day literature begin to beautify life a bit, and as soon as it does begin, life itself will become more beautiful, that is, people will start living quicker, brighter lives, whereas now, just look and see what wretched eyes they have—dull, hazy, frozen.

Some lies are necessary; they are a hidden truth, and without them all men might live on the dreary assumption of the speaker at the end of "In the Steppe": "Nobody is guilty of anything, for we are all of us equally—swine." It is this question of "what is truth?" that is the theme of *The Lower Depths,* the work by which Gorky is still best known outside of Russia.

V I

The fame of this play, however, rests largely on a misinterpretation. It is seldom acted in a way to bring out the author's intention, which is too foreign to Western concepts to be easily accepted. Usually, it is taken to be a lesson in brotherly love: at the nadir of moral degeneracy, human beings are redeemed by the sympathy of a holy wanderer, who brings them the comfort and forgiveness of Christianity. Actually, Gorky had intended to say the opposite of this, as he explained several times: in interviews on the occasion of the first performance and, at some length, in an article written as late as 1933. In the latter, having described four types of "consolers"—the sincere (an extremely rare variety), the professional, the vain, and finally "the most dangerous, clever, well-informed, and eloquent" of them all, the cold-hearted men who cared about nothing so much as their own well-being and peace of mind, and consoled others only because they could not be bothered with complaints—he declared that the "holy" Luke belonged in the last division, and was the villain, not the hero, of his play.

It was Satin who was intended to be the hero, but the effect was muffed, as Gorky himself realized, because in the crucial moments, when he should have occupied the center of the stage, he was not there at all. Satin is in every respect

the opposite of Luke. With native acumen and honest in-
civility he calls Luke "pulp for the toothless," admitting,
however, that in theory, at least, he has the right idea about
man: that man is "large" and free, and must not be ham-
pered. Satin, who sneers when he is sober and is eloquent
when drunk, who is not apart from but very much of the
group, on the spot when he is needed, sensible, and above
all, realistic in his appraisal of what his fellow men can and
cannot do, has a reserved, genuine sympathy with men,
more valuable than Luke's facile, self-protective kindliness.
"You know how to do better than pity," Klesch says to him,
"you know how not to insult." And his rhetorical speech
about man, which begins "What is man? It is not you, not
I, not they . . . no! It is you, I, they, the old man, Napoleon, Mahommed . . . all in one! Do you understand? It
is—immense . . ." is the culminating point of the play.
From Satin's standpoint Luke's pampering consolations,
when they are not positively harmful—as in the case of the
Actor, for whose suicide Satin holds the old commiserator
responsible—are insulting to man. This has always been
Gorky's attitude. The kind of pity which emphasizes man's
helplessness seems degrading to him. And Russia's "holy
pilgrims" he despises. They wander all through the pages
of his books, and their business, with one or two exceptions,
is to cheat. At best they cheat themselves as well as others;
at worst, they know what they are about, and, mercenary
and shrewd, take advantage of credulous men. Gorky's
Luke is such a wanderer, who, from an accumulated store
of sanctified dogma, hands out good advice wherever he
happens to be, to whoever will listen to him. He clucks
sympathetically over men's complaints, tells little moral
tales to illustrate his precepts, and when the wretches he
has been "saving" run afoul of the law and he himself is in
danger of being questioned by the police, slips out unper-
ceived, not unmindful—with all his show of self-effacing,
great-hearted sympathy—of his own safety, for he is traveling without a passport. He is, in short, a hypocrite; his words
are words only. Without himself believing what he preaches,
he is shrewdly and irresponsibly evil, more dangerous than

outright criminals, for he purveys the kind of "truth" men yearn to accept, and so retards their progress.

He is a figure in a parable, for with all its show of "realism," *The Lower Depths* is not a "slice of life" but a social tract, a play of dialogue rather than action, in which what is done is an illustration of what is said. And what is said is a dissertation on the meaning of "truth," as a Soviet critic, Iurii Iuzhovsky, has suggested, pointing out that all the characters of the play are divided into well-marked groups with respect to the kind of truth they believe in: there are those for whom, as for the Actor, Pepel, Natasha, and Nastya, illusion is truth; those, on the contrary, like Bubnov, Klesch, and the Baron, who believe only in the "truth of facts" and delight in pricking the bubble of man's hope— Bubnov with quiet satisfaction, Klesch with bitterness, the Baron with a kind of sensual delight, "sneering out of envy," as Luke says of him; and lastly there are Luke and Satin, who belong to neither category, and whose position Iuzhovsky explains by reference to Lenin's article *What Is to Be Done?*, which was written in the same year as Gorky's drama. "One must daydream," says Lenin in this article, and he quotes Pisarev, the nineteenth-century nihilist critic:

My daydream may be of such a kind as to catch up with the natural course of events, or it may go off completely at a tangent to where the natural course of events can never arrive. In the first instance, the daydream does no harm; it may even support and strengthen the energy of toiling humanity . . . In such daydreams there is nothing that can prevent or paralyze the strength of workers. . . . When there is a point of contact between the daydream and life, then everything is going well . . .

Quoting this, Lenin comments that of this kind of daydream there is unfortunately too little in his time. *The Lower Depths,* says Iuzhovsky, seems to give symbolic form to this distinction: Luke's is a daydream of slavery that leads to a dead end, Satin's is of freedom, which opens a way out; the one goes off "at a tangent," the other has "contact with life."

This examination of men's illusions and the nature of the "truths" they are invited to adopt is wholly practical. Gorky's "truth" and "reality" are humanist, not metaphysical; they have to do with the useful and the possible. All his characters, dissatisfied with their condition, desiring an opportunity to assert themselves in a society that tries to suppress this desire, are vaguely aware that there is some great solution to existence which they have not yet discovered, and the play urges them to seek this great solution. They are boldly, openly immoral, not ashamed to admit crimes, which are not sins—not offenses against themselves, that is, but against something hateful outside themselves—and so, however illegal, are in a sense justifiable as righteous vengeance. The depths to which these men have sunk are social depths; what troubles them is a sense not of guilt but of inadequacy, and to find truth is their only salvation. They need a belief by which to steer their actions and assurance that they are capable of achieving whatever they have a mind to do. Thence the one among them who represents the ethical ideal, Satin, is a man of action, ruthless in his appraisal of individual failings, but with a naïve respect for humanity and an ardent faith in its grandeur, closely involved in the fortunes of his fellow men, but more clear-eyed, far-seeing, and confident than they, and able, therefore, to inspire them with a vision of their power. The high point of his act is a florid oration about Man.

There are extraordinary parallels between *The Lower Depths* and Eugene O'Neill's *The Iceman Cometh*. It may be indeed that in writing his play O'Neill had Gorky's in the back of his mind. But to compare them is to see how immeasurable can be the difference between similar productions of our age, how an almost identical setting and plot can yet exhibit divergences so great as to make two works of the twentieth century seem as unlike each other as, in the early days of Western culture, were those of Byzantium and ancient Greece, divergences that since 1918 have been, on the whole, characteristic of the art of Russia and the West. For this has been a time when, because of radi-

cal differences in philosophic interests and ethical apprais-
als, comparable human situations can appear to be aeons
and worlds apart.

VII

For Gorky there was a truth "that saved" and a truth "that
killed." And there was the lie that degraded, like Luke's
vision of Paradise, which he produced to console the dying
Anna; and the lie that cheated, like the marble halls with
which he deluded the Actor. But there was also the lie of
unrealized ideals, like the prostitute Nastya's inventions
about the youth who had once loved her. The Baron should
not have sneered at the girl; her preposterous falsehoods
were dreams of something "more beautiful" than her life
had given her, they were engendered by an innocence and
nobility incomprehensible to cynics. This was the kind of
lie, thought Gorky, that the times demanded; and, it is this
conviction that makes his plays very different from
Chekhov's, on which they are modeled.

The other day I saw *Uncle Vanya* [he wrote Chekhov in one of
his first letters to him]. I looked on and—cried, like a woman, although I am far from being a nervous person. I came home deafened, crumpled by your play, wrote you a long letter, and tore it
up. . . . For me, it is a terrifying thing, your *Uncle Vanya;* it's an
entirely new aspect of dramatic art, a hammer with which you
knock the empty noddles of the public . . .

He mentions the superb touch in the last act when "after
a long pause, the doctor speaks of the heat of Africa." It
made him "tremble," he writes, "in admiration of your talent
and in fear for people, for our colorless, beggarly life. . . .
Your talent is colossal!" And then he adds:

But what do you propose to achieve by such blows? Will man
be reborn by means of them? We're pitiful people—that's true,

boring people, sullen, loathsome people, and one would have to be a monster of benevolence to love, pity, help such trashy sacks to live. And nevertheless one still feels sorry for people. I am a far from benevolent person, but I bawled at the sight of Vanya and the others like him, althought it's very stupid to bawl and still stupider to talk about it. You know, you seem to me to be colder than the devil toward people in that play. You are indifferent to them, like snow, or a blizzard.

"What do you propose to achieve?" It would have been impossible for Chekhov to explain his unemphatic honesty, his modest ordinary "truth," in terms of moral purpose. Gorky saw things differently. Convinced that, like himself, all men wanted models for behavior and yearned for sermons, he saw the writer's whole duty as encouragement and exhortation. It was an earnestness that led to falsehood. Tolstoy found *The Lower Depths* tricky and full of subjective comment; the characters, he said, were all alike, and no one ever talked the way they did. "One may invent anything one pleases," he said to Chekhov, "but one cannot invent psychology, and what one finds in Gorky is precisely psychological inventions; he describes what he himself has not felt."

With this one is forced to agree, as well as with Mirsky's judgment that "Gorky never wrote either a good drama or a good novel." And the reason is clear. He had to invent psychology, because he could not take time to understand it, to know himself, inspect his own emotions, and so gain insight into others. Such explorations would have distracted him from what he saw as his appointed task; a lofty aim betrayed his art. In 1912, for example, a year before *Childhood* was done, he published a story about his attempted suicide, as if he needed to get this disturbing episode of his past out of the way before he could examine his life in just perspective. Eleven years later he mentioned it in *My Universities:*

In December I decided to kill myself. I tried to describe the motives for this decision in the story, "An Incident in the Life of Makar." But I did not succeed. The story turned out to be awkward, unpleasant, and devoid of inward truth. Among its merits, I think, one may count precisely the absence of that truth. The facts are truthful, but they are interpreted as if not by me, and the story is not about myself. If one disregards the literary value of the story, there is something pleasant in it for me—as if I had stepped over myself.

Very revealing, this pride of Gorky in an artistic failure caused, in his judgment, by a moral victory! The story is unsuccessful because it is "devoid of inward truth," but its merit is due to the very absence of this truth. Here is the central question posed by all his work; and it is a question not only of art but of ethics. There is something immoral, he implies, in revealing an "inward truth" that is unmanly and destructive. As "outward truth" such weakness is a legitimate, indeed a necessary, theme of art, for then it is critically exhibited from a robust, invigorating point of vantage; but as "inward truth" it solicits sympathy with debilitating states of mind. Thence the failure and the triumph of that drab tale with a happy ending, "An Incident in the Life of Makar."

Makar is not a living individual; his thoughts and feelings might be any unhappy young man's. His suicidal mood is not re-created, although the events that led up to it are detailed with care; nor when he lies wounded in the hospital is the atmosphere of delirium communicated, while the delirium itself is factual, a tissue of details with which we are already familiar; they seem to have been photographed rather than transformed by the unconscious. What a poignant story would Chekhov have made of it, what a nightmare, Leonid Andreyev! In Gorky's version, there is but one moving touch. It comes at the end, when Makar, who has been pining for some evidence of genuine affection, is visited by three of his fellow workmen. It is because a "cold emptiness" has formed around him that he has tried to kill himself in the first place, but of all the people he sees in the hospital—the other patients, who reprove him or make fun of him; the professionally callous doctor and nurses; the medical student who visits him only because he is curious about his case; the girl whom he thought he loved, who comes only out of a sense of duty; even the kindly Tartar guard who picked him up and helped bring him to the hospital—of all these, only the three kind-hearted, awkward men really care for him, and make him feel that he "belongs." They are the only ones who talk about the future, who make him realize that what he has done has been a blow to them, that his action has contradicted everything he used to preach:

Laughing, crying, choking with happiness, squeezing two hands of two different men, seeing nothing, and feeling with his whole being that he had got well for the sake of a long and stubborn life, Makar said nothing. And the angry fellow, efficiently drawing the blanket over Makar's naked chest, grumbled: "Yes, brother, he'd talk and talk, and then himself, see what . . . But we mustn't let you catch cold, we're people from the free outdoors . . ."

Beyond the windows snow was thickly falling, burying the past.

Makar has always wanted to feel "useful"; it was because he was "useless" among "useless" people in a "useless" vacuum that life had become unbearable to him. Books had been partly to blame; he had sacrificed sleep to reading, and this reading had estranged him from the world. He had tried to find companionship among other readers, but they made him feel an outsider; "a self-taught fellow . . . from out the people," they would say of him. Now he was among friends at last, his real comrades, and they were proletarians, not intellectuals. The outcome of his despair was an awareness of his solidarity with workingmen. And it was from the new appreciation of their excellence and of their need of him that Gorky was presently to look back upon his life; henceforth, it was for them and in their praise that he was to do all his writing.

How, in view of such interests and such needs, was one to dwell upon oneself, analyze the kind of experience that made one different from others? This would be to fail one's fellow men, to be disloyal to the claims of "comradeship" and "brotherhood." He wanted all those whom he addressed to be stirred as the baker Konovalov had been when he first read him the story of the famous revolutionary peasant leader Stenka Razin. He would not fill their ears with the type of lamentation that had become fashionable in "retrograde" journals. "I am—I," he wrote Leonid Andreyev, having quarreled with him for writing "decadent" pieces.

It is nobody's business what is hurting me, if anything hurts. To display one's scratches to the world, to rub them in public and let the pus run over oneself, to squirt one's bile into people's eyes, as many do, and most disgustingly of all, our cruel genius Feodor Dostoevsky used to do—that is an odious business and harmful, of course.

All of us will die, the world will go on living; it has shown me and fastened onto me much dirt and meanness, but I do not want and will not adopt its abominations. I take, and have taken, what is good in the world, I have no reason to revenge myself on it, no reason to poison men with the shameful spectacle of my wounds and ulcers, to deafen them with my squealing.

"Brotherhood" most certainly does not consist in showing one's brother one's inward nastiness and filth—but if one can't destroy it, at least in keeping tactfully quiet about it.

This was in the somber period that followed the revolution of 1905. Much later, eight years after "October," he wrote Vsevolod Ivanov, who had said something about the superiority of European literature to Russian:

"We are provincial writers?" That is both true and untrue. For a long while I also thought that as craftsmen we were, of course, inferior to Europeans. But now I begin to doubt this. The French got all the way to Proust, who wrote of trivialities in sentences thirty lines long without periods . . .

And again, while Socialist Realism was in the offing, he spoke of Proust as useless and "unbearably talkative":

Life demands a new Balzac, but along comes Marcel Proust and in an undertone relates the excessively long, boring dream of a fleshless, bloodless man—a man who lives outside reality.

Meanwhile, he himself was speaking out in anything but undertones, and art avenged itself on him for scorning Proustian "trivialities" and that self-knowledge through which alone one man may gain understanding of others. His personages, done with a kind of rough impatience, turn out to be not living creatures but skillful copies of men that act out parables, point to certain timely questions, occasionally to the general fates of men, but leave us indifferent to individuals. Nor are his productions, strictly speaking, "problems": nothing in them needs working out, nothing poses difficult questions or leaves anything unanswered. They are moralities, or *exempla*, rather; the stage is always clearly set, the answers are given, not solved.

You know [he says in a letter to Piatnitsky in the fall of 1901], I am going to write a cycle of plays. That's a fact. One: the life of the intelligentsia. A bunch of people without ideals and suddenly, among them, one with an ideal. Fury, crash, howling, rumblings.

Another: semiliterate, urban labor proletariat. An entirely unquotable thing.

A third: a village. This one will be successful and popular. You understand, a mystic dissenter, a rationalist dissenter; the village stagnant, the village literate; rat poison, . . . the rich peasant, beastliness, darkness— and in it, sparks of yearning for a new life.

And still another one: tramps, a Tartar, a Jew, an actor, the proprietress of a night shelter, thieves, a spy, prostitutes. . . . That will be terrifying. I have the plans all made. I see the faces, the figures. Hear the voices, the speeches. Motives of acts are clear, everything is clear . . .

Characters, that is, are conceived in "bunches," plots as the activity of groups, themes as the discordant interests, views, and procedures of these groups, not of individuals: *Petty Tradesmen* is about fathers and sons, *Summer Colonists* and *Children of the Sun*, about dreamers and doers; industrial progress and hidebound provincialism are the theme of *Barbarians*, socialism and the concept of "law" of *Enemies*. These plays are much more clear-cut than the equally moralistic and sociological dramas of Shaw, Ibsen, and Galsworthy, with nothing of Shaw's wit, of Ibsen's splendid characters, of Galsworthy's complex situations. In them desires and philosophies are always representative of means of livelihood or social classes; they entertain no ambiguities as to right and wrong, no doubts regarding men's capacities and responsibilities, no question as to the outcome: the right side wins, or is bound to win in the near future.

The novels, even the best of them—*Foma Gordeyev, Confession, The Life of Matvey Kozhemyakin,* each one centered on a single individual—are all constructed on essentially the same plot and the same idea. The main character "yearns for a new life," struggles against a stagnant environment, and before the end, has a flickering glimpse of a better world than the one he has known, which, he recognizes, may be attained by others even if not by himself. "There, that's how we live," reflects the pathetic, good-hearted Matvey Kozhemyakin, in melancholy bitterness about the dismal place where he has spent his life; and "the more he thinks, the more does life seem to him to resemble a bad dream, in which what is pleasant flares up momentarily in obscure innuendoes." These words might have served as epigraph to the novel about him and to the other novels as well: to *Okurov Town,* which is a prologue to *The Life of Matvey Kozhemyakin;* to *The Artomonov Business,* a kind of distant epilogue to *Foma Gordeyev;* to *The Life of Klim Samghin,* which sketches in, as it were, the historical backdrop to all these dreary pictures of prerevolutionary Russia. Gorky's work is a tireless, and often tiresome, documentation of a single theme: the spiritual drabness of his country. It was Chekhov's favorite theme, also, but Chekhov, having no ready solution, saw it in infinitely varied patterns of comic and tragic irony, in characters who were not only representative of something or someone but very much themselves. Gorky, unfortunately, did have a solution, and a theory of human nature as simple as that of the medieval "humors." In consequence, his characters, measured by the degree of their success in the class struggle, for the sake of which alone they appear to exist, all resemble one another. Even the best drawn and most admirable of them—kind old nurses with their knowledge of folk tales; devoted, wise old men; strong-minded and strong-willed workers; energetic merchants—even they are all copies of each other. They are observed, judged, the values they live by are examined. They submit to, or fight against, forces outside themselves: people, circumstances, ideas, beliefs. But there is not one whose major struggle is an inward one, who wrestles primarily with himself. Life is dull, and people are dull, and only on rare occasions does Gorky make this dullness artistically interesting. Ideas are tested in events, conclusions are pragmatic, reality is reduced to the simplicity of legend. His fiction is almost icon painting, full of devils and angels, with one or two saintly faces among them, gazing from out the crowded company. These are calm, strong, and puzzled, like those who, loving, have come to terms with life but do not understand their world.

The most complex, and most interesting, of them is also the earliest, Foma Gordeyev. A rich merchant's son, brought into the world and reared in the idea of taking over the family enterprise—his father had married a second time for the sole purpose of begetting an heir to carry on the business—Foma finds his environment abysmally tedious and senseless. There is no one to whom he can explain how lonely he is; his attempts to find companionship are desperate and pathetic; and his misery is now and then relieved in wild orgies and mad assaults on those he hates. These bouts culminate in the last episode of the book, where at a party on board a newly launched ship he hurls frenzied abuse at the men gathered there, is overcome by them, tied hand and foot, and taken to an insane asylum. In the epilogue we see this once handsome, rich, powerfully built man reduced to the state of village idiot:

He seems somehow rubbed out, rumpled, and half mad. Nearly always drunk, he puts in an appearance, either gloomy, frowning and his head drooping, or smiling the pitiful, sad smile of an imbecile. . . . Foma walks along the street and someone shouts to him: "Hey, there, prophet! Come here!" Foma very seldom goes up to those who call him; he avoids people and doesn't like to talk to them. But if he does go up, they say to him: "Come now, tell us something about doomsday, will you? Ha-ha-ha! The pro-ophet!"

—an ending in the best tradition of nineteenth-century pathos, that reminds one of Balzac. But Foma lacks the grandeur of Balzac's creations. It would require someone more sympathetic than Gorky with the sufferings of "unimportant" men to develop the tragic possibilities of this essentially warm-hearted being, who longs for a chance to love and wants to be loved, who tries to find some useful channel for his energies, whose undeveloped mind, without interest in reading nor curiosity about the world, is yet endowed with an honest moral earnestness and considerable acumen, of this man of lethargy and passion, gentleness and violence, timidity and arrogance, coarseness and sensitivity, this fiercely indignant orator who, beaten down by the hypocrites he has been accusing, compares himself, brokenly, to a blind owl he had once chased in childhood:

I am lost—through blindness. . . . I have seen much and have grown blind. . . . Like an owl. . . . I was a boy, I remember. . . . I chased an owl in the ravine. . . . She'd fly and bang against something. . . . She was blinded by the sun. . . . Knocked herself out, and perished. . . . And my father then said to me: "Man is like that; sometimes he tosses, tosses about, batters himself, knocks himself out, and flings himself down anywhere—just to rest!"

This many-faceted individual is oversimplified by Gorky, who wanted to portray in him, he wrote a friend,

. . . a healthy, energetic man, seeking scope for his energy, some occupation corresponding to his strength. He is hemmed in. Life oppresses him; he sees that heroes have no place in it, that they are overcome by petty details, as if Hercules, when conquering hydras, had been overcome by a swarm of mosquitoes.

But Foma falls short of this tragic conception, because his social purpose is too clearly pointed. He is so obviously an example that one loses sympathy with him as a man.

There is one memorable occasion in Foma's life, the happiest of all, when he has the sense of being useful, and no longer lonely. It is when he joins a group of workingmen in lifting a heavily laden barge which he himself has sunk in a fit of drunken foolhardiness. At first, feeling it would be unseemly for him, the master, to take part in the operation, he stands by watching enviously. And then, unable to resist the urge to take part in the concerted effort, he plunges into the work, shouting wildly:

His head was spinning, his eyes were bloodshot, he could see nothing and felt only that something was giving way before him, that he would get the better of it, that any minute now he would overthrow something enormous that was blocking his way, would overthrow it, would be victorious and would then breathe easily and freely, full of proud happiness. For the first time in his life, he experienced such an inspiring emotion, and with the whole strength of his famished soul, he drank it down, was intoxicated by it and poured out his joy in loud, exulting shouts in tune with the workmen.

But as soon as the task is done, the men ask him for vodka in recompense of their efforts; and once more he is master, and once more, alone. This episode is moving. It has an authentic ring; obviously Gorky was writing here of a meaningful experience of his own (there is something very like it in his autobiography). But there are few such episodes; and for the most part, his characters perform as typical representatives of social classes. Even their speech is the speech of these classes rather than of individuals: the enlightened, precise, pure language of the nobility and the intelligentsia; the ponderous church locutions and Slavisms of the literate but semieducated merchants; the clergy's modified Church Slavonic; the ungrammatical, brutal, and crudely witty speech of illiterate peasants and workers. Each man is characterized by the way he speaks, and is fully expressed in what he says. There is no devious relationship between the spoken and the meant, no ambiguities, self-deceptions, tortuous semiconscious processes that transfigure words, misrepresent thoughts or emotions; there is no wearing of masks. A man is what he believes; he speaks his mind, is no more than what he says; his beliefs alone make him interesting and it is on them that he is judged. His days are full of talk. In fact, life seems to oscillate between the poles of violence and philosophizing. Men either beat one another or discourse about Truth. And Gorky almost succeeds in persuading us that human relations consist entirely of fighting and discussion.

With all the "philosophizing" in his work, there is, however, little philosophy in it. His was not a speculative mind, and the arguments that fill his pages, unlike the great debates in Tolstoy's and Dostoevsky's novels, are neither spontaneous, nor intense, nor personal, not like the ardent exchanges of Pierre and Andrey in *War and Peace,* or of the Karamazov brothers, or even of Bazarov and Arkady in Turgenev's *Fathers and Sons;* they are not revelations of character but exhibits of doctrines. The "seekers," like Kozhemyakin, examine the theories they stumble on with pitifully limited minds. They want a formula to live by, and the implication is that they are on the right track, that a formula can be found, that so long as they are zealous in their "search," it does not matter if their minds do not go very far. In fact, Gorky is suspicious of theoretical abstractions and is inclined to think them dangerous. After all, theory is imaginative, and imagination is a fault; like fantasy or superstition, it obscures reality and distracts good pilgrims on their journey to Utopia. In nineteenth-century fiction, men began with convictions which, in the course of time, were modified or shattered—tested, at any rate in experience. But Gorky's men, equipped with nothing but unhappiness and wonder and the burden of a dreary environment, start with clean slates and, like Bunyan's Christian, meet helpful or hindering creatures on the way, who advocate conflicting systems for them to ponder and adopt.

Balzac it was who first taught Gorky how sordidness might be made a theme of art, but what Gorky failed to see in Balzac was his adventurous delight in people and the pattern of living; he missed that mystery and ghoulish symbolism in which Balzac's life of "poverty without poetry" is steeped, the grandeur with which he endows the sufferings of miserable souls, that fascination of his with "hidden monstrosities." Gorky insisted on a pettiness without grandeur, a sordidness without mystery. For him all was plain and straight to the eye of judgment, everything drawn up for moral inspection in the clear light of day. Greatness lay in efficient and purposeful rebellion, in concerted effort, in conscious self-sacrifice for the community. In suffering or failure, in a great man's fall from a high station, there was nothing lofty or remarkable. At one time, in 1913, he gave vent to a virulent denunciation of the Moscow Art Theater for staging *The Brothers Karamazov* and *The Possessed.* Dostoevsky, he wrote, was Russia's "evil genius," who "deeply understood and presented with relish two diseases bred in the Russian by his monstrous history, his dreary and humiliating life: the sadistic cruelty of a thoroughly disillusioned nihilist, and its opposite, the masochism of a beaten, frightened creature." It was Feodor Karamazov, he said, whom Dostoevsky knew best of all and whom he reproduced countless times in his novels under various aspects, because, being himself "a man with a sick conscience," he enjoyed portraying this "tangled, disgusting soul . . . an unquestionably Russian soul . . . at once cowardly and impudent, and above all pathologically evil: the soul of Ivan the Terrible . . . a deeply mutilated soul" in which there was "nothing to admire." And as for Ivan Karamazov, he was simply another Oblomov, "who has accepted nihilism for the sake of bodily comfort," whose " 'unacceptance of the universe' is simply the verbal revolt of a lazy man." Dostoevsky saw only the beast and the scoundrel in man, and when he wished to portray something different, he turned sadism into masochism, Karamazovism into Karataevism, and produced Prince Myshkin and Alyosha Karamazov. On the eve of great events, when hopefulness and energy were needed, it was not such travesties of humanity as these that Russians should be treated to. To be sure, "Dostoevsky is great and Tolstoy is a genius, and all of you, gentlemen, are gifted and clever; but Russia and her people are more important than Tolstoy, Dostoevsky and even Pushkin, to say nothing of ourselves."

Gorky had already quarreled with Andreyev for having become "Dostoevskian":

The man who insists on a passive attitude to the world [he had written Andreyev], whoever he may be, is an enemy of mine, because I have insisted all my life on the necessity of an active attitude to life, to people. In this respect, I am fanatical. Many, enchanted by the immoral twaddle of the asiatic nihilist Ivan Karamazov, discourse with utmost meanness about "nonacceptance" of the world, in view of its "cruelty" and "meaninglessness." Were I governor-general, it isn't revolutionaries I would hang, but just these "nonaccepters," because these blatherers are more harmful to the nation than pox-bearing rats.

And in 1915 he wrote a play, *The Old Man,* in which a spiteful sadist, in the guise of a "holy wanderer," breaks up the life of a good man and drives him to suicide. "Suffering is more sacred than work," he preaches, eliciting an angry question, "What's it for?" and a comment on him that, in Gorky's view, was certainly applicable to Dostoevsky:

He considers himself an avenger [says the heroine of the play], he has—suffered! I loathe suffering. There is no truth in it, no! . . . Suffering is his profession, his craft. Oh, there are many like him! They love suffering because it gives them the right to be mean, the right to ruin men's lives. No men are more vainglorious than the unfortunate.

"Russia and her people are more important than . . . even Pushkin." A true artist could not have made this pronouncement, would not have found it necessary to think in terms of such a choice. It echoes Turgenev's fatefully limited Bazarov. And as the credo of a nation's spokesman in the realm of art, it sounds tragically hollow.

VIII

Gorky's triumph as a writer was not his theater nor his fiction, nor certainly his criticism, or theory, of art—but the portraits he drew from life: his grandmother's, notably, and those of Chekhov and Tolstoy. The latter were brief notes, either jotted down at the time of meeting or vividly recollected years later. In them nothing seems to have been invented, and they bring the men to life again, so precisely are words, gestures, expressions recorded. Chekhov is drawn with tenderness, an affectionate understanding that, through his varied moods, catches the essence and the unity of his work and his personality. Tolstoy is done in wondering admiration, a kind of irritated awe. To use his own expression, Gorky "walks around him," watching, listening, but the godlike man eludes him: he is too large, too many-sided. Yet, if he cannot grasp him, he can report on him; and this he performs in a way so astute, witty and level-headed that we seem to hear the great old man, to see the gestures of his hands, to catch even the motions of his mind. This sketch is the work of a discriminating observer who, neither blind nor captious, is awed by, but by no means subservient to, his subject; he wonders at Tolstoy's grandeur but does not pretend to be at home in it. He admires Tolstoy with a somewhat frightened, uneasy, but amused admiration, thinks him "like a god, not a Sabaoth or Olympian, but the kind of Russian god who 'sits on a maple throne under a golden lime tree,' not very majestic, but perhaps more cunning than any other gods"—and resentful of God, "for, being Leo Tolstoy, it is humiliating to have to submit one's will to a streptococcus."

With God he has very suspicious relations; they sometimes remind one of the relations of "two bears in one den."
He reminds me of those pilgrims who all their life long, stick in

hand, walk the earth, traveling thousands of miles from one monastery to another, from one saint's relic to another, terribly homeless and alien to all men and things. The world is not for them, nor
God either. They pray to Him from habit, and in their secret soul
they hate Him—why does He drive them over the earth, from
one end to the other? What for? People are stumps, roots, stones
on the path; one stumbles over them and sometimes is hurt by
them. One can do without them, but it is pleasant sometimes to
surprise a man with one's own unlikeness to him,

as it was pleasant for Tolstoy to confront Gorky, who re-
sented his lordly playfulness, his asking him such questions
as:

What do you think of yourself?
Do you love your wife?
Do you think my son Leo is talented?
How do you like Sophia Andreyevna [Tolstoy's wife]? . . .

"This," Gorky remarks, "is the maliciousness of a 'bogatyr.'
[*bogatyri* are the mighty heroes of folk epics] . . . He is ex-
perimenting, testing something, as if he were going to fight.
It is interesting, but not much to my liking. . . . His interest in me is ethnological. In his eyes I belong to a species
not familiar to him—only that." He is "a cruel rationalist,"
he is "the devil and I am still a babe; he ought to leave me
alone." Tolstoy would quiz him about his dreams, asking
him once to tell him the worst dream he had ever had.
Gorky, who seldom dreamed and then had difficulty in
remembering his dreams, brought forth two that had impressed him. "You are very literary," Tolstoy remarked,
"very! Don't be angry, but that's bad and it will stand in
your way." Although somewhat hurt, Gorky was not resentful. He tried to understand the man:

His silence is impressive, like that of a real hermit driven out
from this world. Although he talks a great deal on his special top-
ics, one feels that he keeps back even more. Some things it is impossible to say. Without doubt, he must have thoughts of which
he is afraid. . . .
At times he has the broad, calm smile of a man who has over-

come something exceptionally difficult or who has long been gnawed by a sharp pain, and suddenly, the pain has gone. . . .

If he were a fish, he would swim, of course, only in the ocean, never coming into inland seas nor especially into the fresh waters of the world's rivers. . . .

It may be that to him the peasant is simply a bad odor; he smells it constantly and must speak of it involuntarily. . . .

He has wonderful hands, such hands as Leonardo da Vinci must have had. With hands such as these it is possible to do anything. Sometimes in speaking, he moves his fingers, gradually folds them into a fist, then suddenly opens it, and at the same time says something good, weighty. . . .

How strange that he loves to play cards! He plays seriously, heatedly. And his hands become as nervous when he takes up the cards as if he held birds in his hands, and not dead pieces of cardboard.

Never did Gorky write anything better than these scattered notes; they are on a par with the portrait of his grandmother. One sees in them his gift for what it really is, the gift of astute observation, of impressionism. Had he tried to expand and unite these fragments in a consecutive narrative, he would have spoiled them, as he spoiled his scattered images of Russia by cementing them into unwieldy novels with the dull mortar of his reasoning. He looked at men with his own eyes, but his thinking about them was borrowed—his moralizing shallow, his ideas not his own. He lacked the ability, which he prized so highly in Chekhov, to express his appreciation of the beautiful through craftsmanship, in the way Chekhov wrote about the hateful and the ugly. He himself could only denounce and exhort, not hint, insinuate, reflect. He was an educator, a reformer, a laborer; he admired craftsmanship, but could not take time to be a craftsman:

Somewhere Nietzsche said [he once wrote Chekhov] all writers are the lackeys of some morality or other! . . . I am a lackey and I serve a mistress whom I don't believe and don't respect. Do I even know her? Perhaps not.

And at another time:

How fine it is that you can regard literature as your primary business in life. I myself, though I feel how fine it is, am incapable of living as you do. I have too many other likes and dislikes. It angers me, but I can't help it.

Thus, although he may have wished to write lyrics, Gorky produced the marches his "mistress" demanded of him. The nation's claims were elementary and urgent, and where the spade was needed, the chisel was out of place. Gorky was like the man in one of his *Tales of Italy*, who, caught with his young son in a furious tempest at sea, roars out to him, above the din of wind and waves, precepts about the conduct of life. "Is this a time to teach me?" cries the boy. "You never did on land." "On land," comes the reply, "I never felt death so near." So Gorky, before the storm, and in it, shouts to his countrymen in the way the old man shouted to his son.

IX

Estimates of Gorky's achievement are naturally, and unfortunately, bound up with political sympathies. A hero in the U.S.S.R., he is a villain to many Russian émigrés, a time-server and hypocrite, as he seemed, for example, to Vladislav Khodasevich, whose close friend he had once been, but who wrote of him in 1940:

He finally sold out—not for money, but to preserve the principal illusion of his life, both for his own sake and for the sake of others. Stubborn and rebellious as he was, he knew that he would not hold out and would go running back to the U.S.S.R., because no matter how the Revolution had turned out, it was the only thing that could guarantee his reputation during his lifetime as the great proletarian writer and leader and after his death assure him of a niche for his ashes in the Kremlin wall. In exchange for that, the Revolution required of him, as it requires of everyone, not honest service, but slavishness and sycophancy. He became a slave and a sycophant. So instead of being a writer and friend of writers, he was transformed into a superintendent of writers. He acquiesced in that too. One could enumerate many, many things which he acquiesced in. To put it briefly—he turned into a direct opposite of that lofty image of himself for the preservation of which he had made his peace with the Soviet regime.

On the evidence of his work and his letters, it is difficult to accept so harsh an interpretation. Gorky did, of course, return to Russia, a friend of Stalin, promulgator of Socialist Realism, exponent of official Soviet ideology—all of which does not necessarily argue that he was "a slave and a sycophant" for the sake of "a niche in the Kremlin wall." His whole life points to the logic of his return and to what looks like submission. For whatever he might dislike in the Soviet regime, whatever indeed might horrify him in it, he thought that, on the whole, its program was good for Russia, and he wanted to have a hand in shaping it, not for his own "niche" but for his country. No man could have been more eager to play an influential role, and yet none could have been less self-regarding. Like the Makar of his autobiographic story, that is, like himself in his youth, he always wanted to "belong," to be listened to, to work with and for men, to bring them out of slavery into freedom, to "build a good life"; and he believed that the exceptional circumstances of his life were clearly a mandate, that they had imposed this task on him as a duty. His very eagerness, of course, could blind him, and his intellectual naïveté could lead him, quite honestly, to views which, had he learned to think independently, he would have recognized as contradictions of his aims. Toward the end of his life, as his letters abundantly prove, he thought his nation was rapidly reaching the goal which he had always envisioned for it. The people were learning, working, creating; the old apathy and greed were gone. When he returned from his trip to Russia in 1928, he wrote:

People have changed greatly in six years, "In haste to live and hurrying to feel" as they have probably never before hastened and hurried.

And speaking later of this trip, in 1935:

And ever since I have lived happily on that energy which constantly, day in day out, enriches the Union of Socialist Republics,
and teaches the proletariat of other nations what must be done,
how life must be rebuilt.

Splendid is our age! [he writes Romain Rolland in 1932]. Splendid in that it coincides with the renaissance of the world's new,
young strength.

And once again:

I have no intention of heaping a pile of papers on your head
. . . but I want to inform you, as fully as possible, of the gleams
of hope in the creativeness of people who learned to write just six,
eight, ten years ago and are already trying their strength in literature—in prose and verse—in graphic arts, in painting. And in all
this one is so happy to note the play of unfettered powers!

On January 10, 1933, to Stanislavsky:

Happiness begins with hatred of unhappiness, with a physical
squeamishness as regards everything that distorts, deforms the
human being, with an inward, organic repulsion from everything
that whines, moans, sighs for the trashy little security that is being
more and more destroyed by the storm of history.
We are living, Konstantin Sergeyvich, in what is a happy land,
where all the conditions essential for every kind of material and
spiritual enrichment are rapidly taking shape, conditions for the
free development of the powers, abilities, talents of her people.

"You are funny," Tolstoy once said to him, "don't be of-
fended—very funny. And it's very strange that you should
still be good-natured when you might well be spiteful. . . .
You're strong. . . . That's good." And after a silence, he
added thoughtfully, "Your mind I do not understand; it's a
very tangled mind, but your heart is sensible . . . yes, a
sensible heart." And indeed—a tangled mind and a good, a
"sensible" heart—that is Gorky, a man of good will, who was
responsible for much that was beneficent and necessary,

and also, unknowingly, for a great deal of harm—a gifted artist, whose art was spoiled by his good intentions. Tolstoy told Chekhov that he thought Gorky "an unkind man" with "the soul of a spy," that Gorky reminded him of "a theological student," who, "forced against his will to take the hood," had "in consequence become embittered toward everybody":

He has come into the land of Canaan, where he feels himself a stranger, watches everything that goes on around him, notices everybody and reports to a god of his own. And his god is a monster, something like a satyr or a water sprite, such as you find in the tales of peasant women.

Tolstoy was right to the extent that Gorky believed in no power beyond man himself, and if he seemed "unkind," if his heart was "sensible" rather than passionate, it was that, convinced of the supremacy of man's power, and so of his dignity and of his absolute responsibility for what he thought and how he lived, he wanted to drive home this truth, to show that it was not faith but brawn that moved mountains, that Nature, as Bazarov had once said, was not a temple but a workshop; and that, since failure was due to self-love and unprincipled, weak-willed dependence on something other than one's self, pity was out of place; the way to encourage men was not to have them look into themselves, to be sorry for themselves, but to make them interested in others. He prided himself on having never complained:

I do not remember that in my youth I ever complained about life; the people among whom my life began loved to complain; but having noticed that they did this shrewdly, to conceal in their complaints their unwillingness to help one another, I tried not to imitate them.

He did not complain, and he told the truth which suited him and which he considered good for others.

Man is master; there is nothing he cannot learn, nothing he cannot do or come to know; his happiness or misery

depends on him alone, and the only destiny that shapes his
ends is his will to work—such was the text of the sermon he
preached his whole life long. He preferred to praise rather
than pity, and to speak of man's conquests of, rather than
his submission to, Nature. Impatient with theory, complexity, "psychologizing," he saw existence in the light of
his unambiguous dogma, and, like the solicitous father of
very small children, told lies to bolster their morale. All men
appeared to him in the guise of the snake and falcon of his
fable; he wanted all of them to be falcons, never doubted
that they could be, and toward the end of his life had the
joy of seeing them so transformed, as he thought. It was
an ardent zeal, a generous humanistic faith that, to his mind,
was more "loving" than Tolstoy's egotistic passion. Ironically
—and he himself was not aware how very ironically—his
idealism expressed itself in falsehood. The choice between
the "truth that saved" and the "truth that killed" could not
always remain conscious. The "truth that saved" devoured
truth as such; the "tangled mind" confounded judgments
of value and ethical problems, and compressed human beings to a formula; it made him increasingly incapable, as
artist and reformer, of seeing how complex were the concepts he reduced to simplicity, how many-sided the world
he wanted to transform, how various the people he sought
to shape to a single pattern.

He never realized his own confusion; his enthusiasm kept
not only others, but himself, from observing the show. He
was never himself, because he never knew himself, for such
knowledge did not seem important to him. He wrote from
moral outrage. Shock and endurance impelled him to creation: the shock of blows to a highly romantic idealism, and,
after the one failure of will, when he attempted suicide, the
capacity to endure such blows without being resigned to
them. Hurried, impatient, assertive, he grasped at knowledge, ethics, truth. He battered life, did not submit to anything; and, having vanquished spiritual torpor, made a virtue
of his means to victory—that arduous single-minded effort
which had saved him—and with native generosity, wanted to
make a gift of it to others. His "philosophy" was an athlete's

respect for the strength he had developed in the face of odds, and his writing a program of spiritual calisthenics. A healthy man, he had no experience of evil in the sense that Dostoevsky or Baudelaire or Gogol or Edgar Allan Poe or Eugene O'Neill had experienced it. He was simply caught in it, and wanted to rid the air of the infection. He was concerned with sanitary measures, his one desire was to uproot the flowers of evil, not to examine their beauty and make them poetic. He prided himself on a stoic refusal to be a purveyor of sordid truth; and although some of his most successful creations are bewildered men, like Foma Gordeyev and Matvey Kozhemyakin, it was the strong, not the weak, with whom he sympathized. In this respect he was like Tolstoy, but without Tolstoy's insight into the complexity of simple strength. And if, like Tolstoy, he too affirmed his faith in the ultimate goodness of man, this assertion was not so much vision or discernment, as command. He ordered people to be perfect. He was "engaged" in life, in the French sense of *engagé;* as a writer his business was to "serve," to rouse, to work for improvement, to be actively involved in the moment; unlike Tolstoy, he did not look upon human beings as moral entities but only as social organisms: they either destroyed or built communities, and their role in society determined their value as men. No individual was so important as his effect on others, no man so admirable but that he must be taken to task if he failed in the example he set and in his influence on others; no friendship so strong but that it should be broken on the grounds of such failure. His own triumph made him bitter toward those who were too self-indulgent to adopt his principles and act upon them. His evaluation of men was based on premises that were the opposite of Tolstoy's. Tolstoy, the divine egotist, made godlike whatever he himself had lived through. Not Gorky. To a man so innately modest as he, no experience of his own could appear to be heroic. Heroism was an ideal which he saw embodied in others or symbolized in legend. He could proclaim it in ardent appreciation, in that rhetoric which was for him a substitute for passion, in those programs for conduct, which took the place of thinking.

His work is loud, but lacks intensity; and, although it seeks to reverse habitual standards of morality, it documents what is already known, does not reveal new realms of perception, makes few demands on the imagination, and has the effect of narrowing, rather than enlarging, one's experience. It is literature of a crushing immediacy. The human situation appears in it as an object for correction. Once its problems are solved, once it is refashioned, will there be anything more to say? To be sure, the world will then be peopled by "creative" spirits, but what they will create, one gathers, will be material improvements and joyous exclamations about themselves and their achievements. Meanwhile, structure, language, description are all centered on the passing moment. It is an empirical attitude that credits mainly the experience of the senses, and while advocating "reason," distrusts the special province of the mind. Reason, in its proper function, examines the data presented to it by sensuous experience. Its processes are deliberate and private. But in Gorky's method, the data are presented not to Reason but to the Will, which is impatient, demands public arenas for its exercise, holds Reason captive, and orders it about. Gorky considered himself more reasonable than Tolstoy and Dostoevsky, who were avowedly anti-intellectual and, as he thought, obscurantist, each in his own way. His own struggle with obfuscating prejudice, his fear of obscurantism and fantasy, his desire for a rationality as clear-cut and "usable" as arithmetic, made intellect loom disproportionately large before him. He respected it with the exaggerated admiration of a flattered acquaintance, not the critical understanding of a friend. And what he did not see was that his great predecessors were clear about the nature of their allegiance, that their scorn of mind came through the mind, that they set its limits only at the brink of the irrational, to which reason itself had brought them, and the scope of which they understood, sharing the exaltation and despair of such poets as Pascal and Dante. To these, of course, Gorky could be no other than indifferent; in his philosophy, Pascal's "reasons of the heart" had no more meaning than the effulgence of divinity in the Mystic Rose of Dante's dream. He felt no inadequacy in observing and interpreting the world he saw, no yearning for transcendental visions; and while advocating reflection and intelligence, did not distinguish between impulse and reflection nor between instinct and intelligence. All the intricacies of which the others were aware, in the relation between ideas, behavior, and beliefs, were rubbed out in his altogether "practical" thinking, in which the rationality he desired was submerged in the evidence of brute fact. He had no quarrel with the mind, but he made fun of men whose minds were "fanciful"; he satirized "thinkers," but made all men "philosophers"—Satin and Luke, Gordeyev, Kozhemyakin, Konovalov, the hero of *Confession,* all the "seekers" and talkers in his stories, plays, and novels.

His satire is most obvious in *The Life of Klim Samghin,* in which he makes his "intellectual" central character an antihero; and it is in this work that the nature of his artistic failure is most obvious. Its theme, the intellectual history of Russia from the end of the nineteenth century to the February Revolution of 1917, was great enough to have inspired a memorable epic of the twentieth century, to be set by the side of Proust's *A la Recherche du Temps Perdu* and Thomas Mann's *Der Zauberberg.* But Gorky was crushed by his subject; he could not compass it:

Am working on *Samghin* [he wrote at the end of 1932]. Between you and me, it is a very difficult business: the material is oppressive. Geysers of material!

And to Romain Rolland in the beginning of the following year:

Am sending you *Samghin* . . . all that has been published. The rest . . . I cannot bring myself to publish. . . . Without in the least posing before you, I can say in complete sincerity, that this endless history of man's attempts to free himself from the coercions of reality, without changing it except through words—this history, I have written ponderously in the extreme, tediously, and altogether—badly . . .

Alas, one must agree. The story, conceived as both a personal history and the history of an age, turns out to be a pious, accurate, and uninspired chronicle, done in the rough, straight, violent piety of the twentieth century, without romantic "nonsense," with people and ideas taken at face value, their emotions hardly differentiated from sensations, their lives tossed from one event to another, and the sum total of their understanding both of themselves and their society, a bright, malicious quip. Flat people, enormously opinionated, ambitious, self-important, they scoff at everything that is beyond them; and in spite of all their bustle, the tremendous events in which they are caught up take place, somehow, independently of them, and are clear to no one. Gorky was, of course, presenting a class that seemed to him ineffectual and justly doomed, so that the dullness and flatness were intentional; but they are not convincing. In his schematic treatment, all ideas, except the Marxist, seem irritating foolishness, and one is left wondering whether it is only certain people who are inadequate as thinkers, or whether thought as such is useless.

As Gorky progressed from his first stories to his epic, his idealistic praise of Man became more and more the praise of a certain class of men, and human qualities were gradually merged with social virtues. His message was always obvious and simple; and what one misses chiefly in his work is that creative faculty as Keats had understood it: "That which is creative must create itself." With Gorky nothing was self-creative; all was conceived in purpose and driven by the will. A courageous man, generous, unselfishly devoted to the public good, his very zeal for men prevented him from making the most of his unquestionable gift. He was modest about his attainments, and despite his enormous fame and influence, was always conscious of deficiency. One finds repeatedly in his letters such comments as the following:

Here I have been writing thirty-five years, and have been satisfied with myself scarce fifteen times.

To Romain Rolland he wrote in 1934:

> I am not in the habit of sending my books to friends. That is not
> due to stinginess, but, really, I don't know why. There is some-
> thing about that rite that embarrasses me. Perhaps it is that, in
> general, I have no very high opinion of my books.

But he did not know why he had failed, congratulating
himself on his defects, and finding fault with others for
possessing the qualities he lacked. A greater novelist than
he might take him as the central figure of a novel of which
betrayal would be the tragic theme, not only the betrayal
of a man by other men, but of a man's unwitting betrayal
of himself.

"It seems to me," wrote Chekhov, "that a time will come
when Gorky's works will be forgotten, but he himself will
hardly be forgotten in a thousand years. So I think—or so it
seems to me—and maybe I am mistaken." This was in 1903,
when Gorky was just starting out. And now, almost sixty
years later, Chekhov still seems right, as always.

2

ALEXANDER BLOK

(*1880-1921*)

I

Alexander Blok was born in 1880, two months before Dostoevsky's death, and his first volume of poems was published in 1904, the year Chekhov died. He himself lived for forty-one years, until 1921, so that his life spans almost exactly the period of revolutionary transition from the Czarist to the Bolshevik regime. Like his great predecessors in Russian literature, like Pushkin and Gogol, as well as Dostoevsky and Chekhov, he too sought to demonstrate the national and historic meaning of what he saw and lived through. But the solutions demanded of him were more difficult than those that had confronted the other writers, none of whom had had to choose between fleeing to a foreign country and staying as an alien in his own; for unlike Gorky and Mayakovsky, Blok had not been prepared by the circumstances of his birth, upbringing, and temperament to be a revolutionary.

He was born into the highest sphere of the Russian intelligentsia. His mother's father was Andrey Nikolaevich Beketov, a renowned botanist and rector of the University of St. Petersburg, whom he described, in an autobiographic sketch of 1915, as "an idealist . . . of a kind that no longer exists." His grandmother he remembered for her gaiety—"she could be happy just because the sun shone, because the weather was good"—for her love of poetry and music, the humorous verses she wrote especially for him, her hatred of Tolstoy's moralizing tracts, and her admirable reading of Chekhov's stories and plays. She was Elizaveta Grigoryevna Karelina, daughter of a well-known traveler and authority on Central Asia, a charming and gifted woman who was personally acquainted with Gogol, Dostoevsky, Tolstoy, and other outstanding Russian writers; and who had herself made a notable contribution to Russian enlightenment through excellent translations of many works of Darwin, Huxley, Thackeray, Dickens, Scott, Balzac, Hugo, Flaubert, Maupassant, Rousseau, and others—"the complete list of her works," said her grandson, "is tremendous"; they came out in inexpensive editions and sold in hundreds of thousands of copies. Blok recalled affectionately the botanical trips that he and his grandfather used to take together, and a little episode that revealed the old man's kindliness and naïveté: once when he saw a peasant lugging away a small birch tree over his shoulder, " 'You are tired,' he said, 'let me help you'; and the obvious fact that the tree had been cut down and stolen from his own wood never entered his head."

Blok's mother, Alexandra Andreyevna, was the youngest of the Beketov daughters. She, too, loved languages and literatures, and, in her turn, translated both poetry and prose; at one time she wrote verse of her own. She married Alexander Lvovich Blok, a brilliant law student, who became professor of government at the University of Warsaw. His ancestors had come to Russia from Germany in the

eighteenth century. His great-great-grandfather, Johan von
Blok, had been in the service of the Empress Elizabeth;
Catherine the Great had made him personal physician to the
Grand Duke Paul, who gave him patents of nobility when
he ascended the throne. The descendants of Johan von
Blok received lands and other gifts from the crown. Not the
least of these favorites, Lev Alexandrovich Blok, the poet's
grandfather, lost his mind two years before his death and
finished his days in an institution.

"In my father's family, literature did not play an important role," Blok wrote. His father himself, however, had
a taste for the arts: he was an accomplished musician, a connoisseur of letters, and a fine stylist who emulated Flaubert.
Yet in the course of his whole life he published "only two
small books, not counting his lithographed lectures," for not
knowing how "to enclose his perpetually evolving ideas
within the concise form he sought," he "labored" the last
twenty years of his life "at a work devoted to the classi-
fication of sciences." In his search for literary perfection
"there was something frightening," writes his son, "as there
was in his whole spiritual and physical aspect." This strange,
gifted man—whom Dostoevsky, it was said, had once compared to Byron—had married Alexandra Andreyevna when
he was twenty-seven and she eighteen, taking her off to Warsaw after a brief wedding trip. Two years later, in 1880, she
was with him when he returned to Petersburg to defend his
doctoral thesis. Her parents, shocked by the transformation
of their vivacious, healthy, mischievous girl into the timid,
emaciated, frightened woman they now saw, persuaded her
to stay with them; and it was in her father's home that on
November 28, 1880, Alexandra Andreyevna gave birth to a
boy, who was christened Alexander. Her husband's love had
proved to be a form of pathological tyranny, and she never
recovered completely from the tormenting years she had
spent with him. Alexander Lvovich, after a mad attempt to
retrieve his son, returned to Warsaw, and the divorce
took place in 1889. Alexander Lvovich married again, and
his second wife was forced to leave him too. Alexandra
Andreyevna also married again—this time a kindly, tolerant

army officer, Franz Feliksovich Kublitsky-Piotukh, a marriage that was not so thrilling as the first, but more peaceful.

The center of attention of an adoring mother and devoted
aunts, the boy spent his early childhood in the Beketov
home in St. Petersburg and in Shakhmatovo, the small property not far from Moscow which the rector had bought
soon after the Emancipation, while his close friend, the
celebrated chemist Dmitry Ivanovich Mendeleev, acquired
Boblovo, a property nearby. There the two families spent
their summers, and young Blok's happiest days were lived
in Shakhmatovo. It was, according to pictures and descriptions, a small landowner's estate, with an old house on a
hill that commanded, from its balcony, a distant view of
typically Russian country, and with a little gateway at the
end of a garden that opened on a path leading to a rivulet
and a valley overgrown with ancient trees. Alexander used
to visit Boblovo, now and then as a boy, more often as a
young man, and in 1903 Dmitry Ivanovich's eldest daughter,
Lyubov Dmitrevna, became his wife.

He was nine years old when his mother married Franz
Feliksovich and moved into army quarters in St. Petersburg;
and he was eleven when she first sent him to school, which
he endured, he said, like a hen whose beak has been chalked
to the ground. He had little in common with his stepfather.
He wrote dutiful letters to his father several times a year,
saw him very rarely, and learned to appreciate him only
after his death, in 1909, when he rushed to a Warsaw
hospital in answer to a hasty summons, and arrived a few
hours too late to see him alive. Then, wandering about the
city in which his father had lived, going over the papers in
his dingy rooms, learning of the esteem in which he had
been held by his students, he gained a sudden, sympathetic
insight into the complexity and tragedy of this unhappy
being, whose striking handsomeness, as well, perhaps, as a
measure of his temperamental violence, he had inherited.
"He was an interesting man, wholehearted, and even
strong," Blok wrote of him to his mother from Warsaw; and,
moved by this new insight into his own past, he began work,
immediately upon his return, on his autobiographical poem,

Retribution (a work of epic scope, which had he lived to finish it would have been one of the great works of European literature).

It was his mother and her family—whose views were as much European as Russian, as much scientific as literary, as much pagan as religious—who most influenced his tastes and ideas. His mother, indeed, was not only devoted and understanding, but also intellectually stimulating. Throughout his life he discussed his poetry with her and valued her advice, and in the early years she and her sister Maria—who was later to write a hagiographical biography of her nephew—were the only ones to see his verse; they took his writing seriously, encouraged him, and had certainly a great deal to do with shaping his gift.

In 1898, at his father's insistence, Blok entered the School of Law of the University of St. Petersburg, but he received permission in 1901 to transfer to the School of Languages. He got his degree in May 1906. "It was only after I finished the University that my own independent life began," he was to say later. "Continuing to write lyric poems, all of which, from the year 1897 on, can be considered as a diary, I wrote my first compositions in dramatic form precisely in the year I finished the University." But although the year of his liberation from the academic was a very fruitful one, important work of his had already appeared in print: a play, *The Puppet Show,* in April of that year, and two years earlier, his first volume of poetry, *Verses on the Beautiful Lady.* This volume, which was itself a rigorous selection, 93 lyrics chosen from 800, he had been writing since boyhood. Some of the earliest poems were published five years later as part of the first edition of his collected works, in a section called *Ante Lucem* (*Before Light*).

Although many of these poems were written at a time of serious student uprisings, when Blok was at the University, they reflect nothing of this turmoil. The student riots were simply annoying to him; they interrupted his studies, and in his letters he would refer sarcastically to the rioters as "choribantes." Once he appeared at oral examinations which his fellow classmates were boycotting: they called him "scoundrel," he answered in kind; and the professor of economics, who had been reduced to tears by the disturbances, gave him "5," the highest grade, after letting him off with an easy question. Such, at least, in the year of the October Revolution, was Blok's humorous recollection of the incident. At the time, his indifference to political events was evident in his letters. "As regards details of the student riots," he would write his father, for example, "I also know of them principally from newspapers (the most accurate source). Individual rumors are so confused, confusing and untruthful, and my mood (in essence) is so detached and opposed to all the passions of the mob, that I shall hardly be able to inform you of anything you do not already know."

The reason the young Blok was indifferent to "the passions of the mob" was that he was completely engrossed in another kind of passion. He was desperately in love with Lyubov Dmitrevna Mendeleeva. For years his whole life was oriented toward meetings with her, and in his diary, whatever occurred before such meetings was designated *A.L.* (Ante Lucem), and what happened afterwards *P.L.* (Post Lucem), to signify that Lyubov Dmitrevna and daylight were one and the same to him. The greater part of his early poems are dedicated in the manuscript to "L.D.M." or have some reference to her. Then came the ecstatic entry in his diary: "Today, the 7th of November 1902, occurred that which never was before, that which I had awaited for four years. I close this notebook as well as the notebook of my verse, this 7th of November (the night of the 7th to the 8th)." The long awaited event was Lyubov Dmitrevna Mendeleeva's consent to marry him. Her answer had settled a question that was, not figuratively, but literally, a matter of life and death, for Blok had made all arrangements to kill himself in case she refused him.

His lyrics, Blok said, should be read as a diary, but as a diary, *Ante Lucem* and the *Verses on the Beautiful Lady* are very far from being a chronicle of daily occurrences in the life of a young man. They are a musical transmutation of spiritual wanderings and complex emotions, love lyrics of

great depth and purity, religious and philosophic in tone,
their passion all the more touching for the restrained music
in which it celebrates ecstatic dreams. The experience is
similar to that which had once produced the *Vita Nuova,*
for just as Beatrice Portinari for Dante, so Lyubov Dmitrevna for Blok seemed not so much a representation, as an
incarnation of all virtue and divinity. The Beautiful Lady
had appeared to him in visions, and was at once the girl
with whom he was in love and a transcendental figure: the
Beloved, the Virgin, unattainable Beauty, the Ideal, his
ability to create as a poet, the concealed archetype of Truth,
a Platonic idea. And presently, as Blok later explained, "She
turned out to be the World Soul" of Vladimir Soloviëv.
Years later, two long entries in his diary for 1918, the beginning of a commentary on his lyrics for a projected annotated
edition of his poems, are the tantalizing opening of a
modern unfinished *Vita Nuova.* They record how in the
summer of 1897, when he was seventeen, he accompanied
his mother to the health resort of Bad Nauheim, where he
fell in love with K.M.S. (Ksenia Mikhailovna Sadovskaya),
a married woman considerably older than he, how there
was nothing for it but to try to forget her; and how in the
following summer he was still in a state of boredom and
dejection, when his mother forced him to visit Boblovo.
Lyubov Dmitrevna, whom he did not remember, although
they had played together as children, made an impression
on him immediately; and he writes of how he "showed off"
before her, and of the amateur theatricals that began that
summer and continued during the next three summers, of
how "severe" and unapproachable she was, of how in 1900
he read Plato and "mysticism began," and of how in the
"mystic summer" of 1901, L.D.M. gradually began to assume an unearthly aspect and in the following winter appeared to him, clearly, as a Vision; then, of how he used to
follow her, unseen, through the streets of Petersburg, sub-
mitting to the pain of being unnoticed and trying to flirt
with another girl in an attempt to lessen this pain; of the
alternation between this misery and the Visions in which he
beheld her as a Heavenly Presence, ascending to a Beyond

to which he could not follow, blessing her in her ascent and developing an "inward armor" to protect himself with "secret knowledge" against her "severity"; of how this condition of being in love deteriorated to something less than a call to the heights, and yet "the object of both was one and the same face," a face that presently took on "the strange semblance of the Russian Venus"; and, finally, of how this state turned to "witchery" and terrifying "premonitions that she would change her aspect." And he shows how the poems he wrote at the time reflected the stages of his love.

I I

Adoration and intense longing are dominant in these poems. The Beautiful Lady is remote, cold, indifferent, and the source of all bliss. She is veiled in an azure, superterrestrial Beyond; she floats like a cloud or melts like the snow. She reveals herself to the poet in the mysterious sound of whispers, of steps, or of voices singing at an immeasurable distance; or she herself is song, or a star, or a planet. The poet has glimpses of her in the gloom or the refulgence of nights or of dawns, on solitary, tangled trails, or on crowded highways. She is an elemental spirit, at home in the distant fog at twilight, in the steppe, in the realm of ghosts and visions, and she will not be lured to the haven of a hearth. She alters her appearance, is "different, faceless, dumb"; she conjures in silence, and he does not know what she will turn into. Or she is young, "golden," walking on a bright path, bathed in sunlight. Sometimes she speaks tenderly, protectively, like a mother. And in her "Beyond" she is nearer than he to the immovable source of life. She is all that is hopeful, all that is light: the song of early spring, the star that shines in daytime, making bright the pavement of the streets; and when she suddenly departs, the poet is in darkness, without God. At such moments he can only beg her to return, or assert his faith that she will rise again "to weld with fire yesterday and tomorrow, closing the mysterious circle of time." The moods of the poems vary in accordance with her caprices; and because she is both real woman and Ideal, she appears sometimes in an atmosphere of dreams that are like fairy tales or medieval visions, and sometimes in the realistic settings of Petersburg streets. The verses are at once solemn, humble, ecstatic, and tender, Petrarchan in their passion for the Unattainable, Dantesque in their fusion of the human and the divine. Sometimes they are so brilliant in color and at once so elaborately and so naïvely reverent, they remind one of old Russian icons; sometimes, in their concreteness and psychological complexity, they suggest Baudelaire or Dostoevsky. In the last analysis, in both her worldly and her visionary manifestations, the Beautiful Lady is the embodiment of the poet's necessity to love, and through love to understand the moving principle of life, or at least to find a meaning to his own existence. The eternal, the fathomless, the immortal, the endless, haunt him like promises of bliss and denials of misery; and although the Beyond, by contrast to the here and now, may be a silent, cold, springless, loveless place, it provides rest from earthly passions, while its vastness counteracts the misery of the small and temporary. For the present is a lying dream, and life itself an old fortuneteller, mysteriously whispering forgotten words. The Beautiful Lady alone is Reality. If she changes, the poet will be thrown back into the irreality of his earthly consciousness, of that entangling dream, the world, from which he has tried to escape into Her presence. That is his greatest fear.

The first impression produced by these poems is of something large and vague, and yet it is remarkable how precise they are in their atmosphere of vagueness. The mystery, the medievalism, the unhappy longings and intimations of divinity; the wanderings, the whispers and prayers, the knocking on doors or windows of shadowy houses, the tangled paths, the temples and monastery walls, the scarlet dawns, and all the varied nights, with "something" floating on a river, with "someone" singing in the distance, "someone" calling from a far-off shore, unseen, unknown, beckoning, whom the poet runs to meet—nothing could express more precisely a complex state of terror, longing, hope, and anxious joy. Blok was not writing here of thoughts or sensations, but of emotions and those indefinite aspirations that we call "spiritual." These were his theme, and clear concepts could be only illustrative of them. Indefiniteness was, therefore, appropriate. But in the sphere of the impalpable he was precise, and this precision lends maturity to the poems of his youth. For although the yearning in them for a nebulous ideal, the hopeless adoration of a Perfect Woman, the turmoil of doubt, the periods of elation and despair, are young and romantic, the clarity and straightness with which the boundary is drawn between vague aims and clear-cut desires, between immeasurable hope and limited attainment—is not young at all. "His strong undeceived intellect," Professor Bowra has said of him, "did not shrink from contrasting the promise of a great occasion with its actual end. He can convey both the illusion which was once his, and his later knowledge of its falsity." This was always true of him. From the beginning, his work leaves one with the impression that he never distorted the experience he wrote about, and that in the telling of it, there was passion and reserve, but neither exaggeration nor understatement. Thus, even in the very poem with which *Ante Lucem* begins, which describes the dark night of the soul, the youthful Blok, unlike many a romantic poet, makes no mistake as to the extent of this darkness. For although it is so profound that love itself cannot dissipate it, the solitary and dejected poet recognizes that his unhappiness does not consume the universe; he knows it is his own and temporary, just as he knows that the night is black, although the moon is shining, and that its cold light will be replaced by the warm light of dawn. So, too, the first of the love songs, as genuinely broken-hearted as any unhappy lover could wish, is so lacking in self-pity, so un-self-centered, that in all its melancholy lyricism it seems to do no more than record a fact, the fact that she whom he loves is so different from him that he cannot know what she feels or thinks, the simple fact, of which the full tragedy is in the bare statement, that he loves but she does not. Other lyrics re-create, through the mere cadence in which episodes are recalled, all the misery of remembering moments of happiness when one knows they will not come again. The details are given literally, but the tone of voice makes them poignant, because it is full of nostalgia. Blok's voice was never to lose the characteristic tone of its youth, a kind of manly reserve, a passion restrained by the capacity to distinguish between the ideal and the actual, between the desirable and the possible, and to recognize, at all times, that the relation of the one to the other is dubious and usually painful. And so, when he appears to be unclear, it is not that he has allowed emotion to blur his meaning, but that he is writing of an experience that is in its essence, obscure.

He does not explain this experience, for he has no patience with analysis. He is not introspective in the manner of Baudelaire, for example, or of Marcel Proust; and his lyrics are, in consequence, dramatic presentations of recondite and intangible perceptions. To make them intelligible, Blok speaks of them in images, words, and rhythms that are familiar. Not afraid of the cliché, he comes to it as if it had never been known before, and revives that original excellence of a phrase or an image which, in the course of time, has made it universally appealing, and therefore trite through being used too much. This he could do because he experienced life and literature in themselves, not primarily as poetic material; and the Romantic tradition, on which he had been brought up and which he respected, did not serve him as a point of departure or inspiration but as sanction for his own observations and moods. The woods, the skies, the meadows of his gold-and-azure landscapes in *Ante Lucem* and *The Beautiful Lady* that, on a hasty reading, might seem to be conventionally romantic were inspired by Shakhmatovo rather than by any literary work; and they are not descriptions but tracings of subjective states, figurative landscapes that stand for a quiet and, somehow, unterrifying mystery, and are as much pictures of the soul as of the earth. Nor are they, properly speaking, similes or metaphors, but only the natural way of expressing a simple perception of unity between subject and object, when some familiar romantic feeling or thought is felt to be, in essence, the same as an equally familiar and romantic aspect of Nature, so that the two are not so much understood to be similar as felt to be one, and the sign of equation between them is obliterated.

But some of these poems are nightmares, images of terror and of death: the poet is followed, in moonlight, by throngs of raging people, their hair on end, gnashing their teeth, beating their breasts; and after them, exhausted ones dragging themselves lifelessly; while before him is a column of fire; and he feels happy and irresponsible as he watches the numberless multitudes and counts their footsteps. Or a man rises out of darkness, walks past him swiftly, to a place where there is neither ice nor fire—a man whose face is concealed, but who turns around suddenly and, for one brief instant, reveals an eye of flame. Especially sinister are the lyrics in which the Double appears: he stands white, importunate, and lifeless in the roadway on a winter night, gazing into the frosty distance; immovable and unconquerable, he stands between the poet and the sky-blue Queen of Earth. Or he is a feeble, trembling, despicable old man whom the poet defies, or drags along with him; he performs secret deeds of horror of which the poet reaps the reward; or he holds him captive, and releases him only that he may return to inevitable torment, inevitable love. One of these lyrics is inscribed in the manuscript as follows: "This poem is dedicated to my other 'I'"; and a diary note records: "I have been split in two. And so I wait, fully conscious, on the forest-fringe—while the other performs a secret deed in far-off fields . . . the murderer-double will do his deed, and drop away, but the whole recompense goes to the onlooker, who has taken no part in the murder. It is a mad idea—but, then, the reward itself is madness. . . ."

Other poems remind one of Gogol's ostensibly simple, "realistic" tales whose commonplace details point to realms of anxiety or terror. In one poem, for example, Blok sketches

a house on a city street. It has a steep stairway that leads
somewhere into the darkness, and there is a commercial sign
over the doorway, "Flowers." Somewhere, on a landing, a
glass door opens, letting out for a moment a stream of
light; up above is a window covered by a motionless curtain, and behind it there is singing, music, dancing. Along
the dimly lighted stair there glides a shadow—and suddenly
the door opens, light streams forth; then all is dark again.
This was the house to which Lyubov Dmitrevna used to go
for drama lessons, while Blok followed and waited in the
silent and deserted street; but we do not need to know this
bit of biography to understand the experience of dejection,
hope, and expectation that the poem conveys. The "real"
house becomes the source of light from which the poet is
shut out and to which he aspires, the unknown and desirable
place visited by the Beautiful Lady; it is built as much of
thought and emotion as of wood and stone, the music and
dancing behind its drawn blinds are those of angels in a
forbidden heaven; it is a symbol, a greatly reserved statement of emotion by virtue of which Blok's love lyric becomes especially affecting, and his "mysticism" gains psychological concreteness. So, too, Baudelaire's imagination
had transformed the ordinariness of cats and smoking pipes,
and, by means of a profound attentiveness to them, made
magnificent the very repetitiousness of sordid settings.
And yet these poems of wonder and of terror betray neither
nervousness nor grievance; they do not sound anxious, although they speak of anxiety. They seem deeply sad, rather,
more filled with praise than with self-pity, and the feeling
of devotion is so characteristic of them, that even in their
expressions of loss, they sound like benedictions. They are
intense, quiet, and worshipful, as if Blok were always moved
by the merits of what he loved, and loved on, even when
the beloved escaped him. Indeed, one might imagine his
saying the opposite of Baudelaire's "*Mon coeur, que jamais
ne visite l'extase,*" changing, "*visite*" to "*relâche.*" For Blok
was always prepared for bliss. When Baudelaire regretted
the passing of summer, it was not so much for love of
the warm sun as through dread of the coming winter; but

Blok's poems speak of winter winds that sing of spring, and winter shadows that stand trustingly by his shoulder. At its deepest, his poetry, even in dejection, rose out of hope and adoration, whereas Baudelaire's was rooted in despair.

Taking them as a whole, one might describe these early poems as the songs of Good and Evil, sung by a good man who is both horrified and fascinated by the evil in himself, conscious of the duality that makes it possible for a man to do what he himself abhors, always straining toward a vision of Perfection, but experiencing joy in the very danger that he may be destroyed before he reaches it. Years later, in a letter to his friend Andrey Bely, he himself said something of the kind:

The drama of my world outlook (to tragedy I have not grown up) consists in this, that I am a *lyrist*. To be a lyrist—is terrifying and joyous. Back of the terror and the joy lurks an abyss, into which one might topple over—and nothing will be left. . . . Were I not led by Unknowable Terror, from which my soul alone protects me, I would not have written a single one of those poems to which you have ascribed some value.

The later poems of the first two volumes are increasingly lyrics of yearning, torment, and passionate doubt, when the Ideal has become at once more dubious and more desirable, as in that famous one, when at the very moment of revelation, with the horizon on fire, and the poet certain of beholding, at last, the Image he has longed for, he fears that she will change her aspect:

> I have forebodings of Thee. Time is going,—
> I fear for all that in Thy face I see.
>
> The sky's aflame, intolerably glowing;
> Silent, I wait in love and agony.
>
> The sky's aflame, draws near Thy apparition,
> But it is strange. Thy look will change on Thee.
>
> And in me Thou dost wake a bold suspicion,—
> Thy face will change from what it used to be.

How I shall fall! how sorrowful and lowly,
Unmastered all my mortal fantasy!

The sky's aflame. Draws near Thy splendour holy,
But it is strange. Thy look will change on Thee.

(*Translated by C. M. Bowra*)

But even at a later stage, when the Beautiful Lady had grown different and appeared to Blok behind a mask of evil, his love was never tinged with blasphemy, so that one might say of him that although he was acquainted with damnation, he was never so completely damned as Baudelaire, and that his happiness was as profound and mysterious as Baudelaire's despair.

I I I

Blok had started to write without any knowledge of literary "schools." Literature had begun for him, he was to say later, not with Baudelaire and the Decadents, but with the literary tastes of his home, where "the *word* was loved and understood in the old-fashioned way" as "*éloquence*," the "dear, ancient *éloquence*" to which he was "indebted to the end of [his] days." In 1901 his mother presented him with a volume of the poetry of Vladimir Soloviëv, the mystic philosopher and poet; and he was amazed to discover that for years he had been writing in the vein of mysticism and symbolism. For a while Soloviëv exercised a strong influence on him in encouraging the natural tendency of his work, since the young Blok was predisposed to religion. At the University he found shocking the rationalism of his professors:

All in all [he wrote his father in 1903], I look forward with pleasure to the end of the university course, because I often detect in it something that is profoundly foreign to me and difficult for me to bear. First of all, there is a line over which not one of my professors will ever step to the day of his death: that is—religious

mysticism. Living by it, as I do, from day to day, I felt myself at
one time persecuted for the right faith. The best that was offered
in place of religion, was grammar. And indeed, the latter does
seem best to me, because the deadest schematic *mos geometricus*
torments me less than sociological and similar attitudes toward
that which to me is sacred.

His closest friends, the poets Serge Soloviëv and Andrey
Bely, were mystics of an ardent stamp. Young Soloviëv was
the son of Michael Soloviëv, brother of the philosopher. His
mother was Alexandra Andreyevna's cousin; the family had
a summer place not far from Shakhmatovo, and the young
men had been acquainted since boyhood. The two mothers
corresponded, and one day Blok's mother sent her cousin
some of his poems. She showed them to Serge, who rap-
turously passed them on to his friend Bely, and he, in his
turn, rhapsodized and made Blok known in literary circles
even before he was published. In January 1904, Blok and
his wife met Bely in Moscow, and the three young men
formed a close friendship; they came together at Petersburg,
in Shakhmatovo; they had intimate discussions, which
meant a great deal to Blok. But presently the two friends
discovered that Blok was not the mystic they had thought
him. For his part, he grew increasingly impatient with their
extravagant notions, and later expressed himself grateful for
the soundness of his upbringing, which had saved him from
their absurdities:

The sane and healthy people by whom I was then [i.e., in child-
hood] surrounded preserved me, I think, from the contagion of
the mystic charlatanism which a few years later became fashionable in certain literary circles.

The dissolution of the triumvirate was hastened, furthermore, by the preposterous cult of Lyubov Dmitrevna as the
Beautiful Lady which Bely and Soloviëv proceeded to
evolve—a cult that really concealed Bely's altogether human infatuation with her. They interpreted her every move,
her every word as freighted with supernatural meaning,
while under cover of worship, perhaps himself hardly real-

izing what he was about, the febrile and sanctimonious
Bely was actually trying to seduce his friend's wife. Blok
was deeply hurt, and this personal disappointment blended
with a larger one to bring a note of disillusionment into his
verse. All that had seemed greatest to him had been reduced to pettiness; he saw men as puppets and the lovely
countryside as a place of swamps and little demons. He
wrote *The Puppet Show, The Violet of Night,* and a collection of lyrics called *Bubbles of Earth,* the title taken
from Banquo's words about the witches in *Macbeth:* "The
earth hath bubbles, as the water has." Serge Soloviëv
thought that the primary reason for their rupture was that
Blok had given up his early idealism and exchanged his
azure worlds for swamps and the Beautiful Lady for an evil
enchantress.

But the mystics were only one set of many that made up
at this time the argumentative, partisan life of literary
Petersburg and Moscow. And Blok found himself drawn
into several groups: those of Sologub, of Vyacheslav Ivanov,
of Merezhkovsky and his wife Zinaïda Hippius. But he never
enjoyed literary disputes, was indifferent to the intrigues
and gossip of cliques, and found altogether unbearable the
clever discussions of "intellectuals." In short, he was not the
kind of man of whom disciples are made. His mind did not
tolerate abstractions; his spirit would not endure dominance;
his whole being revolted against dogma.

I think with pleasure only of *our* apartment in Petersburg [he
wrote his mother at the beginning of 1904]. The Merezhkovskys I
don't want to see at all. Nor all the Petersburg "mystics"—students. . . . I yearn for the holy, the quiet, the white. I want
books; from people in Petersburg I expect nothing but "literary"
discussions at best, and petty mockery or mean insinuations at
worst . . .

Gradually he withdrew from the circles of the intelligentsia
that had tried to absorb him, remaining exquisitely courteous,
but perfectly aloof.

Meanwhile, Russian Symbolism had come into its own
with the publication of Bryusov's *Urbi et Orbi:* Blok was

entranced by it for almost a year, and it had an effect on his writing. It brought him, indirectly, in contact with the work of the French Symbolists, whom Bryusov had incorporated into Russian poetry, and showed him that Symbolism and sociology need not be irreconcilable at all points. Certainly some of his poems of November and December 1903, later included in the collection *Crossroads,* were done under the influence of Bryusov. Such is the one entitled, "From Newspapers," which re-creates dramatically a familiar tragedy, of the kind with which the back pages of newspapers are filled, and reminds one of that earliest of Rimbaud's poems, *"Les Etrennes des Orphelins."* Here, too, little children are orphaned on a cold Christmas day; but Blok's poem is a scene rather than a narrative, and only one-fourth the length of Rimbaud's. Because of this and also because it is full of pity, without the bitterness and sarcasm implied by Rimbaud, it is more tense and poignant. More remarkable is a sixteen-line poem called "The Factory," in which nightmare imagery is turned to social purpose, and with such terrible effect that, understandably enough, the little poem was banned by the censor. The neighboring house, it says, has yellow windows; and toward night, and toward night (the repetition creates a feeling of gloom and of mysterious, monotonous horror), there is the creak of pensive bolts, and people come up to the gates. The gates are tightly shut; and on the wall, and on the wall, an immovable someone, a black someone counts the people, silently. The poet, up in his "heights," hears it all, hears the shouting voice of brass ordering the people to bend their weary backs. They will come in, and scatter, and hoist bags upon their backs. And there will be laughter in the yellow windows, as the wretched beggars are brought in. But how is one to render in English the force of that last word, *proveli,* which means both "to lead through" and "to trick," and suggests also a familiar derivative use of it, "to accompany," especially in the sense of accompanying a coffin to the cemetery? This one word, used to describe the poor let in through factory gates, reverberates with the sinister connotation that they have been maliciously tricked into entering their grave.

This factory was not an imaginary one; Blok could see it from the windows of his apartment—at the time he and his wife were still living in the army quarters of the Kublitsky-Piotukhs in the industrial part of St. Petersburg—and when in 1905 strikes began to take place, he could observe "how a representative of the workers would walk by the lighted windows and how at a single wave of his hand all the lights would go out instantly. . . . This spectacle," writes Maria Beketova, "greatly affected Alexander Alexandrovich."

On the memorable night of January 9, 1905, Blok's step-father was called out to command a detachment of soldiers. Alexander Alexandrovich went out on the street with his mother; they heard how a workman tried to persuade a soldier to dismount, "seeing as how we're all, worker or soldier—the same kind of people," and how the soldier said nothing in reply but was visibly distressed. And Bely, who happened to come to Petersburg on that day, has left an account of Blok's behavior. He had never seen him, he records, in such a state of anger and excitement. The following October, Blok took part in a revolutionary demonstration, carrying a red flag. And yet, at the end of that year, on December 30, he wrote his father:

My connection with the "emancipation movement" expressed itself, alas, almost exclusively in liberal conversations and at one time even in sympathy with the social democrats. Now I retreat more and more, having absorbed all I can of "public opinion," having discarded that which my soul won't accept. And it will accept almost nothing *of this kind*—so let it occupy its proper place, the one toward which it strives. Never shall I become either a revolutionary, or a "builder of life," and not because I see no sense in either the one or the other, but simply, because of the nature, quality, and *theme* of my spiritual experience. . . .

It was not an easy struggle, that between his private world and the public one. But, almost in spite of himself, Blok's consciousness recorded new adventures, and the "theme of his spiritual experience" expanded. Whatever meant little to him he sloughed off, but what impressed him marked him deeply. Thus on November 16, 1905, just one month after he had taken part in the revolutionary procession, he had a dream—"such amazing dreams," he wrote, "occur but once in a year—in two years." He made a magnificent poem of it, *The Violet of Night,* a longish, sing-song narrative, with an irregular rhyme scheme and stanza form, which has something of the uncanny quality of Franz Kafka's work, and is extraordinarily interesting to anyone concerned with the biography of composition, for through it one can trace in detail the transmutation of Blok's anxieties and observations into the stuff of poetry.

He dreams that on a rainy evening, he walked slowly, far out, to the very edge of the city, where the dawn-streaked sky, weary of covering the deeds and thoughts of his fellow citizens, dropped down to a swamp. It may be that his friend was with him, but, if so, he remained silent all the way, whether at his request or because he himself felt gloomy. Whatever the reason, they noticed different things: the friend, fops making love to rouged-up women and girls peeping from yellow-curtained windows. And soon he vanished, which made the dreamer unspeakably happy—for what is there pleasanter than the loss of one's best friends? Passersby became less and less frequent. Only hungry dogs now came his way and the voices of drunken women swearing in the distance; and as his consciousness grew clearer, steps and voices, conversations about the mysteries of various religions, also receded. It became even plainer to him that he had been here before; and had seen, waking, everything he now saw in a dream.

Presently the road descends to a swampy place, where there are no more buildings, and little bridges are thrown from mound to mound across stagnant, rusty water, and the path winds through purplish-green twilight into sloth, dream, and sleep. He crosses the swamp and comes to a small cabin, opens a heavy door, and stands embarrassed, on the threshold. On one of the clumsy benches, lining the walls of the long low hut, at a long table, bending her head over her spinning, sits an ugly girl with a colorless face. He cannot tell her age, nor the color of her hair, nor what her features and her eyes are like. All he knows is that she spins her quiet web, and then, stopping, sits a long while, not looking, not thinking; and also that somewhere he has seen her before, and that she was then straighter, younger, and more beautiful.

And he remembers that everything in the hut was plunged in a sweetish drowsiness, whether because the sleepiness of swamps flowed about his shoulders, or because the air was steeped in the fading scent of the Violet of Night, or because he had not come in wedding costume to the evening festival. He was a beggarly vagabond, frequenter of pubs, while in the hut kings had gathered. But he clearly remembered that once he had made part of their circle, and had drunk from their cups, somewhere amid crags and on fjords, where there is neither sea nor land and only the golden crowns of Scandinavian sovereigns gleam in snowy twilight.

Now he is obliged to bow again to the crowns he had forgotten. He walks around the cabin, pressing the hands of his former comrades, who do not recognize him—and finally notices on a low bench, by an enormous barrel of beer, an old man and an old woman, with tarnished crowns on their greenish, ancient locks. For ages they have sat there, awaiting customary salutations, barely nodding in answer. Having bowed to the king and queen, and received their command to remain, the poet perceives the last bench, in the darkest corner of all.

It is crooked and rickety, and on it, motionless, sits a man, his elbows on his knees, his face in his hands. One can see that, without growing old, changeless, thinking always one thought, he has grieved here for ages. The poet receives no reply to his greeting, but understands, as he looks at him, that he too is fated to sit there by the partly drained mug of beer, in the darkest corner of all—fated to think the same thought, to fold his arms the same way, and to fix his eyes on the hut's distant corner, where, in the shimmering light, by the drowsing regal couple, by the sleeping warriors, by the purposeless spinning, sits the princess of a forgotten land, who is called the Violet of Night.

The poet stays in the hut, while all about him fall into deeper and deeper sleep. The warriors have dropped their armor, the light has faded on the kingly crowns, his solitary neighbor—the beggar who like him was born of noble race and was once, like him, a straight youth, a brave hero, the seducer of northern maids and the singer of Scandinavian legends—has bent over the cup, his head touching the bench and his hands, the floor. A sword has crumbled, clattering; a shield has fallen; the old man and woman lean softly on each other, and the crowns have gone from their heads.

But the princess spins on and on, spins and spins, bending over her work, casting sweet drowsiness over everyone, intoxicating all with the potion of swamps, enveloping all in a fable of night; while she, the Violet, blooms and blooms, breathes the air of the swamps, and her spindle whirls noiselessly and spins and spins and spins.

He grows numb, sleeps, and grieves. And conceals his long thought, and looks on at the streak of the dawn. And minutes pass, or centuries, maybe.

And through his sleep he seems to hear the sea rolling in the distance, and a sound that might be the crying of gulls and of the wind speeding the ships of a happy land. For happiness comes accidentally. Thus he sits in the swamp, while over it, unaging, unchanging, blooms his small lilac flower, which he calls the Violet of Night.

Beyond the swamp, his city remains, with the selfsame evenings and the selfsame dawns. And, undoubtedly, more than once has his friend come home, swaying, and fallen asleep cursing him.

But centuries have gone by, and he has thought through the thought of centuries. He stands at the very edge of the earth, alone and wise, like children. And through the caressing, greenish twilight he hears the circular motion of waves, and the approach of great ships, like tidings of a new land. So the sacred spinning wheel spins the living, momentary dream, that Happiness will come unexpectedly, and will remain, complete and perfect.

This fairy-tale vision of a sleeping kingdom, on the outskirts of the city where he has left his friend, and to which
he is propelled by a force that is both unexplained and
necessary, is a clear symbol of Blok's retreat from the
bustling dissipations of Petersburg to the dream of his
mind, the special "quality and theme of his spiritual experience," the trancelike state in which he meets the ancient
kings and warriors of his ideals, and the fate that spins his
destiny. And if this enchanted realm is rotting in a swamp
and his fate is a delicate poison-flower, and his ancient sovereigns and comrades are enfeebled and lost in sleep, and
even he himself, in the person of his Double, is reduced to
wretched beggary—even so, this is the place of his own
self, and through the vapor and the poison, he hears in it
the promise of salvation, the coming of Unexpected Joy
(this became the title of his next collection of poems). The
symbol has a public as well as a private implication. Privately it marks Blok's impatience with his closest friends
and his break with them—Bely was incensed by the line,
"For what is pleasanter than the loss of one's best friends?";
publicly it is his sense of Russia's stagnation after the failure
of the revolution of 1905, and his faith in her deliverance, a
faith, not unlike Chekhov's, in an imminent, though unde-
fined, change that must pull the country out of apathy. His
irritations with himself and his friends, his longing for a
cathedral-like peace in which his poetry might evolve, became fused in his dream with anxiety about the fate of the
nation, an anxiety that had been forced upon him in a manner more violent than that of intellectual discussion. He
could not solve by rational means the problems that were
here involved, but the private symbolism of a dream was
proof of how inaccessible to debate were his perceptions,
and thus how justifiable his retreat from public matters
and philosophic arguments.

Of course, in discussions of Symbolism the central question is always the relation of appearance to reality, with
the implication that appearance is commonplace and universally perceptible, and reality recondite, hard to come
by and to be expressed only through analogy. "To reveal

in a flash, to make sensible to the heart, the occult reality which the veil of appearances, normal perceptions, easily definable feelings, clear ideas, conceals from us," that, says Marcel Raymond, for example, is the nature of symbolist imagery. To Blok the perceptible and the occult seemed equally real, important, and complex; and his whole life represents a search for meanings through which the reality of both might be expressed. It is not easy, it is perhaps impossible, to tell whether a given image in a poem of his had begun with a vision or a physical perception; and if, as Edmund Wilson has said, "the symbols of the Symbolists are metaphors detached from their subjects," in Blok's case one does not always know what is subject and what metaphor, whether it is the physical perception that should be taken as the event and the vision as its symbol, or the other way round. Dreaming and waking were interchangeable in his experience; he passed so easily, so imperceptibly, from the one to the other that one might say of him either that he was always waking, or always dreaming: never does he seem more lucid than when he writes of nebulous and troubled states, and never more mysterious than when he speaks of what seems perfectly ordinary.

And just as a philosopher's reasoning may reach out to incorporate new elements which extend the initial sphere of his thoughts, so Blok's restless and bemused imagination gathered to itself new elements that enlarged his dream. In *The Violet of Night* the communal image of the sleeping kingdom is added to the basic themes of his earlier poems: to mystery and darkness shot through with flashes of light; to the sordidness of the city and the enchantment of fate; to beggary, princeliness, and the Double; and also to that dominant theme and image which is a continuous thread in the pattern of all his work, the Search and the Road. In the early poems, again and again, Blok speaks of himself as walking or riding along a path, a road, a street. The path is various: misty, moonlit, black, azure, silvery, or scarlet; it winds through woods or on the outskirts of a city; it may be blissful, or terrifying and hard to travel. And whatever is at the end—utter darkness, a mysterious and evil Presence, or the Beautiful Lady—its recurrence emphasizes the experience of wandering, of seeking for a Heavenly Being through a land that is always mysterious in both morning and night, in light and in darkness, and in brilliant weather as well as foul. Its importance is underscored by the persistent repetition of the verb *stremit'sya*, in its several connotations of *rushing to, aspiring, craving, longing,* in a way that seems to give the verses a headlong quality and the pattern of straight lines. But this effect, which re-creates verbally the ardor of the poet's search for the Ideal, is curiously counteracted by a favorite and equally frequent rhyme scheme, wherein a line of the first verse, or stanza, is echoed or repeated in the last—with the force of resolution or completion, or of reinforcing the mood in a prolonged reverberation that produces a circular effect and creates the impression that however inconclusive, nebulous, and disappointing the search, a phase of it has been rounded off and fixed for all time as true in itself. In *The Violet of Night,* the path is sordid. The search is undirected, the end is a morass— and in the rhyme scheme, with its droning repetitions, there is no suggestion of impetuosity or resolution, but only of sleep, and then, of a sudden gentle lilt at the close, when the sleeper awakes from his nightmare and seems to hear the sound of the sea and of approaching ships.

Some six months after the dream that resulted in *The Violet of Night,* in the summer of 1905, Blok wrote a touching lyric in dialogue form about a little boy and a little girl at a puppet show. The children look on excitedly at the performance and speculate as to what will happen to the little clown whom a dreadful devil has grabbed; and when the clown leans over the ramp and shouts: "Help! I am bleeding to death, my beet juice is flowing out of me! I am bandaged with a rag! On my head is a cardboard helmet! In my hand, a wooden sword!," they start crying and the puppet show is closed. Now at the suggestion of a friend, Gregory Chulkov, Blok made a play of this moving little drama of disillusionment, trying his hand at a form of writing that fascinated him. He had always been interested in the theater, ever since the days of the amateur theatricals at

Shakhmatovo and Boblovo, when to Lyubov Dmitrevna's
Juliet and Ophelia he outdid himself in the roles of Romeo
and Hamlet. He even thought of becoming an actor, entering for a while a drama school in St. Petersburg, while
Lyubov Dmitrevna had indeed become a professional actress. *The Puppet Show* was first published in April 1906 in
Chulkov's journal, *Torches,* and acted at the end of that
year under the directorship of Meierhold in the theater
which Komisarzhevskaya had founded two years earlier
and of which Lyubov Dmitrevna was now a member.

In the play the tragedy shifts from spectator to actor, from
onlookers to participants. It is the tragedy of Pierrot, lost
among treacherous, unreal, hypocritical, and self-deluded
people: mystics who at a séance evoke the presence of a
Woman in White, whom they call Death, but whom he
knows to be the Columbine he loves and has been waiting
for; figures at a masked ball, who represent different kinds of
love—romantic, passionate, magical; and finally Harlequin,
who with his gay skipping and jingling seduces Columbine,
and proves that she is made of cardboard. Pierrot goes wandering away with him, but Harlequin, finding both him
and everybody else dull and lifeless, jumps out the window
into what he thinks is the real, large, airy world—and falls
head-on into nothingness: the lovely world, like its inhabitants, turns out to have been painted paper. Through the
hole that he has made, there is only the sky; it changes from
night to dawn, and presently reveals the white-clad figure
of Death. As Pierrot makes toward it with outstretched arms,
it becomes Columbine, and he is on the point of touching
her, when the Author rises between them—a clownish personage who has already broken in upon the action several
times to explain that the actors were not doing what he intended they should do and were taking the play out of his
hands, for he had written "the most realistic of plays,"
which concerned "the mutual love of young souls," and had
never clothed his heroes in the garb of fools. This Author
has never managed to finish any of his speeches: either he
has become embarrassed and sneaked off in the middle of
a sentence, or somebody has seized him by the coattails

and dragged him backstage. Now, triumphantly, he declares
to the audience that his rights have been vindicated, that
the story of his lovers is drawing to its prescribed, happy
end; and he is about to join the hands of his Pierrot and
Columbine, when the scenery swishes up out of sight, the
actors run away, and he, too, walks off, leaving Pierrot
prostrate on the bare stage, mourning for his cardboard
bride. "I am full of sorrow. And you think it's funny?" says
Pierrot, and takes a little pipe out of his pocket and plays a
song "about his pale face, about his hard life, and about
Columbine, his bride."

Here, then, is life that takes its course regardless of an
author's plans. The Author is a silly clown, fooled by a
reality he does not understand; he thought it was simple
and human, but it is all illusory: cardboard people playing
in a paper setting—a bad joke on the one among them who
has taken it seriously. The play is a bitter, graceful parable
on Illusion and Reality, equally applicable to Blok himself,
to Russia, and to mankind. But its metaphysical, ethical,
political theme is made up of references to the actualities of
Blok's own life: his hopes for happiness, his disappointment
in mysticism, his disillusionment with friends, perhaps even
his doubts of his wife's fidelity; in short, his sense that he has
foolishly placed his faith in false beliefs and trusted dolls
that only looked like people. Even the details are actual
episodes recorded in his letters, diaries, and earlier poems.
The Beautiful Lady is now Columbine; a memorable meeting with Lyubov Dmitrevna in the Cathedral is symbolically re-enacted by the first pair of lovers; the masked ball
had actually taken place in 1902—Blok had refused to
go, had stood outside watching the shadows of the dancers
on the drawn blinds, and used the occasion for the first of
his harlequin lyrics, which he sent to Zinaïda Hippius with
the following note: "Meanwhile I am clearing my dense,
lightning-shot atmosphere by means of a cruel harlequin-
ade, the poetic expression of which I am sending you." And
the Temptress, who flashes across the stage in an ardent
dance, was before long to become a reality.

I V

Once while *The Puppet Show* was in rehearsal and doubts had arisen about staging it, Blok wrote Meierhold:

. . . I must stay with your theater, *must* have you do *The Puppet Show;* for *me* it is a moment of *purgation,* the way out of lyric isolation . . .

—a cry that shows what the theater meant to Blok and corroborates his subsequent remark that dramatic composition marked the beginning of his independence. At another time, in an article called "About the Theater," he wrote:

More than any other type of art, the theater gives the lie to the blasphemous abstraction of the formula "art for art's sake." For the theater is the very flesh of art—that lofty sphere wherein "the word is made flesh." That is why nearly everyone, irrespective of tendencies, is agreed on this, that the highest manifestation of creativity is the dramatic.

The theater was for Blok a means of getting in touch with human beings, of breaking the bonds of introspection. And directly after *The Puppet Show* he wrote two more plays: *The King in the Square* and *The Stranger.*

The characters of *The King in the Square* suggest those of the Commedia dell' Arte in their formal symbolism, but unlike them, belong to the present, not to tradition, and stand for contemporary social attitudes rather than for universal types or metaphysical concepts. The scene is the City Square, surrounded by the sea, so as to give it the appearance of being "only an island—an accidental haven for the dramatis personae." It is dominated by the tremendous, majestic figure of The King, and the action takes place in the Morning, Noon, and Night of one crucial day when the Ships are expected to arrive. In anticipation of them, workers are constructing a tower from which to send

rockets by way of greeting, and their hammers are constantly heard off stage. But there are characters who do not
believe in the Ships, like the Clown of Common Sense, who
can only laugh at the folly of popular hopefulness; the
Plotters, who think the people are building their happiness
on a mad daydream; the fops, who are just annoyed by the
silly rumors; and those who are absorbed in love or hunger.
The Clown leaves the scene when everyone seems to have
gone mad.

In all this turmoil of confidence, despair, faith, planning,
superciliousness, the Poet wanders, lost, anxious, dreary, not
knowing what it is he yearns for, but "doomed to yearning." The Architect, whose advice he seeks, tells him to
"live more simply," and not think of the impossible. He
upbraids him for his attitude to the people, for despising
their pettiness, their work, their way of life. "They are better than you," he says, "you breathe neither the sea nor the
dust," you only dream, while they labor and have come to
terms with "the yellow, evil dust" they must live in. "On
your knees before them! . . . Listen, listen to the sound of
the axes . . . Otherwise your heart will grow deaf and
empty . . ."

The Poet falls under the spell of the Architect's Daughter,
who understands the language of his mysterious songs; and
in the evening, as rockets go up to announce the arrival of
the long-awaited Ships, and she mounts the stairs up to the
King, in the belief that (according to ancient legend), if she
gives herself to him, he will come to life, the Poet, too,
ecstatically happy, begins to follow her up the steps. But the
mob, egged on by a man in black, who shouts to them that
they have been fooled, that Common Sense has left them,
that they have power and must destroy, bring down the
columns of the palace, annihilating King, Daughter, Poet,
and part of themselves. Only then do they discover that the
King was made of stone, and the play closes with the
Architect's words:

I sent you my beloved son and you slew him. I sent you another
to console you, my daughter. And you did not spare her. I created

power for you, I carved hard marble—and every day you wondered at the beauty of these ancient locks, the product of my mal-
let. You have shattered my creation, and now your house remains
empty. But tomorrow the world will be green as always, and the
sea will be just as calm.

A faint voice asks:

And who will feed us? Who will give us back our husbands and
children? Who will still our pain?

The Architect:

He who sets the stars in motion will feed you. He who waters
the black earth with rain, He who gathers the clouds over the sea,
The Father will feed you.

And as he descends and is lost in darkness, "the murmur of
the crowd grows stronger and mingles with the murmur of
the sea."

This final stage direction is reminiscent of the end of
Boris Godunov, "the people are silent," and just as Pushkin's words indicated popular horror and a presage of
troubles to come, so Blok's suggest that the people, without
knowing what they do believe, have not much faith in the
Architect's last speech. But what does the Architect mean?
His final diatribe, although strongly suggestive of Church
doctrine, of the Trinity and the Virgin Mary, is not, of
course, a criticism of traditional theology, for the Architect
is not God, but man's creative mind; the Daughter is not
the Virgin Mary, but an embodiment of Beauty and the
Eternal Feminine; and the Son is not Christ, but the
Poet, or man's imagination. The fall of the stone king and
the destruction of the Daughter and the Poet are tragic,
for it is with them that we have sympathized—these "vi-
sionaries," these embodiments of the Beautiful and the
Idealistic—not with the Fool of Common Sense. He appears
in the final act in a priest's garb thrown over his red-and-
gold costume, and once discovered, casts off his disguise
and shouts to the multitude before he leaves it: "Look

at me! I am Reality—in its red-and-gold nakedness! I am many-faced, but bear one name throughout the universe! Common Sense—that is my name. . . . My red gold sings merrily before you! But the merry red gold will bring you death and fire, if you will provoke Common Sense."

The Poet finds himself in the service of an Ideal that is a combination of Beauty, Purity, Power, and Sacrifice for the popular good—and is destroyed by the very populace he would serve, together with the Ideal. But then, he and the Daughter both seem to be serving a lost cause: she does not know that it is a stone image to which she means to give herself, and he is so infatuated with her that he does not see her mistake. The power, then, is in the people, who do not know what to do with it except to destroy, who destroy even their own daughter—whom the Poet worships as "queen," but who assures him that she is not queen at all, but the daughter of the insane crowd—who need a leader, and are, therefore, prey to demagogues. Everyone has given homage to a statue and been ruled by faith in a stone image; and yet we do not approve of those who suspect, or know, the secret. Blok seems to be saying that the act of worship in itself gives power, and that the Poet and the Daughter are proved mistaken only by those who make a greater mistake. Their idea of protecting the King as King, that is, is not wrong. For what will happen now that the people are left without the image of Power? What can they do, except wait for the Architect to build another statue for them to obey, or else be lost, following either cynical Plotters who want good only for themselves, or Common Sense, whose red-and-gold smugness cannot satisfy their craving for the heights? What happens, then, when the Ships come in? The workers, with whom Blok had marched in 1905, were off stage, it must be noted, sending up rockets, when the mob tore down the palace and the King. And what will the Architect's new work be like?

The Stranger, like *The Puppet Show,* grew out of a lyric, a poem of fourteen quatrains rhyming conventionally *a b a b,* written in April 1906. It describes an ordinary pleasure spot of Petersburg where men in derbies take their ladies out walking or rowing on the lake, and where there is a restaurant to which the poet comes night after night. There he sees his only friend reflected in his drinking glass, like him subdued and deafened by the acid and mysterious dampness of the place, while at the neighboring tables stand sleepy waiters, and rabbit-eyed drunkards shout "In vino veritas!" Every evening, at a given hour —or is he only dreaming this?—She enters, dressed in silk, and always alone, walks slowly past the drunkards and sits down by the window. Her silks, her hat with its mournful plumes, her narrow hand covered with rings—all breathe of ancient superstitions. And shackled by a strange sense of nearness, he gazes through her dark veil, and sees an enchanted shore and an enchanted distance. Dark mysteries have been entrusted to him, somebody's sun has been handed him. The acid wine has pierced all the winding inlets of his soul, while bending ostrich feathers sway in his head, and fathomless blue eyes bloom on the distant shore. There lies a treasure in his soul, and he alone has the key. You are right, drunken monster! I know: truth is in wine.

In the play, written about six months later, in November 1906, real settings, real psychology, and surrealist imagery are interwoven with even greater subtlety and intricacy. The three "Visions" of the drama melt into one another in the way of images in dreams, and are held together by the figure of the Poet who takes part in each of them, in the same central and inconclusive way a dreamer takes part in his dreams. The action of the play, indeed, is the dream of Blok, the poet. The three sets, the pub, the solitary bridge at night, and the bourgeois drawing room, are three major realms of his experience: drunken Bohemia, the solitary vision, and "polite society." In all of them he is alone and misunderstood, and in all of them he is in pursuit of an Ideal. In the first Vision the Ideal is a thought and a memory; in the second, it is embodied in an astral phenomenon; and in the third, in a human figure—and always it fascinates, entices, and vanishes. This Ideal is once again the Beautiful Lady, the *Ewige Weibliche*, but with a suggestion of something infernal, as well as heavenly, in her witchery. In the pub—where, incidentally, Hauptmann and Verlaine are among the drinkers—the poet, intoxicated both by his poetic experience and by beer, describes her to the uncomprehending waiter as the dark-veiled Stranger with a narrow hand and swaying feathers in her hat, in whose face have melted the faces of all strangers he has seen in his wanderings on city streets. She rules the universe, and is the one by whom all men are bewitched. In the second Vision she is a fallen star of the first magnitude, "who, on earth, calls herself Maria"; and in the third she is the mysterious, uninvited guest at a commonplace bourgeois party. Throughout, only the Poet loves her and sees her for what she is, for even the Astronomer, who, on the snowy bridge, also beholds her astral magnificence, observes her dazzling descent through the heavens, and is, for the moment, moved to tears, makes practical use of the great spectacle to enhance his reputation among scientists: "Yes," he says to the Poet at the party, "I have inserted a new paragraph in my notes: 'The star Maria has fallen,' " and inquires politely as to the results of his own investigations. "My investigations," says the Poet, "have been inconclusive." He peers into the depths of the room, where the Stranger has stood. His face expresses emptiness and darkness. "Terrible concentration" makes him sway. "But where is Mary? But where is Mary?" asks the fluttering hostess, who wants her guests to go in to supper. "There is no one now by the dark window curtain. Beyond the window, a bright star shines, and blue snow falls, blue as the uniform of the vanished Astronomer."

Here is both lyric poetry and social satire. The social satire is directed against the pettiness of men's preoccupations that makes them blind to the extraordinary and magnificent events that take place among them. And the magnificent events are the embodiment on earth of the Poet's vision, which, "inconclusive" as estimates go, has roused the Poet's emotions and both enhanced and deepened his understanding.

V

The favorite boast of artists that life imitates art might seem to have been made good in the life and work of Blok. Thus, as the Beautiful Lady had taken shape in Lyubov Dmitrevna Mendeleeva, so the Stranger presently found embodiment in a woman of earth. She was the actress Volokhova, whom Blok met at a party in December 1906, while *The Puppet Show* was in rehearsal; she roused in him an overwhelming, tormented infatuation, and inspired some of his best lyrics, among them the cycles *The Snow Mask* and *Faïna*, and his worst play, *The Song of Fate*.

The Snow Mask, composed of thirty lyrics, was written in two weeks, from December 29, 1906, to January 13, 1907. It appeared with the following dedication: "I dedicate these verses to Thee, tall woman in black, with winged eyes, in love with the fires and the darkness of my city of snow." In a letter he said that "the book [was] subjective in the extreme, and would be understandable only to the smallest circle," and in another letter he explained that in it he had sought to express only that which was properly due to verse, not as in his previous collections, where the lyric and the dramatic were mixed together, and that what was properly due to verse was song and lyricism; the rest he was now putting into prose and drama.

The Snow Mask and Faïna are the obverse of the *Verses on the Beautiful Lady*. As the earlier poems had expressed the suffering of Unfulfillment, the hope and passionate search for the Unattained and the Unattainable, these sang the suffering, passion, and ecstasy of fulfillment, hopelessness, destruction, and the knowledge of loss. The rhythm, the imagery, the landscape are all transformed. For this is the country of storms and snows, of night, comets, and falling stars. There are neither flowers nor birds here, and the music is the wind's song and the mysterious trumpet sound of death. The rhythms, like whirling snow, twist, race, and plunge into abysses of dark and restive silence. The only peace here is the peace of frozen wastes and the immobility of death; the only joy is in the headlong flight to self-destruction; the pain is that of torment deliberately inflicted, for the tall dark Woman is as cruel and evil as the Azure Lady had been indifferent and good. The quiet, yearning music of the early poems, with rhymes that return to emphasize the endless circle of unattainable desire, has given place to hurried, nervous, rushing, staccato rhythms and dissonant rhymes, with repetitions that are like blows. They neither bring repose nor resolve questions, but strike and fall apart with abrupt finality, soaring up or sweeping downward, and ending in black chaos.

Blok is writing here from the cyclonic center of his emotions: his heart has been turned to ice and craves to be destroyed; he is rushing through interminable darkness, flying with Her into "a million abysses," while the world's dungeon, the pattern of Endlessness, stretches beneath him; his iron sword is drowned in drifts of snow, he has said farewell to his country and his heart, and ordered away the daughters of paradise, the suns that would have opened the doorway and melted the ice of his cell; he is burning at the stake of the snowy bonfire which She has built for him; but in words that ring with despair, he exults in his fate and proclaims it enviable. Just as the vague but peaceful imagery of the Beautiful Lady poems was appropriate to an anxious but hopeful stage, so the imagery of *The Snow Mask* and *Faïna,* with all that seems exaggerated in it, is also precise. Its vastness, indefiniteness, and magniloquence are appropriate to the turbulence it projects in somewhat the same way as the shapeless forms of Chaos of *Paradise Lost* are exact and appropriate to Milton's view of hell. And everything here takes place in endless stretches of interstellar space, an illimitable darkness lighted up in the fire of shooting stars, or of equally illimitable, dazzling wastes of ice, where ships, with fallen masts, stand frozen. The intoxicating flights, the swoops into abysses take place in stifling, deafening, raging storms, through which come strains of mysterious trumpet calls. It is a world of havoc in which the word "overthrown" occurs time and again: the ships are overthrown; the head of the temptress is thrown back to receive the poet's kisses; or he himself is overthrown, borne on a stream that carries him to destruction—the stream of the elements, and also of spilled wine, and of her hair, for the notion of overthrow is linked to that of scattering and spilling: the dark wine pours out among the worlds, the storm builds and scatters a great white cross, and everything conveys the idea of a shattered man and a shattered world.

The goblet of wine becomes the dome of heaven, and when it is overthrown the universe has fallen, just as the temptress is herself a fallen star, snow storms are cataclysmic, and a moment of infatuation is an eternity of imprisonment. This melting and fusing of the concrete, delimited image of perception with the vast one of the imagination and the uncanny one of dreams re-creates an atmosphere of destructive passion in which events on earth are not compared to but equated with the elemental, just as in the Beautiful Lady poems aspects of nature had been equated with thoughts or feelings to produce an atmosphere of aspiration and love. Here the blackness, the whiteness, the snowy-silver, the commanding trumpet calls have their counterpart on earth in the blackness of her dress, the dark mesh over her shoulders and her sables, her "winged" eyes, shining with the light of stars that never set, her triple tiara, the shackling force of her embrace, her taunts and songs that command obedience and forgetfulness. And the poet himself is the "dark night," and the captive, of a mysterious being whom he at once resents and willingly obeys as a force he does not understand, and who herself is perhaps his own poetic invention, in her turn, a captive, enmeshed in the verse he has woven. Or, on a more earthly plane, both of them are masks: and then their story is a masquerade in which an "evil" mask speaks to a "humble" one. In these dream images, actual nights of drunkenness and passion are present almost casually, almost by implication, as the remote source of a nightmare of helplessness, captivity, and the desired terror of destruction. But their passion is elemental and larger than the individual, so that Blok was wrong in thinking these poems so subjective as to be generally ununderstandable. As a matter of fact, they are more objective than the *Verses on the Beautiful Lady*, although they are inspired by emotions no less intense and deeply centered in the self. His work in the drama had drawn him out of introspection, and the lavish rhetoric of *The Snow Mask* becomes acceptable precisely because its subject is passion itself rather than the raptures of one man.

To a cycle of eleven poems, also dedicated to Volokhova, and written in October 1907—that is, nine months after the period of infatuation and the composition of *The Snow Mask*—Blok prefixed as epigraph five lines from Lermontov's "Gratitude":

> My thanks for all thou gavest through the years:
> For passion's secret torments without end,
> The poisoned kiss, the bitterness of tears,
> The vengeful enemy, the slanderous friend,
> The spirit's ardor in the desert spent . . .

> (*Translated by Avrahm Yarmolinsky*)

and gave a title to each of the lyrics to form the following sentence:

1. I accept
2. In fire
3. And in darkness
4. Under torture
5. In snows
6. And in distant halls
7. And on the brink of the abyss
8. By madness conjure
9. In wild dance
10. And once more humble
11. Abandon myself to thee,

a sentence that draws the emotional graph, the rise to the limit of ecstatic torment and the descent to acceptance and humility, which charts the emotional and musical pattern of *The Snow Mask* as well as of this smaller cycle, and suggests something that impresses one also, though less distinctly, in many individual poems of Blok—namely, that his art has something in common with the ballet, that the symbolism of his language is closer to the meaning given by the rhythm of physical motion, the pattern drawn by the grace of step and gesture, the leaping, gliding, soaring, whirling lines of bodies in a dance, than to the significance of concepts or even of musical tones or the colors and contours of pictures. By contrast to "visual" or "aural" symbolism, one is tempted to call his "kinetic." It is here that one senses best his special gift: an ability to impart the very essence of irrationality.

When he tried to recollect emotion in tranquillity and to explain it reasonably, he became ponderously banal, as for example in *The Song of Fate*. Herman, the hero of this allegory, is compelled to leave his mother and his wife, Elena, in pursuit of a vision and the call of the wind which sounds to him like the Song of Fate itself, so that his departure is hardly a matter of choice, but a superior command. "I have beheld an enormous world, Elena . . . blue, unknown, enticing. . . . I can't go on this way any longer. I am too comfortable in my white, quiet house. Give me strength to bid it farewell and to behold what life is like in the world. Only, O God, preserve in me the fever of a youthful soul and a live conscience." On his journey he succumbs to the spell of the enchantress Faïna, the cruel and pitiable, the powerful and tragic courtesan, surrounded by a crowd of adorers whom she despises and over whom she tyrannizes, and herself subject to a rich and dull old man she does not love. She bewitches Herman, strikes him, and then loves him for a brief space. Their final meeting is on a field in a snowstorm. Herman has fallen asleep there, waiting for her, and would have frozen to death had she not come to wake him. But she must return to her old man, and her "Farewell" is the sound of the wind. Herman thinks himself lost, but along comes a peddler who offers to show him the way. "Just lead me out of here, passerby," says Herman, who does not know where he wants to go. "And then I'll go myself wherever my eyes take me . . ." So the play ends.

Herman's dream has been realized, but with a difference. His first words had been, "I fell asleep again. In my sleep— all was white. I saw a big, white swan; she swam to that shore of the lake, her breast to the setting sun." At the end he has found the whiteness of his dream, but it is the white- ness of storm; the dream is now reality, Faïna has taught him the lesson of Fate, and this lesson turns out to be a na- tional one, for Faïna is not only Fate but also the spirit of the Russian people, as one of her adorers, "a man in spectacles," recognizes:

She has brought us part of the people's soul [he says]. For that, we ought to bow down to the ground before her, and not laugh. We writers live the life of intellectuals, but Russia, immutable in her very being, laughs in our face. . . . An abyss yawns in my soul, when I hear Faïna's songs. These songs are like bonfires— they burn to cinders the arid, feeble, intellectual soul. As I listen to her voice, I feel how weak and insignificant is my voice. It may be that people with a new soul have already come, and are hidden unnoticed somewhere among us. They wait only for a sign. They look straight into Faïna's face when she sings the Song of Fate. Don't listen to the words of that song; listen only to the voice: it sings of our weariness, of the new men who will take our place. It's the free Russian song, gentlemen. The unknown distance it- self, calling us. . . .

Herman has been purified by his experience; his soul has been cleansed of terror and has become one with the soul of the nation, for in obeying the summons of the Song of Fate, sung by the wind, he has been united with his country. The two epigraphs which Blok chose for this work make clear its meaning. The first is Biblical: I John 4:18: "There is no fear in love, but perfect love casteth out fear, because fear hath torment . . ."; the other is Gogol's celebrated passage: "Russia! Russia!—All is open, waste, and flat in thee. . . . Is this not the place for the bogatyr, where there is space for him to unfold and walk about?"; and at one point Herman is made to say: "It may be I am on the threshold of madness . . . or of prophecy! All that has been, all that will be —has gathered about me: as if I were living these days the life of all ages, living the torments of my native land. I remember the terrible days of the battle of Kulikovo."

But Blok was a more interesting person and a greater poet than his Herman, and the cycle of five lyrics, *On the Field of Kulikovo*, which he wrote in 1908, are among the finest in Russian. They re-create the melancholy and majestic landscape of the battlefield: the wide-flowing, fog-veiled river, lazily "grieving" between its banks of yellow clay, the haystacks "grieving" on the steppe, the mist, the clouds, the night over the steppe, with the cry of swans beyond the river, and birds of night circling and soaring in the distance, the feather grass bending to earth in eternal longing; sheet lightning, and a vast silence that envelops even the sounds of battle—details that bring to mind the earliest epic of the Slavs, *The Lay of Igor's Armament*. But these are not poems celebrating the historic battle in which the Moscow Prince, Dmitry Donskoy, defeated the Tartar chief Mamai. The field is ageless, the time is the present as well as the past; the historic occasion stands for what has always existed and will continue to exist, Russia as an entity; and the armored knight on the field of battle is both ancient warrior and modern poet. He is fighter, lover, crusader; and Russia for him is a dearly loved wife with whose hard fate his own is united, who comes to him as a Vision, and calls to him in the voice of crying swans. Images and figures of speech bring echoes of Gogol's rhetoric, as when the poet sings of the prairie mare, flying over the steppe, trampling the feather grass, with slopes and miles flashing by. There is no stopping her. And there is no end to battle. Peace is but a dream glimmering through dust and blood, even the clouds are terror-stricken, and his friend calls to him to sharpen his sword, that he may give his life for a cause that is holy, and not fight the Tartars in vain. In this eternal carnage, on this gloomy stretch of land, over which there is a sky of bloody sunsets and frightened clouds, the knight is not elated, but he is not afraid. Our way, he says to Russia, is through the steppe, through boundless grief. And so, let there be night. We will arrive, will light bonfires on the distant steppe, and in the smoke will gleam the holy banner and the steel of Tartar swords. The tone is tragic, there is no joy of battle in these poems, only grim exhilaration and infinite sadness: *"I véchniyi boyi!"* ("And strife eternal!") *"I net kontsa!"* ("And without end!"); and their grandeur is that of fearlessness and devotion. They were written, said Blok, on the same theme as the *Song of Fate* and an article called "The People and the Intelligentsia"—"I first wrote lyrics, then a play, then an article—all on one theme"—and in the article he explained the battle of Kulikovo as a symbol of the struggle between the people and the intelligentsia, the Russian army of Dmitry Donskoy being the people, a million and a half strong, while the enemy were the several hundred thousand intellectuals.

VI

In February 1909 Lyubov Dmitrevna gave birth to a boy. The expectation of a child had, according to Zinaïda Hippius, transformed Blok. It was the only time, she wrote, that she had seen him really smile, and her description of him during these days, simple, human, with a bright face and a warm voice, is very touching. But the child was born ailing and lived for only eight days, and then Blok "would explain conscientiously why it had been impossible for him to live." In April he went with Lyubov Dmitrevna to Italy, where he wrote his classical *Italian Poems,* and then to Germany, returning in the latter part of June. Near the end of the year, on the first of December, his father died. These two deaths of intimate strangers, who linked him with the past and the future, but neither of whom he had had a chance to know, led him the following summer to begin work on a poem that was to be the story of a family through several generations. Blok's diaries and notes give a good idea of the plans and development of this autobiographic epic, *Retribution*. On February 24, 1911, he jotted down:

My hero's life was uneventful. He lived quietly with his family in the period of Pobedonostev. Silent from childhood, he stored up within himself an anxious, vague excitement. Meanwhile, Tsushima approached and the bloody dawn of January 9. He reacted to everything as a poet; was a mystic; in the surrounding anxiety, detected signs of the end of the world. All events as they unfolded were for him but images of an evolving chaos. Soon his anxiety found a guide: he fell into the company of people from whose lips the words "revolution," "riot," "anarchy," "madness" never ceased to fall. Here were beautiful women with an ever withered rose upon the breast, with lifted head and half-open lips. Wine flowed in streams. Each one acted like a lunatic, each one wanted to destroy the family, the home—both his own and others'. My hero plunged head on into this mad game, into that vaguely tempestuous view of life, that laughed at everything, imagining that it understood everything. One day, his head quite empty, light, irresponsible, but with a protest against his purposeless and destructive existence already lurking in his soul, he ran up the steps of his house.

On the table were two letters: one, perfumed, illiterate and passionate. . . . Then he opened the second. In it he was briefly informed that his father was dying in a Warsaw hospital.

Dropping everything, he rushed to Warsaw. Loneliness in the railway carriage. "Policemen, tracks, street-lamps" . . . First impressions of Warsaw.

Two years later, after a good deal of the poem had been written, he set down the plan for the whole. The hero's story would be taken back to his grandparents and traced within the framework of history: the development of Russian thought and the evolution of the hero's own family. There would be a prologue and four chapters. The narrative would begin with a sketch of "Petersburg at the end of the seventies," would continue through the revolution of 1905— "Red dawns, black nights. . . . The barricade"—and end in an epilogue: "Somewhere in a *poor* room in some city, the boy grows up." The main stages of the boy's development,

Blok conceived in terms of a dance: *"The first mazurka
. . . Second mazurka . . . Third mazurka,"* and the whole
as an interweaving of "Two leitmotifs: one—life progresses,
like infantry, hopelessly. The other—mazurka." The title of
the poem and its epigraph, "Youth—that is Retribution,"
were taken from Ibsen, whom Blok admired and whose influence, as well as Strindberg's, shows itself in psychological
elements of the work, while the concept of evolving generations was borrowed from Zola (Blok referred to his poem
as his "Rougon-Macquart on a small scale"). Of this large
plan, the Prologue was completed, Chapter I (the marriage
of the hero's parents and the child's birth), a brief fragment
of Chapter II (Petersburg in the nineties, the hero's education), and a long fragment of Chapter III (the father's
death). And although in July 1919, Blok prefaced a reading of Chapter III by saying that he felt "neither the need
nor the desire to finish a poem filled with premonitions of
the revolution, at a time when the revolution [was] over," he
was still at work on it the year of his death, and the month
before he died, wrote drafts for the continuation of Chapters II and III. A pity indeed that the grand design was not
completed! But its finished sections are in themselves remarkable.

The Prologue, following epic tradition, states the theme
and calls on a Muse for help. But unlike Homer's, Virgil's,
or Milton's, this theme is not heroic, and the Muse whom
Blok addresses has no name. The beginning is in essence an
apology for poetry, almost the poet's attempt to excuse himself for "singing" at all. "Life," he starts out, "is without beginning and without end"; and in this place of Chance and
ignorance of the Beyond, the poet alone has "faith in beginnings and ends." As a man, "helpless and weak, like everyone," he finds "the world . . . frightening," for "a pillar
of fire stands over" it, "an open-mouthed, thirsty dragon,
over the whole of Europe. Who is to smite him?" But art is
Siegfried's sword, to be wielded only by a fearless hero, a
poet, and "there is always someone singing in the crowd.
. . . And so—I sing."

"Thou who hast conquered Lucifer," he addresses the

Muse, "bless me on this mortal path. Permit me to turn if but one small leaf of the book of life. Permit me, unhurriedly and truthfully, to speak before Thy Face of that which we conceal from ourselves, of that which is alive upon this earth, of how anger grows in hearts, and with anger—youth and freedom, of how in everyone breathes the spirit of the people," for "sons are mirrored in their fathers; and the brief little fragment of a family—two or three links—makes clear the legacy of the past: a new race has matured, the coal has been transformed into a diamond. . . . Strike, then, without knowing rest," so that, "however deep the vein of life may lie," my verse shall reach the buried diamond. "Shatter the rocks, my angry iamb!"

This majestic and touching Prologue, written in 1911, reflects the mood of the years that followed 1905, of which Blok's diary, like Gorky's letters, gives the gloomy record. It is filled with such comments as:

Sameness, apathy. I have forgotten that there are people on the earth.

I am afraid of life, of streets, of everything.

Lyuba propounds that one must work these days, plug away, that never again will one get something for nothing as one used to. Well, I'll try. I'll make an effort. A. M. Remizov is so sallow, so exhausted! And all are like that. Mother is having a hard time, auntie is tired of everything. Will this period ever, ever end.

Everyone is unhappy—rich and poor. The literary section of *Zavett* is devoted to the description of human torments—of many different kinds. . . .

It expresses the mood of those years when, as he recalled later, what was greatest in Russian art had perished:

1910—is the year of the death of Komisarzhevskaya, the death of Vrubel and the death of Tolstoy. With Komisarzhevskaya perished the lyric note on the stage; with Vrubel the tremendous, private world of the artist, his insane doggedness, his insatiable quest —to the point of madness. With Tolstoy died human tenderness— wise humaneness.

Then came new literary movements and debates about art:

I remember the discussions at night out of which emerged a consciousness of the inseparability and the incompatibility of art, life, and politics [different from those of earlier years, for now there was no longer satisfaction with the] fusion of everything into oneness that had been easy and possible in the genuinely mystic darkness of the years preceding the first revolution, and also—in the unreal mystic intoxication that succeeded it.

Now there was only:

the tragic consciousness of the incompatibility and the irreparability of everything, irreconcilable contradictions, demanding reconciliation . . .

These contradictions Blok reconciled in his views of life, art, and the poet's function: life, broader than any understanding of it, art, a valiant affirmation that beneath "accidental features . . . the world is beautiful," the poet's task, "to discover the place of light" so as "to understand darkness." That this task was not private and esoteric is suggested by the nameless Muse whom Blok invokes. His address to her as conqueror of Lucifer recalls the verse in Isaiah 14:12: "How art thou fallen from heaven, O Lucifer, son of the morning! how art thou cut down to the ground, which didst weaken the nations!"; and so identifies the poet as a votary of the Power which champions men against oppressors.

But if he is writing a Rougon-Macquart in miniature, linking the growth of a family with the fortunes of a nation, his evolutionary theme, unlike Zola's, is not scientifically conceived; it is rather a kind of rhythmic and pictorial transmutation of the scientific idea, developed through musical motifs that echo and reverberate in varied contexts of both public and private events. In the psychology of a nation and of individuals, in the rhythm of epochs and of men's emotions, Blok wants to seize that interaction of linear advance and circular return to which he has already given

form in the pattern of his personal lyrics, and which he
senses at the core of the historic process, as well as of his
own experience. The characterizations of social groups, intellectual tendencies, and individual men that make up the
fragments of *Retribution* are held together not through a
consecutive argument, but by means of rhythm and imagery. Blok pictures the nineteenth century as "an iron, a
really cruel age," which threw man into the starless night of
rationalist concepts and petty materialist affairs, an age
when, as a substitute for plague, came neurasthenia, boredom, and spleen, when men banged their heads against the
wall of economic doctrines, and lived on meetings, banks,
federations, after-dinner speeches, purple patches, stocks,
rents, and promissory notes . . . an age not of salons, but
of living rooms, of just plain ladies and not Récamiers, an
age of bourgeois wealth in which machines and cities took
the place of man, and a shrewd power spread the fog of
"humanitarianism" over the world. In that gray, rotten fog,
guns made it impossible for enemies to meet face to face,
and insolence supplanted bravery; "psychosis," heroism;
while flesh withered and the soul went out . . . An age
that has been not a little cursed, and will continue to be
cursed.

But in the twentieth century even blacker and vaster is
the shadow of Lucifer's wing. The roar of destructive machines is tireless day and night, and consciousness is terrified in knowing that all former thoughts and faiths have
been deceptions. Now, too, the first airplane flies into the
desert of unknown spheres. There is disgust with life and a
mad love of it, and passion, and hatred of one's country,
and bloodshed that promises unheard-of changes, unim-
aginable riots. And man? What vistas have opened before
him through the smoke of gunpowder? What does the ceaseless grinding of machines mean to him? Or the whirring of
the airplane?

The resonant chords of these generalizations find resolution in well-articulated scenes, such as the sunny mid-Sep-
tember day of 1878 in St. Petersburg, when the Czarina and
huge crowds greet soldiers returning from the Russo-Tur-

kish war. The warriors come in triumph, and their minds are filled with visions of war, of heroism and adventure. But anyone who has been at war is now and again chilled by the thought: "what's the difference?"—a fateful thought that turns everything into a half-crazy joke. The powers that be hasten to transform those who are no longer pawns into rooks or knights. . . . In all this turmoil—this magnificent, noisy, senseless marching—there is a meeting behind closed doors and drawn blinds. A restrained conversation, full of anxiety and sorrow. And then, the ceremony of crossed swords over a flaming punch bowl, and an ancient Cossack song—a meeting, that is, of revolutionaries.

From this tableau we pass to another: a family of Petersburg aristocrats, somewhat haughty toward all other circles, although power is slipping from their graceful, white hands —a quiet, dignified, ancient family, a charmed circle, in which all that is alien is referred to in quotation marks; "nihilism" does not seem malicious, the spirit of science is compared to religion, and everyone is welcomed, even the nihilist, who, like a gust of wind from a changing world, walks in and insolently asks for vodka. The head of the family, a man of the forties with a Turgenev-like serenity, believes in Enlightenment, and is a connoisseur of wines and food; the French language and Paris are closer to him than Russia, and he is an ardent Westerner in all things—though in soul, an old-time Russian *barin*. This is the rector of the University, the botanist Beketov. He has three daughters: the eldest languishes, waiting for a husband; the second is absorbed in her studies; the third one skips about and sings, a lively and passionate girl, who teases her playmates in school and shocks her teacher. When they grow up, they are taken to a ball. The eldest marries a dishevelled young man who argues with her father about socialism, communism, and various political events, then gradually subsides, becoming a good husband and civil servant.

This tightly packed, delicately ironic, Pushkin-like description of family life is the setting for Blok's superb portrait of his father, who is ominously introduced in a striking image, which recalls a famous passage of Pushkin's

Ruslan and Ludmila: "Go out on the meadow some morning. A hawk wheels about in the pale sky, drawing smoothly one circle after another, searching out a nest poorly concealed in the bushes . . . suddenly, the twittering of birds, a flurry. . . . He listens for a moment, then swoops down on outstretched wings. . . . An anxious cry from neighboring nests, a sorrowful peep of the last fledglings, and soft down flies upon the wind. He seizes his victim in his claws. And, once again, flapping his enormous wings, flies up, drawing circle upon circle, with his famished, homeless eye examining the desert field. Whenever you look up—he circles, circles. . . . Mother Russia, like a bird, frets over her children; but her fate is to have them tortured by hawks."

Beketov takes his three daughters to visit his friend Anna Vrevskoya (actually, Anna Pavlovna Filosofova), to whose home come such men as Dostoevsky to gather material and strength for his *Journal*—"he was at this time, friendly with Pobedonostev"—Polonsky, who reads his poetry here, as well as many professors, writers, artists, both servants and enemies of the Czarist regime, and numbers of young people, some in love with their bewitching hostess, who is enchantingly beautiful and also kind, some sharing her views, some involved in conspiracy. She takes an interest in all problems. Everyone has need of her, and in her presence Slavophils shake hands with Liberals.

Among her habitual guests there is a young scientist whom Dostoevsky notices: "Who is that handsome man? He reminds me of Byron," he says. And everybody follows suit. The ladies whisper: "He is handsome, brilliant. . . . Byron, therefore a demon . . ." He did indeed resemble the proud lord, in the imperious expression of his face, in what might be called his "heavy flame of melancholy." Only, unfortunately, he resembled Byron as a sickly brother sometimes resembles a healthy one. He lacked *will power.* His spirit was bewitched, the flame of action had gone out in him, and consciousness weighed down the efforts of his maddened will.

This bird of prey glances darkly 'round, straightening his

ailing wings, and captivates the youngest daughter, who finds him "so interesting, so bright." The father agrees, and invites him to the house, where he is accepted as one of the family, enchanting everyone by his old-time aristocratic bearing, his free and broad opinions, and the charm of his ardent conversation, in which there is both poetry and science. The contradictions of his nature pass unnoticed in the brilliance of his gifts. A man of extremes, the golden mean always escapes him. "Freedom, law, idealism—all of this was no joking matter to him. But privately, he was afraid—and denied while he affirmed, and affirmed while he denied." Thus in the midst of praise he would grow gloomy, words would suddenly seem useless to him, and he would seek consolation in music. He played the piano, laying "his hands masterfully" on the docile keys, "plucking the sounds like flowers," tearing them "madly, impudently, boldly," like clothes off the body of a woman prepared to give herself. . . . He trembled in his playing as in the ecstasy of sexual union. Yet "there, beyond the musical tempest . . . an image would arise—melancholy, distant, unattainable . . . white wings in azure, and unearthly quietness. . . . But the quiet note would be engulfed in the musical tempest."

And so, what "had to be" occurred. He fascinates the girl. "Promises her a kingdom, without having one." And transforms her home into a prison. Everything that has been dear to her becomes alien and empty; her family, her relatives disgust her. Everyone is in the way. She has almost lost her senses. And he? He takes his time. He has penetration enough to see that the child is in torment, and that it is in his power alone to give her happiness. But his passion has died down, and something whispers: wait! His cold, cruel mind has asserted its rights. And she thinks: "He doesn't love, he's playing with me . . ." "Look, so the bird of prey gathers strength: in a moment he will flap his ailing wing and will descend noiselessly on the meadow to drink the blood of his trembling, terror-maddened victim . . . Such was love in that vampire age that made cripples of those worthy the name of man! Be thrice accursed, pitiful age!"

Another, at this stage, would have shaken the dust off his feet. But this man, too honest to deceive, not proud of his strange temperament, and knowing that to behave like a demon or a Don Juan would be ridiculous, turns bookworm, and while diplomatic conversations about the Balkans are in progress, and there are endless arrests, searches, accusations, and attempted murders, writes a brilliant dissertation, accepts a position at the University of Warsaw, and, already weary in spirit, proposes marriage, and takes his bride away with him. Two years later, as the epoch ends with the "1st of March" (i.e., the assassination of Alexander II), she returns to her father's home, "thin, exhausted, pale, a child in her arms."

Thus, in Chapter I, Blok tells the story of his parents, seeing their individual fortunes against the backdrop of their world: his father is a typical neurotic of the times, affected by the evil force of a decayed Romanticism; and he himself enters life on the verge of a new era. In Chapter II he pictures the Russia of the eighties in an image that continues the figure of the bird of prey, and thus underscores the identity of his own fortunes and the nation's. "Those dim and distant years" were sunk in "sleep and darkness." Pobedonostev spread his owl's wings over Russia, and there was neither day nor night, but only the shadow of his huge wings. Looking into her eyes with the wizard's glassy stare, he had drawn a magic circle about her, and she had fallen asleep to the sound of a wonderful fairy tale, while "the wizard swung the incense-burner with one hand, and with the other, buried living souls." And yet, even asleep and in his power, Russia seemed full of strength.

There follows a humorously bitter sketch of the dullness of Petersburg: rain, wind, mud, foul smells—and the mob shouting greetings to the new Czar; and then a section that seems to be an argument with Pushkin's "The Bronze Horseman," which it rivals in intensity of national feeling and beauty of poetry. But its tone is melancholy rather than majestic: "Why," asks the poet, addressing his "boundless" city, "why didst thou rise above the void?" And does it wake or sleep, the great fleet on the Neva? And what dreams, what tempests, are destined for Russia? A bloody dawn already portends Port Arthur and Tsushima, and January 9.

In Chapter III we are with the son in the train as he speeds to the Warsaw hospital, and arrives in the evening to be told that his father died that afternoon; then, as without emotion he stays alone with the corpse at night, and struggles to get a ring off the stiff hand, he notices the shadows on his father's face, and reads in it the sign of wanderers, of those chased by fate over the earth. At that moment, "the son loved his father for the first, and maybe the last time."

The burial takes place in a cemetery called "Freedom," which leads the poet to a reflective aside: "Yes, we hear the song of freedom when the gravedigger's spade strikes the yellowish clay; when the door of the prison is opened; when we are unfaithful to our wives, and they to us; when, having heard of an insult to someone's rights, we threaten ministers and laws from our well-locked apartments; when capital gains release us from ideals. . . ." The son thinks of his father. He has never known him. They lived in different cities and met only by chance, alien to one another in every way "except, perhaps, the deepest." The father would sometimes visit him, like a guest, his back bent, his eyes red-rimmed. His words were sluggish, often malicious. His mind was cynical, and only now and then a kindly, flattering glance would fall covertly on his son, breaking like a mystery upon their dismal conversation. And now the son recalls how once, in childhood, he drove a pin into his father's arm, and with sudden clarity hears the father's cry of pain resounding in the graveyard. Among the mourners there is an unknown woman who sobs, and leaves without lifting her heavy veil.

The father's rooms reveal the character of this "modern Harpagon," who accumulated all manner of things, ate in a cheap restaurant, kept no servant, ran along the street sidewise in a threadbare little coat, like a hungry dog. But his piano woke sounds of passion, boredom, shame and grief, for he had known other moments, moments of unforgettable power, and held in memory the Demon's wings broken on the crests of mountains, and his enormous eyes. One who has such memories is not like other people. He is sometimes deaf, blind, dumb, and shaken by the poet's tremor. At night, through darkness and falling snow, the son wanders about Warsaw, which slumbers under the Russian yoke, everything in her shouting, Vengeance!, until, exhausted, he returns to the house. And the fragment breaks off with a meditation on night: he who listens to night will find what he has not known in daytime, and will bless everything, having understood that life is infinitely more than Brandt's *quantum satis*; and the world, beautiful, as always.

In his explanatory notes of 1919, Blok declared, in terms that give special meaning to the circling hawks and airplanes of the poem, that the plan had appeared to him in the form of concentric circles, which grew progressively narrower and narrower, until the smallest circle of all began once more to live an independent life, thrusting apart and disjoining its environment, and in its turn affecting the periphery. At the time of composition he had not put this into words, but had sensed it "for the most part, in musical and muscular consciousness." Of "muscular consciousness" he spoke advisedly, he said, because the development of the poem had been closely linked for him with muscular development. In 1911 "French wrestling" had become popular in Petersburg circuses, and he was entranced by the wrestlers, among whom were "some genuine artists," such as one unforgettable Hollander whose "muscular system presented the most perfect musical instrument of rare beauty." He himself was busy with gymnastics, developing his own muscular system, so that he knew whereof he spoke when he explained that: "In systematic [physical labor] . . . the biceps develop first . . . and then, gradually, the more delicate, the more refined, and the rarer mesh of muscles of the chest and the back below the shoulderblades. Just such a rhythmic and gradual growth of muscles was to compose the rhythm of the whole poem," in consonance with its basic theme, "the development of the links of a single family chain." The process was like a wrestler's back, and also like a whirlpool; an individual developed to the farthest reaches marked out by his family and was sucked into the environ-

ment, so that "almost nothing was left of his personality.
. . . There had been a man—and there was a man no
longer, only wretched dull flesh and a little smoldering
soul." But in ever widening circles, succeeding generations
affected the environment, so that from generation to gener-
tion, something obdurate and new "appeared and finally
left its mark." "In such fashion, the family, having experienced the retribution of history, environment, epoch, begins,
in its turn, to create retribution. . . ." It was a notion, said
Blok, that he developed out of his increasing hatred of all
theories of progress. And that accounts for the poem's circular imagery and rhythms: the soaring hawk, the owl's
widespread wings, the wrestler's muscles, the whirlpool, the
wheeling airplane, "mazurka."

Better than any other work, these brilliant fragments reveal Blok's temperament and the nature of his poetic inspiration: the deep unhappiness he had inherited, his experience
of tragedy and sense of guilt, the reconciling gift of poetry
and that self-absorption which was essential for its development. Could he have finished this work, it would have been
one of the great poems of European literature; it is sharp in
historical appraisal, profound in portraiture, unique in form,
and with passages of classic purity that carry on the tradition of Pushkin's narrative style.

VII

In the spring of 1912, while he was gloomily writing *Retribution*, a new acquaintance, M. I. Tereshchenko, a wealthy
patron of the arts, proposed that he do the scenario for a
ballet to be based on the life of Provençal troubadours, for
which Glazunov would compose the music. Blok consented,
and worked on it for almost a year. From ballet it developed
into opera, and from opera into *The Rose and the Cross*, a
drama that contains some of his most graceful and musical
verse, and holds within the outline of a conventional med-

ieval romance, the quintessence of his belief in the nature of poetry.

The story has to do with the ugly, unfortunate, faithful knight Bertrand, loyal to his master and secretly in love with the master's wife, who departs on a hazardous dual mission: for his master, the Count Archimbaüt, he is to search out the whereabouts of Simon de Montfort and his troops, whose help is urgently needed in the Count's struggle with the Albigensians; for his lady, Izora, he is to find the author of a song, certain lines of which will not let her rest. The poet is known only as the Wanderer, and she pines for him. Her husband, meanwhile, advised that she harbors romantic, antireligious notions, shuts her away in a Tower—but releases her when Bertrand, to whom he has promised to grant whatever he asks upon the accomplishment of his mission, returns successfully and requests that she be freed on the first of May to hear the jongleurs who have gathered for the celebration customary on that day. Among these is the Wanderer, whom Bertrand had come upon in weird circumstances in the north of France. He is Gaëtan, the old, eccentric, impoverished Lord of Traumenecke—and not at all the handsome young man Izora had imagined. She faints at the festival, not so much from the pleasure of hearing the song as from disappointment at the unattractiveness of the singer, who vanishes, without trace, as soon as he has finished singing. But now the enemy swoops down on Archimbaüt, and in the battle that ensues Bertrand saves the day, at the price of a serious wound because of which his master relieves him from his night watch. Izora, meanwhile, has decided to take as lover a vain, pampered, empty-headed young retainer whom she is to admit to her room that night. She asks Bertrand to help, and he stands guard by her window, offers the young man his shoulder as a step, and dies just in time for the clanging of his armor, as he falls, to warn the lovers of the Count's approach.

The Cross is the black cross of devotion, the device on Gaëtan's shield; the rose is the black rose of Bertrand's love, transformed into his mortal wound. Izora does not know the value nor the meaning of either. And the tragic situation is that of great love and great gifts thrown away on a capricious pleasure-seeking girl. But for all this, Gaëtan is no less a genius, Bertrand no less noble, nor Izora, for that matter, no less pathetic, longing for romance in the castle of her old, unsympathetic husband.

The theme of the song that had enticed Izora is that "Joy and Sorrow are one," and that this is "the immutable law of the heart." Gaëtan's greatness lies in his having made a song which all men, rich and poor, noblemen and vassals, love to sing because they know that there is truth in its vagueness, and Bertrand's life is a test of this truth and his death a proof of its destructiveness.

Blok read the play act by act to Tereshchenko, of whom he said later that he had *"made"* him finish it, and in his diary he wrote down some of the discussions they used to have at this time. One of these, recorded on October 11, 1912, is particularly significant:

Tereshchenko says that he has never been religious and thinks that everything religion can give is supplied him by art. I began, in answer, to elaborate my usual: the *what* of art is—endlessness, about an unknown on the other side of everything, but empty—destructive, maybe; the *that* of religion is an—*end*, and it is known what its fullness, salvation are about. . . . And of art: do I want to repeat or bring back these moments, when art revealed endlessness to me? No, I could not want this, even did I know how to bring them back. That which is beyond it, one cannot love. (Love—with a capital L.)

Tereshchenko said that art *levels* people (it alone in all the world), that it gives joy or *something* that one cannot even call joy; that he does not understand people who can be interested, e.g., in politics, if they have ever known (have felt) what art is; and that he does not understand people who after "Tristan" fall in love. With all this, arguing, I did not argue, as often happens with me; and specifically: I argued, because I had once known something bigger than art; i.e., not endlessness, but the End, not worlds, but the World; I did not argue, because That I have lost, probably, forever, have *fallen*, have *betrayed*, and I am now indeed an "artist," living not on that which makes life full, but on that which makes it black, terrifying, repulsive. Did not argue, furthermore, because I am a "pessimist" as "everyone agrees," that where I see despair and horror, others see—joy, and maybe even—Joy. I don't know.

The Rose and the Cross is the poetic symbol of the witchery of the *what* of art, and the human failure to attain the *that* of religion, for Blok himself is the unfortunate Bertrand, sacrificing his life to his lady—partly in gratitude, for she had once saved him from death and disgrace—seeking to please her without thought of reward, yearning for the Unattainable whom to adore is bliss, finding joy in the sorrow of his servitude.

When the play was almost finished, he wrote in his diary:

No, in my present state (harshness, angularity, maturity, illness) I am unable and have no right to speak of *more* than the human. My theme—is not at all the "Cross and the Rose"—that I shall not be able to command. Let it be—the human fate of a failure, and if I can manage to "immolate" myself to art, maybe someone will catch a glimpse of *more* through my theme . . .

VIII

Blok was drawn out of his state of dejection by passionate and tragic events. In March 1914, he surrendered for the last time to an infatuation that obsessed and inspired him, falling in love with the singer L. A. Delmas, whom he had heard for the first time that fall in the role of *Carmen,* and to whom he now dedicated the short cycle of poems that bears the name of Bizet's opera. These lyrics are not tumultuous like those of *The Snow Mask* nor reverent like those of the *Verses on the Beautiful Lady.* In them, the poet's love is told in less visionary images and less tempestuous rhythms: in descriptive re-creations of the deep tones and the exquisitely sensitive movements and gestures that had enchanted him on the stage; in figures of speech that are not symbols but similes (for example, like the ocean beneath clouds and lightning in storms, the heart changes color and motion in the tempest of song); and in a reasoned explanation of his love: she will never be his, nor anyone's, she is a law unto herself, she is only light and music, her joy and sorrow are but melody, and that is why he loves her; he is himself like that, he says to her. The images and music of these poems echo the earthy passion of the opera.

Then came the war and the Revolution. In the summer of 1916, Blok was mobilized in the corps of engineers and sent to the region of Pinsk. Back in Petersburg the following spring, and from then on, he was elected and appointed to a variety of official and semiofficial positions. As member of a commission set up by the Provisional Government to investigate activities of Czarist ministers and statesmen, he was present at the interrogations, of which he edited the stenographic report; and as one of a committee to reorganize the Czarist theaters he attended endless meetings and read innumerable plays; then, under the directorship of Gorky, he edited the work of Heine for Gorky's "World Literature," drew up plans for a people's theater, and wrote a historical drama, *Ramses,* for Gorky's projected "Historical Portraits." In addition to all this feverish social activity, he prepared a collected edition of his own poetry and wrote a number of literary articles and lectures, the most remarkable of which were "The Intelligentsia and the Revolution" and "The Decline of Humanism."

Most notably, he produced *The Twelve,* the poem for which he is best known. It is a brief lyric-epic of the Bolshevist Revolution, written at top speed in January 1918, and almost the last of his works. He himself considered it his best because at the time he wrote it, he said two years later, he was living "contemporaneously." More succinctly than any of his other works, this poem condenses Blok's private experience and that of his epoch in a remarkable fusion of the epoch's "music," as he liked to call it, and the "music" of his own emotions. It is a composite portrait of the country at the time of the Revolution, a dramatic symbol of its meaning, and also a summary of the poet's entire life and work—not, however, like the total drawn up below a column of figures, nor like a musical coda, nor the concluding epigram to an edifying story, but like a symphony in which the themes of earlier compositions are found transmuted and combined. The symphony is in itself independent, but it is impossible to understand it without knowing what its author had lived through and written before it, and to have understood it is to have seen his work as a whole.

> Black night
> White snow.
> Wind, wind!
> On his feet no man can stand.
> Wind, wind—
> Over all of God's creation!

it begins, the sound of which in the original,

> Chërnyi výecher
> Bélyi snýeg
> Výeter, výeter!
> No nogahk ne stoit chelovék.
> Výeter, výeter—
> Na vsyëm bózhyem svýete!

with its rhyming of every other line, and the echoing in it of long vowel sounds—vyecher, vyeter, snyeg, bozhyem, and the unrhymed svyete of the last line—creates the effect of wind howling through endless space, while the contrast of the small, hard sounds of the fourth line and the way it almost rhymes, but not quite, with the second, suggests the slipping, miserable attempt of the individual human being to stand up to the storm. This wind, which is not only the actual wind of a Petersburg winter, and not only the allegorical wind of revolution, but also that of Fate and the Russian Karamazov passions, had whistled through other, earlier poems: it had brought faint sounds of the song of the Beautiful Lady; or it had accompanied a dark, indefinite Mystery; or it had come as the voice of despair, or of Time singing at midnight of faded dawn and coming death, or of Fate. An entire collection of lyrics of 1913 was entitled

Of What the Wind Sings, and in Blok's own experience, it is the wind of those cyclonic periods that recurred throughout his life when he composed with the speed and tumult of tempests that swept him off his feet. He said as much in a note about *The Twelve:*

In January 1918 for the last time I gave myself up to the elemental, no less blindly than in January 1907, or in March 1914. [The years of *The Snow Mask, Faïna,* and *Carmen.*] That is why I do not disown what I then wrote, because it was written in consonance with the elemental: for example, for several days, during and after finishing *The Twelve* I experienced physically, aurally, a great noise all around—a blended noise (probably the noise of the old world crashing). . . .

The last line of the first strophe, *"Na vsyëm bózhyem svýete!"* ("Over all of God's creation!"), is a colloquial expression, and it is picked up in the second strophe in the half-scornful, half-affectionate diminutives of folk locutions —a transition to the chief characters of the poem, given in the direct, crude speech and thought of the common men by whom the Revolution is made.

But the action in the beginning is general and vague. There is in the second strophe a hint of a slight mishap; a woman has slipped on the ice and someone has commented on her fall. But who is she? And who is the observer?

> The wind twists and twirls
> The white snow.
> There is ice below;
> Heavy, slippery,—
> Every step
> Slips—ah, the poor little thing!

The scene is indefinite, and as if observed from a distance.

But now it becomes explicit, with the reality of a photograph and the grotesqueness of caricature. An old woman gazes at a banner that hangs from a great rope stretched from building to building, proclaiming: "All Power to the Constituent Assembly." She weeps, not understanding the use of such an enormous banner. How many leggings it would make, she thinks, for all the children who go unclothed, unshod! The old woman, like a hen, has picked her way across the snowdrift. "Oh, Mother of God. These Bolsheviks will be the death of me!" And here is a bourgeois, standing on the street corner, his head hidden in his coat collar; and also a long-haired poet, the "intellectual," the Prophet, muttering, "Traitors! Russia has perished"; a long-robed priest, too, gloomily sneaking away behind the snowdrift—"Do you remember how you used to walk forth, with the cross on your paunch shining on the people?"; and a lady in caracul, slipping on the ice and falling with a crash, just as she was turning to another one to say: "How we wept and wept." These are not the makers of the Revolution, but those who cannot see what it brings, beyond the suffering they themselves must endure. They are opposed to the Revolution, and Blok ridicules their suffering. The gay, cruel wind twirls their skirts, tears at the banner, carries the words of resolutions passed by prostitutes:

> We had a meeting
> There, in that building
> Decided
> Resolved:
> Ten for time, twenty-five for nights
> And nothing less from anybody—
> Come to bed . . .

The night advances, the street grows empty but the wind whistles on. Now only a tramp is left outdoors. Hey, there, beggar; come, let's kiss.

> Bread!
> What's ahead?
> Pass!

> Black, black sky!

Thus the people, lost in darkness, exchange terrified, staccato words.

Anger, gloomy anger
   Seethes in the heart. . . .
Black anger, holy anger. . . .

Comrade!
Watch out!

The first part ends with this symbolic transformation of the blackness of night and the whiteness of snow in the opening lines into the blackness of anger and the whiteness of holiness, while the last two words are a shout of warning which emphasizes the chaotic, perilous state of the city. This is the setting: the storm of revolution, of Russian passions, of righteous anger, which is both dark and light, both violent and holy.

Part Two begins with an almost skipping rhythm:

The wind reels, the snow dances;
A party of twelve men advances.

The wind is now the accompaniment of twelve marching men. They are boisterous soldiers with rumpled caps and cigarettes in mouth, elated by a freedom which means no more to them than a spree. They talk about Van'ka, a former comrade of theirs. He has gone over to the bourgeoisie, they say, and is at that moment in a pub drinking with Kat'ka. But they are pulled up from these thoughts by their duty, or rather by their knowledge that the enemy lurks about: "Revolutionaries, keep in step! The restless enemy is not asleep!" And the Tra-ta-ta of their rifles rings out like a refrain. "Comrade, point your gun; don't be a coward! Let's give Holy Russia a taste of shot! Wooded, hutted, fat-rumped Russia!"

To these ruffians, the "holiness" of Russia is a joke. "Freedom, freedom," they chant gleefully, "without a cross"— "*bez crestá,*" which rhymes with the "Tra-ta-ta" of their guns. And now to the black of night and anger and the white of snow and holiness is added the color of flame, the color of destruction, and maybe of purification. "Ha, ha, ha, without a cross."

Here is evidence of the prophet-poet's grandiloquent "Russia has perished!" for here are the hoodlums, actually shouting in their vulgar way that they are shooting at Russia, thinking of her in the same beastly way they think of their women. But Blok implies, as he has said before, that they will never destroy Russia, with all their shooting and all their beastliness, because Russia is indestructible, and also because they themselves are better than they seem.

Part Three is a *"chastushka,"* that is, a popular jingle composed by factory workers. Here it takes the form of a jaunty marching song, with the traditional diminutives and repetitions of folk poetry:

> As our fellows went away
> With the Reds
> With the Reds
> And their lives to give away . . .

It could be the song that the soldiers themselves are singing. But suddenly it breaks off with the exclamation, *"Gospodi, blagoslovi!"* ("God, bless us!"), giving a poignant glimpse of a mood very different from the bravado they had been flaunting. It is an unexpected sigh or prayer that suggests, in addition to a deeper feeling among the twelve, a broader sentiment, true of all Russians at this time of darkness, misery, heaviness, and elation. It introduces the drama which, developed in the next five sections, is the central episode of the poem.

The Van'ka and Kat'ka of whom the men have been talking now come racing along in a sledge, and the soldiers see them making love: Van'ka, with his idiotic face, twirling his mustache, joking, putting his arm around Kat'ka, and she throwing back her "plump little snout," her little teeth sparkling, pearl-like. One of the soldiers—certainly the one who has muttered earlier, "Come on, Van'ka, you bourgeois son of a bitch, try and kiss my girl"—now mutters more ominously, recalling the gash beneath her breast that he himself has made—"It's still fresh!"—and the officer he once knifed when she went to him; and when the sledge races past, he fires and kills the girl, but misses Van'ka, who escapes. Kat'ka falls on the snow, shot through the head:

> Well, Kat'ka, are you glad?—Not a sound. . . .
> Lie, carrion, on the snowy ground.

And again they pull themselves together, with the reminder that they are revolutionaries and must keep in step.

And so the twelve go marching on; but the murderer, Pet'ka, does not keep in step. Deathly pale, his muffler tight about his neck, he keeps running faster and faster. Then as one of the men tries to console him, he breaks out with memories of his orgies with Kat'ka, of his love, of his guilt. His comrades won't stand for that. They tell him to "shut up," and try to cheer him with the thought of the looting that lies ahead of them. He slows down, tosses his head.

> Lock your doors and windows tight!
> There are looters out tonight.

But the next verse—in the form of a *"plach,"* or folk lament—shows the heaviness of Pet'ka's heart:

> Oh, thou, bitter-woe!
> Boredom drearisome
> Boredom deadly!
>
> Well, I'll pass the time
> pass the time
>
> Well, I'll scratch my pate,
> scratch my pate.
> Sunflower seed I'll
> spit, I'll spit
>
> With my little knife
> I'll slit, I'll slit
>
> Fly away, you bourgeois, like a sparrow.
> Blood will I drink

For my sweetheart,
My black-browed. . . .

Rest, O Lord, the soul of Thy servant. . . .

Misery!

It was with this verse that Blok had started the poem, with
the lines about the knife, which he thought "expressive." In
Russian—

úzh ya nózhichkom
polosnú, polosnú!

—it is cruel and painful with its *zh* and *s* sounds that set
one's teeth on edge, and brutal in understatement: the diminutive form for "knife," and the way the thought of
murder comes on a par with innocuous spitting of sunflower
seeds and bored head-scratching. But "Rest, O Lord, the
soul of Thy servant," with which Pet'ka's song breaks off, is
a line of prayer, and this time it is not a colloquial expletive,
like the earlier *"Gospodi, blagoslovi,"* but the language itself of prayer, while the sound of the last moaning word,
skuchno, prolongs the sense of wretchedness and boredom,
and is but poorly rendered by the English "misery" or any
of its synonyms.

This verse closes the main details of the central tragedy in
the form and language of folk poetry. It is followed by one
which, in conventional quatrains, rhyming *a b a b*, parodies a bourgeois love song, and returns to the picture of the
bourgeois at the street corner with his coat collar about his
ears, and a shivering, mangy cur beside him, its tail between its legs. But mere caricature has here become political satire: the poor bourgeois, who stands "speechless, like a
question," is no longer just an individual, but the whole of
the bourgeoisie, while the hungry, terrified mutt is "the old
world" with nowhere to go and nothing to eat, clinging to
his former master, who himself can do nothing but stand
quaking at a crossroads.

Now the storm grows stronger. It is so dark you cannot
see four steps away. The gloomy Pet'ka is once more admon-

ished by his comrades to be sensible; the refrain by which
they remind themselves to keep alert, "Revolutionaries, keep
in step! The restless enemy is not asleep!," is somewhat
modified: the enemy is now not only "awake" but "near,"
and the final words are a variation of a well-known revolutionary song:

> Forward, forward, forward,
> Workers all.

We have already had the proletarian *chastushka,* the folk
lament, and the bourgeois love song. To these the song of
revolution has now been added, and it marks the transformation of the looting band into a group of workers with a
concerted purpose.

The meter, as well, suggests increasing seriousness and
discipline, as it changes gradually to greater regularity
and a more emphatic beat, while the poem returns from
drama to narration and description:

> . . . So they march, each of the twelve
> And without the name of God
> On they march, into the distance
> Ever ready, pitiless.

They march through blackness, their guns pointed on an
enemy hidden in the storm. But now a red flag waves before
them. Their tramp is steady; they march days and nights,
until in the last section, the twelfth, their pace becomes
majestic: "On, with sovereign step they go!" But they are
disturbed by an unseen presence, by someone lurking about,
a form skimming alongside the houses. "Who is there?" they
shout, "Come on out!" And even their shouts, without losing
realistic vulgarity, sound deeper. But at first it is only the
wind they hear, and only the flag they see waving in front
of them, and the poor mutt, limping at their heels, refusing
to be chased away. They warn whatever "it" is to come
forth and give itself up, or they will shoot. And they do
shoot, but are answered only by an echo calling through

the houses, and by the storm breaking out into long laughter in the whirls of snow.

The poem ends:

> So they march with sovereign tread,
>   Back of them—the hungry cur,
> Out in front—the blood-red flag,
>   There unseen, behind the storm,
>   There unharmed by any shot
> With gentle step above the storm
> In the pearly spray of snow
>   Crowned with wreath of roses white
>   Out in front—steps Jesus Christ.

Thus, through several stages, the disorganized band of rough marauders has been transformed into a holy procession—which brings to mind an image of the Twelve Apostles, led by a Christ they follow but do not see.

This conclusion has puzzled everybody, including Blok himself. On January 29, 1918, the day after he finished the poem, he wrote in his diary: "That Christ goes before them —is undeniable. It is not a question of whether they are worthy of him, but what is terrifying is that he is with them again, and there is no one else as yet; but Another is needed . . ." Later, to the poet Gumilev, who objected that the ending seemed to him to be artificially stuck on, Blok replied: "I don't like the ending of *The Twelve* either. I wish it had a different kind of ending. When I finished I was myself astonished: why Christ? Is it possible it's Christ? But the closer I looked into it, the clearer I saw Christ." And later, in giving instructions to the artist Annenkov, who was illustrating the poem, Blok wrote: "The most concrete thing I can say about Christ: a white spot in front, white as snow, and it looms up in front, half-illusion—persistently; and there, too, flaps the red flag, also looming in the darkness. All this—vexes, attracts, teases, leads on after the spot, which keeps escaping." In another entry in his diary, in answer to protests that the poem had roused (and it became immediately a center of discussion: some among the "intellectuals" saw it as inexcusable praise of barbarism, others among the Marxists, as a satire on the Revolution), Blok wrote:

The Marxists—are the wisest critics, and the Bolshevists are right to fear *The Twelve*. . . . If a real priesthood existed in Russia, and not merely a class of morally dull people belonging to the priestly profession, it would have long since "taken into account" the circumstance that "Christ is with the Red Guard." It is hardly possible to quarrel with this truth, which is obvious to those who read the Bible and think about it. . . . I only stated a fact: if one peers closely into the pillars of snow in this blizzard, one will see "Jesus Christ." But sometimes I myself despise profoundly *that* womanish phantom.

As a matter of fact, the appearance of Christ in *The Twelve* is not surprising. Like all Blok's major images, Christ is here the culmination of a recurrent figure, neither rationally conceived nor accidentally come upon, but rolled up in consciousness in the manner of a great snowball with ever gathering accretions of significance. Blok had read not only the Bible but also Renan. And in November 1912, he noted with regard to a lecture he had heard: "I was especially struck by that part where he spoke of this: *that* when all disputes and contradictions take root in reality and are brought to their logical conclusion, only then will emerge not the Biblical, but the unknown, greater than the Biblical religion of Jesus Christ." In addition, the day before he began work on *The Twelve* he was making plans for a drama about Christ.

But more than that, the experience of this ephemeral, compelling, indistinguishable presence was one of Blok's recurrent and most real experiences, so fundamental, indeed, that all his work could be considered in its light, for it is the uncertain, lurking accompaniment of the three dominant, related themes of his work: the Search, the Road, and the Dream or Vision.

Along the tangled, moonlit paths of *Ante Lucem* and the *Verses on the Beautiful Lady*, through the dismal streets of

Crossroads and *The Violet of Night,* across the vast stretches of land and space of *The Song of Fate* and *The Snow Mask* and the romantic seacoasts of medieval France in *The Rose and the Cross,* the poet or his surrogates wander in search of their Ideal until the Red Guardsmen of *The Twelve* march through the streets of Petersburg, led by the dim, glimmering figure that is the symbol of the greatest ethical ideal so far devised by the Western world. Into this poem Blok had gathered, as into a spiritual last will and testament, the chief preoccupations of his life, and that Christ emerges at the end of it is but a final instance of a lifelong absorption and a lifelong habit, absorption in ideals and the habit of seeing them embodied in dim, alluring visions. If some of his friends of the intelligentsia refused to shake hands with him after they had seen or heard the poem—it was read night after night in theaters and cafés—it was that his twelve marchers were the Russia that Blok, unlike the intellectuals, loved with all her faults, the Russia to whom he had written love songs more tender than any he addressed to women, the Russia he called "my life," "my country," "my poor wife," whose autumn rains were her tears, whose woods and fields were the patterned shawl she wore, who was impoverished, sorrowful, but magnificent and beautiful; and even with all that was false, petty, and disgusting in her, dearer to him than any other corner of the world:

> To sin, unshamed, to lose, unthinking
> The count of careless nights and days,
> And then, while the head aches with drinking,
> Steal to God's house with eyes that glaze;
>
> Thrice to bow down to earth, and seven
> Times cross oneself, and then once more
> With the hot brow, in hope of heaven
> To touch the spittle-covered floor;
>
> With a brass penny's gift dismissing
> The offering, the holy Name
> To mutter with loose lips, in kissing
> The ancient, kiss-worn icon frame;

And to come home, then, and be tricking
Some wretch out of the same small coin,
And with a hiccough to be kicking
A trembling cur in his lean groin;

And where the icon's flame is quaking
Drink tea, and reckon loss and gain,
From the fat chest of drawers taking
The coupons marked with spittle stain;

And sunk in feather beds to smother
In slumber such as bears may know . . .
Dearer to me than every other
Are you, my Russia, even so. . . .

(*Translated by Avrahm Yarmolinsky*)

This was the Russia of "the people," about which Gorky also had written—brutal, thoughtless, hypocritical, not the Russia of the intelligentsia, who had always irritated Blok and who now revolted him: on January 14, 1918, he wrote of them:

Something completely astonishing is taking place (like everything): the "intellectuals," the people who had propounded revolution, "the prophets of revolution" have proved to be its traitors. Cowards, agents provocateurs, parasites of bourgeois scum.

Ten days later, by contrast, he recalled a conversation of the previous day with the peasant poet Essenin, who had described the masses of the people as naïve hooligans who were destructive out of mischief, but like children could always be talked out of their destructiveness. "I asked weren't there some who destroyed in the name of higher values. He says . . . no—" *The Twelve* indicates that, although Blok agreed with Essenin's characterization of the masses as "hooligans," he insisted on "the higher values." So wholehearted was his belief in "the people" and in the grandeur of what was taking place, that he accepted even the looting of his own Shakhmatovo as an act of retribution, as just, and to have been expected in the historic process. He accepted the scorn of the intellectuals and hurled back

at them, after the treaty of Brest-Litovsk, the charge that
Russians were "barbarians."

. . . We will fulfill our historic mission [he wrote in his diary on
January 11]. If with a "democratic peace," at least, you will not
wipe out the shame of your military patriotism, if you will destroy
our revolution, then you are Aryans no longer. And we will open
wide our gates to the East.—We looked on you with the eyes of
Aryans so long as you had a face. But on your mug we will cast
our *slanting*, sly, rapid glance; we will appear as *Asiatics*, and
over you the East will pour.

And, as a kind of furious coda to *The Twelve*, the day
after he finished it, Blok wrote "The Scythians," in which he
gave poetic expression to his rage:

> Millions of you—And multitudes of us.
> Come, try your strength with us!
> Yes, Scythians are we! Yes, Asiatics we—
> With slanting, greedy eyes.—
>
> For you—the centuries, for us—
>   a single hour—

That is, for Europe, there had been centuries of greedy
watchfulness, of waiting for a suitable moment to conquer
the wealthy Orient—where:

> We, like obedient slaves
> Have stood as shield between two breeds
>   at war—

But to that, an end has come, and the old world had better
take warning!

> Old world! While still you rise,
>   While still you languish in sweet torment,
> Oh, pause before the Sphinx, like Oedipus the wise,
>   And contemplate her ancient question.

For Russia is the Sphinx who gazes and gazes on the old
world with the kind of hating, searing love that Europe has

long since forgotten—a many-sided, much-embracing love that includes cold numbers as well as heavenly visions; understands both Gallic sharpness and the gloomy genius of Germany; remembers Paris, Venice, Köln; and loves flesh —its taste, its color, its odor. These Scythians who are accustomed to tame rebellious female slaves as they tame wild horses, breaking their heavy croups—are they to blame if the brittle bones of Europeans crack in their paws? But they are willing to be friends; they invite Europe to come from the horrors of war to their peaceful embrace. If not, they have nothing to lose. They will spread themselves out before Europe over thickets and forests, and will turn on it their fearsome Asiatic snout. For the last time—old world, take thought! For the last time the barbarian lyre calls you to a brotherly feast!

After these poems, something terrible happened to Blok. He said that he could no longer "hear the music of the world," and so could write no more. He continued to serve on committees, to work for Gorky's literary enterprises, to edit his own poems, to write articles and give lectures. But there were no more new poems. The physical circumstances of his life were, of course, difficult in those years. Every day he had to trudge an enormous distance from his house to his place of work. Neither food nor heat was easy to obtain, and living quarters were cramped. Furthermore, Lyuba and her mother-in-law, whose husband died in 1920, did not get on together, and the poet was greatly upset by their quarrels. Equally distressing, and probably more so, were the public events that during the last months of his life made him write in his diary: "Such filth and baseness. . . . Life has changed—(it is different, but not new, not *nuova*); the louse has conquered the whole world; that has already happened and now everything will keep changing, but only in the *opposite* direction, not in the one we lived in, the one we have loved." Besides, he was not well. But he refused to give much attention to his illness, and for too long would not hear of going abroad because that would have been like abandoning Russia in a crisis. When at last he did consent to go and the necessary permits were obtained, he could not be moved. His illness had taken a serious turn in April 1921; in May he was obliged to stay in his room, propped up in bed or in an easy chair to ease his breathing. He died on the seventh of August, 1921.

I X

Numerous accounts of Blok as a person produce, in various ways, the impression of a man intent upon his thought, absorbed in his private vision, and yet neither self-centered nor eccentric, somehow combining almost statuesque aloofness with kindly awareness of, and interest in, others—a man who, in a curious way, is both solitary and in touch with people, who can talk to them enchantingly and of them in a way they recognize as true, although he cannot speak with them; who is indifferent to praise or blame, but glad to be understood. His is a solitude of a very different order from the irremediable isolation of the *poètes maudits*—without the bitterness of Rimbaud, the scorn of Baudelaire, the sought-out despair of Valéry, the melancholy submissiveness of Verlaine—while on the other hand, his concern with human beings is neither the preacher's nor the scientist's nor the reformer's, neither Tolstoy's nor Chekhov's nor Gorky's. He is a poet, and therefore alone, but he suffers from this isolation and overcomes it in successive stages. In his earliest lyrics, he writes of highly individual experience but already in such a way that whoever is familiar with the cult of the Virgin or with fairy tales, or has some understanding of the *Ewige Weibliche*, has an inkling of what his esoteric visions are about. Later, his theory of art explains the poet as a kind of mediator between earth and heaven, a kind of seer whose visions rise out of the ground to take shape in the skies.

He had no desire for popularity, but neither had he any patience with "pure aestheticism," and he frequently expressed such sentiments as the following:

I fear every manifestation of the tendency of "art for art's sake," because such tendencies contradict the very essence of art and because in following it we would, ultimately, lose art. For it is born of the eternal interaction of two strains of music—the music of the creative individuality and the music which sounds in the depths of the people's soul, the soul of the *masses*. Great art is born only of the union of these two electric currents . . .

And so, although his poems, like those of other Symbolists, are allusive, mysterious, evocative, although they make use of private imagery, and convey the indeterminate meanings of music rather than the precise ones of logic, the "dead poets, his ancestors" who "assert their immortality" in his lines are the readily understandable Pushkin, Gogol, and Dostoevsky, rather than the "difficult" Baudelaire, Verlaine, or Mallarmé. Not method so much as aesthetic purpose and moral conviction distinguish him from the masters of French and English Symbolism. Unlike Baudelaire, he was not driven by a desire to escape banality and shock the philistine; unlike Verlaine, he was not absorbed in sensations; unlike Mallarmé, he was charmed neither by obscurity nor the urge to express nonexistence. And Pater's famous phrase, "Not the fruit of experience, but experience itself is the end," could not have been his credo. It was neither experience nor its fruits that he was after, but Truth, some permanent, eternal value that might lend meaning to experience. Obscurity seemed to him a mark of vanity or of poetic deficiency, as he says in one of his early poems, drawing a distinction between the laureled "singer" of strange songs who delights in misty verse, and "the poet," whose goal is Truth, and whose reward is not a laurel wreath, but the glimpse of unknown light beyond new horizons. In answer to his father's mocking letter about his first volume of poems, he wrote:

It seems odd to me that you find my verses unintelligible and that you even accuse me of self-advertising and eroticism. . . . Of course, nearly everyone accuses me of unintelligibility, but the other day I was very happy to hear that the whole book had been understood . . . by altogether simple, "unintellectual" people.

Without praising either the form of my verse, nor indeed anything produced by me, I can say with certainty that well or ill, I wrote my poems about that which is eternal and wholly unquestionable, that which sooner or later must be accepted by everybody (not the verses, but this eternal reality). . . .

And whenever he thought his work insufficiently clear, he willingly provided explanations.

But the fundamental difference between Blok and other modern Symbolists is this: that whereas their perception was based on a sense of irreconcilable dualities—"the absolute laws of the mind and the limiting contingencies of life" for Valéry, existence and nonexistence for Mallarmé, Earth and the Beyond for the early Yeats—Blok's derived from an innate sense of wholeness, a feeling for a unifying principle that he called "music."

In the beginning was music. Music is the world's essence. . . . Culture is the musical rhythm [through which the world grows]. . . . The whole brief history of man, that has remained in our poor memory, is, it would seem, the alternation of epochs—in one of which music dies down, sounds muffled, to gush forth with willful pressure in the one that succeeds it.

So he wrote in his diary in 1919, and developed this theme in "The Decline of Humanism," making explicit what all his work had said by implication, emphasizing, as Tolstoy had done in a different way, the reality of the unanalyzable *substratum* of existence, the matrix of life and the motion of the universe which man's mind cannot grasp, although his whole being is intuitively aware of it.

Blok's attention was centered primarily on the "music" of his emotions, and in his work he found concrete visual equivalents and rhythms to express it. If genuine lyricism is a translation of initial, recondite experience that has no language of its own, Blok's initial experience is the powerful and undirected flux and reflux of emotion, which seems limitless in strength, depth, and duration, principally because it is in essence aimless and larger than its cause. "Every human feeling," Coleridge wrote, "is greater and

larger than the existing cause . . . and this is deeply implied in music, in which there is always something more
and beyond the immediate expression!" Blok knew this,
though he did not and never could have explained it in
Coleridge's terse and brilliant way. Instead, he conveyed
his sense of it, dramatically, as it were, in imagery and
sound. Like Mallarmé, and other Symbolist poets, he sought
to transmit what was "hardly expressible," but unlike the
others, he did not see the "hardly expressible" as the fleeting
and the momentary, but on the contrary as the universal
and enduring. Music and imagery were to him something
other than a means of suggestion or evocation. He had no
such theory as Mallarmé's, that poetry must never *paint*
but only *allude* to objects, and that its proper dominion
was not creation or statement, but the unveiling of the inter-
connections between aspects of things. And if his poetry is
also a study in relations, there is this difference between it
and that of the French Symbolists: that the end of this
study Blok conceived to be not an understanding of inter-
connections but a metaphysical insight that such understanding could yield. What gave him joy was not the pattern of relations itself, but knowledge of what lay back of
them, meaning rather than emotion, insight rather than
pleasure. He believed in the reality of the imperceptible and
the unattainable, and the significance of his life lay in his
quest of this; but, unlike Valéry, he was not afraid to realize
a dream lest the delight of dreaming vanish, and unlike
Mallarmé, he had no desire to express the existence of nonexistence. Mallarmé's theory was the product of an analytic
turn of mind of a kind that was distasteful to Blok, whose
whole bent was away from the questioning, the skeptical,
the rational—which accounts for the immediate, dramatic
quality of his lyrics and the clear-cut lucidity of his images,
which have nothing of the intermelting mobility of Mallarmé's. For Blok did not value indefiniteness, and the
effect of melting and fusing in his poetry is not designed—
not even in *The Snow Mask*—to emphasize imprecision but
to create an impression of exactitude, just as the frequent
extravagance of his imagery is not merely rhetorical but ap-

propriate to the turbulence it symbolizes. His method was direct rather than allusive; his whole attitude tended toward affirmation rather than denial; and the symbols in which he wrote were the expression not of aesthetic theory but of a kind of habit of soul, an emotional and intellectual predisposition to see disparate elements as units. Thus the essence of life *was* music to him, not *like* music; his bride not *like* the Beautiful Lady but, actually, her earthly aspect; an Enchantress was Fate, or a shooting star.

Blok was never consumed, as Valéry had been, for example, with the "mad desire to understand." The mad desire that consumed him was to attain something which he knew existed, without the help of thought; and if Valéry, in the words of Marcel Raymond, sang "a hymn of gratitude to the forces which are active only in the shadow," Blok extolled forces of mystery that were revealed to him in a blinding light. There is something primitive in his sense of the fusion of the natural and the supernatural, in the way the hardest actualities of earth are to him translucent, as if permeated by the light from the realm of the Beautiful Lady. Unlike Yeats, whom in his youth a mere glimpse of the Beyond made miserable and restless on earth, and who called to man to escape with him to the Fairyland of imagination—"Come away, O human child!"—away from the sad earth, which was "more full of weeping" than one could understand, Blok always stayed down below, where visions illuminated life and made it bearable. It was not the sorrow of the world, but the idea of God, that seemed to him incomprehensible; and tragedy to him was not the suffering of man, but the failure of his soul and spirit.

The cadences and images of Blok's poetry are an intimate revelation not only of this fundamentally nonanalytical, affirmative quality of his nature, but of the very traits of temperament that must have shaped it, the pattern itself of his personality which, through varied modulations, displays an essential consistency from the beginning to the end, from the *Verses on the Beautiful Lady* to "The Scythians." All through, like the tempests of his poems blowing over an indestructible land, the forces of passion and of enduring

calm weave the basic design of his life and of his poetry:
the onward rush and circular return in the rhyme scheme
of his early lyrics; the mounting waves of struggle that fall
from crest to trough in the poems of 1907; the moments of
infatuation—with Faïna, Carmen, and the Revolution—followed by periods of dejection; and always, throughout the
tension and the lassitude, there remains the devotion to
Russia, to the Beautiful Lady, and to Lyubov Dmitrevna,
always beneath the raging variations there breathes a lasting quietness, as intense as the moment of passion. These
were, perhaps, manifestations of the antagonistic elements
of character that he had inherited, the demonic violence of
the Bloks and the quiet dignity of the Beketovs, and doubtless it was this that made it possible for him to see "a pair
of wings behind the shoulders of every Red Guardsman."

His poetry reconciled the antagonisms of his nature, and
its imagery is as organic as its rhythms—the visual counterpart of the musical ebb and flow that unites the romantic
and realistic aspects of his vision, as his cadences combine
violence and calm. Thus the shrines and trappings of chival-
ric romance, which stand for desires beyond those life can
satisfy, occur along the roads of a familiar landscape; the
fires and abysses of wildest Romanticism, which symbolize
mad passions, flame and yawn on city streets; the ships of
thought come sailing into imaginable harbors; the bewitching Stranger retains her mystery in an ordinary restaurant;
Christ leads men through an actual blizzard in a real city;
and the wide circles described by a hawk in the sky are the
same as circles made in time by succeeding generations, as
well as the play of muscles on a wrestler's back and the flight
of airplanes that marks the emergence of a historic epoch.
And so close were the instruments of poetry to his thoughts
and feelings, to his intuitive apprehension of life, that Blok
could think of them as the language itself of historic
periods. Thus, for example, having drawn a picture of the
age of which he was writing in *Retribution,* he explained as
follows his selection of the meter for it: "The simplest expressions of the rhythm of that epoch, when the world,
preparing itself for unheard-of events, was so intensively

and continually developing its physical, political and military muscles, was the *iamb*." Could anyone but Blok perceive a whole epoch in terms of pulsations, and these as equivalent to a poetic meter?

It is also this basic difference between affirmation and denial, between, on the one hand, a process of greater and greater inclusion, and, on the other, of rejection that makes for an essential difference between Blok and such a Symbolist as Baudelaire. Nature for Baudelaire became a monstrous compensation for what he had desired and been denied, a giantess of primal lusts, the form of his revenge for the tenderness and care he had not known. And in his celebrated temple of Correspondences, where Nature surrounds man in a forest of symbols, it is the symbols of corruption that are boundless, expansive, ecstatic, while those of innocence are limited and concrete. But Blok's Nature is an infinite extension of what he knows and loves, and evil is limitation, a sin against this infinite. That is why he loves all that soars and flies, and accepts the Revolution because it is "winged." "Here is something else I have understood," he writes on January 18, 1918, "this workers' side of bolshevism, which is with the flying, the winged. This is where they need help. The people have wings, one must help them in skills and knowledge." This is also why the history of Blok's poetry, like that of his spiritual development, is the story of an ever widening circle from an inward world to broader spheres. Probably he would have subscribed to Jean Cocteau's description of the poetic state as comparable to that when, in "great grief" or "great weariness," one dozes without sleeping, and associations take place, "which are neither associations of ideas nor of images nor memories. Rather, they are monsters that meet, secrets that emerge into the light, a whole equivocal and enigmatic world," but the special monsters and secrets that attended him seemed more and more to clarify and simplify his "equivocal and enigmatic world," giving his private nightmares the character of public demonstrations.

Blok has often been called a mystic and a prophet, but it seems to me that he was not a mystic at all. Although he ad-

mired and longed for transcendent vision, his glimpses into
the Beyond were fitful and troubled, with nothing of the
true mystic's ecstasy and certitude; and what he saw there
was so clearly analogous to his earthly experience that one
can hardly call it Revelation. His poetry is hardly the
poetry of trance or vision, nor of "spiritual revelation," and
only occasionally, like "Kubla Khan," the product of "unconscious cerebration." It is the result, rather, of a habit of
ardent, exclusive concentration on the remote reaches of the
self, a listening to its most secret motions, and the skill to
reproduce these motions in language that renders them in
their complex rhythms, colors, forms, and suggested meanings. It is as if the Platonic archetype had here become the
middle term, not the origin of the creative process; and ultimate reality, not universal ideas but private experience—
a characteristically Russian process that one is tempted to
call Platonic Realism. Nor is there anything mysterious or
miraculous in the way some of his poems seem to foretell the
future. In their "prophetic" aspect, they are, really, state-
ments of desires or fears that were fulfilled in his life. For
little of importance happened to Blok through chance
alone, and if his life seemed sometimes to have imitated art,
it was only proof that his desires as poet were urgent, and
his will as man was strong.

About the mystic philosophy of Vladimir Soloviëv he
could probably have written as Coleridge had of those
mystics whose writings had influenced him: "For the writings of these mystics acted in no slight degree to prevent my
mind from being imprisoned within the outline of any
single dogmatic system. They contributed to keep alive the
heart in the *head;* gave me an indistinct, yet stirring and
working presentiment, that all the products of the mere *reflective* faculty partook of Death. . . ." Rational discussion
of what really mattered seemed blasphemous to him, and
although he did not argue in terms of the dualism of mind
and matter, of the difference between life itself and ideas
about life, such distinctions were the very atmosphere in
which his highly individual perceptions developed. It was
"intellectualism" that he found most distasteful, but all

hard and fast formulations, all creeds repelled him. And he was, perhaps, most right about himself when in a remarkably revealing letter of 1907 he wrote to Bely:

> You have wanted and still want to know my "moral, philosophical, religious physiognomy." I do not know how to, literally cannot, reveal it to you without showing it in relation to the events of my life, to my experiences. Some of these events and experiences *nobody in the world knows about.* . . .
> I have no *philosophic credo,* because I am not versed in philosophy; I do not believe in God and I dare not believe, because is it to believe in God to have depressing, lyrical, meager notions of him? I had rather say, so you might understand me better, that I believe, *most particularly,* in myself, that I sense in myself a kind of healthy integrity and the ability to be a *man*—free, independent and honest. *All this I have experienced and bear inside of me.* . . . And here is one of my psychological peculiarities: *I prefer people to ideas.* . . .

Like his Twelve, Blok himself was "without a Cross," wandering through snow and darkness in pursuit of a wavering light. But perhaps it was the blizzard itself that was his goal, and his life a demonstration of Goethe's principle of eternal striving. There is, indeed, something curiously Faustian in the pattern of his life: his absorption in himself; his quest of "the inmost force which binds the world"; his emotional involvements; his social service. It was passion Blok desired, passion in the sense of the elemental, the boundless, the antithesis of pettiness and apathy. Music, unlike reasoning, set no bounds to knowledge, did not enclose itself with protective screens against a limitless world of storms, heavens, and abysses. There was a realm of Fate grander that that of comfortable homes and well-tended gardens; there was misery in loves that could be reckoned; and a brutal, violent revolution was better than clever talk about principles behind closed doors and shuttered windows. The October Revolution meant for him the sweeping away of all the triviality and dullness of the reactionary years that had preceded it, their "abominable desolation . . . insane boredom and senseless idleness"; it was a tor-

rent that had "roared" in 1905 and had then "disappeared
into the earth" and was now "stirring again," with the noise
of "a new music," so that "our lying, dirty, boring, monstrous life" might become "a just and clean, a gay and
beautiful life." In Blok's impassioned rhetoric, and his denunciation of the trivial, one is reminded of Gogol and of
Dostoevsky. Like them, he saw "largeness" of moral intention as peculiarly Russian, but unlike them—for he lived in
an age of reappraisals—he could not be certain that the religion of the past embodied this ideal adequately. The
Vision was here in the whirling columns of snow. But what
was this Vision? Provisionally, it had to be Christ. The
terror of the infinite frightened him as it had frightened
Pascal, but he was exhilarated by it, too, and there was no
question for him of a possible wager with Destiny, no playing safe for the sake of comfort through eternity. Blok
plunged into the destructive element, sought out chaos and
tempests, and sacrificed love for Love. "That which the
most 'healthy' among us call 'life,'" he said, "is only *gossip
about life* . . . the world's morality is bottomless and does
not resemble that which is so called. The world is moved by
music, passion, partiality, strength." It is not self-indulgence
that drove Blok to the "abyss" and the "whirlwinds," but the
necessity to be at one with "life," close to the heart of reality, which he saw as a moral principle that set the world in
motion. And it was in this spirit, with the tragic blindness of
his Poet in *The King in the Square* and the devotion of his
Bertrand in *The Rose and the Cross,* that he threw himself
into the Revolution.

3

VLADIMIR MAYAKOVSKY

(1893-1930)

In an obituary on Alexander Blok, Mayakovsky recalled a meeting he had had with him during the first days of the Revolution:

> I passed by the thin, bent figure of a soldier warming himself by a bonfire. . . . Somebody called me. It was Blok . . .
> I asked him: "Do you like it?"—"It's very good [*Khoroshó*]," said Blok, and then added: "They've burnt my library in the country."
> Well, this "good" and "they burned the library" were two feelings about the revolution interwoven in his poem *The Twelve*. Some read it as a satire on the revolution, others as a glorification of it.

This comment on Blok is characteristic of Mayakovsky. A man who bemoaned the loss of his library could not, in his eyes, be wholly on the side of the Revolution. Blok seemed to him pathetic and inadequate, and when some years later he took Blok's *"Khoroshó"* as the title of a long poem, he did so ironically, in pointed contrast to his own unequivocal endorsement of "1918." Nothing, not even the death of an honored poet, would serve him as reason for unmerited praise. He was honest to the point of brutality. And as for Blok's poetry, although he was artist enough to sense its merit, he denounced the school it represented. Symbolism, he said, had had its day; and he sought to demonstrate, in an essay called "How Verses Are Made," that his own poetry was better, because it was closer to the spirit of the Revolution. Whatever one may think of this estimate, one is bound to accept the fact, for if *The Twelve* is *the* poem of the Revolution, as it has been called, Mayakovsky is its poet. *The Twelve* was, after all, a feat of translation, in which events foreign to the poet's self were rendered in the language of his private music and the imagery of his private dreams. But Mayakovsky did not need to translate. The language, tone, and purpose of the Revolution were his own: the language of the street, the tone of exaltation, the purpose of remaking man and man's society. Unlike Blok, he had not had to overcome distaste for public affairs; he had been immersed in them from the beginning. And he had no patience with half measures, with shades of meaning and reflectiveness. He saw life simply, and believed erroneously that he saw it whole. The world melted away for him about the kernel of his commitments. Everything about him was large, loud, and spectacular. Everything was theater, everything seemed public. He was the voice and the image of Revolutionary Romanticism, and seldom does an age find its embodiment so completely.

I

He was born on the nineteenth of July, 1893, in the village of Bagdadi in western Georgia, the third child and only son of the forester Vladimir Konstantinovich Mayakovsky. The country in which they lived is magnificently picturesque. The mountains there are high, the rivers noisy and rapid, the nights very black; there are furious snow storms and the air is filled with the sound of wailing jackals, barking dogs, and the roar of thunder crashing from crest to crest. Their house was a wooden one at the foot of a mountain, and as a small child, Volodya (to use the affectionate diminutive by which he was called in his family) and his younger sister, Olga, used to clamber up the banks of the Rion to see which of them could climb highest on the rocks and hold on longest to a branch above the torrent—or, squatting on a large stone, they would slide down to its brink.

The Mayakovskys had lived in Georgia for several generations, but they were Russians, and Vladimir Konstantinovich's position was an official one, which made him a member of the ruling class set over a subject population. Nevertheless, his relations with the native inhabitants were unusually cordial. When he rode out on his rounds, people shouted greetings to him; he knew them by name, gave them advice, helped them out with loans from his own meager resources, joked with them in their own language, worked far into the night to accommodate them. And in 1905, when he was asked by the government to take measures to subdue the people, he refused, even though his own place had been broken into and robbed. "All the government clerks here," he wrote his older daughter Ludmila, who was then studying in Moscow, "have received anonymous letters with drawings of coffins, except me." His children shared his sense of justice and his indignation at the repressive acts of government. In school, in Kutaisi, the capital of the province, a center of revolutionary operations, the Georgians were not even permitted to speak their own language, although they were in the majority; and in one of his first drawings the younger Vladimir caricatured a teacher who had called the native dialect a "dog's tongue."

In 1905 his schoolmates elected him delegate to represent his class. He was admired for his ability, his strength, and his fairness—"a desperate fighter," according to one of his fellow students, and "a responsive, kind, reliable comrade. He could stick up for one in trouble." At the age of twelve, that is, he was already an acknowledged leader. During the workers' demonstrations he declaimed inflammatory songs in the streets of the city; and Olga, also deep in revolutionary affairs, wrote Ludmila that Volodya had bought himself ten works of the kind she had herself acquired, books on socialism: they were "very cheap," she said, "10, 15, or 8 kopeks." He himself described what was taking place in a letter to Ludmila:

We had a five-day strike, and then the school was closed four days, because we sang the "Marseillaise" in church. . . . They trained cannon on the school, and in the *real-schule* managed even better: placed cannon in the yard and announced that at the first protest they would not leave a single stone standing on another.

Returning home that summer from Moscow, Ludmila found that she could talk to her little brother as to a grownup. He devoured the illegal literature she had brought with her and added to his repertory of revolutionary poems and songs. It was about this time that he first read Gorky; "The Song of the Stormy Petrel" impressed him especially.

In an excellent memoir, Ludmila Vladimirovna has left an engaging picture of their family: of their big, deep-voiced, hot-tempered father, kind, gay, and fearless, who used to travel unarmed in robber-infested forests on narrow roads that skirted precipices, sleeping in the woods, with his felt coat for cover and his saddle for pillow, and who would quote to his anxious family the Russian proverb: "If you're afraid of wolves, keep out of the woods"; of their mother,

Alexandra Alekseyevna, "thin, frail, and sickly," but possessed of "tremendous endurance and will power," a forthright and exquisite person who "could not tolerate scandalmongering, gossip, prejudice" and who, in contrast to her husband, was self-contained, reserved, always "equable in her relations with people"; and of their brother, who physically resembled both parents, having his mother's features and his father's build and voice. His personality seems also to have combined and intensified the traits of both: the father's love of people and of animals, his independence, leadership, passion, and vigor: the mother's sensitivity, reserve, and strict high-mindedness.

The boy was gifted. Even before he knew his letters, he got by heart much of the work of Pushkin, Lermontov, Nekrasov, and other Russian poets that Ludmila and Alexandra Alekseyevna would read to him. He tagged after them, begging for recitations, and to refuse him was the best means of bringing him to terms when he misbehaved. His memory was prodigious. As a schoolboy he could recite entire pages of Gogol, later of Karl Marx and the whole of *Eugene Onegin*. And presently he was to astonish his audiences by his overwhelming supply of ready quotations. His powerful voice was also to serve him well. When he was an infant, his father, holding him in his arms as he walked up and down the room, would rock him to sleep as he boomed forth Lermontov's "Cossack's Lullaby." "You will deafen the child," the mother would cry in alarm. "Don't worry," Vladimir Konstantinovich used to reply prophetically, "he'll only develop an ear and have a voice like mine." At the age of seven he began to exercise his voice. Near his house enormous clay vessels, used for storing wines, were sunk into the earth. Volodya would climb into an empty one and shout verses from its depths. "Go on farther off, Olya, and listen—how does my voice sound?" Then, having heard of Demosthenes, he emulated his example on the banks of the rushing Rion. In addition, he could draw, and so sharply observant and clever were his cartoons that when he was ten years old Ludmila's drawing master offered to give him lessons free of charge. Everyone was proud of him, made much of him. His rebelliousness involved no conflict with his family: love and revolutionary leadership went together. He was, so to speak, an approved rebel.

The love of opposition, of fighting, of satire came first; the gift of poetry developed later. For six years after 1905 Mayakovsky was absorbed in making a living, in plotting against the government, and in drawing. In 1906 his father died, having pricked his finger in sewing up official documents and contracted blood poisoning. The family now moved to Moscow with Ludmila, and Vladimir continued his schooling there. But with only a pension of ten rubles a month to live on, they had to devise means of making money. Alexandra Alekseevna rented a room to lodgers, and labored with her children at ill-paid handiwork. In cold and semi-darkness they sometimes sat up until morning, decorating little boxes and Easter eggs. "Then we would wash up and go to class, while Volodya took our work to the store. We worked all night to earn two or three rubles, and later the things would be displayed . . . and sold for five or seven rubles." The rented room was usually taken by some poor student, and there Vladimir met his first Bolshevik. "I couldn't be bothered with the child," one of the lodgers recalled. "I remember my momentary surprise when timidly, shyly, fearing he would be refused, he asked for 'something revolutionary' to read. Later he stopped asking, simply took, devoured . . ." and attended secret meetings. "It's all right," the student would say to his comrades, who glanced suspiciously at the boy in the corner, "the landlady's son; he's one of us." Another roomer told him about underground activity and read Plekhanov and Marx with him.

In 1908 he was accepted for work in the Party. He ran errands, distributed proclamations printed on a secret press, and was arrested, but, on the grounds of his minority, released under surveillance. To the Secret Police he was known as "The Tall One," and his comings and goings are meticulously recorded in the dossier which now reposes in the Mayakovsky Museum in Moscow. But on the first of July 1909, he was again arrested, and this time sent to jail. His fellow prisoners elected him their spokesman. He made protests in their behalf, incited demonstrations, and altogether became so unruly that the authorities transferred him after six weeks to solitary confinement in cell number 103 of the severe Butyrki prison, and held him there five months. He was sixteen years old; it was a tedious and painful time. How tedious and painful, one can judge from his subsequent references to it. The number of his prison cell remained unbearable to him. For example, a friend of his recalls how years later he asked in a restaurant to have his coat check changed because its number was 103. And in *I Myself*, an autobiography written in 1922, the rubric for this period reads "Eleven Butyrki Months"; Mayakovsky's memory had more than doubled the actual length of his sentence. Nevertheless, the prison months were valuable.

For me most important period [he wrote in *I Myself*]. After three years of theory and practice began to devour literary works. Read all latest stuff. Symbolists Bely, Balmont. Analyzed formal innovations. But all this was alien to me. Themes and images drawn from life not mine. Tried to write just as well, but about other things. Found that just as well about other things was impossible. Result was banal sobstuff like:

> Forests wear garments of yellow and purple
> Fire of the sun on church cupolas plays—
> I waited: but days in the months were extinguished,
> Hundreds of languorous days.

Wrote whole copybook of such verses. Thanks to the warders for taking it off me, when I was released. Otherwise would have published it. After disposing of contemporary writers, plunged into the classics—Byron, Shakespeare, Tolstoy. Last book—*Anna Karenina*. Didn't finish it. Told at night "get your things ready." So don't know how the Karenin business ended.

He came out of jail convinced that in time he would write better than the so-called "classics." All he needed was "experience in art." "I was half-baked. I needed thorough training." And although his political views had not been shaken, and he was more than ever a Marxist, he knew that if he stayed in the Party he would be doomed to work underground, to write leaflets for the rest of his life, "rearranging ideas taken from books that were correct, but were not the product of my own thinking." It was "all right for others to be in the Party. They had a university behind them." He announced to a comrade that he "wanted to create a socialist art." The comrade laughed at him. "You haven't got the guts," he said. But Mayakovsky "stopped Party work . . . got down to study!"; and since schools and universities were closed to political offenders, turned to painting, serving an apprenticeship in two studios: one, in which he found himself painting "silver tea services" in the company of "young ladies," he soon abandoned; in the other he studied Holbein and worked on "heads" for a whole year under Kelin, "realist . . . very good teacher . . . Firm . . . Couldn't stand anything pretty." Then in August 1911 he passed the entrance examinations to the Moscow Institute of Painting, Sculpture and Architecture. The next year he "became a poet." It happened in the following way.

II

Among the students in the Institute there was a young man who irritated Mayakovsky. He wore a frock coat, carried a lorgnette, looked "insolent," and had something of a reputation as the leader of the Russian Futurists. This was David Burluik. Considerably older than Mayakovsky, he had been exhibiting since 1907, and in the spring of 1910 had brought out the first Futurist anthology, *A Hatchery of Judges*. Subsequently he gave an account of how they became acquainted. "I first met Mayakovsky early in September 1911. An uncombed, unwashed, huge Maypole of a man with an apache's strikingly handsome face pursued me with his jibes and witticisms as 'a cubist.' It almost came to blows." But the youth's show of hostility was, in point of fact, a kind of disguised admiration. Mayakovsky, the rebel, disgusted by the academic timidity of the Institute, where imitation was praised and independence persecuted, saw that Burluik was not an imitator. They became friends. And what finally brought them together was a shared antipathy. The occasion was a symphony concert conducted by Serge Koussevitsky on February 4, 1912:

> Concert. Rachmaninoff. Isle of Corpses. Fled from unbearable melodized boredom. A minute later, Burluik also. Burst out laughing together. Went forth to roam about.
>
> Most memorable night. Talk. From Rachmaninoff boredom to school boredom, from school boredom to the boredom of the whole of classicism. In David—anger of a master who has outdistanced his contemporaries, in me—the passion of a socialist, knowing that the old is inevitably doomed. Russian futurism was born.

That Russian futurism was born on that night is, of course, inexact. But on that night it found its strongest voice. Two weeks later Mayakovsky made his first appearance as a public speaker in a debate on modern art, and in the fall of the same year Burluik discovered the poet in him:

> During the day a poem developed. Bits rather. Poor ones. Never published. Night. Stretenskyi Boulevard. I recite the verses to Burluik, adding—"by a friend of mine." David stops. Looks me up and down. Yaps: "But it's you yourself that wrote them! But you're a poet of genius! . . ." That evening altogether unexpectedly I became a poet.

Next morning Burluik introduced him to someone as "my genius friend, the famous poet Mayakovsky," and taking him aside, "bellowed: 'Now write. Or you'll make a fool of me.'" And so Mayakovsky wrote his first "professional, publishable" poems:

> With lasting love I think of David. Wonderful friend. My real teacher. Burluik made a poet of me. Read me the French and the Germans. Thrust books on me. . . . Would not let me out of his sight. Gave me 50 kopeks daily, so I could write and not starve.

Burluik was enchanted with his new friend. "An unpolished nugget," he wrote about him to Kamensky, the aviator-poet, "aflame with self-assuredness. I have persuaded him that he is a young Jack London. He can recite quantities from memory, among other things, whole pages of *Das Kapital*"; and Kamensky came to Moscow to look at the rough gem. They met in Burluik's apartment: "Gazing at Volodya Mayakovsky through his lorgnette, Burluik called him the Russian Jack London, Martin Eden, Lermontov, Demon, Pushkin, Herman, Dubrovsky, Cervantes, Garibaldi, Columbus, the troubadour of our day. Mayakovsky enjoyed it all enormously."

In December Burluik and Mayakovsky, together with Alexander Krutchënyi and Victor Khlebnikov, who were making bold experiments with words and forms of poetry, produced the now notorious Futurist Manifesto, *A Slap in the Face of Public Taste*. This was the time of Marinetti and Balla in Italy, of Picabia in France, of the 1913 Armory Show in New York. Modern art was scandalizing people everywhere. But nowhere was there anything to equal the crude brashness of the Russian proclamation. As its title indicates, it was intended to insult.

> For readers—Our New First and Unexpected [it begins]. We alone are the face of our Time. We are the mouthpiece of the times in literature.
>
> The past is stifling. The Academy and Pushkin are incomprehensible hieroglyphs.
>
> We must throw Pushkin, Dostoevsky, Tolstoy, etc., from the boat of contemporaneousness.

And it continues with grossly abusive reference to living authors. Balmont is "a perfumed whore"; there is "the filthy slime of books scribbled by numberless Leonid Andreyevs"; "All these Maxim Gorkys, Kuprins, Bloks, Sologubs, Remizovs, Avertchenkos, Chërnyis, Kuzmins, Bunins, etc., etc., would be satisfied with a cottage in the country. That's how destiny rewards tailors." The impudence of this nihilistic language obscures the seriousness of its aim: the right to coin new words, to express new views and new tastes, to talk and judge according to fresh experience and not by ancient rule, to see art as a social force and the artist as the spokesman of his age. It was a demand for artistic honesty: since new things could not be said in old ways, new ways of speaking must be devised.

Mayakovsky's first poems appeared in the Futurists' privately printed collections; and although never so extreme as those of others in the group, who attempted to treat words entirely as expressive sound independent of meaning, they were short virtuoso experiments in grammatical and verse constructions. Mayakovsky broke words up, read them backwards, combined syllables in unexpected ways, found novel puns and peculiar rhymes, and so on—in short, toyed with the Russian language in the same buoyant and imaginative way as James Joyce was soon to play with English. These departures in poetry, like those in other countries at this time, Jules Laforgue's, for instance, or T. S. Eliot's, destroyed logical structure, formed a new syntax, and built effects on allusiveness. Thus Mayakovsky begins a description of night:

> The scarlet and white is cast off and crumpled,
> Into the green are thrown handfuls of ducats,
> To the black palms of confluent windows,
> Cards have been dealt of flaming yellow, . . .

in which adjectives have become nouns, colors are no longer the attributes but the substance of what they represent, metaphors are ingenious, and the whole is a verbal equivalent of new schools of painting, in which an attempt is made to describe well-known objects as line and color only, the way they must appear to the eye when freed from habitual associations.

But from the first what is most striking in Mayakovsky's work is its grotesque anthropomorphism: things appear as people, people as caricatures. Street crowds are a "swift, multicolored cat" that undulates, "enticed by doorways"; "boulevards and city squares do not think it strange" that buildings are "draped in blue togas"; the rain is "cross-eyed"; anchors are "earrings in the ears of deaf ships"; "a magician pulls rails out of a tramway's maw"; a fog "chews tasteless people"; the Neva is a two-humped camel wearily driven to the sea; "a bald street lamp lasciviously draws a black stocking off the street," etc. This, of course, is a cartoonist's manner, which reminds one that Mayakovsky was a caricaturist before he became a poet. It is a device that Gogol liked; and indeed Mayakovsky's exaggerated images remind one of Gogol's, for they too are used for both comic and uncanny effects. At bottom, however, they are the reverse of Gogol's, which, as the Formalist critic Yurii Tinyanov has pointed out, are comic through their transformation of people into things and terrifying in their manner of presenting motion as demonic, and in showing all life to be on the threshold of the supernatural, whereas in Mayakovsky's case the opposite is true. With him, things act like people; immobility, not motion, is dreadful; and the horrifying is always human, not supernatural. It has been suggested that this fascination with mobility was generally true of artists at the beginning of the twentieth century and that it reflected the strong impression that science had made on them. But Mayakovsky's work bears a special stamp; with all its humor, his world of animated objects is full of pain.

A short play in verse, *The Tragedy of Vladimir Mayakovsky,* sums up the characteristic tendencies of his first period. It was directed, managed, produced, and acted by its author; and in the memoirs of a stage director, A. Mgebrov, we have an account of its performance in St. Petersburg on December 2, 1913. The curtain went up, he relates, on a dimly lighted stage with a black cardboard backdrop, and although it was hard to tell what this backdrop was meant to represent, "strangely enough, it was impressive. There was motion in it, and a lot of blood. Possibly I have never seen a city more real than what I saw on that cardboard." On to this gloomy setting came Mayakovsky in ordinary dress, without make-up. "He seemed to be above the crowd, above the city—the city's son, to whom the city had raised a monument." He began:

Is it for you to understand,
why I,
calmly,
through thunders of jeers,
bear my soul on a platter
to the feast of future years,
I,
trickling down the unshaved cheek of city squares,
an unnecessary tear,
the last of the poets,
perhaps.

He had walked through alleys of stone, over which the face of dreariness hung, the sky wept inconsolably, and a "cloud-lette had a bit of a grimace in the small fold of its mouth, as if a woman had expected a child, but God had flung her a crooked little idiot." It was a world of ugliness, suffering, and brutality; and he wanted to comfort people:

Come all to me
who clawed at silence,
who groaned
because tight is the noose of noondays.

He would comfort them, if they would first help him: patch his soul "to keep the emptiness from oozing out," fill him again, for he had been "milked" and was dry as stone. And if they wished, he would dance for their amusement.

The people gathered, "coming out slowly, like animated dolls," dragging in shop signs that were their food: a tin herring, an enormous gold loaf, folds of yellow velvet; and the poet promised them a festival:

The barefoot cutter of diamond verses,
I've swept the down in strangers' houses,
and will today a world feast kindle
of these so rich and motley beggars.

But no, this was no time for festivals. Neither he nor his world was ready for them. "Let be!" says an ancient man, several thousand years old, "I see in you a tortured cry, crucified on the cross of laughter. An enormous grief lies on the city and hundreds of little griefs—out of the sky a crazed god looks down, shouting of cruel vengeance, while in your little souls there is but a worn-out sigh. Let be!" The Man without an Ear reports that a "legend of torments" has stretched over cities; a huge woman, "the black care of ages," ranges about; she spits, and her spittle is transformed into enormous cripples; the musician's hands are caught in "the enraged white teeth of piano keys"; even side streets have rolled up their sleeves to fight, and his own grief increases "inexplicably, anxiously, like a tear on the face of a dog that is weeping"; the cripples, terrified by the soulless tyrants, things, decide to smash them. But what is the soul? asks Mayakovsky. He himself has walked the earth on swollen feet, searching for it, to place its "healing flowers" on "the wounds, his lips." And one day, as a matter of fact, he did find her, the soul:

> Out she came
> in a light blue dressing gown,
> said:
> "Sit down!
> I've been long expecting you,
> Won't you have some tea?"

"You yourselves," says Mayakovsky, "all you people, are but bells on the bonnet of God." There is no difference, that is, between men and things; and this is now borne out by the Man without an Eye and a Leg who hobbles in to announce an incredible revolt in the city. Things have broken away from their places, and, yelling, have stormed the streets.

In the second act, Mayakovsky, in another city, dressed in a toga and wreathed with laurel, has been proclaimed "prince," and people with strange bundles crowd in to see him. They approach shyly, bringing their gifts. "Here is my little tear, take it," says a woman, "I don't need it, but it's silky and white, made of the threads of eyes"; a second one: "A mere nothing, my son is dying; here's another tear. Use it on a slipper, it will make a pretty buckle"; and a third:

"Never mind that I am dirty, I'll wash and will be cleaner. Here's my tear, a huge, idle one." Then before the terrified poet, appears the Man with Two Kisses, who, juggling a pair of balls, tells the following story:

A big dirty man
was given two kisses.
He was an awkward man,
didn't know
what to do with them,
where to put them.
The city,
all festive,
sang alleluias
in churches;
people came forth to put on pretty things.
But the man's place was cold,
and there were holes in his shoe soles.
He picked out a kiss,
the one that was larger,
and put it on, like a rubber.
The frost, though, was cruel,
and bit his toes.
"Very well,"
the man said in anger,
"I will throw away these unnecessary kisses!"
He threw them away.
And suddenly
the kiss grew little ears,
began spinning 'round,
in a thin little voice, it cried:
"I want my mother!"
The man was frightened.
In the rags of his soul
he wrapped the trembling little body,
and carried it home
to set it in a light blue frame.
Long he rummaged among suitcases in the dust
(looking for the little frame).
Glanced 'round—
The kiss was lying on the couch,
huge,

fat,
grown,
laughing,
carrying on!
"My God!"
wept the man,
"I never thought I'd get so tired.
I must hang myself!"
And while he was hanging,
nasty,
pitiful,
in the woman's boudoir
—a factory without smoke and chimneys—
millions of kisses were manufactured,
all kinds,
big,
little,
on the fleshy levers of smacking lips.

What is there in this crude and soulless world to assuage men's grief? Mayakovsky, the Poet, who wanted to make life a festival for men, is instead overwhelmed by their woes. What is he to do with their suffering, he who has asked them to help him? At the end he gathers up their tears and goes away, dragging himself "farther up, to the north," to fling his burden where "the fingers of waves tear the breast of the ocean," to "the dark god of thunders, at the source of bestial faiths."

At the beginning of the play, writes Mgebrov, "the audience tried laughing, but its laughter stopped abruptly. Why? Why because all this wasn't a bit funny." But at the end, according to a newspaper account, the people hooted. "Never mind," they cried, as Mayakovsky, excited and confused, was gathering up the tears of men into an enormous canvas bag. "Don't bother! Don't go away!" And no wonder. Mayakovsky's rhetoric was too strident; his role of self-elected martyr created the impression that he only desired to love others but really loved himself alone. And yet the play was poignant; his sympathy with men might not have been genuine, but his own suffering was, suffering that came of an obsessive sense of horror, disgust, and above all, of loneliness and great ambition. Mayakovsky, much like Baudelaire and his successors, saw his tragedy as that of the Poet in an alien world; but, unlike the *poètes maudits,* he was not satisfied with defining himself in relation to others and in withdrawing from them as a being apart; he wanted to change the world to make it better, and to be accepted by men as teacher and leader. He demanded a social role, and it may be that his insistent anthropomorph-ism, his exaggerated use of the "pathetic fallacy," reflected this willful desire to be at one with his world. Incapable of humility, compromise, or submissiveness, he willed not only men but the inanimate universe to speak his language. This was the ground plan for what was to follow. Mayakovsky's work was built up with remarkable consistency; it grew as a tall building grows, not as a living organism develops. There was in it, up to the end, the same concern with self-definition, the same questioning of his role as poet, the same troubled analysis of his relations to the masses of men —and with it all, an extraordinarily domineering longing for service and for martyrdom. From first to last Mayakovsky tried arrogantly and willfully to make himself a scapegoat.

I I I

The activities and behavior of the Futurists, who set out to shock people and make themselves conspicuous, had a good deal to do in shaping his attitude to the world. Solemnly, in single file, these young men would parade on crowded streets, dressed in outlandish outfits, with decorated faces— Kamensky had an airplane painted on his, Burluik, a dog that wiggled on his fat cheek. Mayakovsky went unpainted but sported a striped, loose-fitting, yellow blouse. On lecture platforms, while their audiences stamped, jeered, and shouted, they talked quietly at table, over glasses of tea that had been brought them on a huge platter. When the

exasperated public demanded to share their discussion, Burluik lectured on Cézanne, Manet, Picasso; the others read
and explained the poetry that they and their friends were
writing.

The hall was filled to overflowing [one reads in a characteristic
news report of one such performance]. The tickets had all been
sold. A phalanx of policemen with a constable and a police officer
separated those unhappily without tickets from the ones on whom
fate had smiled. Heroes of the evening appeared here and there,
fanning the impatience of an already excited public. The most
heroic of them all was dressed in an artistic yellow-black blouse,
striped and beltless. . . . He started right off with the matter in
hand: "We are wrecking the old world. . . . You hate us! . . ."

The "most heroic" was Mayakovsky, and his yellow blouse
soon became famous all over Russia.

At times the Futurists provoked more than jeers. There
was, for example, the notable evening of October 19, 1913,
when Mayakovsky, by way of greeting, hurled at the well-
heeled audience that had arrived for the opening of the Pink
Lantern, the Futurist cabaret, his abusive "Take It!," a
poem that begins: "In an hour, one by one, your flabby fat
will trickle out into the clean side street." They booed,
whistled, shook their fists, women fainted, men offered to
fight. Mayakovsky stood his ground, "like a fighter with a
hand grenade stuck in his belt," as he was described on
another occasion when, with the same poem, he put to rout
a select group of influential persons, gathered by his
friends in the hope of advancing him with publishers.
At this later time his friend Korney Chukovsky realized that
no kind of truce was possible between these people and the
poet, that Mayakovsky's "hatred of their rotten world"
was no mere "poetic declaration," but "the sole content of
his whole life."

In December 1913 the Futurists set off on a three-month
lecture tour, visiting some fifteen cities and towns in the
south of Russia. They followed the procedure they had inaugurated in Petersburg, and devised even more fantastic

stunts to stimulate discussion. In Kiev, for example (where their theater was guarded by mounted police—"The scoundrels! They've involved even horses in their dirty business," Mayakovsky said), they had a grand piano hoisted by cables above the platform, and there it hung throughout the performance. "Why is the piano up there?" people shouted. "Wait to the end, and you will see." And at the close of the session, "Well, why did you put the piano up there?" "So you'd want to find out and stay to the end." Mayakovsky had an ingrained sense of drama, and the gift of quick, impudent repartee. "Why are you dressed in a yellow blouse?" "So as not to look like you," he would reply, quietly sipping tea. "Mayakovsky, do you think we're all of us idiots?" Mayakovsky, in gentle surprise: "How can you! Why all? So far—I can see only one in front of me." "Mayakovsky, your poetry will be dead tomorrow. You yourself will be forgotten. Immortality is not for you." "Well, I'll tell you what. You drop in in a thousand years or so, and we'll talk it over." "Mayakovsky, your poems don't excite, don't warm, don't infect." "My poems are neither the sea, nor a stove, nor the plague." "Mayakovsky, I read your poems with a friend of mine; we couldn't understand a thing." "One should have clever friends." And so on. It was boorish, but it was lively. Mayakovsky teased, insulted, startled his listeners, and gradually made his point: that poetry was something more than prettiness and idle amusement.

In one place, for example, where the audience was divided in loud approval and disapproval, and several dangerously obstreperous persons had to be ejected from the hall, Mayakovsky continued unperturbed, reciting alternately perfectly intelligible verse and some that was quite incomprehensible. He came to the following lines of Khlebnikov, which in those days must have been puzzling and shocking in their apparent lack of consecutiveness:

> On Ezeli Island—
> You and I daydreaming,
> I was in Kamchatka,

> You your gloves were rumpling.
> From the height of Altai,
> "My darling," said I.

And his rendition of the last line was so masterful that it unleashed a storm of applause. The auditorium was subdued, and Mayakovsky, now knowing himself in command, read by contrast some of the saccharine verses of the immensely popular Igor Severyanin. When the delighted audience begged for more, he produced his own work instead. Severyanin, he said, is "chocolate, but I am the Black Sea. We have different things to do; he flutters around princesses, but I am 'The barefoot cutter of diamond verses,'" and so on from *The Tragedy of Vladimir Mayakovsky*, greeted with a crash of applause.

" 'Really, now, it is better, isn't it?' (Applause. Shouts of 'Severyanin!')." Mayakovsky resumed "the bass clanging" of his own resounding lines, then switched again to the tinkling Severyanin, and the audience clamored for more.

"You like the artistic way I dish up Severyanin?"

"Yes! Very much!"

"But his verse isn't much. Not so good as mine!"

"Better! Best of all!"

"That's an optical illusion. Compare:

> "Ladies and Gentlemen!
> Stop!
> How can you really?
> Even the alleys have rolled up their shirt-
>   sleeves to fight,
> And my grief increases,
> anxiously, uncomprehended,
> like a tear on the face of a dog that is
>   weeping."

Mayakovsky had demonstrated the difference between jingling affectation and resonant, conversational, serious verse. That night the poets were accompanied to their rooms by a group of excited young people. In Tiflis, in his own Georgia, where Mayakovsky spoke a word of greeting in the native dialect, he was given an ovation. Guardedly enthusiastic comments began to appear in the press. "I won't deny it," wrote one correspondent, "I enjoyed sitting in that over-crowded, passion-torn theater."

These audiences had been previously treated to readings of another kind. There had been Balmont, who "behaved as if he were in some special realm, and read not to people, but to visions that surrounded him"; Sologub, who with a "weariness like the satiety of much experience in his every feature" resembled "a visionary civil servant, a man of Peters-burg addicted to daydreaming, courteous and imperturb-able," who any moment might "shut his eyes and stop, for-getting everybody"; Severyanin, "with the elongated face of an international snob, and a long-stemmed lily in his hand." After such exhibitions of the aloof and the effete, Maya-kovsky, with his blunt talk, his virile, deep-voiced, tousle-headed earnestness, his reading of poetry not "for himself" but "as if he threw open the gates and invited everyone to enter the poem" was like the impact of a blow or the in-timacy of a handshake. His "warm, powerful, aggressive" voice passed over his audiences "like a hot flatiron over snow." But it was not his voice alone, nor the "natural per-suasiveness" of his gestures and the perfect ease with which he commanded the stage, "without any pose, without the slightest effort," nor even the readiness and directness of his speeches, which, whether he had actually been challenged by his hearers or not, were never monologues but always discussions—more than all this, it was an elusive sense of "a tragic strain" back of the brilliance and the im-pudence that made him so extraordinarily magnetic, some-thing "incomprehensible, unfounded, negated by his youth, by his successful boldness, but none the less clearly per-ceptible. . . . And it was this, perhaps, that distinguished him from everybody else and drew one to him so strongly."

The poets were still on tour when they read that Mari-netti, arriving in Moscow, had denounced Russian Futur-ists as "savages, and not men of the future." They decided to confront their calumniator, and on February 13, 1914, appeared at his lecture. The chairman, alarmed by the unexpected advent of the three Russian savages, proposed at the close of Marinetti's speech that the discussion be conducted in French. "This is a public muzzling of the Russian Futurists," shouted Mayakovsky, and the chairman, to avoid further unpleasantness, adjourned the meeting. Two days later the newspaper *Nov'* carried a letter to the editor, in which Mayakovsky forcibly denied the current allegation that Russian Futurism derived from the Italian: "Futurism," he wrote, "is a social movement, born of the big city, which itself destroys all national differences. . . . That's all there is to the story about the teacher and his pupils."

By the time they had fulfilled their speaking engagements, at the end of March 1914, Mayakovsky and Burluik had been expelled from the Moscow Institute of Painting, Sculpture and Architecture, which, because of their behavior, had forbidden its members to make public appearances. They had made Russian Futurism notorious, and wholly unacceptable, not only to academies but also to publishers. Therefore, they continued to bring out their work in private editions; but while Kamensky and Burluik had something to live on, Mayakovsky did not. He existed for weeks on sausage that, marked off into daily rations, dangled from the ceiling of his room, and sometimes hunger forced him to eat a whole week's allotment at a sitting. This nobody knew. He published occasional essays on art, and was at work on a big poem when, in July, war was declared.

IV

His big poem had been inspired, or as Mayakovsky would have said, "commanded," by love. The poets were in Odessa when for the first time in his life he fell in love. It was a sudden, violent passion. The girl, Maria Aleksandrovna Denisova, was beautiful. She reminded Burluik of the Gioconda. Before a week was out, on the eve of their scheduled departure, Mayakovsky asked her to marry him. The tour was in danger. But on the appointed day Mayakovsky came back to his worried friends. "Let's go," he said. Maria Aleksandrovna had refused him; she was engaged to somebody else. On the train to Kishinev, Mayakovsky looked out the window, humming over and over again a well-known line of Severyanin: "It happened by the sea." Then, with a gloomy smile, recited, stressing each word:

> It happened
> It happened in Odessa,

and in a quarter of an hour read out the beginning of what was presently to take shape as *The Cloud in Trousers*. The war and other work intervened, and the poem was not finished until two years later. It turned out to be a remarkably original production, a love poem that from its lyrical beginnings evolved into a treatise on society. It was divided into four parts, the meaning of which Mayakovsky later designated as: "down with your love," "down with your art," "down with your society," "down with your religion." A prologue announces the theme:

> Your thought
> dreaming in a softened brain,
> a fattened lackey on a dirty couch,
> with my heart's bloody rag I'll vex,
> will, impudent and acid,
> of fun have my fill.
>
> There is not a gray hair in my soul,
> and there is no old man's tenderness in it!
> I've thundered the world with the might of
> > my voice,
> and handsome I go,
> in age, twenty-two.
>
> O tender ones!
> You sing your love on violins
> The crude lays his on kettledrums.

But none of you, like me, could manage this:
to turn you inside out, and make yourself
all lips.

You, from your parlor,
come and learn,
batiste young woman,
in the angels' league clerking sedately;
and you, your lips calmly leafing,
like a cook the pages of her book.

If you wish it,
fleshy mad I'll be,
or, like the sky changing its colors,
if you wish,
irreproachably tender, I'll be,
not a man, but a cloud in trousers.

I've no belief in a flowery Nice.
Those I now reglorify
are men like hospitals long lain upon,
and women, like proverbs, outworn.

Part I is about the initial experience of spurned love:

You think this is the raving of malaria?
It happened,
it happened
in Odessa.
"I will come at four,"
said Maria.
Eight
Nine
Ten.

Then the candelabra laugh and neigh at his drooping back.
And who would recognize him now?

The veined colossus
groans and writhes.
What might a clod like that desire?
But there is much the clod desires.

Enormous, he bends at the window, his "forehead melts the windowpane," wondering: Will there be love or not? And of what kind? A big love or a little one?

> No doubt a tiny
> peaceful lovelet.
>
> She shies away from auto horns,
> she likes the little bells of trams.

But midnight, racing with a knife, has caught the hour, and twelve falls, like "the head of the executed from the block."

> Again and again
> he thrusts his face into the pockmarked
> > face of rain,
> sprayed by the thunder of the city's surf.
> Gray raindrops on the windowpane,
> whine in chorus
> and grimace,
> as if the gargoyles of Notre Dame
> were wailing.

And now he hears, a nerve has jumped like a sick man from his bed; then many nerves big and little set up a frantic dance, knocking down the plaster in the room below, until their legs give way—when suddenly, *she* walks in. "Tormenting the suede of gloves, 'You know,' she says. 'I'm getting married'":

> Well, go ahead—
> Never mind—
> I can bear it.
> See how quiet I am—
> like a dead man's pulse.
>
> Remember?
> You said:
> "Jack London,
> money,
> love,

passion"—
But I saw one thing only—
you, the Gioconda,
that must be stolen!

And so:

Hello! Who's there? Mamma? Mamma! Your son is mar-
velously ill! Mamma, his heart is on fire. Tell his sisters he
has nowhere to go. Every word, even the jokes he disgorges
fling themselves out like naked prostitutes from a burning
public house. People sniff. They smell something roasting.
They send helmeted firemen. Mamma, tell them boots are
not allowed, tell them, one climbs with caresses up a heart
that is on fire. I myself will pump out the tears from my eyes.
I'll lean against my ribs and jump. I'll jump! I'll jump! But
the ribs have fallen. There is no jumping out of one's heart.
Mamma, I can't sing. Burnt little figures of words tumble
out of the skull. Thus fear will grasp at heaven,

he closes, invoking the terrible image of the upraised arms
on the *Lusitania,* and the "hundred-eyed glow" that from
the harbor breaks into the quiet of people's homes. At least,
he hopes, his last cry, the cry of those who burn, will moan
itself out through the century. D. S. Mirsky has commented
on the peculiar mannerism of this poem, its elaboration of
commonplace figures of speech to grotesque lengths, as characteristic of Mayakovsky. And it is remarkable that these
verbal games, these jumping nerves equipped with legs, this
burning heart that calls forth a fire brigade, complete with
boots and helmets, do not destroy the emotion they ridicule. But this is a stoic kind of fun making, and it underscores and doubles the pain. "Down with your love!" Mayakovsky means to say in Part I.

"Down with your art!" he says in Part II, to a blind, snob-
bish society, whose poetry is as petty as its love, whose poetic language, suitable only for "some kind of brew of love
and nightingales," lets the street writhe tongueless with
nothing to shout or talk with. Plump taxis and bony cabs

stick swelling in her throat. Yet when, after a tremendous effort, the crowd has been spat out into the squares, the street, which should be scourging god in archangelic choirs, squats down and yells: "Let's eat!" In the mouth, little corpses of dead words decay. Only two of them grow fat, "bastards" and "borsch," and soggy, sobbing poets wonder how with two such words they are to sing of love and young ladies, and a floweret in dew. Thousands run after them: students, prostitutes, clerks. "Stop," shouts Mayakovsky, "you're not beggars!"

> Is it to them one must go in humility:
> "Help me!"
> Of them
> implore a hymn
> and eloquence?
> We ourselves creators are
> in the flaming hymn
> of noise, of factory, and laboratory.
>
> What is Faust to me
> in fairy-tale rockets
> gliding with Mephistopheles on the parquet
> of heaven!
> I,
> golden-lipped,
> whose every word
> reanimates the soul,
> and celebrates the flesh,
> I tell you:
> that of living dust the smallest grain
> is preciouser by far than anything I've made
> or any time will make.

He calls himself the day's "crooked-lipped Zarathustra," the prophet of men, "prisoners of the leprous city," who are worthy of song:

> What matters it
> there are none like us,
> pockmarked with soot,
> in Homers and in Ovids?

I know
the sun itself bedimmed would be
could it but see
the gold mines
of our souls.

. . .

I,
who today am laughed at
like a long, scabrous anecdote,
behold over the mountains of time advancing
one whom nobody else has seen.
There, where the eyes of men drop, dock-tailed,
leader of hungry hordes,
wreathed in the revolution's crown of thorns,
looms the year 'sixteen.
And I, among you, its precursor am.
Wherever pain is, I am.
Myself have crucified on every drop
of flowing tears.

And when
with rebellion
his advent proclaiming,
you will come forth, the savior greeting,
I will draw out my soul for you,
and trample on it, to make it big,
and give it, blood red, to you for a
                    banner.

"Down with your society!" he cries in Part III, a vapid
society that still prefers Barabbas to Christ, and that brings
madhouses to Mayakovsky's mind. In a world where a yellow blouse must hide one's soul, he has gone forth with the
sun as a monocle, leading Napoleon like a dog on a chain,
and has called on men to "take their hands out of their pockets, and snatch a stone, a knife, or a bomb, or, if armless, to
strike with their foreheads." But after a sunset "red as the
'Marseillaise,'" night has come and the sky is "once more
playing Judas, with a handful of treason-sprayed stars."
Down, he cries, with your society that has plunged into
night the promise of its first revolt!

Finally, "Down with your religion!" There is now another Maria whom the poet invokes:

> Maria! Maria! Maria!
>
> Let me in, Maria!
> I cannot stay out on the streets!
> You don't want to?
> You're waiting
> for my cheeks to grow hollow?

Maria lets him in:

> Maria!
> The poet of sonnets sings of Tiana,
> but I,
> all of me flesh,
> all of me man,
> beg simply your body
> as Christians beg
> "give us this day
> our daily bread."
>
> Maria, give!

And he promises to cherish her body as a solitary, unwanted soldier, chopped up in war, guards and loves his one remaining leg.

> Maria,
> You don't want to?
>
> Then,
> darkly and gloomily once again
> I'll take my heart,
> with tears sprinkled over,
> and drag it,
> as to his kennel,
> a dog
> drags his paw
> that a train has run over.

Then, when my term of years has been danced through to the end, I'll climb forth, filthy from nights spent in gutters, and will whisper to God: Listen, Mr. God, aren't you tired of casting your kindly eyes day after day over this heavenly cranberry juice? Let's build a merry-go-round on the tree of good and evil in a paradise of little Eves. No? You won't? You shake your shaggy head? You think that that One with wings, behind you, knows what love is? I am an angel, too. All-powerful, you invented a pair of arms, gave each man a head, why did you not fix things so that, without suffering, a man might kiss and kiss and kiss?

He pulls out a knife and storms heaven, threatening the angels:

> Let me in!
> You won't stop me!
>
> . . .
>
> See!
> The stars once more
> have beheaded in slaughter
> and crimsoned the sky
> in gore.
> Hey you!
> Sky!
> Off with your hat!
> I'm coming!
> I!
>
> Silence.
> The universe is sleeping,
> an enormous ear,
> laid on a star-clawed paw.

Thus all injustices are implicated in Mayakovsky's private pain; and, knowing the universe to be indifferent, denouncing a world of hypocrites, prudes, and sanctimonious believers, where the idea of love is formed on the model of "liqueur glass" Severyanins, where art is puerile, society tyrannical, and religion absurd, with its worship of a god who has created man to suffer for his natural desires, he rebels against the false beliefs that make men blind to their possibilities and to their wretchedness.

He first called this poem *The Thirteenth Apostle,* and then changed the title because of the censor's objections. "When I arrived with this work at the censor's," he recounted years later, "they asked me: 'Do you want to be sent to hard labor?' I replied, 'On no account; that would not be satisfactory by any means.' They then crossed out six of my pages, including the title. That's about where the title came from. They asked me how I could combine lyricism and great coarseness. Then I said: 'All right, I'll be like mad, if you wish, or if you wish, I will be most tender, not a man, but a cloud in trousers.'" He added his prologue, the mutilated poem appeared "all feathery" in 1915 as *The Cloud in Trousers,* and retained this title in subsequent editions, because, said Mayakovsky, he had got used to it.

V

At the beginning of the war, Mayakovsky had been rejected by the army as "unreliable"; later, when the need for men became acute, he was drafted, but evaded service and, through Gorky's influence, received a nominal post in the Automotive School of Petersburg that left him ample time for writing. His laconic entry about these years in *I Myself* explains his changing attitude.

1914
War. Took it excitedly. At first thought of it in its decorative and noisy aspects. Poem, "War Declared." Drew posters to order.

August. First engagement. The horror of war stared us in the face. War hideous. To speak about the war, must see it. Tried to enroll as volunteer. Not accepted—unreliable. . . .

Winter. Disgust and hatred of war. . . . Lost all interest in Art.

1915
Called Up. Taken into army. Did not want to go to front. Pretended I was draughtsman. At night learned from engineer how to draw auto designs.

If he was now serving a government he had fought against, it was not that he had relinquished his revolutionary principles but that he was overwhelmed by the sheer horror of war, by the amount of suffering which it entailed. He did several long poems, gave lectures, wrote articles, squibs for government posters, pieces for the humorous journal *Satyrikon*, to which he became a regular contributor. By 1917 he had already achieved fame as a revolutionary poet. When the Revolution came, he tripled his activity, and for five years there was little about himself. "To the streets, Futurists, drummers, poets," he shouted, "the streets are our brushes, the public squares are our palettes!" The poet was a worker like other workers, as useful as the woodcutter, the fisherman, the ironmonger. All were equal, all comrade workers, proletarians in body and soul. The poet was a factory, a factory without chimneys, perhaps, but it was harder without chimneys.

For five years Mayakovsky became almost literally a factory. During the war, a peculiarly Russian form of folk art was revived for propaganda purposes. This was the *lubók*, a crude woodcut that had been introduced by peasant craftsmen in the eighteenth century. Originally concerned with religious and folk themes, it gradually turned to political satire and in the middle of the nineteenth century was censored by the government, which ordered quantities of carved blocks to be destroyed and permitted only a few selected publishing houses to make new ones. Millions were now manufactured, cheap illustrations with worthless jingles, so that the word *lubók* became synonymous with "trash." Tolstoy once tried to revive the genuine peasant prints, began himself to write the texts, and got such great painters as Repin interested in the venture. But his attempts came to nothing. When the government decided to utilize the genre, Mayakovsky was employed to produce rhymed squibs, which he turned out all through the summer of 1914. Later, Gorky proposed to him and the artist A. A. Radakov that they use it for revolutionary purposes. "From Gorky's we went directly to my studio," Radakov relates, "where Mayakovsky immediately made three new sketches." Skillful satires on the deposed Czar, they were the first in a series of countless posters, pamphlets, and cartoons.

The most astonishing of these were the famous ROSTA (Russian Telegraphic Agency) windows. When in 1919 paper, together with other commodities, had become scarce, and Lenin was advocating the use of wall newspapers, the Telegraphic Company in Moscow hit upon the scheme of utilizing its windows for news and propaganda. The first exhibit appeared in August 1919. The following month, Mayakovsky was invited to contribute. He worked there until February 1922, and in that time produced, according to his own estimate, "about 3000 posters and 6000 titles." Each poster consisted of six or more drawings, and the "titles" were accompanying rhymes. Other artists worked with him, but most of the drawings and themes were his own, and all were submitted to him for approval. Each day the old "window" was torn down and a new one put in its place. When a method of stencil reproduction was devised, whereby as many as 150 copies could be printed at one time, they were dispatched to some fifty cities in all parts of Russia. They have never been collected, only a fraction has been published, and many are doubtless lost. It was feverish work, "without rest," Mayakovsky was to recall. "The speed of machines was required of us. Sometimes a wire would reach us about a victory at the front, and forty minutes or an hour later the news would be out on the street in a colored poster." They worked in a large, unheated room. Mayakovsky used a log for pillow, so as not to oversleep the few hours he allowed himself. When in the summer of 1921 he commuted daily from Pushkino to Moscow, he would jot down in the train fifteen or twenty news items, and would sometimes arrive at ROSTA with verses already made up. Dispatches, decrees, slogans on all possible subjects—political, military, social, hygienic, whatever had to be made known —were transformed into verse that often incorporated the exact wording of the original reports. Mayakovsky used the devices of folk art to insure popular appeal. The drawings were like the characteristic *lubók,* clear, simple, laconic, with sharply contrasted colors and neither perspective nor shading. The rhymes were usually parodies of well-known fairy tales, songs, or proverbs; they seconded the vigorous sketches and made their point with crude wit. In one poster, for example, a caricature of Mayakovsky shouting to a Red Army man, "This is what the Powers bring to the People," is followed by four sketches: a grave, with the caption, "Land for the people"; a gallows, "Freedom for the workers"; a jail, "An abode for the homeless"; and a blow in the face from an enormous fist, "Food for the hungry." Then there is a picture of a soldier on guard, who is told: "That's what the White army is like. Don't submit to it! Smash it!" On the same order, but more carefully executed, were Mayakovsky's propagandist pamphlets and his children's books.

VI

The major poems of these years, *War and the Universe, Mystery-Bouffe, 150,000,000,* employ the same methods on an epic scale. All of them are gigantic cartoons. In *War and the Universe* (the title is a pun on *War and Peace,* the Russian words for "peace" and "universe" being the same, except for a slight difference in spelling in the old orthography), the world is pictured as a decaying corpse, eaten away by a golden-pawed microbe; also, as a coliseum watched by the dull eyes of gray-haired oceans, by the "severe, eternal arbiter," the sun, and by stars that burn with curiosity; Europe is a flaming chandelier; and the earth is so thoroughly soaked in blood that once a workman in Rostov, wanting water for his samovar, found red liquid flowing in all pipes. Now, as battalion is heaped upon battalion, death, a noseless Taglioni, dances on the carrion— and in a rotting train car there are four legs and forty men. One day in 1916, Alexander Blok jotted down in his diary: "Mayakovsky phoned. He complained of Moscow poets and said he had written altogether too much that was horrifying about the war; one ought to verify, they say it's not so dreadful. All this—with his habitual grimace, but back of it, apparently something genuine—(as I had thought before)." Mayakovsky was doubtless at work on *War and the Universe* when he called.

Two years later, to celebrate "October," Mayakovsky wrote *Mystery-Bouffe,* the first Soviet drama, subtitled "A Heroic, Epic, and Satiric Representation of Our Epoch." The curtain goes up on two Eskimos, a hunter and a fisherman, who sit by an open fire, watching a leaking globe, out of which survivors drop: "seven pairs of the Clean": an Abyssinian negus, an Indian rajah, a Turkish pasha, a Russian merchant, a Chinaman, a well-fed Persian, a fat Frenchman, an Australian with his wife, a priest, a German officer, an Italian officer, an American, and a student; and six pairs of the Unclean, making seven with the Eskimos: a chimneysweep, a lamplighter, a chauffeur, a seamstress, a miner, a carpenter, a farm hand, a servant, a shoemaker, a smith, a baker, and a laundress. Recovering from the shock of their fall, the Clean organize a meeting, and persuade the Unclean to build an Ark. Once aboard, with lands crashing on all sides, they hit upon a scheme: appoint the negus king and have him commandeer all the food brought him by the Unclean, whom they then rob and bind, but presently release, and invite to discuss the establishment of a republic, when, having discovered that the negus has devoured everything himself, they throw him overboard. "You will be citizens of the democratic republic," they say, "you will catch walruses, make shoes, and bake rolls . . . and the thirteen of us—God rest the negus' soul—shall be ministers and secretaries. To work! And we to our pens!" They sit at table, record what is brought them, and eat it up. When the Unclean demand their share, "Why all the fuss?" ask the ministers. "We are dividing things equally: one gets the doughnut, the other the hole—that is the meaning of a democratic republic." And so the Unclean throw the Clean overboard, and sail in harmony upon the flood.

One day it seems to them they see Mt. Ararat. But they are wrong. It is no mountain, but a man moving toward them upon the waters. It must be Christ, they think, and if it is, they are resolved to keep him off the Ark, for in the past he has always turned his back on them. "Hey," they shout to him, "who are you?" He replies that he is "the most ordinary man":

Who am I?
I am the woodcutter
of the deep woods
of thought,
wreathed in the vines of bookmen,
skilled carpenter
of human souls,
stonecutter of men's hearts.

. . .

You're waiting for Ararats?
There are no Ararats.
None at all.
You dreamed them in your sleep.
And if
the mountain does not go to Mahomet,
the devil with it.
It's not of Christ's paradise I shout to you,
where keepers of Lent lap tea without sugar.
It is of real earthy heaven I shout.

. . .

My paradise is for all
but the poor in spirit,
not for those,
bloated like moons
in great fasts.
It is easier for a camel to pass through the
                eye of a needle
than for one of these elephants
to come unto me.

Come to me,
thou who hast calmly knifed thine enemy
and gone from the corpse singing!
Come, thou unforgiving,
thou shalt be first
to enter my kingdom of heaven.

Come thou, great lover of men, cast about by
        all kinds of loves,
in whose veins darts the demon of mutiny,
for thee, untiring in thy love, is
my kingdom of heaven.
Come all, who are not rotating mills,
each of ye for whom life is unbearable and
        narrow,
be it known unto thee:
for thee
is my kingdom of heaven.

The Most Ordinary Man vanishes, and we next meet the Unclean on their trip to Hell, where they terrify Beelzebub and his devils with accounts of how workers live on earth. "Your silly hell is honey to us, who have machines and culture." Next they climb to Heaven, where in preparation for their arrival a cloud is milked and another sliced, and where the Saints—among whom are Christ, Tolstoy, and Jean Jacques Rousseau—line up to receive them. They arrive exhausted and are not refreshed by the heavenly bread and wine. They ask the angels about the life they lead, advise them to install an elevator, if they travel to earth so often, and, tired out, feeling cheated, they work their way back through the clouds. Now they find themselves at city gates, through which they see machines, locomotives, cars, all wreathed in sunlit rainbows. These things come forth to greet them, bearing bread and salt. "This is the earth," they say, "this is no dream; this will not vanish."

What do you mean—the earth?
The earth is dirt,
The earth is night.

The Unclean are afraid that the bread will bite, that the machines will cut them. But, persuaded to come in, they find themselves on real earth among friends. And this cartoon version of Marxist history, dramatizing the economic and political exploitation of the proletariat, the false promises

of religion, the triumph of technology, concludes with a resounding hymn to labor.

Mayakovsky's anthropomorphism had by now become the
symbol of a materialist philosophy. Inanimate objects, alive
and powerful, were the support of the proletariat, the enemy of the capitalist. Their role was all important in 150,000,-
000, a long poem, published anonymously in 1919 (the
title was the population of Russia in that year) to emphasize
its claim to having been written by the country itself: "150,-
000,000 are the makers of this poem. Its rhythm is a bullet,
its rhyme is fire sweeping from building to building. 150,-
000,000 speak with my lips. This edition is printed with human steps on the paper of city squares." Its theme is the
struggle of East and West, and it begins with a tremendous
gathering of forces: things, animals, and men, "millions of
workers, millions of laborers and servants," who together make
up Russia, Ivan, whose arm is the Neva, the soles of whose
feet are the Caspian steppes, and who suddenly looms up
in Chicago, a city all electro-dynamo-mechanical, which
has 14,000 streets with 700 alleys running out of each, every
one the length of a year's journey by train, a city so bright
that the sun is but a penny candle to it. Here Royal Street
leads to the hotel where Woodrow Wilson lives, so huge a
hotel that from any given spot, one can see but a small corner of it, and to climb all its stairs, one had better start
young, and even so without hope of reaching the top before
old age. As for Wilson himself, he is a giant of immeasurable
height, with cheeks of such preternatural softness they seem
to beg you to lie down on them, and clothing of the subtlest
stuff of poetical dreaming, so fine it might not be there at
all. All Americans are his subjects, and they say proudly, "I
am an American subject. I am a free American citizen."
Ivan appears, heralded by all kinds of wild rumors and a
panic on the stock exchange, and there is a combat between
him and Wilson. Wilson fights with four-trigger revolvers
and a sword that has seventy blades, Ivan with his bare
hands. Wilson slashes Ivan four miles down from his shoulder, but Ivan turns out to be the Trojan horse. Instead of
blood, a man emerges from his wound. Then more climb

out, then houses, battleships, horses. Half the world now sings the Red hymn, the other half, the White: "God save Wilson, mighty, imperious." New weapons are brought into the fight. There is a great battle of things: skyscrapers, meat, and furniture. People are trampled by wardrobes, pierced by table legs. Then Wilson brings on Hunger, which cracks cities like nuts, Ruin, Disease, and finally, his last weapon, an army of *isms:* Democratism, Humanism. *Ism* goes marching after *ism,* professor after professor, priests, terrorizing people with Hell, enticing them with Heaven, poets, flying skyward to shoot from the heights as from airplanes. Wilson backs up against the sun, trying to push it back, and is burnt up.

Then comes a festival in a year of endless zeros, the feast of a classless society. Buildings are hung with flags; and the world's triumphant requiem is sung by men, beasts, and rivers in memory of "the hungry, the poor, and those shot on the soul's barricades—painters, singers, poets." Finally:

> The world's parade was breaking up slowly,
> for the soul is not frenzied by ancient grief.
> Sorrow
> to peace
> is
> by years orchestrated,
> and in song is cast up to the skies.
> As echoes of voices were still resounding
> of the deaths of some,
> of eternal remembrance,
> people
> already
> in streets' manifold gleaming,
> a minute were rolling with joy painted over.
> Roll on, then, through concord of singing.
> Flourish, earth, in thrashing and sowing.
> This is for thee—
> the bloodstained Iliad of revolutions,
> of hungry years the Odyssey for thee.

VII

In these years of frantic activity Mayakovsky had been able to use his satiric gift in a new way. He had become a kind of official spokesman. He could now praise and teach, as well as denounce. His work was not only useful but essential. He had stepped into that position of leadership which he had always felt to be his by rights; and one senses his exuberance in the gusto and the good-natured humor of his squibs, his posters, and his epic caricatures. He had made the language of the street acceptable as poetry; and there can be no question but that he enjoyed his public role. It seemed to his friends that he had never been so happy; the Revolution had absorbed him completely, he had had no time to think about himself.

Nevertheless, an important part of him remained unexpressed. He was in love with Lila Brik; and this was a much more serious and lasting attachment than that first passion which hardly outlived the composition of the poem it had inspired. They had first met in July 1915, an occasion recorded in *I Myself: "Most Joyful Date.* Made acquaintance of L.Y. and O. M. Brik." Lila Yurievna, Ossip Mikhailovich's wife, was an actress, beautiful, clever, much admired. Like Turgenev with the Viardots, Mayakovsky became a friend of the Briks, in the same kind of tormenting relationship that lasted the rest of his life. Ossip Mikhailovich published Mayakovsky's work, made anthologies of it, wrote about it, brought out even such passionately jealous poems as "The Backbone Flute," which was dedicated to his wife. This poem, written in 1915, a few months after *The Cloud in Trousers,* is, like all of Mayakovsky's love poems, tragic and anguished; but in it, for the first time suicide appears as a serious possibility. Mayakovsky represents himself here as playing a concert on "the flute of his own spine." It may be, he says, his last concert, for more and more often he thinks of closing his life with the period of a bullet. He feels he must apologize for dwelling on so personal a theme as love at a time of public disaster. But even in these days, he says, "when the sky itself has forgotten its blueness, when drunk with blood, the battle goes reeling like Bacchus, the Germans, in dying, have Goethe's Gretchen on their lips and the French smile if they think of Traviata's kiss." And he himself could not avoid the personal issue. It was obsessive; it forced its way even into *War and the Universe,* which ends with a vision of his private bliss in a universal Utopia. Cities are restored, the dead resurrected, nations are at peace, and there is such brilliance, song and fragrance that "even a fairy tale of Andersen's is a mere puppy crawling at the foot of this dawning day." With his great eyes man looks the earth over, his head reaching mountains; and as Mayakovsky himself, awkward, enormous, saunters through these wonders, "she" comes to him:

> Greetings, beloved!
>
> Each hair I fondle,
> curly,
> and golden.
> Oh, what winds
> out of what south
> have worked this marvel on a heart entombed?
> Your eyes in flower
> two meadows are;
> in them I tumble,
> a joyful child.

To his country's and the Party's demands Mayakovsky could respond devotedly. But placards and cartoons can make little of a man's private experience; they have no use for his sense of his own individuality. They may require enthusiasm, wit, and imaginativeness; they may call on his convictions and his skill, but they leave his essential being untouched. The public role erases the private one. For Mayakovsky success and popularity themselves stirred up an ironic awareness of the disparity between the self-assured, gay face he showed to others and the bitterly unhappy and

helpless man he knew himself to be. Time and again he
sought to erase the difference between his public and his
private being by looking on himself as an exemplar of all
men, a kind of mythical figure who embodied all human suffering and hope. In *The Tragedy of Vladimir Mayakovsky*
he had seen himself as Poet, in "The Backbone Flute," as
Lover. Then, in a Whitmanesque poem of 1916, called *Man,*
he and Man were one. As such, he was more wonderful than
any supernatural wonder. Walk around him:

> On each side
> marvel at the five-beamed radiance
> called "arms."
> A pair of magnificent arms!
> Notice:
> I can move them from right to left,
> and from left to right.
>
> .   .   .
>
> Open the skull's jewel box;
> Within sparkles
> the mind, most priceless,
> Is there anything
> I cannot do?
> If you wish,
> I can invent a new
> animal.
> It will walk
> three-legged,
> double-tailed.

He has a beautiful red tongue, and the "O-ho-ho!" of his
voice can fly to the heights and come down softly again, a
falcon to the poet's will. Indeed, he cannot recount all the
wonders that are in him. To change summer to winter, water
into wine, there is an extraordinary clot beating under the
wool of his vest. He, this incredible miracle of the twentieth
century, has raised his heart like a flag, and palmers have
withdrawn from the tomb of the Lord to come to him; the
ancient Mecca has been emptied of the faithful. But this
glory is lost in the world's corruption. "Arms!" he had
boasted. They're for a gun. His tongue is covered in the spit

of slander. Astride his brain is "Law" and on his heart the chain, "Religion." He is a prisoner. There is no ransom for him. The cursed earth has manacled him. Riveted to his leg is the ball of the globe, and around him men, beasts, and things are drowning in a whirlpool of gold that rushes foaming from all meridians, and in the middle of which, on an island, lives imperturbably the Ruler of All, "my rival, my unconquerable foe." Exquisitely dressed, with daintiest polka dots on his delicate stockings, in striped trousers and a tie of yo-ho colors spreading itself from his bull neck over his belly's circumference, he is hailed in all languages:

> B-rra-vo!
> Eviva!
> Banzay!
> Urah!
> Hoch!
> Hip-hip!
> Vive!
> Hosannah!

And Mayakovsky loses to him the woman he loves. She too goes with the crowd to kiss his diamond-ringed hand, bending over the three hairs that bristle from under the stone: *The Flute* one of them is called; *The Cloud,* another; the third by the name of his most recent creation.

The theme of suicide is now fantastically developed. Mayakovsky's heart "yearns for a shot," his throat "craves a razor." He goes to a druggist:

> Druggist!
> Druggist!
> Druggist!
> Where,
> at the last
> will the heart
> outwear its woe?
> Is there a home for the jealous?
> Is it in fields of limitless heavens,
> or in Sahara's delirium,
> or in the desert of lunatic ardors?

Back of the walls of phials,
there are so many mysteries!
You know the highest equities.
Druggist,
let me lead my soul out
painlessly
into infinity.

The druggist reaches for the skull and crossbones labeled
"poison," but before he can hand it to him, the ceiling
opens up, and the immortal Mayakovsky floats smoothly
around the counter and out above the houses. Over the
heads of gaping crowds, over a church he flies, over woods,
up through clouds. Then, *Stop!*

Mayakovsky is in Heaven. He throws himself down on a
cloud and looks about "the fair surroundings." Everything
"sparkles, shines, gleams." There is a rustle of bodiless creatures gliding along and the sound of a Verdi melody. He
peeps through a slit in the clouds and beholds angels singing. One of these detaches itself and courteously inquires:
"Well, Vladimir Vladimirovich, how do you like the infinite?"
"And I reply with equal courtesy: 'The infinite is splendid.
The infinite is a joy!'" At first, however, he finds his new
abode rather irritating—there is nowhere he can drink tea
and have newspapers with his tea—but gradually he gets
used to it, and joins others in receiving new arrivals:

How do you do, Vladimir Vladimirovich.
How do you do, Abraham Vassilyevitch.
Well, how did you die?
All right?
Comfortably?

He goes on a tour of Heaven and views the "central station
of all phenomena, . . . the chief warehouse of all kinds of
rays," the "place where burnt-out stars are thrown," and
examines an ancient anonymous blueprint, the first unsuccessful project for the universe. He learns to like it all: "Everything is serious. Everyone is busy. One angel mends
clouds, another brings fuel for the sun's furnace. All are

exceedingly quiet, well behaved, organized according to rank. Nobody pushes; of course, there is nothing to push with." So seas of time pass over him, and after untold centuries—thousands, millions of years—he gets bored and descends to earth. Once more he sees rubles dancing through the cities in their various, familiar guises: devil, god, idea—all led by the ballet master of the earthly can-can. He comes to a street he seems to recognize and asks a passerby if it is Zhukovsky Street. No, he is told. For thousands of years it has been known as Mayakovsky Street. It was here the poet shot himself at the door of his beloved. Mayakovsky, through the habit he has acquired in heaven, flies into a bedroom where "she," young as ever, is in bed with her husband. They wake up. It isn't she after all. Mayakovsky is in a stranger's room. What, then, has happened to "her"? About her, he learns, there is a legend: when he killed himself, she jumped out of the window after him into the street. Where is he to go now, handcuffed as he is in the millenniums of love? He asks to be taken back to the dull stretches of heaven.

VIII

For five years after this there were no more poems about himself. When in 1921 his friend Aseyev requested that he send him a new poem, Mayakovsky replied, quoting a well-known gypsy love song: " 'You ask songs of me, but I have no more songs.' For a year and a half I've taken no rhymes into my mouth—(as you know, pen in hand I've never taken)." As soon as he did take rhymes into his mouth again, it was to talk about himself, in the most explicit of his self-portraits, which he called "I Love." He speaks in it of his childhood, when he wandered idly on the banks of the Rion, sprawled in the open without burden of shirt or shoes, while the sun marveled: "How is there room in that yard's length for me and the river and the thousand-foot cliffs?";

when, in his teens, he passed from school into jail and would have given everything on earth for a spot of sunlight on the prison wall. After this,

> What can desire of Boulogne forests mean to me?
> What to me are sighs on views upon the sea?

What are curly poodle lyricists to him who was taught by the street and the jail, and learned the alphabet by leafing through the tin and iron pages of signboards? In his universities he mastered the language of buildings and street cars, not French and arithmetic; and all his geography and history and whatever else he learned was not intended for polite chatter with the ladies; he talked with houses and with water towers. When he was grown, he knocked about, hands in pockets, staring, stifled in the embrace of Moscow's endless streets:

> O, how many of them,
> only of springs,
> are in twenty years heaped in the ardent one!
> Their unspent weight is simply unbearable,
> not just
> in verse,
> but really unbearable.

He was immense, he loathed restraint; and having felt so much, longed so much, endured so much, he could have no patience with frivolity and pettiness.

What came of his childhood and youth? Bloated, exhausted with the love and the poetry in him,

> More than permitted is,
> more than is needed,
> as if
> hung upon sleep in poetic delirium,
> the clot of the heart had swelled, a colossus,
> love—a colossus,
> colossus—hatred.

He bore its weight like an athlete, and shouted like the village tocsin calling to a fire: "Here it is! here! take it!" The ladies sprang away from him:

> We'd like something smaller,
> something that's tango like.

Then "she" came, saw in all his enormousness only a little boy, and took his heart and played with it, as a little girl plays with a ball. Others looked on: "To love such an one? She must be from the zoo, a lion tamer." But for him:

> It's gone,
> the yoke!
> Out of my wits with joy
> I pranced.
> Leaped like an Indian in a wedding dance.
> So gay it was,
> so light for me.

Now he can no more take back his heart than he could, all by himself, haul the grand piano down from the floor upstairs, still less the fireproof cabinet. Like a rich banker he has hidden his wealth, his love, in her, the fireproof safe, and only now and then he dips into his treasure, taking a smile or half a smile. But fleets, even they sail into harbors; the train, even it, comes to a station. Pushkin's miserly knight goes down to his cellar and feasts his eyes, and rummages in his treasure. "So I, beloved, to you return. Mine is this heart. I feast my eyes upon mine own." And the conclusion:

> Neither quarrels
> nor miles
> will wash love away.
>
> I love—
> immutably and truly!

This was written early in 1922, at the close of the busy years, when Lila Brik worked with him on the ROSTA windows, and acted with him in his film scenarios. But a twelve-month later, the most complex of his lyrical epics showed, if not a repudiation of this love, at least a kind of condemnation of it as selfish. That year had been full enough. He was invited to become a permanent contributor to *Izvestia;* and the first poem he published there, a satire on Committee meetings, was publicly praised by Lenin, who said he did not know how it stood "as poetry, but as for politics," he vouched that it was "absolutely correct." Other satiric poems followed. In the spring he established a publishing house, which that fall brought out a two-volume anthology of his poetry, *Thirteen Years of Work.* In October he made his first trip to France and Germany, he wrote a cycle of poems called *Paris,* published a collection of his works in Berlin, and upon his return to Russia in mid-December gave lectures about his trip. It was at this time also that he founded a new journal, *LEF* (Left Front of Art). Then at the very end of the year, in the last days of December, he shut himself up in his room, contrary to his habit, and wrote his poem. Victor Shklovsky has given the following account of its genesis: "Many people were always correcting Mayakovsky, advising him, explaining to him what one should and what one should not do. Everyone explained to him that one mustn't write about love. The discussion began in 1916." That year, according to Lila Brik, Mayakovsky had written "a long poem, *Don Juan.* I didn't know that it was being written. Volodya recited it to me all of a sudden, as we were walking in the street, the whole of it, by heart. I got angry, because it was again about love. How was it he hadn't tired of the subject? Volodya snatched the manuscript from his pocket, tore it to bits, and let it fly on the wind along Zhukovsky Street."

I X

That is why the remarkable poem of 1923 is called *About What? About This.* Its fine prologue discusses that "small, private," unmentionable theme, sung "not just once, nor five times"—a theme that has made him again go round and round like a squirrel in its cage, an inescapable and all-pervasive theme: a prayer to Buddha contains it, and it sharpens the Negro's blade against his master. It is a theme that will come to a cripple and command him to write. It comes and orders: "Truth!" It comes and orders: "Beauty!" It is a theme that will come unworn down the ages, commanding: "From now on look on me!" It is a cunning theme. It dives under events and, in the secret places of instinct, prepares for a spring. Just try and forget it! It will grasp and shake you, will make souls tumble out of their skins. To him it came in anger, looked in disgust at his daily life, thundered, rubbed out all other themes, and alone became inseparably close. It stepped up to the heart with a knife, from heart to the temples it hammered. It darkened the day, and ordered the head to beat out a rhythm. "The name of this theme is: . . . !"

No simple love song or love story is this poem inscribed "to her and to me," but an anxious probing into the nature of love. It proceeds in surrealist fashion, with intermelting scenes, like a film by Jean Cocteau. There is first a telephone conversation. The ringing of the phone is like an assault or an earthquake:

> This something squealing, this something ringing
> shot at the walls, seeking to wreck them.
> Small tinklings in thousands from walls ricocheting
> rolled under chairs and under the beds.
> From ceiling to floor, the huge bell slapped down;
> and then, once again, the ringing ball-giant,

hitting the floor, flew up to the ceiling,
and rained to the bottom in splinters of ringings.
Glass upon glass, damper on damper
stretched out to ring in tone with the phone.
The house was a rattle
in a little hand shaken.
In a flood of ringing drowned the phone.

The conversation itself is a duel between "her" and "him."
The cook, who answers the phone, is her second, measuring
the distance between them, as she goes to announce his call.
He waits in a universal stillness; everything stops: those
making reports at meetings stand transfixed, mouths open,
unable to complete their words and gestures; sirens, wheels,
human steps—all have stopped. The world has receded:
Moscow, the fields beyond Moscow, the sea, the straight
mountains beyond the sea—the whole universe looks as if
seen through the wrong end of binoculars. Only the field of
combat is near, and Time, the doctor, with his infinite band-
age of healing death. Finally, more terrible than bullets, a
word crawls along the wire, a monster from the epoch of
troglodytes. Perhaps, however, there was no monster; perhaps the troglodyte was but his own face reflected in the
telephone.

This is what can happen to a man. Shaggy in the fur of
his shirt, what is he doing with telephones? Away with
him where he belongs, to his own kind, in icy seas! Do bears
weep? If they do, it must be just like this: muzzles in air,
they howl, and having howled, lie down in their lair. His
bed goes gently floating on the waters he has wept. He
climbs on to a slab of ice, his pillow, and rowing with his
paw, floats out to the river. How empty it is! How the wind
howls in pursuit from Ladoga! He rages on his ice-cake
pillow and senses one thing only: he must pass under the
arcs of his bed, or maybe it's under a bridge, and vaguely
remembers that all this has been before: the wind, and he,
and this very river. He turns back. On the bridge, immovable, terrible, stands Man— He, against the background of
flaming skies, the man that he himself once tied there. He

hears his own voice praying, pleading: "Vladimir! Stop! Don't leave me! For seven years I've stood here looking on these waters, tied to the railing by the ropes of my verse." Seven years ago He should have been permitted "to smash his heart against these wharves." And He warns him that if he has "wormed his way" into "their caste, eating, kissing, growing a paunch," he will not escape. "I'll find you, torment you, finish you!" The thunderous voice pursues him as he flees: "You thought you'd trade the shimmering Neva. You can't exchange it—not 'til the grave!" In a panic, the bear cries through the storm: "Help! Help! Help! Help! There on the bridge, on the Neva, stands Man!"

Shouting, he floats down to the "insultingly big" ocean, when all of a sudden, an island of cushions springs up under him and he becomes aware that there are no seas at all, that there is only dry land for miles around, dry and a bit dampened by snow. What land is this? It seems to be Green-lap-love-landia. Calling, he runs along streets he recognizes, falls, and is greeted with obscene curses. "What are your eyes for? Has NEP made you blind?" It's Christmas Eve. They think he is a mummer. He seems to them to be only dressed up as a bear. A misunderstanding! But here is someone coming toward him, with the moon making a halo 'round his head. At a distance, he looks like Jesus, but nearer—no, he is younger, gentler—a young Communist. He clasps his hands as if in prayer, he waves his arms as if addressing a meeting. The snow is cotton; he walks on the snow. The snow is gilded! What could be baser? The boy walks on, his eyes on the sunset; and suddenly stops, steel in the silk of his hands; looks at the sunset an hour, and is robbed by the wind, which carries away a note from him: "Farewell. I am ending my life. Please do not blame me!" "How he resembles me!" Dreadful, but one must. The bear pulls off the boy's bloodstained jacket, struggles into it, shaves the fur off his paws and snout, and sees in the glass of ice that he looks just like the boy. And so he runs to the "family burrow." "Volodya! For Christmas! What joy! What joy!" But as he passes from the dark entrance hall into the lighted room, "Volodya! Lord! what is this? You're all crimson. Show me

the collar! . . ." "Never mind, mamma. I'll wash it at home.
That's not the point. My dears! My loved ones! You love me?
Yes? Then listen! Auntie! Sisters! Mamma! Put out the lights
on the Christmas tree! Lock the house! . . . Let's go immediately. It isn't far—only some 600 short versts. We'll be
there in the wink of an eye. He's waiting." "Volodya, darling, calm yourself!" And he answers furiously: "Well, then!
You've traded love for tea? You replace love by the darning
of socks?" But, of course, the whole universe is now family
strewn—Germany, America, the Sahara even. And here,
where

> the scourging, the judging October had thundered,
> you have disposed yourselves,
> have set out your dishes
> under its flame-feathered wing.
>
>   . . .
>
> Chicken love!
>   Love of brood hens!

Out he goes in a rage, and meets himself on the street, his
arms full of presents, striding along between houses with
lighted Christmas trees; and walks into a party. Drinking,
greetings, gaiety. Everything is exactly as it has been for
centuries. And worst of all, his double, he himself, is there.
He has come unexpectedly, and the host apologizes: had he
only known! But he had thought him at home, with his
people. His home! What was his home? Just now he floated
from it, on the ice, his pillow. He has used delicate words
and he has groaned terribly; he has rung lyrical bells, has
begged, has threatened, has pleaded and agitated. After all,
a poet's work is important. Even if he is a bear—to put it
crudely, one takes the hide, makes a lining of rhymes, and
there's a winter coat for you! Now, by the fireplace, with
coffee and smoking, for only ten minutes, but before it's too
late, they listen, smiling, to the famous mummer. Some, in
their cups, are even touched. When he tries to get away, they
will not let him. To eat, to drink, to drink, to eat—and then
to cards! To hell with theory! NEP is practical. But—he's a
Futurist! At him, then! And so poetic quarrels come pouring

in, while HE, Man, stands there, nailed to the railing, stands and believes that before long his time will come. Remembering Him, the poet fights again, but, strange to say, his words evaporate, his bass is silenced in mosquito trills. No wonder! Moscow has long since become the Island of the Dead. Its quiet measures are cypresses, guardians of night.

He is alone and lost, when, as with a hatchet one enters a dream, a sudden memory comes to him: here is the longing, there the corner—round it, *she*. If only, as before, he could again fly up to her window in poetry! But these are other times; pressed to the wall's dampness, step by step, like Raskolnikov after the murder, he climbs the stairs, making way for guests. And hears the piano tinkling, and shouting, singing, laughing. They're dancing the one-step. He stands by the wall.

> Let life become delirium—
> Just not her voice
> unbearable!
> I've given the day,
>   the year I've given
> to daily dreariness,
> in this madness stifling.
> It has eaten out life
>   in thin smoke of apartments.
> I shouted:
>   resolve!
>   from your floors!
>   to the pavements!
> I ran from the call of wide open windows,
> loving, I ran—
>   never mind it was sideways,
> never mind it was only in rhyme,
>   in footsteps of night.
> Only so does one stitch,
>   and souls become poems,
> if by verses one loves;
>   but in prose I am dumb.
> There now, I
>   cannot speak it,
>   do not know how to.

But where, my darling,
where, my beloved,
where
in song
is my love betrayed?
Here
every sound
is a call,
a confession.
And only from song—not a word may be thrown.

In all his cursing, her name is untouched. He begs her to respond to his verse, to run with him to the bridge. He himself is determined to go, having conquered himself.

But that moment in the roar of a tempest Man's thundering voice reaches him: "Stop! From beyond seven years I have come. From 600 versts. I order: let be! . . . What can you do alone? I await the whole of mankind. Seven years I have stood on the bridge. I will stand there two hundred, scorned and laughed at, standing for all, praying for all."

Finally, the poet, an old man, in "some kind of Montmartre," surrounded by prostitutes, while the walls reel in a two-step, climbs up on a table; and everyone knows that he will call to them to go somewhere, to save someone. From France he rises, a gray cinematic shadow, in the electric current of remembrance to bid a last farewell to eastern lands. And finds himself caught on the cupola of Ivan the Great in the Kremlin. He balances precariously up there, afraid of falling again into the old Christmas horror. And now he is over the Caucasus, and bristling crowds come to see him. They spit on their palms and slap his face, the ladies throw their gloves at him. "I am not bothering you. Why all these insults? I am only a poem, I am only a soul." But they shout to him from below: "No, you've been our enemy a hundred years. Another such got caught—a hussar!" They fire at him, at a hundred paces, at ten, at two, charge after charge.

The battle is finished; happiness bubbles. Relishing the details, they walk slowly away. And only on the Kremlin, the rags of the poet are a small red flag that glows in the wind. The sky as before, is starlit with lyrics. In astonishment the Great Bear looks down, recognizing her brother. And carries him over the Ararat ages, as an ark on the flood of heaven. The sun shines on mountains, days smile from the pier. The ark arrives. But Mayakovsky bends in grief over the globe, hating, unable to accept the pettiness, the slavishness he sees there. Their bullets have not silenced him. It will be long before they sing a requiem to his talent. Wherever he dies, he will die singing. In whatever hole he lies down, he will be worthy of lying beneath the red flag. And yet, whatever one dies for, death is death. It's terrible not to love; it's frightful not to dare. If one believed in the after-life, it would be easy—one need only stretch one's arm and in a second a bullet would take one there. What is he to do if with his whole heart he believes in this world, this life, even though as he looks back upon it he can find but some ten tolerable days at most, at "its very bottom," his childhood?

Yet death is not the end. There will be resurrection. With the clarity of a hallucination, he sees a great, quiet chemist leafing through a book, "the world," and coming to the twentieth century. Whom shall he resurrect? Well, here is Mayakovsky. He will pass him by for a more interesting man. But Mayakovsky will plead with him: "Resurrect me! I never lived out my life on earth, nor loved through all the love that was in me. Seven feet tall I was. Yet what I did, a plant louse might have done!" He will be useful if resurrected. He can clean, wash, and sweep, he can be gay, and even though in this age people "bare their teeth only to grab and chatter," who knows, a joke might come in handy. Also, he has loved animals; so, best of all, let him be keeper in a zoo. She too loved animals, and maybe one day she will come to the zoo, smiling, just as she does in the picture in the table drawer. She is beautiful. She will certainly be resurrected. Then, in the thirtieth century, they will catch up on all the love they had not loved. "Resurrect! I want to live my life through!" And this won't be, until love is all of life, not a servant to marriage, home, bread, lust, not until he can claim as relatives at least the universe as father, the earth, at least, as mother.

This most intimate, and most despairing, of all his poems, exhibits more clearly than anything else the heart of Mayakovsky's misery, which was not just the unhappiness of a tormenting love affair, though the pain involved in it was real enough, but the agony of isolation, a spiritual isolation that seems to have grown deeper with the years and to have become incurable. Formerly, when Mayakovsky raged against his world, he was denouncing a class of men he loathed and whom he hoped either to overthrow or to reform. But now, those who were closest to him—his family, the woman he loved, the whole society he had fought for— had sunk into the despised ways of life from which he had wanted to save them. Mayakovsky's was the tragedy of the romantic idealist. He believed what he willed to believe, refusing to distinguish between possibility and reality. He was the kind of thinker whom Herzen, in *From the Other Shore,* had once reproached for failing to understand human beings and for imposing on people the tyranny of his ideals. There was, however, an all-important difference between these dreamers and Mayakovsky. Herzen's idealists ran away, and in self-pitying exile fulminated against the world they had left; Mayakovsky was wholly dependent on his countrymen: his thought, his poetry were bound up in his activity among them. Either he was to live with them, or not at all. He could not run away except in death; and since he was not a man to compromise, the possibility of suicide kept recurring to him. After all, his young idealistic self had already been killed; Man, his mature self, ready to wait long ages for the millennium, had no need of him; his fame had brought him enmity and persecution; even his friends valued him only as one who could entertain them a few minutes after dinner.

X

A year later, in 1924, Lenin's death forced Mayakovsky to forget himself again. On January 27, Lenin was buried. Mayakovsky attended the funeral, then for over six months studied his writings and steeped himself in the history of bolshevism. The following October he completed a long commemorative poem, *Vladimir Ilych Lenin,* which he dedicated to the Russian Communist Party.

It begins in somber eloquence with a heavy, rhythmic fall on the word "time," the reiteration of which sounds like the tocsin's knell, and announces the central, historic meaning of the poem.

> It's time—
> > of Lenin the tale I begin.
> Not for the reason
> > that sorrow
> > > has failed us.
> Time,
> > because
> > > keenest anguish has grown
> to become clear
> > definable pain.
> Time,.
> > Lenin's slogans
> > > to unfurl again.

Men, says Mayakovsky, are boats, to whose sides in the course of a lifetime cling all kinds of seaweed, shells, and slime; and to cleanse himself of these he comes to Lenin before sailing further on into the revolution. Afraid, as a boy fears hypocrisy, that little wreaths of glistening verse may cover Lenin's wise, enormous brow, that mausoleums and processions may drown his great simplicity in saccharine ointment, he writes as his heart has voted and duty commanded. But how poor is the factory of words and measures! Where shall suitable ones be found to explain this man? There are none large enough. We have seven days, we have twelve hours. And when the clock and the calendar are too small for events, we say "an epoch," or "an era." At night we sleep; we act in the daytime. But if someone comes along who can direct events, we say "a prophet," we say "a genius." But Lenin was himself an era, an era that every man had seen with his own eyes passing through doorways, his head not even touching the lintel. He will not be given the purely official honors paid to others. It will not be said of him, as of others, that he was "leader by the grace of God." For he is genuinely mourned; "hearts are chilled by a real pain," as this most earthy of all men is buried, a man who had the same weaknesses, the same illnesses as those of ordinary men, and held dear what they hold dear. And yet, he, Mayakovsky, and not he alone, would have given his life to preserve a single breath of his. Whence came he, who was he, this most human of all men?

He was, to Mayakovsky, the incarnation of men's hopes. He had been prophesied by starving workers of capitalist cities all the way from Russia to Patagonia. To account for him and to praise him, one must recite the story of society. And this Mayakovsky proceeds to do in a cartoon history of industrial man, reminiscent of *Mystery-Bouffe*. He does this, he says, for the sake of future children, who will ask: "What is 'capitalism'?" And explains: to begin with, Capitalism was a good fellow. He worked, not afraid of soiling his shirt front, threw away the feudal tights that were too small for him, flourished in revolutions, and even hummed the "Marseillaise." He invented machines, and swallowed kingdoms and nobilities with all their crowns and eagles, but then grew bloated like the Biblical calf, licking his chops with his parliament tongue; in time, like his ledger, he became large and soft, built an incredible palace with Empire floor, rococo ceiling, walls Louis XIV; he made ethics, aesthetics, and other nonsense his domestic servants, sold to old women the holes from the nails on the cross of the Lord and feathers from the tail of the Holy Ghost; and so, fat and flabby, went to bed across the path of history. There was no way to walk or ride around him. He had to be blown up!

Time gave birth to brother Karl, who revealed the law of history, set the workman on his feet, and as he was writing his last lines, certainly had a vision of the Kremlin. The proletariat grew up. Anger became rebellion, rebellion revolution. Even now the walls of the Paris cemetery call workers to unite. Capitalism swelled to a hedgehog, bristling with contradictions, strong in bayonets—and the ghost of communism stalked over Europe. Because of all this, in the depths of Simbirsk, Lenin, an ordinary little boy, was born.

There was an illiterate workingman, who hadn't even learned his letters, but he heard Lenin speak, and so knew everything. There were Siberian peasants whose little village was taken away from them. They had never read Lenin, nor heard him speak, but they were Leninists.

Take a bird's-eye view of Russia. She is striped with blue rivers as with the marks of a thousand rods, and bluer even than her rivers are the bruises of her serfdom, and sorer even than hard-labor mines, the bondage of the factory bench. There have been richer, wiser, more beautiful countries— but none so full of pain as Russia. Not every blow, however, is wiped off a cheek. Rebels take up bombs, revolvers. The Populist Alexander, Ulyanov's brother, is hanged as the Czar's would-be assassin; and seventeen-year-old Ilych takes up his cause. With Socialism in view, he preaches gradualness: yesterday just four of us, today four hundred, tomorrow a thousand. The Party grows, Lenin's twin brother. When we say Lenin, we mean the Party. When we say the Party, we mean Lenin.

There came the failure of 1905. The intelligentsia locks itself in, burns incense, lights candles, searches for God; Plekhanov whimpers, "It's your own fault. You were not ready. No point in taking up arms in vain," but Lenin replies with a hearty, loud, "No! Arms you should have taken, but more energetically, more resolutely." Then, in the terrible year '14, when Imperialism, with naked paunch, knee-deep in blood, made earth a mountain of iron scrap and human rags, a single man, bald, with high cheekbones, raised his voice louder than all cannonades: "Enough! Let us turn the war of nations into civil war!" At war's end, he was the only victor.

He read in Switzerland about the Russian tempest and its premier, and arrived from the Finland Station:

> —Comrades!—
>> and over the heads of
>>> the first hundreds
> he stretched
>> his onward
>>> leading arm.

Under his guidance followed the well-known events of the October Revolution and of the subsequent years. With NEP, a sudden veering of the ship, which brought "the colossus of Soviet Republics" sailing from disaster "into Construction docks." Then, suddenly, the news: "Ilych has had a stroke!"

On January 2 the year beheld what a whole century will not see again, a weeping Bolshevik. There was a meeting of the Soviets. The delegates came in, sat down, exchanged jokes. Time to open! Why the delay? What is the matter with Kalinin? The ceiling descended like a crow's wing, and the lights of the chandeliers went black. Kalinin, tears on his cheeks and whiskers, mastering himself, got up, announced: "Yesterday—at 6:50 died Comrade Lenin."

Through the sieve of newspapers, print blackened snow. Like a bullet came the news to the workman at the bench. The peasant, who had more than once looked in the face of death, turned away from the womenfolk but was betrayed by the fist-smeared dirt on his cheek. Even men of flint bit their lip.

And now were a magician to proclaim that Lenin would awake if all of us should die, people would jump singing to death. But there is no magic. There is only the dead Lenin, bent shoulders, a coffin.

Yet even in death Lenin is a uniting force. And Mayakovsky is "happy": "I know—from now on and forever this minute is in me. I am happy that I am a small part of this power, that even the tears in my eyes are the tears of all men." The rites are finished. A gun is fired—maybe a thousand guns. But all this firing seems no louder than the clinking change in a beggar's pocket. There is the coffin, mute and motionless; we by the coffin, men's representatives.

Evenly breathing, heavily stepping, they leave the square all with one thought: It will be hard without Lenin! Who will replace him? But the answer comes from everywhere: workers, peasants, sailors, all join the ranks; and the death of Ilych itself becomes a great organizer. The banner is raised by a million arms, and Lenin calls through its every fold: "Proletarians, close ranks for the final battle! Slaves, straighten your backs and knees. Long live the Revolution, the only great war of all those known to history!"

Utterance such as this may strike a nonbeliever as naïve, dull, and meretricious. Nevertheless, Mayakovsky's sincerity cannot be questioned. If his enthusiasm sounds forced it is because it is adulterated by propaganda. But this is the "correct" Marxist attitude: and the poem both expounds the official view of history, and stands as an example of the official doctrine of art. It is not only a declaration, but an act, of faith. Mayakovsky had succeeded in creating a socialist art, but the irony of his situation was that while he had set out to break away from pamphleteering so as to keep from parroting others and work out his own ideas, he found himself so devoted to a rigid doctrine that in its service he squandered his gift of original creation.

XI

The very nature of his faith imposed on Mayakovsky the necessity of pleasing others; it obligated him to play a public role, and although temperamentally he was by no means opposed to this, there was that in his passionate nature which craved another kind of satisfaction, and a more in-

timate mode of expression. There can be no question but
that the tension generated by these unreconciled, and probably unacknowledged, demands lay at the heart of his
tragedy. He enjoyed his fame, but it enslaved him, and in a
way he could not admit, reduced his stature. At one time
the universe was part of him, now he was part of the world.
Once he had worn the sun as a monocle or offered it tea,
now he was a citizen of the U.S.S.R., the poet of socialism,
ruler and legislator of Soviet letters, an important actor in a
drama of momentous events. However proud he might be
of his role, it was not so vast and free as his imagination had
once conceived it. He was no longer the center of his major
poems—not until the end; and the work of his last years was
largely objective, almost entirely satiric, and much of it
based on his travels, for beginning with 1922, as soon as
circumstances permitted and the ROSTA work came to an
end, he made yearly excursions either abroad or in Russia.
At one time he had planned to go around the world, but he
gave that up, and a voyage to America was the longest of
his trips. He was in France and Germany for a month or
two every year but one from 1922 to 1929, sometimes stopping in Poland and Czechoslovakia; and from 1924, he
visited numerous cities in Russia on extensive lecture tours.
He traveled in Russia because he was much in demand, and
he went abroad to get a perspective on Russia. There was
nothing relaxed in these journeys. It was not for rest and
distraction that they were undertaken. "It is essential for me
to travel," he wrote, "contact with living things is to me almost a substitute for reading books. Traveling absorbs the
reader of today. Instead of invented points of interest about
dull things, images and metaphors, one has things that are
interesting in themselves." Europe, exhibiting the type of
regime Russia had overthrown, provided him rich material
for laughter; and his portraits of European dignitaries were
so insulting that the *London Morning Post* once recom-
mended that he be prosecuted for a libelous poem on Lord
Curzon.

In 1925, after several previous attempts, when he was
unable to procure a visa, Mayakovsky visited America,

crossing on a small Spanish ship that sailed from St. Nazaire to Havana and Mexico. In the United States Embassy in Mexico City he was asked: "Moscow. Is that in Poland?" " 'No,' I answered, 'it's in the U.S.S.R.' " "Not the slightest impression. They gave me a visa." He saw Havana, Vera Cruz, Mexico City, Laredo; was entertained by Diego Rivera, who took him directly from the station to the Museum, and showed him his own unfinished work at the Ministry of Public Education; watched a bullfight; walked about the streets; ran into one or two Russian immigrants, and met several Comrades at the head of the small but growing Mexican Communist Party. In the United States he gave lecture readings under the auspices of Russian organizations in New York, Philadelphia, Cleveland, Chicago, and Detroit. He was interviewed for the *New York Times* by Michael Gold.

Upon his return to Russia, after a six months' absence, he published several poems about his trip and a small prose work, *My Discovery of America,* in an introduction to which he gave a fair estimate of his qualifications as a writer of travel books: "I have lived entirely too little to be exact and detailed in describing particulars; I have lived sufficiently little to convey generalities accurately." His comments, without being profound, are penetrating and amusing, as, for example, the little poem in which he sketches six nuns aboard ship: all of them straight as a rope, sober, clean as boracic acid, mumbling day and night, noon and morning, yawning as one, coming to the table in squadron formation, and after dinner marching off to the washroom in unison, so that if Christ came down from the cross and found himself among them, he would hang himself from boredom. Or his remarks about Mexico City, where:

. . . the car competes with the bus, and cars of different makes compete with one another. This competition, because of the more than passionate temperament of Spanish drivers, takes on, positively, the aspect of battle. Car chases car, cars together chase the bus, and all, as one, ride up sidewalks, hunting down rash pedestrians. . . . The driver in Mexico is not held responsible for mutilations (take care of yourself!) and for this reason the average length of life there without mutilations is ten years. Once every ten years each man is run over. True, there are those who haven't been run over for twenty years, but that compensates for those who are run over every five.

There are also more serious passages:

You will look in vain in New York for that system, orderliness, speed, cold-bloodedness, made famous in literature and cartoons. You see a mass of people sauntering aimlessly in the streets. Each will stop and talk to you on any subject you please. If you look up at the sky and stand still a moment, a crowd will gather round you. . . . The capacity to be distracted by something other than the stock market reconciles me mightily to the New York crowd.

About architecture in the United States, he remarks that "Americans build as if they were for the thousandth time performing a most fascinating play that they have learned thoroughly," and that "with all their grandiose construction," the height of American skyscrapers, their comfort and spaciousness—"houses in America produce, on the whole, a strange impression of impermanence."

There is, along with ridicule and disgust, an attempt at fairness, a kind of condescending tolerance, and sometimes even genuine admiration. Mayakovsky takes the trouble, for example, to qualify the "irresponsible commonplaces" which every schoolboy knows: that America is "a land of dollars, of imperialist jackals, etc." A land of dollars, of course, but not of speculators chasing dollars as Russians did in 1919 when the ruble was falling, or Germans in 1922 when the mark was crashing and "men worth thousands and millions would refrain from eating their morning bun, in the hope that by evening it would be cheaper." Americans are not miserly, and although it is true that for them "God is dollar, dollar Father, dollar Holy Ghost," theirs is not "the penny-pinching avarice of men" who "accumulate a little sum" so they can "plant daisies in a garden and install electric lights in the hen houses of their favorite brooders. . . . No! There is poetry" in their feeling about the dollar. The American sees spring in the green of a dollar bill. It affords him "aesthetic delight." "In meeting you, the American does not say indifferently, 'Good morning.' He shouts to you sympathetically, 'Make money?' and walks by. The American does not say vaguely: 'You look well (or ill) today.' The American formulates his greeting more precisely: 'You look like two cents today' or 'You look like a million dollars.'"

Mayakovsky admires engineering. Humbly as a believer whose faith has been shaken comes into a church, and proudly as a fame-drunk conqueror enters a ruined city, he walks up Brooklyn Bridge. Like a stupid artist gazing with love on the museum's Madonna, he stands there beneath a sky of stars and looks on New York. He is proud of this steel mile; his visions have come to life in it. If the world were destroyed and it alone remained, a geologist a hundred years hence could reconstruct the present. He would say: this steel paw connected seas and prairies; it came after the age of steam, when people were already flying airplanes and shouting over radios. Here life for some was carefree, for others, a long whine. From here the jobless threw themselves head first into the river. Here Mayakovsky stood, composing verses. . . . Brooklyn Bridge, yes, . . . it's quite a thing!

But with all its poetry, its skill and largeness, there are ugliness and inhumanity in America. The jobless jump into the river; Negroes are lynched; there is "the odious spectacle" of the stockyards in Chicago; there is the fantastic efficiency and oppression of the Ford factory in Detroit. The lesson of America is that the days for glorifying bare technology are gone, that the time has come for harnessing it in the interests of humanity. The days of delight in the noise of machines have passed; it is now time to install sound absorbers: "We poets have to talk in railway cars"; to recognize that division of labor destroys the quality of man; to assimilate American industrial methods and use them for something better. It may be fantasy, says Mayakovsky, but it seems to him that presently America will be the moneylender of the world, and as "the last armed defender of the hopeless bourgeois business" will come in conflict with the U.S.S.R. Then, history will write a novel called *The Struggle of Two Worlds* in the style of H. G. Wells. And he ends on a Voltairian note: back in France, it seems to him that the little houses, miserable shacks by comparison with American structures, and the bits of closely cultivated land are the height of culture by the side of the "bivouac state, the grabbing nature of American life. Yet all the way up to Rouen, on endless country roads of chestnut trees, in the most thickly settled corner of France, we came across only one automobile."

XII

In 1926 Mayakovsky had just started on a trip to the south of Russia when the news reached him of Essenin's suicide. The two men had met years before, and from the start had not liked each other. To Mayakovsky, Essenin seemed grossly affected, and his work so perniciously reactionary that "Esseninism" became for him a term of abuse. For his part, Essenin seems to have hated Mayakovsky with a kind of pathological fury: he could not bear to hear his name mentioned, and he tore up his books.

Essenin's death, however, provoked Mayakovsky to write one of his finest poems, and he tells the story of its composition in the essay *How Verses are Made*. He was shocked by the news, grieved, as a man is naturally grieved by a human tragedy. And yet, as he recalled his acquaintance with Essenin and especially his last glimpse of him, drunk and almost unrecognizable because of drink, the end seemed logical to him, and in time, no doubt, he would have dismissed it from his mind. But the morning papers published Essenin's final lines, the verses he had written with his blood in the hotel room where he had slashed his wrists. These verses transformed his death into "a literary fact." They were dangerous, and they could be combated only in verse. And so, "the command was given" him to write. But first he had to get away from the provincial Russia which was Essenin's setting. He wrote his poem "To Sergey Essenin" only three months later.

It is, like *Vladimir Ilych Lenin*, a threnody in which the lyric, personal note of grief is drowned out in the rhetoric of impersonal argument. In each case the man is mourned not as a private individual but as the embodiment, or representative, of a sphere of life. The poem to Essenin is a passionate argument on aesthetics, building up to the climax of a final couplet, which paraphrases and answers his suicide lines. Mayakovsky is sadly amazed by his action. Had he run out of ink? Perhaps if there had been some in his hotel room, he would not have needed his own blood to write with. He should have lived on to instruct talentless versifiers and teach them to stop mumbling and rumpling the poetic line. While so much rot was being produced, there was a great deal to be done: life was still to be made over and then it must be sung. True, times were hard for a writer, but what great man had ever chosen a path easier and better than this? The word was leader of man's power. And since our planet was ill equipped for pleasure, it was the poet's duty to wrest happiness from the future. Essenin had written at the end:

> To die in our world is nothing novel,
> But neither is there novelty in living.

Mayakovsky countered with:

> It is not hard to die in our world,
> Harder is it, by far, to make our life.

XIII

For Mayakovsky himself, it seemed, there could be no question of stopping. Now that the period of spectacular revolu-

tionary heroism had gone, men must be shown that their
inconspicuous labor was as heroic and important as the self-
sacrifice of the early days when they had "gone through fire
and the cannon's mouth." So he had written in 1923, praising the miners of Kursk, the first in Soviet Russia to obtain
iron ore. "What do you care about statues, lectures, mono-
graphs done in your honor? . . . Yours will be a greater
monument: a million chimneys weaving the pattern of your
names" in the industrialized land of the future.

> The doors to fame
> > are narrow doors,
> but however narrow,
> you will enter for all time,
> > you of Kursk,
> hauling lumps of iron
> > from the mine.

Men must not lose sight, Mayakovsky kept insisting, of
the grand socialist design, through which alone each man
could hope for what all men desired. Communal effort and
faith in one's country must not be relaxed. NEP was a
temporary measure, not a return to the ideas and methods
the Revolution had overthrown. This was what he said and
persuaded himself that he believed; but he was finding a
self-seeking pettiness everywhere, a love of comfort, a
mood of sentimental melancholy. Young poets were imitating Essenin. And Mayakovsky satirized, criticized, stormed.

His public had changed from that which had jeered at
him in 1913. The students, peasants, factory workers who
now jammed the halls to hear him no longer came as to a
vaudeville show. They still argued, and showered him with
questions, but they respected him. The man on the street
knew him and liked him. One day in Odessa, for example, a
stevedore, "without so much as a how-do-you-do" shouted:
"You tell Gosizdat to make a cheaper edition of your
Lenin"! Poets brought him their work for criticism; in one
city alone sixteen of them came to his room. Back in Moscow
and Leningrad, Mayakovsky reported all this. The very
word "provinces," he said, had become archaic. His former

audiences, first "the thick cream, then the whipped cream of the city," used to leave the lecture hall long before the end, to retrieve their boots and fur coats in the lobby, and you'd never see them again. Now, "the real audience, the real recital [began] only the next day."

There was all this, but there was also meanness, the same old *poshlost'* that Gogol and Dostoevsky had denounced years ago. It was now Mayakovsky's turn. He lashed out against it in poems, speeches, plays. It was the theme of his most amusing comedies, *The Bed Bug* (1928) and *The Bath House* (1929), in which Gogolian caricatures serve to satirize the moral degeneracy of Party members, models of greed, pettiness, idleness, of the very evils, that is, for which communism denounces the bourgeoisie. In *The Bed Bug,* the central character is a one-time workingman who by means of an advantageous marriage has decided to enter upon a life of ease; in *The Bath House* he is the pompous, frivolous, and stupid head of a governmental bureau. But, unlike Gogol, Mayakovsky is not basically concerned with human vices or weaknesses, nor is he carried away by the dramatic possibilities of an absurd situation. What interests him is men's beliefs about society and about the place they hold in it; and although his starting point is the society he knows, he is concerned with its implications in the abstract: not with society itself, but with its historic significance. Thus in both plays he transports us from the present into the distant future. *The Bath House* deals with a time machine (suggested certainly by H. G. Wells) and introduces a Phosphorescent Woman of the year 2030, who flies into the present to select those worthy of the future; and in *The Bed Bug* a man is defrosted fifty years after he has been congealed in a cake of ice.

But this type of vision had always been a favorite satiric device of Mayakovsky. He seems to have needed the perspective of ages to assess his own epoch, and of eternity to come to terms with his life. It is even possible that he had come to believe what, to begin with, had been merely a literary convention, that a favorite fantasy had become something more to him than a daydream of Utopia. Through a kind of self-hypnosis he seems to have persuaded himself that time, like matter, could be subjected to human control. Roman Jakobson has told how, in the spring of 1920, he attempted, as best he could, to explain to Mayakovsky the theory of relativity:

The release of energy, the problem of time, the question of whether speed that exceeds the speed of light may not describe an orbit in time, all this fascinated Mayakovsky. Rarely have I seen him so attentive and entranced. "Don't you think," he asked suddenly, "that in this way immortality will be attained?" I looked at him in astonishment. . . . "I am absolutely convinced that there will be no death. The dead will be resurrected. I will find a physicist who will expound Einstein's book to me point by point . . ."

The scientist of his *Bath House* describes "the grandiose idea" on which he is at work as a matter of transferring time from the status of a metaphysical substance, or "noumenon," to a "reality subject to chemical and physical effects." Time, he says, is a great river, a Volga into which "we used to be thrown at birth to float like logs and flounder about and swim with the current"; but now this Volga was subject to the human will. When critics objected to Mayakovsky's invention as puerile, he gave them a more mundane explanation: "No, Comrades," he said, "we are fulfilling our five-year plan in four years—that, in its own way, is a time-machine."

Whatever one might think of the fantastic element in these plays, one would have to be extraordinarily solemn to remain impervious to their humor. They are full of absurdity: verbal play, ridiculous people, preposterous situations. The satire in them provokes guffaws rather than sneers. The names themselves are comic: Prisipkin suggests "a rash," and its socially ambitious owner changes it to the musical Pierre Skripkin, from *skripka*, "violin"; there is Elizaveta Renaissance, the manicurist whom Prisipkin marries; Pobedonosikov, the bureaucrat of *The Bath House*, whose name is a ridiculous diminutive of Pobedonostev, the formidable Procurator of the Holy Synod under Alexander II.

There are such scenes as the one of a rehearsal, when the director, to please Pobedonosikov, organizes a symbolic pantomime: "Stand here, Comrade Capital . . . Dance over all with the air of class mastery . . . Skip over to the left in the attitude of the Second International . . . Breathe your last effectively! Produce picturesque spasms!" There are remarks such as Prisipkin's declaration that he is "opposed to all petty bourgeois stuff—canaries and the like," and, being "a man of large demands," is interested in a wardrobe with a mirror; or such as his best man's objections, at his wedding, to Oleg Bayan's manner of playing the piano: if he plays on the black keys only, it means he is slighting the proletariat, if he favors the white ones, he is giving preference to reactionaries, if he plays on both white and black, he is collaborating. There is in *The Bed Bug* Prisipkin's resurrection. It is voted by the nation in accordance with a law of 1965 that declares human life to be immutable, but is undertaken with every possible safeguard against contamination, for an epidemic of toadyism is known to have been widespread in 1929; yet in spite of all precautions, the epidemic rages out of control: hospitals are filled with inebriates, poisoned by the fumes of the beer Prisipkin demands; the dogs of the town have gone mad: they no longer play and bark, but only stand on their hind legs, begging; couples go about in strange gyrations, called "the fox trot"; rows of girls skip in unison to a mechanical rhythm; and young women are in a peculiar state of imbecility that used to be known as "being in love." Then it is discovered that Prisipkin, the cause of this contagion, need not have been resurrected at all, for he is not *homo sapiens,* but only resembles him. Actually, he is *Philistinus vulgaris,* good only as food for the rare specimen of *bed-bugus normalis* that has crawled off his body and been recaptured with great difficulty. The two of them belong, as a matter of fact, to the same species of parasite, the only difference between them being that Philistinus lives on the body politic, while bedbugus lives on Philistinus. "Both inhabit the moldy mattresses of time. When *bed-bugus normalis* has grown fat on the body of a single man, he falls under the bed. When *Philis-*

tinus vulgaris has grown fat on humanity, he falls on the bed. That is the only difference between them!" They are caged and exhibited in the zoo. But Prisipkin, invited to say a few words, suddenly notices not the stage audience of 1979, but the real audience in the theater. "Citizens! Brothers!" he cries. "My own kinsmen! Where have you come from? When were you all defrosted? Why am I the only one caged in?" Confusion on the stage. Prisipkin is locked in again and his cage curtained. The Director makes apologies: "Excuse it, comrades. . . . Excuse it. . . . The insect is tired. The noise and light have brought him to a state of hallucination. Please calm yourselves. It's nothing serious. It will be all right tomorrow. . . . Leave quietly, citizens. Until tomorrow. Music, a march!"

In *The Bath House* there is the scientist's desperate pursuit of Pobedonosikov, whose help he needs to save from calamity an envoy from the future: he and his helpers have received a message from fifty years ahead, that a visitor is to arrive the next day, but an explosion has accompanied the message, indicating that an obstacle is in the way; they must, therefore, shift their gear to a higher atmospheric level. For this, money and people are needed immediately, but they cannot get a hearing from Pobedonosikov, in whose anteroom a long line of petitioners is kept waiting and put off with various excuses, while in the inner sanctum the great man dictates a speech to his secretary, and on the pretext of urgent business, is busy securing railroad tickets for himself and an international adventuress, Mesaillansova. The speech he is dictating begins with a discourse on tramways, passes without transition to remarks on Tolstoy, then to Pushkin, and his secretary, Miss Underton, is discharged for having called his attention to these discrepancies; "no self-criticism, if you please!" he commands, "Tolstoy, Pushkin, and even Byron, if you like—are all of them, though at different times, subjects of jubilees." She is to take the whole of his article, and cut it up under appropriate headings as occasion requires. The scientists, foiled in every maneuver to get his attention, start carrying the machine to his apartment when the crucial moment is at hand. But the machine explodes on the landing, and the Phosphorescent Woman emerges at the moment Pobedonosikov is taking leave of his wife to join Mesaillansova. When he beholds Her, he orders his assistant, Optimistenko, to find out from the bureau whether such a thing is possible, and meanwhile uses diplomacy: "Of course," he says to Her, "I have been already informed of this occurrence. . . . The matter is being already discussed in committee. . . ." The Bureau declares that the event is impossible, but when nonetheless a flight into the Future appears imminent, Pobedonosikov arrives with masses of luggage, prepared to take up in the Future the position he holds in the present. He is amazed to discover that he has been left behind, "overthrown by the machine of time." "All right! All right!" he says, "let them try swimming about for a while without a leader! . . . I retreat into private life to write my memoirs." He is sure, at least, of Mesaillansova. But even she leaves him; and as the curtain falls, he asks in the manner reminiscent of Famusov in *The Misfortune of Being Clever:* "She, and you, and the author—what did you mean to say by all this? That communism doesn't need me and people like me?"

Both plays roused virulent discussion, *The Bath House* especially. "The audience split apart in a way that was positively funny," Mayakovsky wrote Lila Brik, "some say they were never so bored, others, they have never had such a good time."

XIV

Not only had Mayakovsky's audiences changed, but also his critics and the way they criticized. Formerly, a general laziness and conservatism had to be fought. Opposition was based on taste and habit, opponents sneered or ignored. But now opposition was based on "principles," and its aim was power and control. All artists were organized in groups, the groups fought one another viciously, and influenced the public. It was a natural development of Marxist aesthetics;

and Mayakovsky himself, with his dogmatic views and extravagant intolerance, was to a degree responsible for the new situation. But Mayakovsky was never petty; he lived for what he loved, and spoke what he believed. Now literary discussions had degenerated into squabbles. On the one hand, he was taken to task for being "difficult"—the Futurist label still clung to him; on the other, for having turned from poet to hack—his very popularity was held against him. To the first type of critic he had alluded in *About What? About This;* of the second, he wrote in *I Myself:*

1926
In my work I am consciously becoming a newspaperman. Feuilletons, slogans. Poets badger me but can't do newspaper stuff themselves, for the most part getting their stuff published in irresponsible supplements. To me their lyrical trash is funny, it's so easy to write like that and it interests no one save the spouse.

Unsuccessfully he tried to restore these squabbles to a plane of intellectual integrity. Three times he changed the policy of LEF in accordance with what he considered to be legitimate demands made on art by a changing society: in 1926, abandoning an "outworn" revolutionary Futurism for a "socially constructive" program, LEF became "The New LEF"; in 1929, in a further move from "aestheticism" to "communism," it was changed to REF; finally, in 1930, REF joined RAPP. The controversies were as logical, and as trivial, as those of medieval scholastics. But they involved tragedy. Enemies were made, talent was crushed by men with no genuine interest in art but a desire to dominate, and even friends fell out with one another in an atmosphere of acrimony and hairsplitting. "We began to quarrel easily," wrote Shklovsky of this period, "and to make up with difficulty. For mere nothings I quarrelled with L. Brik. When a man is weak, or a movement is coming to an end, death requires but a trifling pretext." And there are always small men on hand to needle those of greater stature. At a literary gathering, a neurasthenic youth says casually to Mayakovsky:

"Mayakovsky, history shows that all good poets came to bad ends; either they were killed, or they themselves . . . So, when will you shoot yourself?" Mayakovsky, with a shudder of disgust, replies slowly: "If fools ask me about this often enough, I had indeed better shoot myself."

Mayakovsky was not well. For some three years his throat had bothered him. On November 26, 1926, he had written Lila Brik:

I travel like mad. Have already read in Voronezh, Rostov, Taganrog, again in Rostov, Novocherkask and again in Rostov. Now I am in Krasnodar. This evening I'll be not reading, but croaking. I beg the sponsors not to take me to Novorossiysk, but the sponsors beg me to go in addition to Stavropol. Reading is a bit hard. I read every day. For example, Saturday I read in Novocherkask at night from 8:30 to 12:45; they asked me to appear again at 8:00 A.M. at the University and at 10:00 at the Cavalry Regiment. That I had to refuse, because at 10 I went to Rostov and read in the RAPP from 1:30 to 4:50, and already at 5:30 at the Lenin shops, with no possibility of refusing: it was for workers and without pay!

Early in September 1927 three of his engagements were canceled, because he had had an attack of grippe; one again in November, several in February, March, and April 1928, when he was confined to bed for about a month. In January 1929 five engagements were canceled. Mayakovsky was afraid he might be losing his voice. "I can't go on without my voice," he would say. Doctors told him he was nervously exhausted and advised a six months' rest.

On December 30, 1929, his friends gave him a party in honor of the exhibit he had organized, "Twenty Years of Work," which was about to open. They decorated his apartment, acted out charades of his poems, begged him to recite. But Mayakovsky was gloomy; contrary to his wont he would not be persuaded, until at last, late at night, he recited an early poem of his about a horse that falls on a slippery street and is surrounded by a jeering crowd. Mayakovsky helps it up, consoles it: "Don't cry," he says, "we are all of us, in a way, horses," and the horse trots off happily, feeling itself a child again. Had any of his friends heard at this time what Shklovsky reported later: "He used to say" that "horses, not being endowed with the gift of words, never explain themselves, do not define their attitudes, and for this reason are not given to suicide"? Now, as his friends applauded, "All this is old," he said, "old! I am sick of it. But there are new verses clambering out of me. . . . A real poem! You'll see —The best I've written," and he went into another room, where for a long while he stood leaning on a bureau, holding an unfinished glass of tea. "There was something helpless, solitary, poignant in him, that no one as yet understood," writes his friend Kassil'.

Two months later, at the opening of the exhibit, Mayakovsky read his new poem, "At the Top of My Voice," the beginning of a long work he did not finish, and of which nothing is known except that it was to have had a second prologue of a "lyrical" nature. It is addressed to "posterity," because, he said, being "a determined man," he did not wish to wait for what critics in the future would say about him but wanted "to talk to posterity" himself. It is his last estimate of himself, and there is a majesty in it that recalls Pushkin's "Monument":

> My verse shall come to you over the crests of ages,
> Over the heads of poets and of states—
> Not as an arrow, though,
> > > in lyrical love hunt,
> Nor as a rubbed out coin reaches a numismatic's lot,
> And not as light of perished stars arrives.
> The labor of my verse
> > will tear
> > > the mass of years,
> And will appear
> > crude,
> > > visible,
> > > > and weighty,
> As down to us,
> > those aqueducts have come
> That slaves of Rome
> > built centuries ago.

The exhibition took up several large rooms, filled with Mayakovsky's books and posters. But on the opening night, no one had been delegated to introduce him, and hardly a poet came to hear him. On March 25, Mayakovsky spoke at the exhibit:

I have labored all my life, but not to make pretty little things and to caress men's ears. And somehow matters have always turned out in such a way as to create unpleasantness for everybody. My basic work is to curse and ridicule whatever seems wrong to me and twenty years of my literary work have been in large part—to put it in plain language—a literary face punching, not in the literal, but in the best sense of the word!

He talked about his purpose and explained his reasons for organizing the exhibit. Toward the end he remarked:

I have come to you today quite ill. I don't know what's happening to my throat. I may have to stop reading aloud for a long time. Today may be one of my last evenings.

The magazine *Press and Revolution* informed Mayakovsky that its next issue would have a portrait of him and an editorial greeting. But on the ninth of April, a delegation arrived with excuses: the editor had ordered the portrait and greeting torn out of the already printed copies. "Trifles," Shklovsky remarks about this incident, "but an army of infantry may not march in step over a steel bridge." On the tenth of April Mayakovsky agreed to speak on the fifteenth and again on the nineteenth. On the eleventh, at a gathering where he was scheduled to speak, he did not appear, and telephoned to excuse himself on grounds of illness. On the twelfth he attended two meetings, one in the morning and one in the afternoon; and on the thirteenth had a telephone conversation about a proposed trip to Leningrad together with other writers. The next morning, April 14, there was to be a business meeting in his apartment. But at 10:15 he shot himself. The message that he left, addressed "To Everybody" was dated April 12. It read in part:

Blame no one for my death, and please don't gossip. The deceased disliked that awfully.

Mama, sisters and comrades—forgive me—it's not the right way. (I don't recommend it to others)—but I have no way out. Lila—love me.

Comrade government, my family is Lila Brik, mama, my sisters, and Veronica Vitol'dovna Polonskaya.

If you arrange a decent life for them—thanks.

The verses I began please give the Briks; they will understand.

The verses were:

> It is past one
> > and you must be in bed.
> The milky way,
> > a silver Oka,
> > > lies upon the night.
> I am in no haste,
> > and with a wire's flash
> There is no need
> > to wake and trouble you.
> As they say,
> > the incident is closed,
> The love-boat
> > has crashed upon day-to-day life.
> With you
> > we have settled accounts
> > > and need not rehearse
> Mutual sorrows,
> > offenses,
> > > and hurts.
> So long,
> > Vladimir Mayakovsky.

> Comrades of VAPP,* don't think me cowardly.
> Seriously—there is nothing to be done.
> > Greetings.
> Tell Ermilov, it's too bad he removed the slogan: We
> should have fought it out.
> > V.M.

* All-Union Association of Proletarian Writers, not RAPP, Russian Association of Proletarian Writers.

In my table there are 2000 rubles; send them in for taxes.
The rest you will get from Giz [that is, The Government
                                        Publishing House].
                                        V.M.

There were also some unfinished verses in a notebook:

Behold, beloved, what silence in the world.
Night has banked heaven with a gift of stars
In hours like these one grows, and talks to all creation,
    to centuries, and history.

And next to them:

The sea's receding,
The sea is sleeping,

in which there is a play on words:

"receding"—*v spyat'*
"sleeping"—*spat'*.

The slogan removed by Ermilov was, among others, in the
theater where *The Bath House* was being performed. Obviously Mayakovsky did not want it thought that he bore a
grudge or had lost the will to fight. Why did he kill himself? There had, of course, been disappointments. "Like
Pushkin before his wedding," writes Shklovsky, "Mayakovsky sought ordinary ways to happiness: made the acquaintance of young dramatists, watched how they lived," tried to
find friends in RAPP, hoped for a woman's love. He had not
found the happiness he sought: the young dramatists talked
another language, the women he loved did not love him, he
had enemies whose criticism amounted to persecution, and
he was ill. It is not difficult, in short, to reckon up the circumstances and occasions, the shoals on which his life had
crashed, but they are not the current that had driven it.
Certainly it is absurd to think, as some have done, that he
"died for love" in the sentimentally romantic sense. The
"love-boat" was he himself, not a love affair. "Men are boats,"
he had written in his poem on Lenin, using a metaphor in-

spired perhaps by Rimbaud's *Le Bateau Ivre;* he himself was a vessel of earthly and human love, and the current of his complex nature had carried the boat to its logical doom. The "real reason," of course, can never be fully known. But one cannot help noting the obsession with suicide that recurs persistently in his work. He was lured by the idea, and his eloquent denunciations of it may be due to the power of its attraction for him. This is what prompted Pasternak to speak of "that pedantry with which the will sometimes follows a road known to be inevitable." Roman Jakobson, in tracing this suicidal obsession, has pointed out that a painful sense of the difference between the *I* and the *non-I* can be detected throughout his work. And indeed much of his poetry, as well as the conscious effort of his entire life, can be seen as an attempt to get the better of this experience of estrangement.

X V

At the end he must have realized that his loneliness was irremediable, and he died, as he had lived, with a grim joke about himself and a word of explanation that explained nothing. There is no more tragic poet than he in Russian literature, and it will not do to hold society, nor even individuals, responsible for his tragedy; it was not by his world, but by himself that he felt oppressed, and it is difficult to imagine any external circumstances that would have brought him happiness. He was endowed with a violence of passion that can be neither satisfied nor subdued, that both sues for sympathy and rejects it, that sees the world as too small for it, and strives perpetually to transcend the limitations by which it feels itself hemmed in. He felt himself enormous and unnecessary, and turning self-pity to defiance, forestalled sympathy by mocking both himself and others. He craved the dominance of martyrdom, and forced his mind to submit to the dictates of a scheme that claimed all his loyalty. "What would you do," he once asked Aseyev, "if the state decreed that all poetry must be written in iambs?" "I simply couldn't," said Aseyev. "Well, I," retorted Mayakovsky, "I would write in iambs."

Even his earliest, impudent and boastful poems express desolation. "I go and solitary weep that crossroads crucify policemen" may look like surrealist fun, but in the context, where the poet's "trampled soul" is a pavement on which "the soles of madmen stamp the prints of rude, crude words" and "the crooked necks" of city towers "have grown cold" in a "cloud's noose," it becomes an image of helplessness. Cities hang, their guardians crucified, the poet's soul is in shreds, "the rags of a torn cloud in a burnt-out sky," caught "on the rusty cross of a belfry"; and he is "solitary, like the last eye of a man on his way to the blind." In a later poem, called "Cheap Sale," he will trade, he says, all that his soul rules over—and its riches are immeasurable—his immortality itself, and all the splendor in which eternity will clothe him, for one kind, human word. And elsewhere he calls himself an ostrich trying to hide its head in the feathers of stanzas, rhymes, and meters. There is a terrible, naked honesty in verses such as this; if they seem fantastic, it is because suffering has twisted reality into images of horror.

Of all Russian writers, Gogol was the favorite of his youth. He must have sensed in him his own variety of loneliness, the kind that turned what was not himself into the monstrous, the cruel, and the alien. Like Gogol, he was a humorist, but it can be as truthfully said of him as of Gogol that those who think him funny do not know how to read him. Gogol's laughter, as he himself explained, was the product of despair; he escaped from depression into an imaginary world of absurdity, but he never proclaimed his misery so openly as Mayakovsky, for he had accepted his alienation to this extent at least, that he had no desire to exhibit it. Mayakovsky, on the other hand, instead of fleeing to a never-never land, caricatured his own experience. He remained the central figure of his tragic work, instead of obliterating himself in fantastic tales as Gogol had done. For since he had never fully accepted the difference between the *I* and the *non-I*, he wanted to explain himself and to unite himself to the world of men and things. There is, of course, this all-important difference between them, that whereas at the heart of Gogol's unhappiness lay a sense of loss and inadequacy, Mayakovsky's self-pity was based on a feeling of power, of an insufficiently appreciated grandeur. His tragedy had in it an element of paradox; it was the inarticulateness of the outspoken, the tragedy of those who seek to relieve pain by trying to explain it, although they know that pain is incommunicable and that when it is past cure, no one can be of help. A cry of pain is without purpose; and much of Mayakovsky's best work is in essence such a cry, disguised though it is as rational protest.

He was not clear about himself, and was a mixture of honesty and falsehood, of imperious willfulness and dependence, of freedom and enslavement. Yet, consciously, he was nothing if not honest. His denunciations of society, of art, of morals and ideas were rooted in a loathing of pretense. It was honesty that made him blunt: the world was crude and ugly, his own experience was bitter; he despised artists who insisted on sweetness, and hated all men who loved comfort of body and ease of mind. There was much in him of the nineteenth-century Russian nihilists, of Turgenev's Bazarov. But he was not so independent as they. He needed people not only for approval but for self-realization, and belonged to the type of rebel whom Albert Camus has called the Dandy, the man who does not know that he exists unless others can serve him as mirrors, who "acts his life, because he is incapable of living," for whom "to be alone is equivalent to being nothing," and who is always obliged to astonish others by negating their values, for he can define himself only by means of opposition. A desperate relationship is set up between the Dandy and his public. He demands approval and rejects it at one and the same time; he pleads and he abuses; he declares his love of men but holds them at arm's length. If he is a Rimbaud, his solitude becomes a habit, his scorn of men a principle of integration and a way of life. He has needed an audience up to a point only; he can, when he wishes, step off the boards and lead another kind of life. In a gesture of supreme mockery, he becomes what he despises. But Mayakovsky was always on stage, unable to retire; and all who knew him seem to have been struck by something profoundly discordant between the man himself and his appearance in public: the yellow blouse and the gesture of bravado concealed something they did not understand; the jester's role hinted at tragedy but deterred one from taking the tragic mask seriously. Boris Pasternak remarked that not content with taking one role, Mayakovsky acted the whole of life and with such careless disdain that his performance was terrifying, and Roman Jakobson has called his poetry "a scenario according to which he acted out the film of his life." The episodes of this scenario are well defined: childhood in Georgia and the revolution of 1905; Moscow, with Party work and jail; the beginning of poetry; the "Golgotha" of the Futurist tour; first love; World War; Lila Brik; Revolution; NEP; trips abroad; the death of Lenin; lecture tours, illness, suicide. But both scenario and life were built on a process of mystification, that "playing with reality" which Boris Eichenbaum has shown to be the essence of Gogol's work. When Mayakovsky pictured himself as Man or Poet, as the martyred savior of humanity, or as the sun's comrade, he was indulging in a kind of solemn, baffling joke on the order of his other grotesques: the gruesome images of the bleeding world in *War and the Universe,* the huge fantasy of warring objects and the duel of giants in *150,000,000,* the pictorial caricature of history and religion in *Mystery-Bouffe.* All are exaggerations intended to teach a lesson. As pictures they are unambiguous; all is black and white in them, there are no complexities here, there is no shading. But they are jokes. And the theatrical pose was a similarly jesting riddle: on the one hand, a dramatic caricature that told others what they were to think of him, and on the other, a mask that saved him from the necessity of introspection and fooled him into believing that he knew himself. Whatever the motive—pride, vanity, or despair—this necessity to conceal lay at the heart of his work, although it appeared in the semblance of self-exposure.

Negation was the principle of Mayakovsky's life; and parody, which is a form of negation, was something more with him than a favorite trick of art. It was an ingrained habit of thought. His image of himself as a tragic hero was really a parody of the traditional concept of tragedy. From his point of view neither *hubris* nor *hamartia* was involved in his situation. Cruelly created to be man by a non-beneficent and nonexistent god, he was a representative of the human condition, the flaw in which was due to God, not man; man could not sin through pride, since no moral sanction was higher than his own, and the deadliest sin, therefore, was not pride but an absence of it, not a challenge of divinity but the relinquishment of effort and ambition to challenge. In his tragic role Mayakovsky was defiant and self-sufficient. He passed judgment on himself, annihilated death, and talked to posterity. But he parodied even his own idea of tragedy when, attempting to achieve something like comic catharsis, he burlesqued his suffering and presented himself as a kind of *miles gloriosus,* simulating absurdly the attributes of gods or nature. He did not manage to obtain what he desired; his performance was gravely earnest, even at its most preposterous; if he "stepped on the throat of his own song" he could not stamp it out, and his ultimate parody of artistic revelation lies in the doubt with which he leaves us as to how much of his clowning he intended to be taken seriously.

Ridicule absolved him of cosmic terror, and his anthropomorphism took rise in the opposite feeling from that which is usually presumed to motivate it. Usually, it would seem, the darker, the less explicable, the more awful an asspect of nature, the more does man seek to humanize it, wishing to diminish his fear of the incomprehensible by seeing it as human. But Mayakovsky's anthropomorphism is either a kind of camaraderie in which man fraternizes with nature, animals, and things, or a ghoulish force that turns what is perfectly familiar into something ominous and sinister. In his use of the pathetic fallacy, it is not nature that responds to man's experience, but man who sympathizes with nature—since in his view of life man is all-encompassing and nature is part of him, not he of nature. When he wishes to present whatever seems to transcend men's limitations—greater powers, greater achievements than theirs—he neither elevates the human being to the rank of deity nor invests him with supernatural qualities but, in a way that parodies heroic myth, extends men's capacities within the realm of nature and confers earthly status on the superhuman: the stars and planets are his brothers, the universe is an animal, the soul wears a dressing gown, Christ is not God but the Most Ordinary Man; but the future is a place into which man can fly as easily as he can cross the ocean or divert the course of a river; and the completely human Lenin is in himself an era.

And yet, although negation was the heart of Mayakovsky's thought, he was not a Satanist of the romantic school who loved denial for its own sake. He loathed assent and had an imperative need to assert himself through contradiction, but his negation was not absolute, not like Rimbaud's, for instance. It was provoked by a respect for justice, and was aimed not so much at a transvaluation of values as at a redefinition of men's attitudes. He plotted, denounced, and blasphemed in the name of right, truth, and independence. Like Rimbaud, he wished to turn habitual concepts upside down, to shock men out of complacency; the stance of opposition was in itself important to him, and he delighted in blasphemy. But the blasphemy of *Une Saison en Enfer* has a suave elegance that Mayakovsky's lacks, for it is the witty statement of a personal experience, of one man's conclusions about human history and human ideals, whereas the parody of Christ and the Beatitudes in *Mystery-Bouffe*, for example, or the conclusion of *The Cloud in Trousers*, or the sketch of heaven in *About What? About This* are didactic, and purposefully grotesque, for they are tools in an ideological battle, not private visions. Mayakovsky and Rimbaud were kindred spirits, but in their most intimate experience they were each other's opposites. Rimbaud thought himself endowed with superhuman qualities which, being man, he was doomed to lose; from his idealistic heights he must come down to earth:

> Moi! moi qui me suis dit mage ou ange,
> dispensé de toute morale, je suis rendu
> au sol, avec un devoir à chercher, et la
> realité rugueuse à étreindre! Paysan!

Mayakovsky, on the other hand, who held that there was nothing greater than to be simply man, felt in himself angelic qualities and powers that transcended the earth. He might have paraphrased Rimbaud as follows:

> Moi! moi qui me suis dit homme et laboureur,
> privé de tout bien-être, je suis rendu au ciel,
> avec un rêve à chercher, et un infini, calme
> et doux, à traverser! Ange!

Rimbaud's negation was absolute, because it came of an embittered sense of loss; Mayakovsky's was a tentative first step on his way to the grand affirmation of a universal Utopia.

His art was public through and through: in purpose, form, even in process of composition. He seldom composed pencil in hand, but was always at work. Once his sister ran into him on the street; he waved her off: "Don't interrupt me. I am writing." And once when someone asked him how he worked: "It's this way," he said, "I walk along. And all of a sudden a big desk appears in the air before me. I sit down at it, and start writing." Korney Chukovsky, whom he visited in Kuokala when he was composing *The Cloud in Trousers,* has described him at work: "He would sometimes stop, light a cigarette, sink in thought. Sometimes he'd gallop off as if storm driven, leaping from stone to stone; but most often he walked along like a lunatic, with an uneven stride, spreading wide his enormous legs . . . and never for a moment stopped talking to himself in a concentrated, quiet conversation." Once a poor peasant was terrified into frantic flight, when he saw this creature marching toward

him over the dunes. Not only, that is, did Mayakovsky write
for the street, he wrote in the street; and his verse swings to
the rhythm of his stride and bears the accent of his heavy
step and the casualness of informal meetings. Loud, determined, staccato, beating with the pulse of the day, there is
no intimacy in it, nothing of that "inner life" that Mayakovsky seems to have denied himself for the sake of an audience
of which he was always aware. Powerful and defiant, he
believed himself free, but he never could or would have
said, like Beethoven about his quartets, that he was writing
for himself. If he dreamed, he paid no attention to his
dreams. Even his surrealist effects were consciously contrived; nothing welled up unasked from the unconscious,
and his visions of the future give the impression of having
come not of insight, but of fantastic desire. When from
painting the real he passed to the imaginary, he refused
to note the transition or admit the irrationality of his visions.
Just as he himself had become indistinguishable from the
part he had undertaken to play, so hyperbole, which he had
originally adopted as an artistic device, came to stand in his
mind for reality. His will was stronger than his judgment. His
thought was as rhetorical as his style; his poetry, his life,
and his reasoning were passionate and narrow. An immod-
erate and violent man, he had no capacity for analysis or
detachment; he did not criticize, he damned; he did not
love, but worshiped; he could hate and despise, but not dislike. He was intransigent in his opinions, and as uncompromising in his relations with himself as with others. He
made his reason fight unhappiness and his public voice
shout down the private one. If he confused the two, mistaking ventriloquism for his own speech, and, at the last,
was stifled by the heroic puppet that masked the man in
him, he did not know it. His work was a process of willful
exclusion, and it is strong by reason of its passion, not its
wisdom. Sometimes it seems the poetry of a nihilist Beethoven, without Beethoven's melody or lightness, but with his
power to record the grandeur of rebellious suffering. And
sometimes it reminds one of those primitive sculptures, massive and rough, that seem to express the anguish of a child

helplessly possessed by an overwhelming emotion. His self-analyses indicate a struggle between a sense of his own greatness and his desire to be at one with the masses of men. But he has nothing of that large, generous ease, that undiscriminating joy in life which Whitman makes a virtue and the basis of his love of men. Mayakovsky is all tension, striving, willing. He is united with humanity not in feeling, but on principle. The principle is the magnet of his vigorous emotions, and it is therefore passionately argued. A megalomaniac image is made to express the nature of humanity. It was as if a Russian Rimbaud had tried to make himself the Whitman of the proletarian revolution.

It is an indication of Mayakovsky's complex and paradoxical nature that he should have combined the characteristics of two such opposite souls as Walt Whitman and Rimbaud. He knew neither English nor French, but Burluik introduced him to Rimbaud and Chukovsky to Whitman, whom he was translating; and such was Mayakovsky's feeling for language that he could grasp the texture of even a foreign poet's speech. He offered Chukovsky, for example, valuable suggestions for his Whitman. His own poetry often reminds one of Whitman's. Like his, it is made to be spoken and has a similar loose, oratorical structure, the long line, the marked, emphatic beat, the calculated crudeness, and there are passages in it which unmistakably echo Whitman. But Whitman's long rhythms are Biblical; Mayakovsky's re-create the cadence of his own steps. Whitman's praise of man, his exultation in the body, his love of humankind must certainly have appealed to Mayakovsky. Yet in 150,000,000 he pictures him derisively as "rocking a cradle in imperceptible rhythm" and bearing the highest title which Americans bestow on a poet, "honored smoother of ladies' wrinkles." He was too much of a rebel to tolerate Whitman's open-hearted geniality. Never could he have been a Good Gray Poet; and even if like Whitman he loved things and men in the abstract, his feeling for them was not exactly comradely; his pride in them and in himself was too involved in suffering to be joyous; the violence of his love resembled hatred. In his rebelliousness he was closer to Rimbaud.

But his was a primal, Promethean revolt that took place in the void and was itself a kind of parody. There was no Zeus for him to defy, and, unlike Rimbaud, he had never believed in the God whom he addressed. His blasphemy was, in effect, denunciation of men's folly and a cry of resentment for his own suffering. He addressed himself to a nothingness, a cosmic injustice that had once been given a name, and which men worshiped as good—and he pitied men for adoring this embodiment of tyranny, and, wanting to cure them of error and to lead them out of torment, courted them in the dual capacity of martyr and jester; if they wished, he would dance for their amusement, or, like Gorky's Danko, would give them his heart as a banner. It was as if, oppressed by his immensity, he could be at ease only on the stage, where he tried to make himself intelligible by pretending to be grotesque. There he had postured, a lonely giant, unconscious of the irony that made the role he played more tragic than he realized. He addressed himself to large crowds, talked to the masses in their own language, all Russia knew him. Yet these people were not his real audience. The real one he invented, imaginatively transforming the men before him into a concept of Humanity. And even as he served the needs of the moment among actual people in a given place, he was shouting to the future through the void of his crowded auditoriums. He neither saw nor knew the men for whom he wished to sacrifice himself. It was as if through some impossible metamorphosis Prometheus had become Narcissus; instead of bringing men fire, Mayakovsky was himself consumed, and what he saw before him was not, as he thought, the men he had endowed with their most precious possession, but his own flaming image.

He had made himself all will, and gloried in self-immolation; and there is a dreadful logic in his progress up to his final assertion of supreme self-mastery and freedom, when, having assembled his life work for all to see, he died at thirty-seven, at the same age as Pushkin, and also in a kind of duel. He had managed by means of enormous labor—it was labor he boasted of, not inspiration—to create a Socialist Art. He was proud of it, and like the god of the Deists, having done his work and seen that it was good, retreated from it, sure of its survival.

As artist, Mayakovsky was the opposite of the Shakespeare once described by Coleridge as one who "first studied patiently, meditated deeply, understood minutely, till knowledge, become habitual and intuitive, wedded itself to his habitual feelings." Mayakovsky had respect for neither meditation nor patience. Instead of study and minute understanding, he pounced on events and molded them in the roughly hewn formulas of reason-masked prejudice. Nevertheless, his loud rhetoric, inflated imagery, propagandist simplifications, his broken rhythms and brutal words achieve aesthetic wholeness, because they contain in themselves their reason for being. There is grandeur in them, and the strength of immediacy, the sense, that is, of something lived, not borrowed from talk about life. They express the upheaval, willfulness, and negation which are the mark of his day; and neither the bold, bright way he used the language of the street, nor the raw agony of his impassioned love, nor his crude but pointed wit are likely to be soon forgotten.

His limitations are the limitations of the revolutionary temper, and more than a revolutionist Mayakovsky never claimed nor desired to be. When from rebel he passed to revolutionary, he changed from outlaw to architect, acquired, that is, a plan for action and a social purpose. But a revolutionary can have no truck with either sentiment or metaphysics. Mayakovsky could not have accepted that "anguish" and "absurdity" which Existentialists have announced to be man's "condition." The revolutionary deals briefly with such matters: he cuts the Gordian knot of man's predicament, and gives the rope to the hangman. He may discover that he cannot jump out of his heart, but he also knows that it is in his power to make the heart stop beating. This assumption of a defiant fortitude compels him to the greatest effort of which he is capable, and making a virtue of extreme positions, leads to fanaticism and martyrdom. There is hardly a better example of it than the achievement of Vladimir Mayakovsky and his real tragedy, which he himself, its blind protagonist, could understand but dimly.

4

LEONID LEONOV

(1899-   )

In 1932 an article on Leonov in the Soviet Encyclopedia
spoke disparagingly of his early work as having been "abstract" in the manner of the Symbolists and influenced by
Dostoevsky, and congratulated him on having "surmounted"
Dostoevsky. Leonov, then thirty-three years old, had been
publishing for about ten years. He had begun with short
stories; had written a play, *Untilovsk,* and four novels,
The Badgers, The Thief, Sot' (translated as *Soviet River*),
and *Skutarevsky,* which had brought him to the attention of
the public and elicited the praise of Gorky, who declared
that the writing of this very gifted young man would one day
merit "serious study," if he abandoned his "aestheticism"
and turned his vigorous prose to good account.

Leonov's earliest work was not social-minded. His stories were stylistic experiments, inspired by a purely literary interest. Some were fairy tales, "Buriga," "The Wooden Queen," "The Jack of Diamonds," "Valya's Doll," in which woodland sprites or playthings figured as main characters; others were essays in various forms: in the uncanny and the grotesquely humorous, "Egorushka's Destruction" and "An Incident with Jacob Pichunk"; in the Biblical parable and the Oriental prose poem, "Ham's Departure," "Khalil," "Tuatamur"; in pathos, "The End of an Insignificant Man," "Petushikhin Notch"; in satire, "A Record of Certain Episodes Made in the Town of Gogulev by Andrey Petrovich Kovyakin." All were derivative; manifestly Leonov was "playing the sedulous ape," copying E.T.A. Hoffmann, Remizov, Blok, Leskov, Gogol, Dostoevsky, Gorky. Endowed with an unusually acquisitive ear, he enjoyed making the most of his verbal facility, mastering dialects —including Tartar for the sake of "Tuatamur"—steeping himself in all manner of rhythmic prose; interested, in short, in making himself a writer. He gives the impression of one for whom the activity—one is tempted to say the game—of writing was, initially, more important than any theme, much less any "message." No personal experience, no belief compelled him. He tried out subjects and styles, was dexterous in playing with artistic effects; but since he was a man of neither passion nor conviction, his work, unlike Blok's, Mayakovsky's, Pasternak's, even Gorky's and Sholokhov's, was the work of a follower, not a leader.

The stories with which he began were semiserious, gently tender, romantically pathetic. And there was implicit in them a teasing, insoluble comparison between the artificial and the real, between the game and actual being, between toys or fairy-tale creatures and real men and women. When the black chessboard queen becomes a woman with whom a chess player falls in love and then turns out to be the bride of his best friend, "Even in chess," he remarks, "as I have long since felt, the kind of situation must exist in which a woman is unfaithful only for the sake of unfaithfulness, a situation in which there is mystery and all kinds of magic."

A fancy such as this, on the borderline between the dream and actuality, is the kind that Blok and the Symbolists were using to express their most intimately evanescent, their most complicated experiences. In Leonov's hands it turns to sentimentality and triteness; and the manner in which a potentially original and personal theme is here made platitudinous is indicative of a characteristic duality of Leonov's mind: fascination with excursions into unknown realms on the one hand, and desire for comfort on the other. Leonov was affected by the atmosphere of experimentation which prevailed when he started to write, just as later he was to fall in with another dominant tendency. But his experiments were differently motivated from those of the introspective Symbolists, or of such speculative novelists as Pilnyak and Olësha, or even of such limelight seekers as Mayakovsky. There was less boldness in him, a kind of cautious effacement of personality, an unwillingness to cultivate whatever capacity for individual experience he might have had. From the first, he seems eager to use his unquestionable cleverness not to impose himself but to get a hearing, and without being natively devoid of distinctiveness and intensity, chooses to suppress the one and to dilute the other.

He was published in experimental journals—*Shipovnik, Literaturnaya Misl', Krug, Russkiy Sovremennik;* in a literary quarrel with Vakhtangov, he defended what was later scornfully referred to as "personal psychologism"; and when in 1927 he was asked by an interviewer: "Whose method, among classical writers, do you consider most appropriate for depicting our contemporary world?" he answered, "F.M. Dostoevsky's, given sufficient strength and understanding." Three years later, however, on a similar occasion, he replied that although he himself had learned most from Dostoevsky, "by the irony of fate" he had "flunked" because of him. Dostoevsky's psychological analysis was "static," he had decided, not suitable for describing the contemporary world, and his style was "long drawn out, verbose." Between these two opinions had come friendship with and encouragement from Gorky, and the publication of the Dostoevskian novel which had "flunked" him, *The Thief.* Now his consciousness became a battleground on which Dostoevsky and Gorky fought for his allegiance. Gorky scored an easy victory. For despite his earlier enthusiasm, Dostoevsky had never been firmly entrenched in his mind. It had been Dostoevsky's trappings and gestures that had impressed Leonov, not his essence; and just as from Leskov he had borrowed the form of the *skaz* (i.e., of the extended anecdote, comically related in semiliterate speech) but not that starkness of tragedy which makes Leskov's work powerful, and from Gogol the element of grotesque humor but not his sense of terror, so he had caught Dostoevsky's fascination with complex and abnormal states of mind but nothing of his philosophic depth or psychological imaginativeness.

And yet, however naïve his use of Dostoevsky, he was apparently more deeply stirred by him than by the other writers whom he imitated, for in the works that lean most heavily on Dostoevsky, there is a subjective strain, a touch of intimacy, which has always been rare with Leonov, and which was completely "surmounted," it would seem, under the influence of Gorky and other Soviet commentators. Strongly Dostoevskian was the short story of 1922, "The End of an Insignificant Man." It had to do with a geologist, Likharëv, who, caught in the hard days that followed the Revolution, obliged to endure cold, hunger, illness, and intellectual isolation, becomes involved with a set of "arty" characters, whose pretentious arguments are a cover for mental chaos and the absence of moral principles, and who finds it all but impossible to continue his writing; but having returned to it, Likharëv is persuaded by a demonic hallucination, a "Fop" who visits him during his heart attacks, that his work is of no importance, while the paper it is written on might serve a useful purpose in warming his room. Although the "Fop" is an obvious replica of Ivan Karamazov's bourgeois devil, though he talks and looks and acts like him, and has the same function of belittling a thinker's efforts and forcing him to doubt himself, the scene in which Likharëv burns his manuscript is genuinely moving. So also is another Dostoevskian episode, his sister's death. This occurs at the moment when, at long last, Likharëv has found it possible to resume his work. He is so engrossed in it that when his sick sister calls to him, he selfishly refuses to be interrupted; and she, realizing the situation, stifles her cries of pain and, to spare him the death agony, sends him out on a fictitious errand. He goes, aware of the ruse, but, too cowardly and selfish not to take advantage of it, wanders about the streets until he knows she must have died. Passages such as this indicate that Leonov had a feeling for the intricacies and ironies of Dostoevsky's moral situations, the poignant tragedy of his pathetically isolated men, but more for the Dostoevsky of *Poor Folk* than of the major novels.

In "The End of an Insignificant Man," just as in *Poor Folk*, society forms the background for the pitiful individual. But in *The Badgers*, his first novel, which followed immediately upon this story, Leonov reversed the design and made a social theme its center. He dealt here with one aspect of the establishment of Soviet power, the struggle between city and country, which he represented in the fortunes of two brothers, Simon and Paul Rakleev, who, taken as children from their native village to Moscow, part company there and meet again only at the end of the story. Paul, rebelling against maltreatment at the hands of his employer, runs away to become a factory worker and a Communist; Simon, after a period in the army, returns to the village, ends up as leader of a guerilla band that defies the Bolsheviks, and is in the outcome confronted by his brother, who, transformed into Comrade Anton, has arrived as commander of a punitive expedition. After a hazardous and daring struggle, Simon submits to the new power: the forward-looking Communist city has overcome the backward, recalcitrant country.

Leonov, the son of a village poet who had been exiled to Siberia for some Marxist publications, had embraced bolshevism without question, but the Revolution, which came when he was nineteen, and the civil war seem to have appealed primarily to his love of excitement. In both subject and design, *The Badgers* is a fairly obvious adventure story, while its contrast between city and country is a clever variant on a very popular, an all-pervasive theme in the post-revolutionary period, the difference between past and present, a novel that is entertaining enough, but so dispersed in feeling and idea that it can be neither moving nor convincing. There are stirring bits of writing in it: the history of the village which, in an atmosphere of Gogolian grotesquery, takes one back to its brutal origins in serfdom, the Dickens-like picture of Moscow's ancient commercial quarter, a whole gallery of eccentrics and adventurers. What it lacks is understanding of men. "I've become curious about men," says Comrade Anton toward the end. "Yes, brother, there is more that is incomprehensible than understandable in people. The other day, in fact, it occurred to me: maybe man shouldn't exist at all? If some specimen is no good—away with it. That's simple. But, in this case, you can't say away with it. . . . What's one to do? Man, brother, is a historical necessity." This might have been Leonov himself speaking. He too seems puzzled by and interested in this ununderstandable "historical necessity," called man. But he is equally concerned with the mechanics of making a captivating story out of this "necessity." To achieve this end, he contrives a peculiarly inconsecutive form of narration, with flashbacks, interpolations, disappearances and re-emergences of characters, and evolves something on the order of a disorganized mosaic.

Thus the story begins with Yegor Brikin arriving in his native village and returning to Moscow with the two sons of an impoverished neighbor; it shifts to the boys, and Yegor drops out, to reappear suddenly much later as a deserter from the army. One of the sons, having been briefly shown in Moscow, with an inserted report about his early childhood, is made to run away and, after a fleeting glimpse, is lost sight of again until the very end, when he re-enters with a new name, in time to bring the story to a close. So also with less important figures: Peter Bikhalov, the Moscow grocer's son, emerges once from prison to see his father, then vanishes and pops up again as a Soviet leader after the Revolution; Nastya Sekretova, the girl with whom Simon falls in love, is forgotten after her marriage to another man, and unexpectedly comes into view much later to join the band of outlaws in Simon's village; her friend Katya drops out completely and is but casually mentioned once again as having gone to work in "Gubkom," while Mishka Zhibanda seems to have been invented on purpose to complicate her love story. There is virtuosity in this, but the meaning of the novel does not require such obliquities of plot.

After *The Badgers* came *The Thief*. Its central figure, the passionate Mitka Vekshin, is modeled on Dmitry Karamazov and is, like Raskolnikov, an honest criminal who is ultimately regenerated; the woman he loves, Man'ka Dolomonova, nicknamed Viuga (i.e., blizzard), reminds one of both Grushenka and Nastasya Fillipovna (as well as of the enchantress who inspired Blok's *Snow Mask* and *Faïna*). Manyukin is another Marmeladov, and there are several more minor personages in the tradition of Dostoevsky's insulted and injured. It was noted by Gorky that in this novel one had, as with Dostoevsky, "the elemental riot of instinct," and by others that the idea of the contradictions between the individual and society was basic in the book; that its leading characters were "individualists" and "sufferers" whose suffering "purified" their souls; that all of them were more or less unbalanced and full of reflectiveness, doubt, and inward struggle; and that structurally its main figures, like Dostoevsky's, served as "crooked mirrors" in which the others were reflected, so that they came to play an almost symbolic role, Manyukin standing for the "disintegration of personality," Ageyka for the "descent of the individual to crime," Pchkov for rejection of the world, etc. Today Leonov is spoken of as having been influenced by the "psychologism" of the twenties, and *The Thief* does not appear in the six-volume edition of his collected works. But although *The Thief* is so obviously Dostoevskian that it often reads like a pastiche, Leonov's differences from Dostoevsky are more striking than the similarities. He writes for a different reason; his interests, themes, emphases are all different. The intricate plot of this novel, more intricate than that of *The Badgers*, and more justifiably so, is closer to André Gide's structures than to Dostoevsky's; and its basic theme, which, elaborating the speculations of his early stories, is a musing on how art is related to life, is also Gide's kind of theme, not Dostoevsky's. Like that of *The Counterfeiters* it is developed on two levels: there is the story itself of Mitka Vekshin, the thief, and the story that the writer Firsov writes about him, the "real" events and their literary version proceeding along parallel lines. The characters themselves want to be written about; they take the writer into their confidence and comment on his work both while it is in process and afterwards, while Firsov is more than an observer: he takes part in the action, even, to a degree, manipulates events, and his book about Mitka comes out before Mitka's story is finished. All this creates an atmosphere of mystification, in which a drama of guilt and passion is acted out. The implication is that however close to life the writer may think himself to be, however much involved he may be in it, life itself escapes him. For his involvement is never complete; and with all the influence he may exercise, he is primarily an observer and commentator, not an actor.

But another kind of artist is introduced in this novel, one whose art is not of the intellect but of skill and daring. And so often does Leonov subsequently return to the experience represented by this type of artist that, as one soon realizes, it must be fraught with symbolic import for him, must stand in his mind for some cherished ideal, perhaps the one most intimately cherished of all. Like that moment in Thomas Hardy's *Under the Greenwood Tree,* when the plaintive cry of "the small bird being killed by an owl" pierces the stillness and passes "into the silence without mingling with it," so in *The Thief* there is an incident which, though it has no vital bearing on the plot, remains most memorable and most poignant. This is an episode which concerns Mitka's sister Tanya, who, having been lost for many years, is finally rediscovered as the famous Guella Vel'ton, a daring performer on the trapeze, the chief attraction of a traveling circus. Her act is called *shtrabat* and we are told that it was considered old-fashioned, but Vel'ton had complicated it with hazardous details, and her unaffected grace welded the whole of it into the complete triumph of a youthful, skillful body. . . . Her agility rose to deadly daring that gave *shtrabat* a cruel and terrible beauty.

She had been trained in this work by a pathetic, lonely old clown, part of whose story is given as follows:

At the height of his career he earned his bread with his "little ones." In circus language this is called "strap-turning the mill." Head down, his feet grasping the trapeze, he held the strap in his teeth and slowly unwound his children who hung on it. A rapid drum roll, as at executions, accompanied the fateful moments. In the buzzing shaft of the spotlight the children fluttered about, over the sand, the pitiable tinsel of their wings glistening: butterflies! . . . The calamity was trite, as if invented by a bad author. When the mill was unwound, the piece of strap which is clenched in the teeth, and which had rotted, tore apart, and the butterflies fluttered to the sand. An agitated, uniformed attendant was already running toward them, but the father hung with the bit of strap in his teeth, afraid to understand its sudden lightness.

Tanya also dies in the performance of her act. Before stepping into the arena for what is to be the last time, she says to the old clown—she who is now famous, who is "that night the center of attention, precisely she herself and not the mysterious name of her performance":

"You know, I still haven't got used to the idea that I am a regular circus performer. My whole life seems an attempt to do what is impossible for man to do. I love my work, Pugel, because I know how much labor I put into it when I first started. How I cried when I couldn't do it! . . . Do you remember? . . . Work, when you love it, is jolly; then even failures are jolly."

There follows a description of Tanya beneath the enormous dome, gracefully poised on the trapeze, fastening herself to it in the midst of thunderous applause, her body "yearning to fly."

With quickened consciousness Tanya measured the distance to
that point in the air beyond which the noose would not permit
her to go. A colossal recklessness took possession of the artist as
she glanced at the rows, where like a mountain of vegetables,
human faces lay close together; a terrible fear floated up from
them. The moment split into a thousand particles and they
crumbled into other moments, imperceptible to the mind. Tanya
darted down, and it was as if time had stopped. Then, everyone
saw the light blue, longish body hanging like a faded flower; but
this in no way entered their consciousness. Tanya hung there;
dead, she seemed to be looking at the dead light of the lampion;
the noose had lifted her chin.

This episode appears to be unintentionally symbolic, not of
Leonov's themes but of himself, the only instance in all his
productions when unconscious experience has been permitted to take conscious, artistic form. Just as the pitiful cry
of the unseen bird expressed all Hardy's bitterness at the
tragedy of innocent and helpless creatures and was the most
intense note in his book, although its suggestion of fatal
cruelty was not borne out in the story, so Tanya's death, in
my opinion, strikes the central, deepest note of Leonov's
work, and is emotionally, if not structurally, the climax of
The Thief. In somewhat the same way as the poor, anonymous small bird sums up the core of Hardy's tragic tales,
the irrational and irremediable suffering of inoffensive creatures, and as the leap from a high tower, the sudden fall,
and the moment of vision or dazzling illumination stand in
Dostoevsky's work for passion or a supreme act of will, so
the perilous circus stunt seems to express Leonov—the daring exploit that requires skill and training as well as courage,
an artistic defiance of death, in which a human being attempts to do what is superhuman before a frightened and
fascinated audience. Presently, as the sound of Dostoevsky's
voice recedes to be replaced by Gorky's, this symbol is
metamorphosed into a useful and rational form, suitable for
conveying the message of Socialist Realism.

But Tanya and Pugel are episodic characters, and when
The Thief was published, critical attention was given not to
them but to Mitka. Lunacharsky, among others, found him

a disturbing figure: how was it, he asked, that a man who had served in the Red Army could turn out to be an apolitical, antisocial thief? Later on Leonov explained his hero as representing the erroneous outlook of the bourgeoise. In Mitka, he said, he had

wished to embody the elemental source of human passions and to picture the individual, elemental phenomena of our revolution. Mitka's desires were of the most egotistic kind and having satisfied them, he did not know what else he wanted. It is this that makes for the narrowness of his outlook and his lack of culture. In childhood he had dreamed of chocolate and, thanks to the revolution, he got it; he had dreamed of sleeping in a royal bed and his desire was fulfilled. And then what? It is here that the tragedy of his inward emptiness became manifest, the drama of cultural development. . . . Mitka presents the question of the cultural revolution in a primitive way and expresses it too simply.

But that was in 1930. In 1927 Leonov was still under the influence of classical literature, which, he said, "had given what was best and unforgettable about man, about his faith, his strivings, mistakes, joys and disappointments." "Classical literature," he had said at that time, was "first of all literature about everyman, unattached to temporary circumstances of age, place, nationality, and so on. All these circumstances are but material for the creation of the eternal image of man on earth." It was in terms of this "classical" concept that Leonov had written *The Thief*, and it was precisely this "classical" concept that he was now persuaded to reject. For according to Marxist doctrine, men, far from being independent of such ephemeral factors as time, place, the social class to which they belong and the work they do, are formed by them; there is no "man" in general. And so, four years after he had created his "elemental" Dostoevskian hero, Leonov explained him away as a symbol of the false, "uncultured," egoistic attitudes of the old regime, and from then on saw to it that his novels were optimistic, his heroes "positive," and always shown in relation to their socially useful occupations. He himself became absorbed in the communal work of Soviet writers: he made speeches, attended

meetings, in 1929 was elected chairman of the Writers'
Union; he preached the doctrine of the artist's role as molder
of his society, and tried to practice what he preached. In the
winter of 1927-28, with a correspondent of *Pravda,* he made
a trip to the site of a large construction project in the wilderness of the north. In the spring of 1930 he visited Turkmenia
with the first "writers' brigade." "It is time for the Soviet
writer to transform himself from observer of socialist construction to active participator in it," he declared, and wrote
the novel *Sot'* (*Soviet River*), after the first of these expeditions, and the novelette, *Locusts,* after the second. Both
conformed to the main theme of Soviet literature at the time,
"Socialist Reconstruction."

Soviet River, which was published in 1929, seems to have
inaugurated a whole series of novels about the first five-
year plan, the best known of which are: Marietta Shagin-
ian's *Hydrocentral,* 1931; Gladkov's *Cement,* 1932; Katayev's *Time, Forward!,* 1932. In Leonov's work it represents
a marked change in his ideal of the heroic. The central
figures of his two previous novels were outlaws, and
although it was implied at the end of each story that they
had become integrated members of the new social order, in
neither case was this outcome quite clear or entirely convincing. Leonov, indulging his love of passion, had made
them romantic figures in tales of adventure, a type of
Robin Hood in *The Badgers,* a noble criminal in a kind of
roman policier in *The Thief.* In both works, the contemporary scene of revolution served to set off incidents of violent
love, intrigue, cloak-and-dagger mystery. Now this imaginative riot was made to serve a social purpose: tempestuous,
elemental nature supplanted man's elemental passions. In
Soviet River we are given splendid descriptions of the virgin forests of the North, in *Locusts* of the Southern Asiatic
plains. And from now on floods, fires, plagues rage through
Leonov's pages, while human feelings either degenerate
from passion to sentimentality, or are controlled out of
existence. For now that the days of revolutionary romanticism have gone, that the storm has blown over and the
time for building has come, his heroes are no longer isolated

individuals who try to assert themselves in an alien world.
They too have changed from the chaotic adventurers of an
unsettled epoch to the staunch, upstanding pillars of a new
society.

Such is Uvadyev, the hero of *Soviet River*—a tough-
minded, practical man, respected by everyone and loved
by no one, tactless, brutally direct, laconic, and a thorough
Marxist. "Your Peter the Great," he says to an enthusiast,
"was a mere craftsman, he didn't have the Marxist
approach." "The Soul," he says again, is a "quaint word.
. . . You see, I know what calico, bread, paper, soap are.
. . . I've either made them, or eaten them, or held them
in my hand. . . . I know them by color and by touch. But
the soul, well, I don't know what the soul is at all. What's
it made of? Where is it sold?" He hates the spring, "that
rowdy female, who misbehaves along the roads and whose
voice in the gurgling streams sounds as if she had a cold.
He disliked in general whatever crumbled beneath the
crude trowels of his reason, and if his mind retained the
memory of some little valley in springtime, with dandelion-
sprinkled slopes, he was ashamed of this, the most confused
page" of his life, the page that had been filled with marriage
and romance. He is a determined man, and a lucky one. In
prerevolutionary days, after a year's imprisonment for con-
spiratorial activity, he had returned in better shape than
ever; drafted in the First World War, he carried on Communist propaganda in the army and was not caught, came
out without so much as a scratch, and escaped court-mar-
tial when the empire fell. "He was truly lucky, this obstinate
and quiet man, this dray horse of the revolution." To him is
delegated the management of an ambitious project: the
building of a paper mill in the uncharted expanses of Siberia. To get the work done, he must combat both wild
nature and recalcitrant humanity—superstitious peasants,
stubborn monks, intriguing and unperceptive colleagues—
and he must cope with the swerving and veering of those
responsible for National Planning. "You're not afraid?" he
is asked when he first comes to the forbidding land. "Eyes
frighten one," he answers, "but hands work." And after a

year's arduous and patient struggle, he sits alone on a height above the river, watching the lights go on in the new factory settlement.

A half-hour later wet snow began to cover the man. . . . His shoulders and knees grew white, snow melted on his hands, and still he did not leave, although evening had come. Peering with sharp, dispassionate eyes into the darkness of March, he gazed perhaps on cities that were to rise out of this dizzy waste, and felt in them a flowery breeze playing with a little girl's wavy hair, a little girl whose features were familiar; perhaps all that he saw seemed to him a naïve picture in Katya's ABC, printed on the paper of his manufacture a hundred years hence. . . . But from this spot it was very clear that the face of Sot' was changing and that the people in it, too, had changed.

The imaginary Katya stands, of course, for the Russia of the future, and Uvadyev's meditations remind one of Mayakovsky's dream of a Soviet utopia, a realm of love and peace when struggle has ended. Is there not also here an echo of Pushkin's portrait of the heroic builder of Russia, though now a regal and imperious Peter has become the Marxist "dray horse of the revolution"? The book ends, as Pushkin's "Bronze Horseman" had begun, on the vision of a new Russia emerging from the wilderness.

Obviously, in these days of reconstruction, there was room for heroism but not for heroics, nor for torments of doubt. The heroes of the times were to be quiet men who neither vacillated, nor indulged their moods and feelings, nor dreamed any but realizable dreams. Mayakovsky was telling the miners of Kursk that their names would streak the sky in the smoke of the thousand chimneys which their labor was building, a monument more glorious than poems or statues. And Uvadyev, calm, devoted in his work, with a heart so stout that its "wounds healed faster than a scratch on the hand," is distinguished from his colleagues: the dreamy Favorov, the visionary Potemkin, the kind and loving Zheglov. Although Suzanna, to whom he is attracted, compares him to Pechorin, Lermontov's Byronic hero, he is actually— in his single-mindedness, his disregard of others' feelings, his firm self-control—more like Turgenev's Bazarov. Whether he is meant to be attractive or not is beside the point; he is necessary, and so a hero. This is also true, with variations, of the central figures in Leonov's other novels: of Peter Maronov in *Locusts,* of Matvey Nikolaevich Skutarevsky in the novel that is named for him, of Kurilov in *Road to the Ocean,* of Vikhrov in *The Russian Forest.* Their private lives, what there is of them, have significance only in relation to the part they play as public figures: Skutarevsky as a renowned physicist, Kurilov as a railroad engineer, Vikhrov as professor of forestry in the University of Moscow, and with one exception, they are old or middle-aged, concerned with teaching the young, setting them an example, building a world that is meant for them.

Even the exception, young Peter Maronov, grows up, in the course of what is essentially a *Bildungsroman,* to the Communist conception of ethical maturity. His story, *Locusts,* seems to me to be the watershed of Leonov's productions, his last attempt to deal with anything like psychological complexity. And although it originated as a journalistic enterprise, it is more personal than the others. Peter Maronov is subjectively drawn; his experience, like Tanya's in *The Thief,* strikes one as a mirror of the author's own in a later stage of his development, when fully realized intention has come to seem more praiseworthy than instinctive performance. Tanya's self-forgetfulness and moral strength were instinctive, motivated by an artist's love of art; Maronov's is a conscious achievement that involves a clearly understood reversal of values: the discarding of heroic, romantic individualism in favor of the Marxist doctrine of self-fulfillment in communal effort. Maronov, to begin with, yearns to take part in some vitally important national enterprise. Too young to have had a share in "the holy struggle with which his epoch started," he accompanies to Murmansk his older brother who has fled there in an attempt to recover from an unhappy love affair, and stays until his brother's death in that lonely, glacial region, yearning to write a famous book on an as yet unchosen theme. He then

journeys to Turkmenia—the opposite extreme of Russia—
where, he has been told, there is useful work to be done.
His motives, however, are not altogether selfless, because
there, in the "Russian Cairo," managing vast cotton plan-
tations, is Mazel', he who won away the unforgettable Ida
whose name his brother invoked when he was dying. Peter,
fascinated by this instance of fatal love, wants to see for
himself the irresistible beauty that inspired it. And so it is
really desire for adventure and exoticism that brings him
South. But arriving on the banks of the Amu in a cold driz-
zle, he finds no flowering tamarisks, no phantom rosiness
there, and Ida turns out to be a self-assured, unemotional,
promiscuous woman, for whom the very word "love" is outmoded. "That word," she says, "spells weakness. Therefore,
if I find it necessary, I will have relations, quite simply, with
Akiamov, with Zudin, with you . . . without any torments or lacerations of the heart." Side by side with this disillusionment—and even more important—is the experience
which teaches Maronov to correct his youthful notions of
heroism. He engages in fighting the plagues of locusts by
which Turkmenia is ravaged, a danger very different from
the perils he encountered in the North. There he hunted
bears, traveling far out on the ice, knowing "the hopelessness of thousand-verst stretches of snow"; there "attention
was centered on the self," while here, by contrast, in this
"locust Verdun," the self "crumbles ineffectually." What
Peter learns to appreciate is the silent heroism of men battling disaster. "Come," he says to Mazel', whose cotton he
is helping to save and who had been his brother's friend before becoming his successful rival, "let me show you amazing things—men first of all," men as they are when "they
are working seven times beyond their strength . . . unshaved . . . enraged . . . terrifying." These are the true
heroes, who do what must be done silently, "with clenched
teeth." Maronov returns North a new man, having cast out
the memory of his lovelorn brother, having supplanted subjective cravings with a sense of social obligation, and replaced the image of an all-powerful, tyrannical beauty with

a knowledge of man's power in the face of disaster. In sum, he has shed romantic notions and adopted in their stead what is presumably a realistic view of life.

Leonov's description of the locust plague is more than gifted reporting: it is an impressive paean to the grandeur and poetry of elemental catastrophe. In his scientific recital of the onrushing clouds of devastation, there is something that reminds one of Thomas Mann's account of the onslaught of disease in *The Magic Mountain*. In both instances, exact detail serves an artistic purpose; it is heaped up to create tension, to underscore the tragedy of man challenged by death to a contest that calls forth his utmost effort and all his resources. Leonov's battle, of course, is differently conceived; death does not threaten man immediately but through the source of his livelihood, not individually but in multitudes, and it is conquered by masses of men, whose concerted effort (in accord with Soviet ideology) is bound to be strong enough to meet any threat. Tanya's drooping, light blue figure can no longer be permitted to hang pathetically in the noose of a slight error of judgment, which is more decisive than skill and daring; it must be made to glow with the force of an ideal and rouse onlookers not to pity and terror but to awareness of their capacities and of the greatness of their fellow men.

In *Locusts* Leonov's interest in the doubting, searching mind is discarded once for all. Henceforth his novels do not present mental conflicts, but exhibit "right" and "wrong" attitudes. Like Peter Maronov, Leonov himself seems to have returned from Turkmenia with all problems solved; and now his work, however turbulent the theme, is bathed in the aura of spiritual comfort. No longer do his heroes encounter difficulties within themselves. Skutarevsky, Kurilov, Vikhrov are obliged to deal with envious, ambitious, unprincipled men, but they themselves are pure of heart and sure of mind. And this is eminently true of the war books, whose central characters have the enemy to fight but not themselves. Men of courage, resourcefulness, determination, unselfishness, their merit is not capacity for decision but devotion. Their personal misfortunes redound to their glory, their apparent failures turn to victories. They are, in short, the verbal equivalent of government posters that call for sacrifices in the name of people, land, ideals. Leonov's work becomes filled with examples of stoicism and discussions of heroism. In *The Orchards of Polovchansk,* a play written and produced just before the Second World War, an old man's youngest, and favorite, son, who has been expected home on leave, is reported dead. He had been a frogman, assigned to spy on enemy craft, and had perished in line of duty. What the stunned father finds to say when the message is brought him, is: "He didn't, then, accomplish his mission?" And he is told, by way of consolation, that the task will be completed by others, that his son was not the only one in service. The old man's ways are certainly not the ways of Job, but of Lars Porsena. The same is true of the parents in the war play, *Invasion,* and of their son, who, under the impact of enemy brutality, is transformed from a moral weakling to a hero-martyr, permitting himself to be tortured to death for another's sake.

So also with a whole group of men in *The Taking of Velikoshumsk.* Written in 1944, this novelette deals with an episode in the defeat of the Germans in the Ukraine. Its action centers on an armored tank with its personnel of four men, their adopted kitten, and the general in command. Structurally, it is a counterpart of Leonov's four-act plays, its action clearly divisible into: Act One—Dawn to Dusk of December 21; Act Two—Day and Night of the 22nd; Act Three—Morning of the 23rd; Act Four—Afternoon and Evening of the 23rd. Act One is prologue, Acts Three and Four, epilogue. The main action, concentrated in Act Two, that is, December 22nd, is the day which marks the turning point of the war, so that a single episode is made to represent the entire conflict; the tank, the whole army; and the handful of soldiers, the Russian people united in a supreme effort to repel the enemy; while the heightened tension of each incident is made the summary of each man's life. The acrobat's leap, the ultimate test of skill and courage before the eyes of fascinated onlookers, has now been enlarged to include an entire country. The performer is an ordinary man,

made heroic by the role in which he is cast; and the onlooker is related to him through a feeling other than the
more or less altruistic sympathy of any one human being
for any other. He is no longer detached, but completely involved in an exploit, the outcome of which will determine his
own fate; his position is, in essence, the same as the performer's. As for the performer, he who had been previously
a victim sacrificed to an idle demand for amusement, has
now become a savior; his sacrifice is called for by something more imperative and immediate than the thrill of vicariously experienced jeopardy, and his own motivation
has changed from responsibility to his art to responsibility
to his nation, from pride in skill to love of justice and a
sense of identification with the masses of his countrymen.
The fighters are righting a wrong, moved by the same desire
for retribution which animates the whole land of Russia.

This change of motive and of involvement is due, to be
sure, to a difference of theme. But it also corresponds to a
change in Leonov's position as artist. He himself had been at
first a skilled performer, staking his reputation on a daring
feat to delight an audience. He had now become patriot
and propagandist, performing for the nation, as one of the
nation, interpreting and following the "Social Command."
His most famous productions followed *Locusts* and *Soviet
River*. There was *Skutarevsky*, 1930-1933; *Road to the
Ocean*, 1935; a series of war plays from 1936 to 1943; *The
Taking of Velikoshumsk*, 1944; and lastly his longest novel,
The Russian Forest, 1950-1953. All conform to the formula
of Socialist Realism, "national in content, socialist in form."
All deal with the trials, the hardships, the fortitude, and the
triumph of Russian patriots. All "look into the future," all
end happily, and all are constructed on one basic plot: a
"good" main character; that is, an upright and useful Soviet
citizen, having been obliged to struggle against a "bad"
set of treacherous men—usually foreigners and their allies
among prerevolutionary, disaffected Russians—unmasks their
devious plots, and helps save the country.

In short, they are eminently satisfactory to Soviet officialdom: optimistic, patriotic, and sufficiently detached from

dangerous controversy to insure Leonov's own safety and popularity. What is obviously lacking in them is artistic inspiration and a critical sense of literary values. The most ambitious, *Road to the Ocean* and *The Russian Forest,* are a hodgepodge of history, journalism, adventure and detective story, prophecy of utopia, Marxist propaganda. Leonov's early interest in technical virtuosity shows itself here in structural intricacies and tricks of narrative. For example, in *Road to the Ocean* what is first presented as "reality" becomes mystifyingly a "story"; Leonov himself suddenly walks into his narrative as the friend of his hero, with whom he has long discussions, and some of his remarks are corrected in footnotes by the character he has invented; there are numerous flashbacks, and a good deal of crudely obvious symbolism. The title, *The Russian Forest,* is a pun on the word *L'ess,* which is used in its dual meaning of "woodland" and "scaffolding," so as to signify at once the resources of Russia and her reconstruction after the war—and these in both their spiritual and physical aspects: patriotic youngsters grow up like the strong saplings of the country's great forests to replace the fine old pines that have been cut down, and their labor and patriotic zeal are the scaffolding from which the bombed-out cities are being rebuilt. In a similar figure of speech, the road to the ocean is a highway to the future; the ocean is the space that separates the present from the future, and it is ready for navigation by the intrepid men of Soviet Russia. As for the characters, they are neither types of human qualities nor actual human beings. Intended to be real, they are so studiously employed in waving flags and shouting slogans, or in villainously tripping up those who do, that it is hard to take them seriously.

Among Soviet authors, Leonov stands out for what Gorky called his "strong, clear, juicy" prose, and for his genuine feeling for elemental forces. His writing throbs with the excited sense of the chaotic and destructive violence of nature which stimulates man to incredible exertion. He needs enthusiasm to write, and it is adventure, danger, the utmost straining of nerve and muscle that rouse him to enthusiasm. But he cannot let nature stand alone. Like the medieval theologians for whom gross earth had meaning only as an allegory of the divine—the shining sun signified Jesus Christ, the unplowed field the unregenerate mind of man, and the frisking lambs in spring the happily converted heathen—so Leonov sees swarming locusts as "the enemy," floods and fires as unbridled passion, and the forest as the greatness of Russia's land and people. Nature rages in his novels only that man may subdue it, the Russian man, that is, the good citizen of the U.S.S.R., who conquers it in time of peace as he conquers enemy nations in time of war. Clearly enough, Leonov's predilections jibe with the official demands of the state, and it is unlikely that he has needed to change himself to become accepted; he has simply utilized a native admiration for strenuously won success to both political and literary advantage. Early in his career, his docile, acquisitive mind had welcomed a publicly authorized theory and method; it gave him opportunity to indulge his thirst for knowledge, his verbal facility, and a genially unreflective optimism. Gorky's formula had proffered, in effect, the means of letting the mind rest, while giving it the illusion of discovery. Once the subject was supplied, the method indicated, the feeling ordained—once, in short, Leonov had adopted Socialist Realism—it became his duty to do what he most liked to do: extol great enterprise and the valor of his countrymen, assimilate their modes of speech, and acquire information about their processes of labor. His duties and tastes so happily coinciding, he followed his inclinations and filled his works with narratives of success, portraits of victorious men, and borrowed erudition: disquisitions on lumbering and forestry, on power plants and railroads, with settings and dialects that ranged over the length and breadth of Russia, and a whole gallery of scientists with their stores of specialized knowledge of engineering, surgery, mathematics, theoretical physics—not to mention more recondite fields, such as the history of chronometry. Thus for an understanding of power transmission one might read *Skutarevsky*, for railroad engineering *Road to the Ocean*, for the theory of conserva-

tion and the practice of forestry *The Russian Forest*, and
any novel or play for a lesson in elevated patriotism.

On this basis, Leonov has accomplished now and then
something like *tours de force*, as when in *The Taking of
Velikoshumsk*, he succeeds in endowing an armored tank
with personality and in making it convincingly the hero of
a decisive battle; or as when in *The Russian Forest*, a long,
uninterrupted university lecture becomes the eloquent kernel of an epic tale of war and reconstruction. The latter instance is structurally reminiscent of Dostoevsky. Does not
"The Legend of the Grand Inquisitor" stand in the same
relation to *The Brothers Karamazov* as Vikhrov's lecture
does to *The Russian Forest*? But here, as always with
Leonov, the literary echo is purely stylistic. In substance
and feeling, nothing could be further from Dostoevsky,
or for that matter from any other important Russian writer
of the past, since the one element that most inspired Russian
literature in its great period was precisely that to which
Socialist Realism gives least encouragement and for which
no doctrine can make provision: an interest in human beings in themselves, not only as exemplars of a prescribed
morality, mere ciphers in an ideological ledger, as Leonov's
people always are, even at their most complex—like those
three elder brothers conceived in the womb of Socialist
Realism, Skutarevsky, Kurilov, Vikhrov, with their marked
family resemblance to one another and to their Marxist
progenitors Lenin and Gorky. If it be objected that all
fictional heroes represent ethical ideals, that Pierre Bezukhov and Andrey Bolkonsky, Prince Myshkin and Ivan Karamazov might also be entered in an account book of virtues
and vices, the answer is that these men were not created for
purposes of illustration and that the difference in artistic
method between them and Leonov's creations is like the
difference in logic between induction and deduction. Nowhere in Leonov's novels will one find any revealing comment on the human situation, any subtlety, novelty, or
convincing portraiture. His characters are contrived images
of human beings. At first, wanderers in search of something
they can prize, victims of accident, fate, or circumstance,

dissatisfied or miserable rather than unhappy, uncommitted and uninvolved, engaged in play, fantasy, invention, they entertain, pretend, and cheat; their personalities and opinions clash, but they are incapable of passionate debate, and life flows on somewhere beyond and beside them; then, having been made masters of events, "engineers of human souls," they still remain incomplete, peripheral beings of whom life demands a part of themselves only, making use of their specialties, not of their whole selves. There is not one among them whose action involves the entire man. They are cleverly constructed plaster models of civic virtue, presented not in sympathetic understanding, but through a haze of sentimental kindliness toward suffering, which casts a rosy glow on the horizon. This rosy glow is obligatory; it brightens the foreground, shows life *sub specie utopiae,* makes tragedy impossible.

And yet, through the stereotypes of theme and manner a more personal pattern emerges, the pattern of a romantic admiration for what is individually heroic. The acrobat's fatal act, of course, cannot be meaningful to one who rejects the whole concept of tragedy and does not believe in chance or fate, for whom man himself is fate, tragedy only a sentimental term for weakness, and life is interesting, important, and "true" only when humanity, through supreme ingenuity and effort, wins against tremendous odds. Tanya's leap into the void beneath the dome of a circus tent becomes the aviator's flight into enemy-infested skies or into interstellar space; or it is transformed into the bold experiments of the far-seeing scientist, or the endurance and intrepidity of men and women on perilous missions in wartime. What is man to Leonov? More and more what society wants, or judges him to be, and less and less what he is to himself—a development which is indicative of Leonov's own process of increasing conformity to public demand.

If, however, Leonov is praised in the Soviet Union for his "correctness," is hailed as the "patriot-author," and is held up as an example of one who has been able to overcome the initial error of his views, it must be admitted, in all fairness, that his eminence has been come by honestly. For however

strong his love of popularity, he cannot be called a time
server. His is apparently the more complicated case of a
man who, in need of ready-made dogma, develops, through
ambition coupled with the honest weakness of self-distrust,
a moral sense so resilient and an intelligence so flexible
that the one can adopt astonishing reversals of belief and the
other provide ready justifications for them. There is even
something like logic in his development, a kind of organic
progression from a degree of independence to complete submission. When the critics of his early work, and Gorky most
of all, pointed out the "right," indeed the only acceptable,
direction to him, he followed it eagerly, since he wanted to
be told where to go. His is not, therefore, the story of coercion but of persuasion, operating on a gifted, acquisitive,
adaptable being, as curious about ideas as any literary mind
of Soviet Russia, the quickest to grasp the ins and outs of
scientific enterprises, to catch the forms and intonations of
dialects, and to appreciate all processes of reason—all, that
is, except that of independent thought, of which he has
never been capable. At no time was Leonov's thinking
vigorous and original, nor his disposition rebellious. The in-
quiring attitude and the preoccupation with philosophic
questions, exhibited in his early stories, were soon abandoned in favor of accumulating facts; the possibility of rigorous thinking was relinquished for the easier process of
gathering information; and an inclination to irony, pathos,
and tragedy was replaced by a simple-minded acceptance
of men's feelings and a formula for judging human events.
By no means merely facile, but intelligent and gifted, Leonov
is a very interesting example of talent that lacks independence and needs to lean on well-formulated, officially accepted articles of faith. Nor is it so paradoxical as on the
surface it might seem to be, that the best established of
Soviet "realists" is, at bottom, an aesthete attracted to
schemes of writing rather than to the substance of art.

The truth of the matter seems to be that Leonov is interested in neither people nor ideas, that his major concerns are and always have been dogmatic to a degree, that
this was true even in his early work when he experimented

with forms of narrative in the manner of his favorite authors, and that this has remained true when experiments in propaganda have succeeded experiments in style. In both stages he has been concerned with effectiveness, not with the matter but the manner of discourse. Intellectual and moral questions were early solved for him; he asked, and the answers were given. There had been a brief moment when restless outlawry, perilous amusements, and uncontrollable passion had seemed enchanting to him. But this was soon made purposeful, and a serious social aim reduced artistic intention to frivolity. For seriousness in "realistic" works is impossible when, as in fairy tales, everything must end happily, whatever outcome may be demanded by the logic of characters and events. At the beginning Leonov had been inspired by that which for the artist is the most serious of all frivolities, the essential, gratuitous delight in invention and expressiveness, although in his case the very nature of delight had been dictated by the favored literary mood at the time of his debut. Then, still moved by the desire to be in favor, and under the influence of an aestheticism which confuses art and propaganda and recognizes no other legitimate motive than the will to "serve" the nation by elucidating and inculcating official dogma, he transformed entertainment to usefulness, drowned his art in mistaken patriotism, and diluted his affection for hard-won achievement and his love of exciting adventure to an insipid, childlike optimism.

But if one sees in his work a progressive relinquishment of fantasy, of the personal vision, of independent speculation, if one sees him as having been persuaded by the enticements of a popular philosophy to reverse his views and interests, one is also bound to recognize that what he gave up never constituted that imperative necessity which rules genuine artists. One cannot see him as another Mayakovsky who "stepped on the throat of his own song." Mayakovsky, having had much to lose, was inspired by his very martyrdom to creative vigor. Exalting at the top of his voice the agony of his self-willed repression, he made himself a tragic hero and endowed literature with the eloquent utterance of his pain and his will. But Leonov has had only a desire to sing, no song to step on, nor much more than his playfulness to sacrifice. If his reversal has reduced a genuine, if timid, gift to commonplace, he has been either unaware of the loss or has thought himself well compensated by the rewards of comfort. At any rate, he seems to have accepted his descent to public favor without qualm or protest. Of the true state of mind of one who has written so little about himself, it is, naturally, impossible to tell. And it may be that the progressive loss of gaiety and humor in Leonov's work, its increasingly ponderous discursiveness, are signs of some unhappiness. But this is pure conjecture. Outwardly there is nothing to indicate dissatisfaction. His themes are the "right" themes, and they are dealt with in the "right" way.

The solemn commonplaceness of his views shows up in the pronouncements he is called upon to make from time to time. There is, by way of example, an article of 1956 in *Literaturnaya Gazetta,* called "Talent and Labor," in which he lays down the law to aspiring authors. He tells them that talent is essential, forming 60 percent of the process of production, the other 40 percent consisting of "culture, the will to work, the ability to work, and many other qualities"; that first of all a writer must be a great man, since writing and thinking are one, and thought is the product of heart, mind, social consciousness, love of country, and the desire not to receive but to give; that the writer is a leader, watched with "jealous hope by a million fellow citizens" whom he labors to instruct and stimulate; that his every book must be a "cultural event," inviting men "into the future," having "something to share with a humanity that pines for knowledge." Do not rush into print, Leonov admonishes the young writer. Remember that literature, the most important instrument of progress, must stand on a level with the greatest discoveries of the times. It must be not only informative, but nourishing, contain not only facts but "the most valuable vitamins of spiritual life"; and only such books have a right to live as it would be shameful not to have translated into "the languages of all nations and peoples" and not to know as one knows Dostoevsky and

Tolstoy. But the task of today's writer, he goes on, is not the same as that of his forebears, whose heroes had no part in the processes of labor and who, therefore, were not obliged to describe their means of livelihood. The hero of Soviet literature, by contrast, is a worker, "tied to his epoch by his profession"; and the Soviet author must accompany him to the laboratory, the workshop, the field, and must learn his trade if he is to understand his psychology.

Today's writer must know a great deal. And although he may not be able to assimilate "everything that mankind has achieved culturally in thousands of years," he must know how to get at the information he needs, where to look for it on library shelves. He must have a lively interest in his surroundings, be well informed on all scientific achievements: astrophysics, biology, automation, telemechanism, etc., and he must master each aspect he studies so thoroughly that once he has written on it, no one can take it up again "for at least ten years." He must ask himself whether his book gives a glimpse into the future and determine, without fail, whether it has but "a one-hundred-thousandth particle of the importance" that attaches to some such grandiose invention as the cyclotron. He must fill his notebooks, and know how to use them; cast off ballast, so his theme will soar and not sink to the bottom; make an exact preliminary plan, logical, graphic, geographic, and he must make it lean and economical: "eliminate unnecessary fat. . . . One mustn't eat indiscriminately, not even the very attractive food that life puts before one." He must make the reader participate in the events he deals with. If he is presenting something difficult to understand, a new industrial process, for example, he must lead up to it gradually by means of "interesting episodes." The writer's craft is very like the examining magistrate's: a given piece of life is to be thoroughly investigated until it is known from every angle; then it must be presented in such unmistakable and palatable fashion that the reader will assimilate it easily and draw the right conclusions from it by himself, without having to be dragged to them by the "lassos of calligraphy." But although "calligraphy" is unnecessary, for to embellish

"Socialist Humanism" is to tie a bow on Mt. Everest, the writer must write and rewrite. He must "work, work, and work," like Flaubert and the French classicists, for whom writing was "a passion and an act of heroism"; must give attention to form (a need for calories does not preclude the art of cooking; it is important not only that the ingredients be fresh but that one know how to prepare them); must emulate the magic language of his Russian predecessors, and to this end must listen respectfully to the speech of the folk. "For a literary man there is no sweeter music." But though he must learn from it, he must beware of phonetic imitation. Apart from talent, then, a writer must have "culture, ability to work, and health." His life must be as disciplined as an athlete's, for he must work eighteen hours a day, without holidays or vacations, and even in periods of discouragement must adhere to the motto *Nulla dies sine linea.*

There is nothing in this *apologia pro laboro suo* to contradict the Party line, but what makes Leonov somewhat different from other loyal adherents of the regime is the frequent liveliness of his expression and his emphasis on the importance of form and language. When he speaks of how nineteenth-century writers used the Russian tongue, he attains eloquence. His thought, however, does not rise above trite practicality; and Flaubert, whom he admires, might have said of his theory what he once said of Zola's, that it was *"profondément farce,"* while his plays and novels, like Zola's, and for much the same reason, are also, to the eye of art, eminently successful failures.

5

MIKHAIL SHOLOKHOV
(1905-   )

I

Well, that little of which Gregory had dreamed through sleepless nights had come to pass. He stood at the gate of his own home, he held his son in his arms.

That was all he had left in life, all that for the time being made him kin to the soil and to this whole vast world that lay shining beneath a chilly sun.

So ends *The Quiet Don*. Gregory has had his last hollow dream. The gate before which he stands opens on a house that is no longer his; it has been taken over by his sister and her husband, Mishka Koshevoy, the honored Bolshevik. The son Gregory holds in his arms did not at first recognize his father in the disheveled man who climbed up the river bank to confront him, nor did he show much joy at his return: it is Uncle Misha to whom he is now devoted. Gregory knows that when he enters the house it will be to die. He wills it so, for he is through with life and, after a long struggle, has come "home" to give himself up.

No other ending would have been appropriate to this novel, of which Gregory Melekhov is the tragic hero. He loses because bolshevism wins in a contest as clearly predetermined as that of Lucifer with Jehovah or Prometheus with Zeus, for Gregory's opponent, the Historical Necessity of Marxism, is no less powerful than the gods of Hebraic and Greek legend. His failure to recognize its greatness, the doubts that made him waver in his allegiance constitute his tragic flaw. And if his fate is that of thousands caught in a battle they did not will and could not understand, it represents the tragedy of fatal error and resembles the doom of ancient myths with the mysterious justice of their supernatural punishments.

Gregory is a sympathetic character, a vigorous, passionate, and fearless man, who acts according to an independent code of ethics, defying injustice, brutality, and oppression as he understands them. He disobeys his father and flouts the opinion of his neighbors to live with the woman he loves; in the army, when the authorities are guilty of outrage, he refuses to submit to them; twice he is narrowly prevented from shooting a superior officer who has mistreated prisoners; once he forces open the doors of a jail in which innocent people have been locked up. He is several times rebuked or demoted for insubordination. He acts impetuously, provoked by pride or a sense of justice, by love or hatred. These are the reasons for what he does, but beyond an ingrained sense of right and wrong, he has no philosophy, no doctrine of means and ends to justify a present evil as a step toward a future good. And that is why, living at a time when traditional morality no longer suffices and a man is forced to choose among ethical systems that may violate innate convictions, Gregory's loyalties are uncertain and he is forced by events to give his allegiance first to one side, then another. To begin with, he fights for the Czar, unquestioningly, as duty bound; then, shaken by the madness in which he must take part—the malice, the viciousness, the injustice, the sadism, the spectacle of mutilations and pitiable deaths to which he contributes—he joins the Reds, persuaded by their theories of pacifism and equality, and also because he feels he has more in common with them than with their enemies. But soon he turns against them, revolted by the cruelty of the Communist general he serves; is won over by the Separatists, who argue that Cossack freedom is imperiled by both Whites and Reds; then, to avenge the vandalism that has ravaged his home, he joins the White Army, and when that has been broken up, a band of outlaws in a last, desperate spurt to freedom, because, as he says, "an evil liberty is better than a good jail." Thus during seven years of World War, Revolution, and civil war, Gregory has fought in the Imperial Army, the Red Army, the White Army of the Don, Wrangel's army, and finally with a band of terrorists. He has fought courageously, been wounded a dozen times and more, has received decorations, commanded thousands of men and won renown as an able leader. Whenever he has changed sides, it has been for the sake of justice or of freedom; but, at the end, he has found neither. Never has he been convinced that any of the causes he has followed was so supremely right that it could not be questioned. Contemptuous of public opinion, a law unto himself and a rebel not on principle but as his desires and his sense of decency, dignity, and fair play dictate from moment to moment, he has been loyal to himself alone; and it is this quality of independence that Sholokhov presents as his fatal error.

Clearly, Gregory is meant to be pitied as heroes are pitied for having fallen through errors as great as their natures. But it is Mishka Koshevoy whom we are invited to accept as the ideal required by a cruel age, Mishka who is at opposite poles from the proud and rebellious Gregory—an unpretentious fellow, from early boyhood dutifully supporting his widowed mother, reading Marx, fighting always on the side of the Reds, and ending up as commissar of the local soviet, a calm and steady character who has a good and sufficient reason for everything he does. In the course of the civil war, he sets fire to the houses of the prosperous members of his district, leads forth its old inhabitants to imprisonment and execution, captures and shoots Gregory's older brother, and goes about all these activities with the same rationality and confidence with which he courts and marries Gregory's sister. Stoic harshness has replaced in him a native inclination to gentleness, and loyalty to the Party has channeled his private sentiments. Gregory, by contrast, is semiliterate, has not read Marx, and has no conception of the historic meaning of the events in which he is caught up. Ideas about communism drop on him as suddenly as war itself. He first encounters them when a fellow patient in a hospital to which he is sent early in World War I expounds to him the notion that if all governments were in the hands of workers there would be no war. Presently he hears from others that communism is as bad as czarism, that Cossacks should have a government of their own. Dissatisfied with life, unable to answer any argument, much less evolve a theory of his own, Gregory feels lost among these doctrines as in "a snow storm on the steppe." "Life will make you see," he is told, "and will not only make you see, but will give you a shove to one side or the other." So indeed it turns out. And as he is thrown from side to side, he becomes more and more confused in thought the while he grows more skilled in combat, until at the moment of his greatest military triumph, he is overcome by despair, takes to drink, and falls screaming on the battlefield in a frenzy of guilt. By contrast to Mishka, Gregory has grown with the years from a kind of careless and callow toughness to anguish and a mature capacity for tenderness. Once, before the end, Gregory had returned home, wanting, after years of war, only to live in peace, till the land, care for his orphaned children. Mishka sent him packing. He could not trust the likes of him, he said:

"I know all about your heroics. I've heard of them. You've ruined a lot of our fighters. That's why I can't bear to look at you. Things like that can't be forgotten."

"You've got a long memory [Gregory replied]. You killed

brother Peter, but somehow I don't remind you of it. If everything's to be remembered, we've got to live like wolves."

In this, as elsewhere, Mishka is supposed to be right. But
he is a pale creature by the side of Gregory, whom Sholokhov had not perhaps, at first, intended to make quite so attractive as he turned out to be.

And this may indicate an unacknowledged discord in
Sholokhov's work, a conflict between dogma and humaneness, almost as if he himself were a Gregory trying to become Mishka. For however cold its doctrine, in feeling *The
Quiet Don* is grandly romantic. The love story of Gregory
and Aksinia is done on a heroic scale, the descriptions of the
land are prose lyrics inspired by authentic passion, and
there is tenderness and humor in individual episodes. All
this spontaneous delight, however, is held in check by a
dutiful pragmatism, for which nothing may be considered
valuable except in so far as it is directed to an end. The end
is the victory of bolshevism, and Sholokhov's purpose is to
display its excellence. His righteousness constricts an inborn
poetry and narrows his appreciation of men in such a way
that, in the last analysis, all that is spontaneous seems inconclusive and extraneous to the main design, hard
driven by the demands of a moral. The book is about men,
but how a man feels or thinks, how he grows, what concepts or imaginings have formed his mind or generated his
emotions, are matters with which Sholokhov is less concerned than with what men think, what it is right for them
to think, with what they feel and what it is right for them
to feel under given circumstances, rather than in how
thoughts and feelings take shape. His understanding of men
is thoroughly materialistic. In his view, no free play of emotions, no chaos of feeling, seeking form and direction,
impinges on the world. An emotion cannot be unattached;
it is created by an object, and there is nothing interesting
in it except as it eventuates in action. His art is based on
this materialism. Simple, concrete, it produces an effect of
brute immediacy. His epic is a sequence of episodes; its
theme is a moment in history; its plot is, in essence, a story

of flight and pursuit. Experience in it is not a thought, but a blow. Everything is sharply defined, clearly delimited; bodies and faces, details of action are minutely drawn. Men are seen in gestures that represent not the pattern of mind and character, as they do with Tolstoy, but the demands of a given situation.

Comparisons between Sholokhov and Tolstoy are often made. *The Quiet Don* is referred to as the Soviet *War and Peace,* of which it seems to celebrate the centenary; *War and Peace* begins in the summer of 1805, rises to the crucial year 1812, and closes in 1820, and *The Quiet Don* begins in the summer of 1912 and ends in 1920. These dates, to be sure, are imposed by history, not by artistic design. Nevertheless, Tolstoy is always in the background. *The Quiet Don* is full of stylistic and structural echoes of *War and Peace,* and once, in the course of it, Tolstoy is explicitly mentioned. This happens in an episode which, though but tenuously related to the plot, has a meaning that reaches back, beyond its place in the story, to something fundamental.

One day at the front, Gregory finds a slim notebook on the body of a young Cossack who has been slain by the Germans.* Thinking it may be important, he takes it to headquarters. But it turns out to be not in the least important, nothing more than the private diary of the boy, a piteous record of the last five months of his life: an unfortunate love affair while he was a university student in Moscow; the draft into the army; the bit of fighting he saw before he was killed. The girl in question has already figured briefly in the narrative, the depraved young daughter of a rich merchant in Gregory's district. The part she plays is slight, however, and the young Cossack remains unknown except for these notes, which the officers read aloud and laugh at. In one of his last entries the young man mentions Tolstoy:

In Tolstoy's *War and Peace* [he writes], there is a place where he speaks of the line between two enemy armies—the line of the

---

* This episode is one of those omitted in the English translation.

unknown, that separates, as it were, the living from the dead. The squadron in which Nicholas Rostov was serving is about to attack, and Rostov makes mental note of this line. I recalled this passage of the novel today with special clarity, because this morning at dawn we attacked the Germans. . . .

He then describes the engagement, making note, very much in Tolstoy's manner, of everything that strikes his senses: the odor of pine needles, of oats; the snorting of horses, the way their hoofs scatter "juicy dew" off the oats, the chilliness of dawn, the sound of enemy fire, as if "the scented pines were burning" above them, then the tremor of "a pitiable, limp, dry 'hurrah,' " and "silence pierced by machine guns"; the appearance of the infantry in flight, "baggy, gray figures" in their "pancake-like" battle caps and rough, knee-length boots, and "the precise, hoarse little laugh" of the German guns; then their own ranks, quickly formed on the left flank of the fleeing infantry, his horse racing into the fight, with ears held back so tightly they looked as if one could not have pried them away from his head. "I glanced back—I saw behind me the commander of the regiment and two officers. There it is: that line dividing the living from the dead. There it is: the grandiose madness!" And now he saw his squadron commander in the act of killing an enemy soldier:

Before my eyes, the squadron commander, Chernetzov, cut down a German hussar. I saw how one of the Cossacks of the sixth squadron chased a German, and, losing his wits, slashed the neck of his horse. Pieces of hide sprang away from the leaping sword. . . . No, this is impossible! There is no name for this! When we returned I saw the face of Chernetzov—intent, restrainedly happy. There he sat—not on horseback, but at cards— after the murder of a man. He will go far, the squadron leader Chernetzov. He's gifted!

All this is heartfelt, but derivative. The bookish style is as pathetic as the writer's brief life, its careful language as alien to his native Cossack speech as he himself had been in Moscow to his home on the Don. He has grown "civilized" and introspective; his literary manner, borrowed from Tolstoy, is a contemplative retreat. Out of it, at a distance, he looks at the events he lives through. But the experience of Nicholas Rostov, which he invokes, is not at all like his own, while Gregory Melekhov's is still more different.

The passage in *War and Peace* to which he refers is the battle in which Nicholas is wounded:

The squadron in which Rostov was serving had scarcely time to mount before it was halted facing the enemy. Again, as at the Enns bridge, there was nothing between the squadron and the enemy, and again that terrible dividing line of uncertainty and fear—resembling the line separating the living from the dead—lay between them. All were conscious of this unseen line, and the question whether they would cross it agitated them all. . . .

"If only they would be quick!" thought Rostov, feeling that at last the time had come to experience the joy of an attack. . . .

The order to attack is given. There is the sound of shots and a prolonged "Hur-a-a-ah!"

"Let anyone come my way now," thought Rostov, driving his spurs into Rook. . . . Ahead, the enemy was already visible. Suddenly something like a birch broom seemed to sweep over the squadron. Rostov raised his saber, ready to strike, but at that instant the trooper Nikitenko, who was galloping ahead, shot away from him, and Rostov felt as in a dream that he continued to be carried forward with unnatural speed but yet stayed in the same spot. . . .

"How is it I am not moving? I have fallen, I am killed. . . ."

These observations are hardly the kind that Nicholas would have written or talked about. Indeed, they are not observations at all, but feelings and impressions. What he thinks is happening is not what is actually happening, and the pathos of the incident lies precisely in our sense of his being lost, in our seeing more clearly than he sees and in knowing what he does not know. And yet, it is through his

mind only that we look; details beyond his state of semicon-
sciousness are vague. True enough, we never see Sholokhov's
young Cossack in battle; we have only read his report of it,
but in this report we are impressed not by the haziness but
by the exactness of his mind. Even in the heat of battle, details have been engraved on it with absolute precision.

This is also true of Melekhov's first encounter. He was
serving his regular term in the army when war broke out.
First there were rumors of Austrians massing troops on the
border, then, one summer day, in a peaceful countryside,
his company crossed the border. His detachment, sent on
ahead, stole through a deserted village, like a beast of prey,
then climbed a hillock. From the top they saw the enemy.
"What a lot of them there are!" gasped Gregory's companion. "The rest were silent, all gripped in the fist of the selfsame feeling. Gregory listened to the rapid beating of his
heart (as if some small but heavy creature, there, in the
left side of his chest, were marking time) . . ." Ordered to
report the discovery, Gregory gallops back to the commander:

The commander snatches his sword from the scabbard, its tip
gives out a pale blue spark.
"Co-o-ompany!" The sword bends to the right, to the left, and
falls forward, stopping in mid-air above the horse's pricked-up
ears. "Scatter like lava and advance!"—Gregory mentally trans-
lates the wordless command. "Lances ready, swords away, to the
attack, forward march!"—the captain shouts the order, and gives
his horse the rein.
Dully gasped the earth, crucified under the countless hoofs.

And now the tempo quickens; the tensely quiet overture
modulates into a gallop, as bullets whistle and men fall
wounded. Convulsively, Gregory presses the wooden end
of the bayonet to his side, his hand sweating as if it had
been rubbed in a slimy liquid. Bullets force him to bend
his head close to his mount's neck, his nostrils are filled with
the acrid smell of horse sweat. As through misty field glasses,
he sees a line of trenches and masses of running men. And
within:

There, in the middle of Gregory's chest, that which before the attack had hurriedly pumped blood, seemed to have ossified. He felt nothing except the ringing in his ears and pain in the toe of his left foot. His thoughts, unraveled by fear, wound a tangled, heavy, freezing skein in his head.

Then, "as with a diamond on glass," bits of what he sees are cut on his memory: the pink gums and bared rows of teeth of a fallen horse, the distorted mouth and protruding eyes of a man he does not hear but whose cry, he knows, had been inhumanly savage. A tall, blond-browed Austrian fires at him at close range, the bullet grazes his cheek, and Gregory drives his lance into the enemy with such force that half of it enters his body:

Gregory had not had time after the blow to pull out the lance and was letting it fall under the weight of the sinking body, feeling through it the body's fluttering and convulsions, seeing how the Austrian, bending far back—only the sharp, unshaved point of his chin was visible—fingered and scratched the stick with twisted fingers.

Gregory lets go the lance, grasps his sword, turns his horse around, not knowing why, and, driven to a fever by the insanity about him, gallops after a fleeing, disarmed Austrian, who, beside himself with fear, swaying, runs along a garden fence, his cap clasped in his fist. Gregory can see the fleshy crease at the back of his neck and the wet line of his shirt collar, and although it is awkward for him to strike with his left hand, "he leans over in the saddle, and holding his sword at an angle, lowers it on the Austrian's temple. The Austrian, without crying out, presses his palms to the wound and wheels about with his back to the railing." Gregory sees the look of terror in his eyes, sees him sinking slowly, hears the gurgling groan in his throat; squinting, he strikes again and slits the skull in half. "The Austrian fell, spreading out his hands, as if he had slipped," and the halves of his skull struck the pavement with a dull thud. Gregory's horse snorts and carries him out to the middle of the road. Another horse gallops by, dragging a dead Cossack whose foot is caught in the stirrup, "and the horse drew the bruised, naked body, shaking it along the stones. Gregory saw only the red streak of the leg band and the torn green blouse, beaten up into a ball above the head." And suddenly he is overcome by a great sense of heaviness. "Leaden heaviness filled his head." Men rushed by him: a wounded man was carried past in a greatcoat, a crowd of captive Austrians were driven by. "Their faces ran together in Gregory's eyes into a jelly-like, gray-colored blot." Not knowing why, Gregory goes back to look at the man he has cut down. There he lies, with his dirty palm stretched out as if for alms, and his face looks small to Gregory,

almost childlike, in spite of the drooping mustache and the tormented—whether from suffering or a former, joyless life—twisted, severe mouth.

"Hey, you!" shouted an unknown Cossack officer, as he rode past in the middle of the street.

Gregory glanced at his white, dust-spattered cockade and, stumbling, went to his horse. His step was heavy and uncertain, as if he carried a burden on his back that was beyond his strength; disgust and astonishment crushed his soul. He took the notched stirrup in his hands, and for a long time could not lift his foot that had grown heavy.

Like Rostov's, and unlike the unknown Cossack's, Gregory Melekhov's experience is immediate and individual. It is primarily the experience of shock and it is not involved in moralizing. The young Cossack had not known how to see with his own eyes. He looked through those of the author he admired, wrote the kind of thing that would interest the friend for whose eye he had intended his diary, made piously commonplace remarks. His version of battle, examined through a haze of "literature," is a step removed from what actually took place. Sholokhov no doubt meant it to be a pitying satire on the archaic, clouded vision of the "cultivated" man. But Gregory's experience, like the Cossack's and unlike Rostov's, is precise in detail and the effect it creates is not so much of pathos as of horror. Even when Gregory sees things in a haze, it is not his vague impressions we are given, but the exact image of what he himself has not seen clearly. The effect is pictorial and sensuous, for we are not identified with the character; we are observers of a scene of which he is himself a part. This is sensationalism in both the current and the root meaning of the word. And it is a trait peculiar to Sholokhov, who points things out to make us shudder, a method that indicates not only stylistic but philosophical and psychological differences between him and Tolstoy.

Tolstoy's realism was the result of skilled analysis; his simplicity was the height of sophistication. He studied the world with the same uncompromising severity with which he looked into himself; he understood others through self-knowledge, and his writing was an attempt to define himself in relation to others and to his world. It was a deep but troubled introspectiveness that made his greatness, and his finest creations project the problem by which he was always tormented: how to preserve the precious insights of intuition and curb an inveterate impulse to dissect, which seemed to him destructive. His celebrated method of "*otstranenie*," of "making things strange"—of seeing everything, that is, as if it had never been seen before—depended on this acute self-awareness; his work, however realistic in effect, is in essence subjective, and always speculative. That is why the world of his novels appears through the eyes of men and women who approach it with the notions and interests characteristic of their personalities. Like Tolstoy himself, they have questions to ask of life. They come to it with certain expectations, and the meaning of their experience lies in the interaction between what they anticipate and what the world presents. Thus Rostov, galloping into battle, has preconceived notions of what a battle should be and expectations of the part he is to play in it; and this is also true of the older and wiser Andrey Bolkonsky, and even of the absent-minded Pierre Bezukhov, who wanders through life in the same abstracted way in which he strays onto the field of Borodino, his thoughts entangled in enormous problems he always yearns to solve. To Tolstoy's men and women, action and sensuous perceptions are a testing ground of

ideas; all that happens physically corroborates them or per-
turbs the mind. For Sholokhov the opposite is true. Occurrences in the physical realm are primary and most important. The mind, like the body, reacts automatically to the
blows that overwhelm it. The senses are not subordinate to
the imagination. Meaning and value reside in the physical
world, and little exists beyond the evidence of sight, hearing, taste, smell, touch. Gregory, to be sure, is confronted
by ideas and vacillates between doctrines, but these are for
him no different from events in the physical world. He is
mentally unprepared for what he will have to live through;
and everything—battles, ideas, even love—descends on him
with the force of sudden, shattering collisions. Everything
comes as shock, not the shock of disillusionment, but that of
surprise. Nothing has been foreseen, and Gregory is darkly
driven through a nightmare of the unexpected.

It is, then, in the realm of consciousness, in the role of the
mind's debate with itself, that one detects a basic difference between Tolstoy's realism and Sholokhov's. Sholokhov
seems to have no quarrel with himself, and the disharmony
one notices in his work does not appear to have engaged his
consciousness. He has neither the habit nor the need to
look inward; he does not have to fight his mind; his work
proceeds from a kind of unobtrusive solidity, a calm self-
assuredness. He is a chronicler of events and is not identified with any of his characters, as Tolstoy is, for example,
with his Pierre Bezukhov and his Andrey Bolkonsky. Sure
of himself, untroubled in his relations with others, Sholokhov
is not an actor in the drama but an invisible, sympathetic
member of the group he writes about. Reflectiveness is alien
to him, perhaps even distasteful. He ascribes it to such men
as his pathetic young diarist, whom he does not know well
nor care to know better, or to his tragically mistaken Gregory, whose puzzled and unproductive oscillation between
schemes of belief can hardly be called "thinking." Such men
Sholokhov either pities or despises; they are out of touch
with the true and the real. But even those he admires, his
Communist leaders, do not wrestle with the ideas they in-
culcate; their "thinking" is a ready acceptance of a philos-

ophy, the rightness of which they take to be self-evident. Nor is it ever suggested that thought might involve anything more than the adoption of ready-made doctrines, or that discussion can be anything other than a violent clash of opinions. For the most part, his characters act without inward strife. Their choices are predetermined by habit, tradition, or unwavering prejudice. No room is left for individual interpretation; there is no examination of principles, there is only a well defined "truth" on the one hand, and on the other, that which lies outside it and is therefore false. Reason can add nothing to the prescriptions of doctrine, and he who hesitates is lost indeed. It is remarkable, when one thinks of it, that a story which is concerned with nothing less than a radical revaluation of traditional concepts, symbolized in a man whose fate hinges on the choices he makes among ideas—that in a story of this kind there should be nothing of that poetry and passion of debate which one finds in *War and Peace,* not to speak of Dostoevsky's novels. But, of course, this is consistent with a view which assumes that truth is limited and incontrovertible, and that the selection of beliefs is, therefore, not an intellectual but a moral act.

What are Gregory's convictions in the end? To what state of mind and feeling have his thoughts and passions brought him? This is not clear, nor does it matter. What a man does and what happens to him is more interesting than what happens within him. The only criterion by which he can be fairly judged is the role he has played in society. By this standard Gregory has been proved guilty. His doom, like that of every tragic hero, reflects the nature of his guilt. If justice demands that the punishment of Oedipus' inward crime be self-inflicted, so that the form it takes, the blinding, the exile, become physical manifestations of a spiritual blindness and alienation; if Ivan Karamazov's error of the mind is paid for by the mind, and his brother Mitya's sin of passion can be redeemed only by his emotions—so Gregory's political fault is punished by society. Like the pagans of Dante's limbo, Gregory is pitiful and wrong, excluded from a Utopia which he has not had the foresight to revere. But

where else in epic or romance does the victory of a group
overshadow so completely the defeat of an individual?
In *The Iliad* the moral triumph of Achilles surpasses the
military triumph of the Greeks, and the grandeur of Hector
ennobles the Trojans; in *The Aeneid* the destiny of an empire hangs on the fortunes of one man; in *The Song of
Roland* a single champion restores his France to honor; in
The Lay of Igor's Armament a hero's escape from captivity
is the climax of his nation's fate; in *War and Peace* the
spiritual growth of Pierre Bezukhov and Andrey Bolkonsky
is no less important than the defeat of Napoleon; and in
medieval lives of saints, a man's martyrdom in this world is
but a means to eternal salvation. At all times, the fate of
individuals has been the focus of interest. Now this fate is
shown as unimportant. It is the group that matters; the ideal
man is the social servant; and the willful individual, embodied in Gregory, is denounced as tragically mistaken. His
failure is complete and without compensation, and all that
made him unique is implicitly damned: passion, rebelliousness, pride, the will to put principles to the test and to
change allegiance as conscience may exact. In a moral
order that takes discipline and submissiveness to be the
highest virtues, sympathy for a man like Gregory, who hesitates at the crossroads, cannot be allowed. And one can
only marvel at the rapidity with which in a revolutionary
epoch the ideal of revolt has been suppressed.

Gregory stirs our pity but does not move our reason; his
passionate life, twisting in tangled and devious ways, leads
nowhere beyond itself. And yet, as a representative of the
old order, he might have been a Great Antagonist, a Satan,
a Prometheus, or at least an Iago. But Sholokhov's scheme
demands that the undistinguished be praised. His Gregory
is not, and could not be, permitted to dazzle. The brilliance
of Milton's Satan makes God's creation and even God himself seem dull, Iago has a depth of pettiness worthy of Othel-
lo's largeness. There is greatness in their evil, but for Sholokhov the unique must be conceived as small, Gregory's rebellion must appear pitiable, and Mishka's virtues the kind
of which most men are capable. Grandeur belongs to the

masses, and the only individuals in whom it can be embodied are those who have understood the laws of historical necessity and ordered their lives accordingly. In this again we find a sharp contrast to Tolstoy, who, while pleased to debunk "greatness," counterbalanced his caricature of Napoleon by his paean to Kutuzov and his praise of Pierre, showing humbleness and simplicity to be magnificent, and thus changing the concept of grandeur without relinquishing it. But Sholokhov levels, or refutes, the admiration he arouses; his Communist heroes—such as Bunchuk, the account of whose love of Anna Pogudko is one of the most touching passages in the novel, or Podtelkov, whose execution is memorably harrowing—are either piteous or obscured by the horror of their fate, and the ideal Mishka Koshevoy, with all his pleasant boyishness and stoic virtues, turns out to be a prig and a bore. Tolstoy knew how to make the commonplace poetic, Sholokhov can only sentimentalize it. His real heroes, as a matter of fact, are not living characters at all, but idols: Marx, Lenin, and Stalin, who do not appear in his books, but are spoken of and quoted with reverence.

It is not by virtue of an ideal that Sholokhov holds us entranced, but by the passions of his men and women, by his vigorous love of the land, and by the sheer fascination of horror. The love story of Gregory and Aksinia is as powerful as any love story of romantic legend. It has no "meaning" as Tolstoy's love stories have meaning; it stands by itself, overwhelming and complete. It is the glory of the book. Nowhere else does Sholokhov's gift appear more clearly, nowhere else does one see so well how feeling may be shown pictorially—compact, unanalyzed—in the graphic utterance of actions and gestures. It is an earthy love. And the whole book is earthy; it feels and smells of the soil. The seasons here are the timepiece by which the fortunes of individuals and history itself are clocked. Men are attached to the earth physically and emotionally, and the setting of their lives is never forgotten.

We first meet Gregory at dawn of a spring day on a fishing expedition with his father; the stars fade, the mist looms over the river and creeps into the ravines "like a gray, head-less snake." As the first year comes full circle, Gregory and Aksinia have become lovers, and have tried to put a stop to their love; Gregory has married Natalie and left her to return to Aksinia, Natalie has attempted suicide; and the Communist Shtockman has taken up residence in the village. All this takes place not so much against the background of nature as within nature. The dramatic action is part of the summer work in the fields, the first chill of autumn, the slowly coming winter, and the breaking of ice on the Don in the spring. Human events acquire a kind of depth and solidity for having been accompanied by winds, snow, clouds, rain, and sun. The turmoil of men is steeped in the calm of this unanxious rolling around of the seasons; and in the exact center of the book there comes an eloquent ad-dress to the steppe that gives the effect of a bright stone over the main entrance of the edifice, bringing to a focus the color diffused in the veined blocks of which it is built. It is the only time in this work that Sholokhov speaks in the first person:

The feather grass ripened. For many miles the steppe arrayed itself in swaying silver. It bent springily to the wind that rushed upon it, ruffled, heaped it up, drove it now southward, now west-ward in dove-gray waves. Where the flowing stream of air ran by, the feather grass bowed prayerfully, and a black trail stretched a long while upon its old, gray spine.

The varicolored grasses flowered and withered. On the crests of hills, joyless, burnt-out wormwood drooped to earth. The brief nights faded quickly. At night innumerable stars shone in the coal black sky; the moon, the Cossacks' "little sun," darken-ing to its wane, gave forth a stingy, pallid light; the vast Milky Way mingled with other starry paths. The acrid air was close, the wind dry, smelling of wormwood; the earth, also steeped in the bitterness of the almighty wormwood, yearned for cool-ness. Trodden by neither hoof nor foot, rippled the proud starry roads; the wheat-gold of stars, not rising, not yielding the joy of sprouting shoots, perished in the dry sky, black as the black earth; the moon, a dried-out salt marsh—and drought over the steppe; dead grass with the white, ceaseless, silver struggle of the quail above it, and the metallic ring of grasshoppers. . . .

And in the daytime—heat, sultriness, misty haze. In the faded blue of heaven—a pitiless sky, cloudless, and the brown steely arcs of the kite's outspread wings. Blinding and irresistible shines the feather grass along the steppe; the hot brown grass sends up a smoky vapor, camel-hued; the kite, careening, floats in the blue —below, his enormous shadow slips noiselessly over the grass.

Siskins whistle languidly and hoarsely. On the yellowing slopes of burrows, marmots doze. The steppe is hot but dead, and everything around is motionless and transparent. Even the graveyard, on the boundary of the visible, is fantastic and hazy, like a dream. . . .

Beloved steppe! A bitter wind settles on the manes of mares and colts. The horse's snort is dry and salty with the wind, and breathing in the salty, bitter scent, the horse chews its silky lips and neighs, tasting on them the tang of wind and sun. Beloved steppe, beneath the low-hanging sky of the Don! The windings of ravines, of plains, of red-clay valleys, the expanse of feather grass, traced with the nest-like markings of a horse's hoof, the funeral mounds in wise silence, guarding buried Cossack glory. . . . Low I bow before thee, and filially kiss thy fresh soil, Cossack steppe of the Don, unrusting, watered with blood!

This prose poem with its melancholy tone, its love and pity for a land "watered with blood," belongs to a long, patriotic tradition that goes back to *The Lay of Igor's Armament* and includes some of the finest pages in Russian literature: Gogol's celebrated descriptions of the Ukraine, Turgenev's of northern Russia, Blok's cycle, *On The Field of Kulikovo*. Sholokhov's, like these, is a love song to the land. It is symbolic of his sorrow at the misery of the years he is writing about. It gathers up into a musical statement the essence of the book, underscoring what is perhaps most true of it, that, despite its "ideology," it is not a treatise but a song. Indeed, *The Quiet Don* shares the characteristic qualities of the primitive epic. It is lyric, objective, and devout: lyric in that it is not analytic and is filled with enthusiasm about life, objective in that the author is not identified with any of his characters and takes no part in the action, devout in that it is dedicated to an unquestioned faith. But lyricism, objectivity, and devotion differ in direction and degree in accordance with the beliefs to which they are given. And Sholokhov's beliefs are given to a doctrine which, asserting the primacy of social values, cannot accept as valid any experience that is only subjective.

Nevertheless, his view of men is lyrical, his feeling about the land is sensuous and personal, and he seems to be endowed with so much good-natured tolerance that even his condemnation of men is tinged with kindness. He does not appear to belong to an age of anxiety. But he writes in an age of total horror for people whose imagination, fed on anguish, has grown insatiable. His audience, men and women of the twentieth century, have not only been inured to pain but have developed a craving for it, and he does not blink at the suffering that all of them have known either directly or vicariously. Tolstoy's work belonged, if not to a gentler era, at least to one in which extreme brutality was not habitual. When pain occurs in *War and Peace* it is poignant and appalling, partly because it is rare; the work is not saturated in physical anguish. To Sholokhov, wounds, convulsions, death throes, self-inflicted mutilations are the order of the day, and he records them minutely. Not callously, however, convinced as he is that in the outcome all misery will be redeemed. He is optimistic because his goal is sure, and because there is nothing imponderable in his view of life. This is not the same as Tolstoy's happiness, nor Homer's enjoyment of all that exists. Tolstoy's morality was, in essence, hedonistic. Happiness was his theme, and happiness not as a future possibility, a social goal, but as an actuality, experienced in ordinary moments of evanescent pleasure, which were the purpose and standard of life. Homer's delight was in the moral strength of men and their physical vigor and joy in living. But Sholokhov is pleased and hopeful because men know how to endure. There is a greater sense of loss and pity in *The Iliad* than in *The Quiet Don,* and a greater reticence. When Homer pauses to describe a wound, his description has little to do with suffering; the wound is almost independent of the wounded man:

With this he hurled his spear, and Athene guided it on to Pandarus' nose near the eye. It went crashing among his white teeth. The bronze point cut through the root of his tongue, coming out under his chin, and his glistening armor rang rattling round him as he fell heavily to the ground. The horses started aside for fear, and he was reft of life and strength.

It is not suffering but death that Homer emphasizes, and he is full of pity: young men fall "like high pine trees to the ground," their bright armor rattles round them, their death destroys their parents' hopes for them, where "many Trojans and Achaeans" lie "stretched side by side face downwards upon the earth." Homer grieved for unfulfillment, for the loss of those who should still have lived; to Tolstoy physical suffering is sometimes a revelation of personality or a means of spiritual discovery; to Dante, that poet of torment, suffering is a moral symbol, an instrument of divine justice. Only in our day and age does physical agony seem to have become important in itself.

This is in keeping with a materialistic, pragmatic view of life. Sholokhov does not venture outside the bounds of his observation into a realm of meanings. His work could not be summed up, as *War and Peace* is summed up in the conclusions at which Pierre and Andrey ultimately arrive, taught by experiences of love and death. Gregory's love shows him nothing except its strength, and death and suffering soon become too habitual to teach a lesson. Because Sholokhov's people approach the world without preconceptions, they meet it without wonder, and are driven through life but do not learn from it. As the years of horror pile up, those who are not killed grow hard; the fit are callous. What Santayana once called "the blind tendency of action" is Sholokhov's concern. History itself is no more to him than a clearly perceptible march of events, the meaning of which is immediate, specific, unequivocal. Events are what they are, accurately recorded in the impressions of those involved in them and in official documents. Such intricate problems as the nature of consciousness in its relation to brute fact, as the possibility of the mind's fully knowing anything beyond itself, which led Tolstoy to think of history as but a murky window on elusive truth, such problems and concepts are of necessity foreign to a Marxist. Tolstoy took nothing for granted, and when he propounded a philosophy, he was also announcing a discovery. But Sholokhov's doctrine is not his own. He is not a discoverer in the realm of thought but a missionary among missionaries, seeking not so much to explain as to impose an idea, the validity of which he believes to have been proved in action. *War and Peace* and *The Iliad* are more than tales of how the Russians conquered Napoleon and the Greeks the Trojans: these historic moments are part of an ampler theme, and through them we enter that realm of the imagination in which a poet can speak to all men in all times. But *The Quiet Don* is the story of how the Reds defeated the Whites, and neither pretends nor aspires to be anything more. Sholokhov stands firmly on the ground by the Don, and we remain there with him, unprovoked and uninvited to venture beyond. But what strikes us is that the fine descriptions to which we are treated, the vivid dramatic scenes, the sketches of men and women, the racy conversations, are all slices of life rather than full experiences, broken pieces, as it were, unrelated and irrelevant to the central thought. They have come from the depths, but have been flung aside and, unlike the episodes of *War and Peace* or *The Iliad,* are not borne on the current of the spontaneous delight which inspired them. For the current has been deflected, the stream has been diffused and has run aground. A formidable dam of rigid principles has blocked its flow.

There can be no doubt that Sholokhov's gift is genuine and exceptional, neither can his sincerity be called in question. He is perhaps the most wholeheartedly Communist of all Communist writers, and certainly the most popular and honored in the Soviet Union, recipient of the highest awards his country can bestow on artists, deputy to the Supreme Soviet, member of the Academy of Sciences. On the occasion of his fiftieth birthday, the *Literaturnaya Gazetta* announced that in the U.S.S.R. his novels had been published in four hundred and twenty-one editions, totaling twenty million seven hundred and seventy-three thousand copies, and at the Twentieth Party Congress he delivered a major address which, according to reports, was received with rapturous applause. Himself a Don Cossack, he has always been identified with his people; he writes in their language, from their point of view, and he has made them known to the rest of Russia. Nothing of the kind had been done before. Gogol had romanticized the Cossacks in *Taras Bulba*, Tolstoy had written of them from the standpoint of a sophisticated Moscow citizen; in Gorky's work, as in Eisenstein's film *Potemkin*, they appear as the Czar's most reliable tools of oppression. With Sholokhov, they are no longer primitive, fairy-tale heroes nor models of mechanized brutality, but real men and women. Yet Sholokhov's importance lies not so much in his regionalism as in his communism. He has sung the legend of an age. And although his theme of War and Revolution is common among Soviet writers, there is no other work like *The Quiet Don*. Sholokhov's voice is unique. It is a voice that seems to sing unwaveringly of a loved country and a cherished faith; it has the ring of certitude. Nevertheless, in *The Quiet Don* one is disturbed by something like a quaver in this voice, a deep-seated discrepancy between conviction and emotion, which is nowhere openly expressed and of which the author himself is doubtless unaware.

Sholokhov's social pragmatism colors his whole work. It is an outlook that can, and does, require that an individual do violence to himself if the common good demands this of him: commit acts that he finds repulsive, school himself to ruthlessness, learn to murder as a duty and extol his murders as right. We know we should admire Mishka Koshevoy. And yet, when he lords it over Gregory in a way we are meant to applaud, he offends our aesthetic perceptions as well as our moral sense. Something, one feels, is wrong here. Something has been twisted or left out. It has been Sholokhov's romanticism that moved us, and his voice, in spite of all the horrors it recited, has sounded mostly kind. How could he end by praising callousness? Mediocrity he could praise: he seems a man to suffer fools gladly. Brutality, too, as a tragic necessity to which a man must steel himself at times: he is a stoic. But brutality as such, brutality in itself? Yet here is Mishka, who performs too easily and blithely what his position demands. Gregory is to him not a person but an enemy, and although they had been boyhood friends he has no qualms in sending him to death. Enemies must be destroyed. Is this Sholokhov speaking? One's sympathy remains with Gregory, who has not been able to school himself to inhumanity. And one wonders. Is Sholokhov's voice quite so self-assured as it has seemed? The quaver one detects in it argues something discordant and unbalanced, as if its cadences and timbre were inappropriate to his theme. Is it, perhaps, that artistic inspiration and civic duty have not been fully integrated here, and that for this reason his finest achievement is a portrait of a man he condemns? Gregory, we are given to understand, has been forced to suppress qualities that would have made him a valuable member of the Communist Party; only in the world of communism could his generosity, directness, and integrity have been fully expressed and appreciated. And the question suddenly presents itself: is not Gregory, unintentionally, a portrait of his creator in reverse, of Sholokhov the Party man, who in the ardor of his belief has lost more than he knows, whose romantic appreciation of life, which verges on the sentimental, and his native easygoing kindliness have been inhibited by his allegiance to a cause that imposes the terrible obligation of preaching hatred? The unintended moral ascendancy of the rebellious and defeated Gregory over the pious and victorious Mishka may be then a demonstration that sometimes, in defiance of the artist's will but by virtue of his nature, art and humanism can triumph over dogma.

As is usually true of fine works of art, *The Quiet Don* admits of various interpretations. "It is inconceivable," writes Professor Ernest Simmons, for example, "that Sholokhov expected his readers, even within the Soviet Union, to prefer the Bolshevik monster [i.e., Mishka Koshevoy] to the tragic Gregory Melekhov." Indeed, this does seem inconceivable when one confronts the paltriness of the "monster" with the splendor of Gregory, that "Hamlet of the Steppe." As artistic conceptions they are incommensurable. But that other aspect of Sholokhov's art, which militates against his art, his stubborn and naïve loyalty to bolshevism, makes it by no means clear that his intentions always coincide with his artistic intuition. Gregory is magnificent by virtue of his strength, justice, and independence. The character he most closely resembles in Russian fiction is Dmitry Karamazov. But his tragedy is occasioned by the nature of the society with which he is involved; it is the tragedy of an independent and solitary man in a world that has no place for solitude and independence. Mishka Koshevoy, on the other hand, is attuned to this world, and however paltry he may appear by the side of the great-souled Gregory, he is, of the two, the one who in Sholokhov's philosophy is the more nearly "right." There are finer men among Sholokhov's Communists, but none more loyal than this young fanatic, whose rigid callousness, however revolting it may appear to Western readers, is to Sholokhov a commendable, if excessive, mark of zeal. Mishka may exaggerate, but his direction is correct; the Party is foremost in his thoughts, he serves it as he must, and such service demands ruthlessness. Later it became possible for Sholokhov to denounce this kind of inhumanity, but that was only after Stalin had stamped it as the sin of "leftist deviationism."

II

Whatever the interpretation, the excellence of *The Quiet Don* cannot be questioned. It is a splendid novel, not only by comparison with other products of Soviet fiction, but by any standard, and certainly superior to any of Gorky's or Leonov's. Nor has Sholokhov himself done anything to equal it. Before it, he had written a number of short stories; but good as many of them are, they are chiefly interesting as premonitions of his masterpiece, while the fiction that has followed is distinctly inferior to it.

Sholokhov's strength is passion, his weakness sentimentality and prejudice. His early stories, first published in 1925
as *Tales of the Don* (to be later incorporated in a larger
collection, *The Azure Steppe*), deal with battles, murders,
and adventures of the kind he himself experienced or witnessed in his native province on the Don during the civil
war which followed the October Revolution. Written with
ferocity, as if through clenched teeth, as starkly grim as the
old Border Ballads of Scotland, they are about the pathos of
loss, the tragedy of conflict, about fathers at war with sons,
brothers with one another, about all those excruciating
divisions that unavoidably accompany civil wars. For if bolshevism is the principle that divides fathers and children, it
is not of ideas or philosophies that Sholokhov writes primarily, but of passions; ideas, social doctrines are but the
basis and the background of these. As for the Cossack region itself, he knows it too well to perpetuate the traditional
fairy-tale legend of it. To his accustomed eye, it is not a
country of romantic enchantment but of a grandiose,
gloomy bitterness; his Don, unlike Gorky's sea, does not
"laugh," and the vast, desolate steppe is an austere land, as
harsh as the lives of the men who live upon it. He sees it
realistically, and writes of it with somber majesty:

The steppe is broad, and no one has measured it. Many roads
and paths run through it. Darker than dark is the autumn night,
and rain will wash clean away the traces of horse hoofs.

So ends an episode in which a zealous young shepherd is set
upon and murdered by the kulaks whose unfairness he has
exposed in a Bolshevik newspaper. And in conclusion of another tale:

The night fell starless, wolvish. Beyond the Don faded the
lilac steppe. On a hillock—back of the tempestuous young growth
of wheat, in a ravine washed through by springtime waters,
among windfallen trees, in the drunken odor of rotted leaves, a
she-wolf dropped her litter in the night; she moaned like a woman
in childbirth, gnawed the blood-drenched sand beneath her, and
licking her first, damp, rough cub, heard nearby in the hollow,

in the thickets of brushwood—two husky gunshots and a human cry.

She listened to it, pricking up her ears, and in answer to the brief, moaning cry, the she-wolf howled hoarsely and brokenly.

The shots she heard were fired at two Red prisoners, Ignat and his father Pakhomich, whom we had just seen behind barbed wire taking final leave of their family. The wild beast howls its acknowledgment of the savagery of men.

There is here, as there was to be later in *The Quiet Don*, the same remarkable combination of tenderness and brutality, of sweetness that sometimes borders on the sentimental, and with it, savage rigidity—the attitude, quite possibly, of a man whom necessity has inured to harshness, who has been made cruel by his very love, by a protective, pitying tenderness for the innocent and the helpless, because of whose suffering he harbors an implacable hatred for everything that makes them suffer and describes their pain with relentless cruelty. Of animals he writes with a charm that he reserves entirely for them, as, for instance, in a story called "The Colt." The tale begins:

In bright daylight, next to the dung heap, thickly covered with emerald flies, his head thrust forward, his front legs outstretched, he climbed out of his mother's belly and right above him saw the delicate dove-colored, melting little ball of bursting shrapnel; the screeching roar threw his small, wet body under his mother's legs. Terror was the first emotion he experienced here on earth.

There in the midst of battle, the colt is in the way, and the squadron commander orders the soldier Trofim to destroy it. But Trofim cannot bring himself to do this.

"Listen [he says to a comrade]. The devil take him! Let him live by his dam. For a while, and so on. . . . After the war, he'll do for plowing, maybe. And the commander, just in case, will have to understand the situation, because he needs milk and has to suck. . . . The commander himself once sucked a nipple; you and I sucked too, since that's the custom—and so, that's that!"

A month later however, the commanding officer brings the matter up again:

"Your colt, you do away with it! It creates panic in battle. . . . I look at it, and my hand trembles. . . . I can't kill. All because he has a homelike look—and in war that sort of thing is not allowed. . . . The heart turns from stone into a mop." [The officer] smiled reflectively. "You understand, Trofim, that tail of his, well, that is, . . . he lays it on his back, kicks up, and the tail— it's like a fox's. . . . A remarkable tail!"

At the end, when the detachment is crossing the Don to engage the enemy, the colt is caught in a whirlpool. Trofim sees it struggling, hears its pitiful neigh, gets to it too late to save it, and as he pulls out its carcass, is shot by the enemy.

Sholokhov is equally tender in writing of children. But then his pity, as gentle as Thomas Hardy's, becomes more easily sentimental. Hardy's feeling is compassion for man's helplessness in the grip of a transcendent and unhuman fate. Sholokhov does not believe in any supernatural power, any fate that subjects men to suffering they themselves cannot remedy, and that is why his pity is accompanied by hatred, and not awe. The suffering he sees is humanly inflicted. His villains are simply men, whose minds and hearts have been perverted by a wrong attitude to life. And a note of heroics comes to spoil his mood of affectionate sympathy. The little men of his stories undertake dangerous missions, dream of Lenin, and are rewarded by membership in the Komsomol. And although their naïve reasoning and courage are authentic enough, they are naïvely presented, as in the case for example, of the hero-worshiping eight-year-old Mishka in a story called "Rapscallion" (*"Nakhalënok"*). He reminds one of Nicholas and Petya Rostov. But Tolstoy's youngsters are shown from the standpoint of maturity; and in the perspective of older, broader experience, their infatuations appear pathetically absurd, or absurdly tragic. Sholokhov's Mishka, on the other hand, is seen with wholehearted, uncritical approval. He is meant to edify as well as charm; his elders are supposed to share, or applaud, his point of view. So thoroughly has Sholokhov identified himself with the requirements and mentality of the simple people he writes for, that his instructive tales of good little Communist heroes appear to have been done not only about children, but for them.

There is no complexity in these passionate tales, no detachment, no reflectiveness. The people are obvious: neither more nor less than their desires, habits, and work. Quite simply and ingenuously, bolshevism is presented through them as a heroic force that liberates the oppressed, restores human rights to those who have been robbed of them, shows up the callousness and greed of exploiters. The Cossack population of which Sholokhov writes is divided into three parts: the kulaks, that is, landowners, rich enough to hire labor; the poor, who are obliged to hire themselves out and have few, if any, possessions; and the middle group (the *serednyaki*), who have some little property but must work it themselves. The kulaks are naturally sworn enemies of Communists; the poor are enemies of the rich and furious defenders of bolshevism, which they support with the ardor and loyalty of martyrs; the *serednyaki* are an uncertain quantity, courted by both sides. Moral groupings coincide with the economic: the poor are good: industrious, faithful, open-minded, brave, kind, honorable; the rich are evil: lazy, callous, narrow, dishonest; those in the middle are a disturbed and vacillating lot. And no theorist of Marxism could fail to be delighted with the ever present implication that a man is made by the kind of labor he performs. There are a few exceptions to this arrangement; once in a while, the pathos of sheer humanity transcends party and class divisions, as for example in a story ironically entitled "Alien Blood," in which an old couple nurse back to life a wounded Red Army soldier, and become attached to him as to their own and only son, who has been killed in fighting the Reds. But such situations are rare. Usually, in Sholokhov's primitive community, where literacy is low, passions intense, the concept of legality practically nonexistent, and "justice" a matter of vendettas, where memory records tales of capricious and sadistic brutality, and the class war is exhibited in its simplest, least controversial form, bolshevism means not only justice, but enlightenment, education, freedom from superstition. And yet, despite such obviously weighted scales, these early stories are, even to the non-Marxist, humanly plausible and appealing, so clearly do they take rise in passionate conviction, so powerfully do they convey the sense of an intimate and sympathetic knowledge of men.

Communism to Sholokhov is not one possible way of life among many, but the only primordial, incontrovertible Truth. He did not choose it, as Gorky for example, had chosen it after weighing the merits of other systems. He was always a Bolshevik at heart, even in boyhood, long before he was taken into the Party. On that occasion in 1930, he said to the "electors": "I was born on the Don, there I grew up, went to school, was shaped as man and writer, was brought up as a member of the Communist Party." Born in 1905 in the Don Cossack village of Veshenskaya, the son of a Cossack cattle trader, he entered school the year the First World War broke out, and closed his formal education in 1918. "I was in a boy's school in one of the provincial towns of the province of Voronezh," he writes. "In 1918 when the German forces of occupation came to that city, I left school and went home. After that it became impossible to go on studying, since the region of the Don became the arena of the most furious civil conflict." In 1920 he joined the Red forces and fought various antirevolutionary bands that invaded his territory: "I was in service and knocked about the country of the Don. We chased the bands, and the bands chased us. . . . Everything was as usual. One was forced into all kinds of tight spots." Thus, in 1922, when this fighting came to an end and he was only seventeen years old, Sholokhov had already lived through several years of savage war. He now went to Moscow in the hope of continuing his education there, but unable to do so for some reason, took on work as a common laborer and began to write for publication. He placed three sketches in a Komsomol paper in 1923 and 1924, and was "discovered" by the Bolshevik novelist Serafimovich, who contributed an introduction to the *Tales of the Don*, and later helped him in publishing *The Quiet Don*, which began to appear in 1928. By the time it was completed, in 1940, Sholokhov had undertaken another large novel.

In 1930, the year he was made a Party member, a speech of Stalin's inspired him to write *Virgin Soil Upturned,* of which the first part was finished in 1931 and the second only some thirty years later, in 1959, and published serially in February and March of 1960 (translated as *Harvest on the Don*). Meanwhile, in conformity with the demands of Soviet officialdom, Sholokhov made extensive revisions both of *The Quiet Don* and of the finished part of his new novel; and during the Second World War engaged in journalism and propaganda. His philosophy of art and method of work are suggested in his own statement about *Virgin Soil Upturned:*

I wrote [the first part of] *Virgin Soil Upturned* in 1930, hot on the track of events that were still fresh in memory. But when, under the influence of fresh impressions, I . . . brought the first part to the end, I was faced with a dilemma: at the moment it was not this that seemed fundamental any longer, not this that moved the reader. You're writing about how kolkhozes were formed, but the current problem is work-days. And after workdays, the question of sabotage in 1932 will arise. Events outgrow, outreach human beings; and therein lies the difficulty of our task.

The novelist's business, that is, is the same as the journalist's. He too must deal with immediate, pressing concerns. In 1930, when these concerns were centered on the new five-year plan, Sholokhov took as his theme, its most vital phase, agricultural collectivization, and presented in his novel a typical section of the Cossack population, faced with all the difficulties that naturally arose when the attempt was made to communize farmland: enmity of foreigners and Whites, opposition of property owners, failings of the Party leaders themselves. There was plotting, sabotage, greed, lethargy, and also excessive zeal. The inhabitants of his "Gremyachiy Log" prefer to slaughter their livestock than give it up to the central management; one of their most respected citizens is treacherously harboring spies and revolutionaries; one of the Soviet leaders, appointed by the Central Committee to carry out Party orders, is too lenient with kulaks, another one is too harsh. The action takes place between January and the fall of 1930, and the climax of the book is the publication in March of Stalin's "Dizzy with Success," which had given Sholokhov the idea for his story in the first place. This speech was a denunciation of Communists who were so eager to advance collectivization that they resorted to inhuman measures, alienating the farmers they were supposed to win over. Sholokhov set out to explain how such "deviations" came about; and in so doing, created probably the most complicated of all his characters, the neurotic, fanatical Nagul'nov, a tragic fellow, very different from the shallow and self-righteous Mishka Koshevoy of *The Quiet Don*. Brought to trial for "leftist deviation," and found guilty, he is pitifully lost, uncomprehending:

"I won't give up my Party ticket [he shouts to the presiding officer]. Where am I to go without the Party? And what for? No, I won't give up my Party ticket! I've given my whole life, my whole life . . ." And suddenly he grew agitated, and like an old man, pathetically and senselessly, his hands fumbling on the table, began to mumble hurriedly, inaudibly, his words all tangled up. "In that case you'd better shoot. . . . There's nothing left. . . . I've no need of life now, put me out of it too. . . ."

His lonely trek home, over the desolate steppe, when he contemplates suicide, is very moving. In short, we are made to sympathize with Nagul'nov, his cruelty and eccentricities notwithstanding, and are pleased when, subsequently, he is readmitted to the Party. But he is not the hero of the piece. The hero, Davidov, is a very different kind of man: honest, brave, level-headed, amicable, unassuming. He and Nagul'nov are friends, and together with a third companion, Razmëtnov, constitute an object lesson in the virtues and defects of Soviet leadership.

Like *The Quiet Don* and most of the short stories, *Virgin Soil Upturned* also ends tragically: the heroes die. Yet, as a whole, this work is lighter in tone than the others, in keeping with its purpose, which is to picture the triumph of enlightenment and good-natured comradeship over wily machinations and temperamental faults. It is appropriate to this hopeful theme that a mood of happiness prevail over pain and tragedy. That is why, no doubt, there is more laughter here than in anything else that Sholokhov has written, why he brings into this book a superbly humorous old fogy, Grandpa Shchukar', garrulous, boastful, loyal, a kind of *miles gloriosus,* Sancho Panza, and one of Thomas Hardy's rustics rolled into one, and becomes so enchanted with him that, destroying the unity of his narrative, he allots a goodly fourth of the Second Part to the dear fellow's irrepressible arguments and stories. Once, at an important meeting, when Shchukar's chatter keeps vital business from being transacted, and he is finally ejected by means of a clever ruse, one of those present thinks, laughing to himself, as he sees him led away, "And yet, if, God forbid, the old man should die, it would be dreary without him. . . ."

That is the old man's excuse for being and for taking up so much space and time. In these difficult, solemn days of "socialist construction," with all their hardship, treachery, ignorance, theft, murder, there is nonetheless too much solemnity, Sholokhov is saying. For in spite of trouble, things are going well, and it is high time to have a bit of fun.

More clearly partisan than his other fictions, imbued with the happy optimism prescribed by Socialist Realism, *Virgin Soil Upturned* is a story of collective triumph over private losses, a tale of adventure and group action, not, in spite of Shchukar' and Nagul'nov, of individuals. Psychological complexities may be suggested in it but they are not worked out. The Bolsheviks win against sly and ruthless enemies; the best men are, unfortunately, murdered, but others come to take their place, and meanwhile a whole community is united in a kolkhoz and some of its members are taken into the Party. The intention is clearly propagandist; the vicious plotters have been unmasked, a new kolkhoz has been formed in spite of them, and it bears Stalin's name. But once again a strength of feeling gains a partial victory over utilitarian aims; and although none of the heroes can so much as touch Gregory Melekhov's largeness of nature, strength of independence, and emotional depth, although the loves in which they are involved are tawdry by comparison with Gregory's passion—although, in sum, there is nothing in this work in the least comparable to the tragic grandeur of *The Quiet Don*—what saves it from the general run of officially prescribed fiction is the skill, if not the depth, of its portraiture and the poetry of its landscapes. As in the early stories, there is something touching, genuine, and endearing about the characters, however obviously they may be used to point a moral. Old Shchukar', for example, is no mere clown. In the epilogue it is he who, more keenly than anyone else, feels the loss of Davidov and Nagul'nov. After their death, he is a changed man: silent, unsociable, more than ever inclined to tears. Their funeral has been too much for him; he takes to his bed and when he gets up again, four days later, is slightly paralyzed. Unable, in consequence, to continue with his old job, he is selected to be night watchman; and we last see him hunched up on his bench, sighing, crossing himself, and weeping all through an impenetrably black night, while flocks of cranes cry and moan until the dawn —lovable to the end and exceptionally pathetic by contrast to his former humorous self.

The final word, however, is given to Andrey Razmëtnov, who has now taken Davidov's place at the head of the kolkhoz. After many years as widower, and an interval of living with a woman who was not his wife, he has recently married again. In 1918, in revenge for his having joined the Reds, the White soldiers of his village raped his first wife; and she, unable to stand the disgrace, committed suicide. Now he bends over her grave:

Far beyond the Don, heavy storm clouds were gathering, streaks of lightning cut the sky slantwise, scarce audibly the thunder rumbled. "But I love you even to this day, my never-to-be-forgotten, the only one in my whole life. . . . You see, there's never time enough. . . . We don't meet often. . . . If you can, forgive me all my evil . . . all I've done to insult you in your death."

He stood a long while with uncovered head, as if listening to something and awaiting an answer, stood motionless, bent down like an old man. A warm wind blew in his face, a warm rain began to fall. . . . Beyond the Don, sheet lightning flashed white, and Razmëtnov's somber, joyless eyes no longer looked down on the crumbling corner of the small, dear grave, but out to where, beyond the invisible selvage of the horizon, half the sky was lighted up in scarlet flame, and, majestic and violent, as in the heat of summertime, awakening somnolent nature back to life, the final storm of that year approached.

The final storm, that is, of the year 1930, which in the realm of human relations was also one of storms, a year of strained effort, of the testing of men's characters and loyalties, the settling of old accounts. Now men could look ahead to a promising future, but this did not mean that they should, even if they could, blot out the memory of the past. Such is the import of Razmëtnov's meditation on what happened long ago, and of his looking up from the grave of the beloved woman, whose murderers he has not forgiven, to the tempestuous sky with its symbolic storm and promise of peace.

This message is in keeping with other recent works of Sholokhov, such as a short story of 1942, for example, called "The Science of Hatred," a lieutenant's calm, coldly told account of his imprisonment by the Germans, of their sadistic enjoyment in humiliating, beating, taunting, and killing pitifully defenseless, wounded, and starving prisoners of war. It is because he has experienced all this that, in the place where he sits at the end of a day's battle, Lieutenant Gerasim's face turns pale and darkens with hatred when a group of German prisoners is marched past him. These wretches may, or may not, be individually responsible for the outrages he has himself experienced; collectively, they are the same men, and so they can expect no mercy. Similarly, in "A Word about the Fatherland," Sholokhov wrote in 1948:

My dear friend and fellow countryman! Let not our hatred of even the conquered enemy grow cold! But may it seethe and

boil in our hearts with tenfold fury against those for whom no
name exists in human speech, who are not yet satisfied with the
profits taken from the blood of millions, who in blind, satanic
madness are preparing a new war for suffering mankind! . . .
Enemies remain enemies: some simply slander, slander with an
impudence characteristic of them, in a crude, primitive way;
others hastily draw out of dusty archives thoroughly moth-eaten
arguments about "the enigma of the Slavic soul," about "Russian
fanaticism"; and shamefully covering their pitifulness and meanness with these outworn garments, pretend that they are quite
unable to understand whence comes the all-conquering might of
the Soviet people.

And should one miss the allusion here to the United States,
one comes upon a passage that speaks of the "most preda-
tory" of imperialisms, the American, "like a spider . . . disgustingly bloated since the Second World War." By contrast
there is the glorious Russian people: "To be the loyal son of
such a people and such a Party, is this not, my friend, the
greatest happiness on earth for us and our contemporaries?"
It is understandable that such intransigent hatred should
be preached in time of war, but for Sholokhov a state of war
has always existed, and an ever present memory of injustice is at the heart of everything he has written. It is the
standpoint from which he looks at history; in his eyes, indeed, it seems to take the place of history. The remembrance
of things past is for him a remembrance of cruelty, and
history a record of justifiable, indeed, of noble vengeance:
vengeance on serfdom in his early stories, on Czarism in
The Quiet Don, on the enemies of bolshevism in *Virgin
Soil Upturned,* on Germans in "The Science of Hatred." Nor
need one expect a change of attitude in his projected large
novel, *They Fought for Their Country,* of which only fragments have so far appeared.

A stubborn, tenacious chauvinism is characteristic of
Sholokhov, a fierce hatred for all men alien to his own people. When he writes about those he loves, his tone is warm
and sentimental, as it is in a story of 1957, "A Man's Fate."
Like "The Science of Hatred," this is also a first-person narrative by a man who has suffered excrutiatingly during the

war. On a muddy day in early spring, as the writer sits waiting for a boat to ferry him across the river, a ragged man and a little boy come up to him. They are trudging to another town, and they stop off with the stranger for a rest. With sardonic matter-of-factness, the man, Andrey Sokolov, recites his tragic history: how the war deprived him of all that he held dear—his wife, his children, the little house he had built with the savings of ten years' hard work. The child with him is another victim of the war, an orphaned waif he has met by accident and adopted. Thus, without forgetting the frightful past, do survivors join forces and rebuild their lives. The story ends as abruptly as it began, with the arrival of the boatman and the travelers going their separate ways:

"Good-by, brother, good luck!"
"And good luck to you, too . . ."
With heavy sorrow I looked after them. . . . All might have gone well with our parting, but little Ivan, having gone a few steps, stumbling along with his little fat legs, turned his face to me abruptly and waved his little pink hand. And suddenly it was as if a soft, but clawed, paw had tightened itself about my heart, and I turned away quickly.

Sokolov had told him of his recurrent nightmares about his dead family, and of how although he never wept in the day, many a morning he found his pillow wet with tears. "No," the writer concludes,

. . . it is not only in their sleep, they weep, the middle-aged men, whose hair has turned gray during the years of war. They weep even in their waking hours. The important thing here is for you to know when to turn away in time. The chief thing is not to wound a child's heart, so he won't see how a man's scalding, stingy tear comes running down your cheek.

It would hardly be wrong to say that of all important Russian authors, Sholokhov is intellectually the most limited. If he has tears for the affairs of men, they are reserved for a very small part of the world's population, the Don Cossacks to whom he belongs, and but a section of these, the Bolsheviks among them. The rest of humanity are enemy aliens, and he is interested in them only as hostile forces to be fought and conquered. But if he is not a man of thought, he is a man of feeling. Passion is his theme—primitive, unrestrained, unreflective, the passions of love and of hatred, the excitement of battle, the violence of death, and also the sorrow of loss, the tenderness of pity. His knowledge and interests are restricted, but because he writes only of what he knows intimately and cares about intensely, his work is very different from Leonov's studious investigations or Gorky's expositions. Neither ethnography nor journalism, it is done from the heart, and is powerful in *The Quiet Don,* some of the early stories, and certain passages of *Virgin Soil Upturned.* But often this heart is too enmeshed in immediate sorrows, and then the necessary distance between suffering man and creative artist is destroyed, the fine tragic sense diluted, and the stark poetry reduced to tearful pathos and petulant resentment.

6

BORIS PASTERNAK AND THE
POEMS OF YURII ZHIVAGO

(1890-1960)

I

It was one o'clock in the morning when Lara, who had been pretending, really did fall asleep. Her nightdress and Katenka's and the bed linen, all freshly changed, shone clean, pressed, lacy. Even in those years Lara somehow managed to get things starched.

A blissful stillness surrounded Yurii Andreyevich; it was filled with happiness and breathed sweetly with life. The lamplight fell in quiet yellow on the white sheets of paper and swam like a spot of gold on the surface of the ink in the inkwell. Outside the window the frosty night was light blue. Yurii Andreyevich stepped into the neighboring cold, unlighted room, from which the outdoors could be seen more clearly, and looked out the window. The light of a full moon drew together the snowy meadow as with the tangible stickiness of egg white or white paint. The splendor of the frosty night was inexpressible. Peace was in the doctor's soul. He turned to the light, warmly heated room, and began to write.

In a scrawling hand, taking care that the appearance of what was written might express the living motion of his hand and not lose individuality, growing numb and soulless, he remembered and set down in steadily improving versions the best defined and most memorable of his poems, "Star of the Nativity," "Winter Night," and a good many others of the same kind, that were later forgotten, mislaid, and never found again by anyone.

This is the moment when Doctor Zhivago, fleeing with Lara and her little girl from Yuriatin, seeks precarious safety in the isolated, deserted Varykino, and finds brief respite there from the chaos of World War, Revolution, and civil war, which for years has tossed him from loss to loss and hardship to hardship. It is short-lived, this interval of peace, this blissful moment of creativity, love, and hard-won warmth, this white-gold-azure sphere of snow and moonlight, lamplight and clean linen, in which, as in a bubble, the little family is enclosed. Coming, as it does, on the brink of extinction, it is an epitome of life itself, or, at any rate, of the happiness and meaning that a man is able to snare and hold in the course of it. It is the most treasurable of all Zhivago's days, the pinnacle of his happiness, and—because some of his poems do survive—it is the one that assures him immortality; in the poems that he is writing, he himself, and all that made him what he is, are to remain alive after he is dead.

The two poems mentioned by name, "Star of the Nativity" and "Winter Night," both had their inception at the same instant on a remarkable night a long time before. The war had not yet come, nor the Revolution. Zhivago was in his early twenties, he was finishing his medical studies at the university, and was interested in poetry. It was Christmastime. He was on his way to a party with Tonya, the girl with whom, after the death of his parents, he had been brought up. Anna Ivanovna, Tonya's mother, was gravely ill, but she had insisted that they go to the party; and in bidding them good-by, had joined their hands and given them her blessing. Thus, unexpectedly and suddenly, they found themselves engaged, and this seemed strange, but also natural, desirable, and inevitable. That night also Larissa Guishar, a girl of a different upbringing and from another class of society, set out, a revolver concealed in her muff, to the flat of her seducer Komarovsky. She was desperately in need of money, was going to ask him for it, and would shoot him if he insulted her. He was not at home, and she pursued him to the party to which he had gone, making her way through dark streets encased in ice "thick as the glass of broken beer bottles" underfoot, and on either side, smearing the windows as with chalk, so that "over their opaque surfaces gleamed colored reflections of Christmas trees and the shadows of merrymakers, as if the people in the street were being shown misty pictures on white sheets hung before a magic lantern." Lara, making her way through this unreal world of dim reflections, like those of Plato's cave, has a sudden impulse to drop in on her fiancé, Pasha Antipov. She tells him that she is in difficulties, that they must be married soon, and as she does so, asks him to put out the lamp and light a candle:

Lara liked to talk in semidarkness by the light of candles. Pasha always reserved for her an unopened package of them. He exchanged the burnt stub in the candlestick for a whole, new one, placed it on the window sill and lighted it. The flame sputtered in the wax, shot out in all directions in crackling sparks, and drew itself up into a small straight arrow. A soft light filled the room. At the level of the candle, a little dark eye melted in the ice on the pane.

There is something mysterious in this minute spot on the frosty window; the small, black, flame-made eye has the uncanny effect of some living consciousness, some concentrated inward world of passion, peering out into the frozen, indifferent, and unconscious outside world with its formless, distant shadows. And it is at this instant that young Yurii Zhivago and Tonya come driving by:

They were driving along Kammergerskaya Street. Yura [this is the affectionate diminutive of Yurii] noticed a black, melted slit in the icy incrustation of one window. Through the slit a candle flame was shining; it reached the street almost with the consciousness of a gaze, as if the flame were spying on the riders and awaited someone.

"A candle burned on the table, a candle burned!" Yurii whispered to himself the beginning of something vague, unformed, in the hope that the rest would come of itself, without compulsion. It did not come.

It did not come, because Yurii could not as yet appreciate the magic of this moment, could not know that the unseen presences behind that pane of glass were to be entangled with himself, that the candle had been lighted for the woman who, through a series of the most incredible coincidences, was to become the center of his life.

A few weeks earlier Anna Ivanovna had had a conversation with him about life, death, and resurrection. She was very weak, was not expected to live. "Death may come any minute now," she had said to Yurii, tears streaming down her cheeks, "when you go to have your tooth pulled, you're frightened: it hurts, you prepare yourself. But now it's not a tooth, it's you, the whole of you, your whole life. . . . Tell me something. Console me." And Yurii, on the spur of the moment, found himself delivering an impromptu lecture, the point of which was that the meaning of life on earth and of life after death was a matter of consciousness: when one is alive, except in illness, one has a sense of oneself only in external manifestations: in what one does, and what one is to others. "Man in other men is the soul of man," he says. Consciousness, turned inward, is poison; consciousness turned outward is light. It "lights the way before us, so we shall not stumble." It is "the lighting of a flare before an oncoming locomotive." Perhaps he now noticed the candle in Pasha's window because the image of the outward-breaking light had occurred to him so recently. Perhaps. But if so, if the objective world had tendered him an image of his thought, he did not know it. The line of verse about the candle arrived inexplicably and sank deep in the mind, to re-emerge, only after a long dormition, as the mysterious refrain of a poignant lyric. Consciously, he was for the moment occupied with another idea. He was thinking of Alexander Blok, about whom he had promised to write an article for a student paper:

Suddenly it occurred to Yura that Blok was the manifestation of Christmas in all phases of Russian life, in the daily urban life of a northern city and in the latest literature, beneath the sky of a contemporary street and around the lighted Christmas tree in the living room of the present era. He thought that there was no necessity for any kind of article about Blok, that one need simply write a Russian Adoration of the Magi, like that of the Dutch, with frost, wolves, and a dark pine forest.

Now in Varykino, more than a decade later, with "frost, wolves, and a dark pine forest" actually present, the two poems, and a score of others, are written. "Star of the Nativity" turns out to be the first of a series on the life of Christ, "Winter Night," one of several that re-create passages in Zhivago's experience. The religious and the secular poems complement each other, are indeed a commentary on each other, and together they are a summary and interpretation of the whole novel, the ultimate knot of that long, looped, much-knotted thread which is Zhivago's story, the last stop on the circular, crisscrossed highway of his journey, which seems, but only seems, to bring him back to the place from which he started; it is the final station on that railroad track he follows, where, at the last, nothing of the long trip has been forgotten, where the passing moments of many lives through many years have come together for all eternity in a final, all-embracing and intricate truth. Structurally, "The Poems of Doctor Zhivago," which follow "The Epilogue," are the conclusive, necessary resolution, the final chord in which a wandering melody has come to rest. It is a scheme which is, so far as I know, unique in fiction. Other novelists have been concerned with writers and their work, but none, with the possible exception of Pushkin, has taken his stand on so profoundly, so essentially aesthetic a position, and Pushkin's attitude is always implicit, never so overtly demonstrated. Pushkin steps into his narratives in playful asides, tells you jokingly about himself as artist and about what he understands art to be; but it is not so much in what he says as in the style of his verse and the structure of his narratives that one realizes how profoundly aesthetic is his outlook on the world; it is simply that whatever his subject, he writes like a man who is in all respects, and every inch, an artist. Other poets, of whom James Joyce is the most notable instance, adopt a more extreme position. To them art is completely autonomous, and not just the fruit of rationality, balance, and detachment. In their writing, words are no longer mere instruments of expression or communication, but the substance, the theme itself, of their work. Pasternak differs from all these in being always concerned, and especially in *Doctor Zhivago*, with dramatizing what he conceives to be the function of art. And this function he sees as nothing less than the means whereby the experience of individuals is made permanent as well as comprehensible. In other words, art to him is the very principle of concreteness, intelligibility, and perpetuity; without it, men's inward lives, evanescent as dreams, would vanish without trace. Were it not for his poems, all that Yurii Zhivago has lived through, his observations and his dreams, his thoughts and emotions, would remain unformulated and ununderstood, and would die with him. The poems show how even slight and wholly personal incidents become significant, how a casual episode turns into a human value, and so endures beyond the life of any one man.

In "Star of the Nativity," Zhivago achieves what he had wanted to do from the first as a tribute to Alexander Blok: he paints a Russian Adoration of the Magi in the style of the Dutch. The landscape is Russian, but the simple reverence of the poem, its close attention to commonplace details belong both to the Dutch masters and to the tradition of Russian realism. The ordinary animals, the ordinary people, Mary's arrangements, like any housekeeper's for receiving guests, are the setting for the earthly marvel, watched over by the supernatural star. The poem celebrates, in grateful wonder, the miracle of Christianity that endows the simplest men with the gift of magic.

"Winter Night" is also full of wonder, but this is the wonder of amazement:

> It snowed and snowed throughout the land
> Snow swept from end to end,
> A candle burned on the stand,
> A candle burned.

Snowflakes fall on the window sill like summer insects flying to a flame, circles and arrows are sculptured by the storm on window panes, and shadows are cast up to the lighted ceiling, shadows of

> Crossed arms, crossed legs,
> Of fate, the crossing;

two little shoes fall to the floor, making a noise, and candle wax drips tears upon a dress—

> And all was lost in snowy murk
> All white and hoary.
> A candle burned on the stand,
> A candle burned.

The flame is shaken by a draught from a corner, and, angel-like, temptation's fever raises its wings crosswise.

> It snowed all February through,
> And almost always
> A candle burned on the stand,
> A candle burned.

The ways of Fate shape an unpredictable, mysterious design; they are inexplicable and teach no lesson. The whole novel, indeed, all of Pasternak's work, may be said to follow the two lines of wonder represented by these poems, the pagan and the Christian, which, however divergent they may be in the moral sphere, are but different ways of judging the same spectacle, the universal lot of man since the beginning of history. Poetry gives voice to them both: to the pagan, in the drama of events; to the Christian, in terms of a myth. They are so voiced in the poems of Yurii Zhivago, while in the epic itself of his life, pagan Fate, general and inscrutable, and Christian principles, explicable and individual, are woven, like his poems, into a complicated tissue of obscurity and clearness. Even as a schoolboy, we are told,

> Yura had dreamed of writing prose, of doing a book descriptive of life, in which he might include what had been most astonishing in all he had had a chance to see and think through. But for such a book he was still too young, and so he wrote verses instead, like a painter who, during a whole lifetime, might make sketches for a large canvas he has envisaged.

Yura never does achieve the prose work he has dreamed of. Pasternak writes it for him, but in the way in which he would have done it, as a lyric poet, like himself. That is why the long story is a series of intense episodes, united, paradoxically, in their very separateness, each of them complete in itself and, so far as plot is concerned, related to others only by the merest chance. Coincidence, which plays a major role, far from being a structural flaw, is a symbol of Pasternak's awe before the play of Fate.

The poem about the lighted candle could have been written only when the experience of many years had shown Zhivago the wonder of that night's events, not the least wonderful of which was the sheer accident of his having driven past the sign of his destiny and having sensed it, all unconsciously, in terms of a poetic line, as if in some transcendental sphere it had been determined that Fate should gaze on Yurii and that he should take note of that gaze without understanding it. This, now in Varykino, he can recognize, remembering also that on that night Anna Ivanovna had died, that on that night he himself had first become aware of Tonya as his future wife, that on that night also he saw Lara, whom he had seen just once before, in boyhood, and then too in melodramatic circumstances, and that the man with whom he had seen her then and whom she had this time tried to kill, he now recognized as the lawyer who had been involved in his father's fortunes and was largely responsible for his death. But the full intricacy of this night's magic could not be revealed even to him. He did not know that by the lighted candle of his poem Lara and Pasha had arrived at a decision to get married. Nor could he know how well Lara—and also without knowing why—had remembered that candle by the frosty window, while Lara, for her part, cannot be aware of the mysterious appositeness of her remarking as she wakes up while Zhivago is still writing: "And you are still burning and warming yourself, my bright little candle!"

The idyl of Varykino is interrupted by Komarovsky, who reappears to save Lara from danger, inducing her to leave with him and persuading Zhivago to promise, falsely, that he will follow. They never see each other again, and of this Zhivago has a premonition: "Farewell," he whispers, waiting for a last glimpse of the departing sleigh, "farewell, my only loved one, and lost forever. . . . Farewell until the next world." We see Lara for the last time some eight years later by Yurii's coffin. It is by sheer accident that she has come upon it, and it is also by accident that it stands in Pasha's former room in Kammergerskaya Street. Looking on the face of the man she has loved, in the room of the one she once loved even more, Lara meditates that

No one is left. One is dead. The other killed himself. And only he remains alive who should have been killed, on whose life she had made an attempt, but missed. . . . Ah, but that was at Christmastime, and before the contemplated shooting of that monster of meanness, there had been a conversation with the boy Pasha in this very room; and of Yura, to whom people are now bidding farewell, there was as yet no trace in her life.

And she began to strain her memory in an attempt to reproduce that Christmas talk with Pashenka, but could remember nothing except the candle burning on the window sill and the little circle that had melted near it in the icy bark of the pane.

How could she imagine that the dead man who lay here on the table had seen that little eye as he drove past along the street, and had noticed the candle? That in that flame, seen from the outside—'A candle burned on the table, a candle burned'—the predestined course of his life had its beginning.

Lara remembers the candle, not what she and Pasha had talked about on that night, remembers, that is, not the consciously adopted plan of her life but the symbolic sign of destiny she never fully understands, the design of which was being shaped that moment in a crossing of lines that transcended her consciousness. In Pasternak's highly integrated world, a room forms a whole with that which is outside its windows, a man's soul is what he is "in others"; thoughts and emotions are part of the Nature in which they take place, "subject" and "object" are one, and the angel wings of Fate cast great shadows by the light of candles on the ceilings of small rooms. There is no need to search for allegorical meanings in such circumstances as these, to try to explain in terms of allegory or any kind of legend such events, for example, as the uncanny intrusion of Samdeviatov, who chances to meet Zhivago and Lara in a difficult moment of their lives and gives them much necessary help, nor the still more wonderful advent of Evgraf, Yurii's supernatural half-brother. The one is a beneficent accident of a kind that to Pasternak is a habitual part of life's mystery; the other embodies an abstraction for which it is hard to find a name: in part Evgraf is Zhivago's poetic inspiration, but more than that, he is whatever it may be that shakes the kaleidoscope of human lives, and, standing apart, is alone capable of seeing their pattern, a manipulator like Pasternak himself, who, tossing the bright fragments of Zhivago's fortunes, is the only one for whom it is possible to know the full significance of Lara's lighted candle.

The book is full of inexplicable chance encounters that play in and out of understandable events in elaborate counterpoint. At the outset of the novel, for example, Nikolay Nikolaevich Vedenyapin, Yura's uncle and guardian, has brought his young nephew on a visit to Ivan Ivanovich Voskoboynikov, pedagogue and popularizer. A schoolboy, Nika Dudorov, lives with Voskoboynikov, and the eleven-year-old Yura has looked forward to seeing him; but Nika eludes him, and while the boys go their separate ways and Ivan Ivanovich exchanges views on man and God with

Nikolay Nikolaevich, the five o'clock express rushes past on the far side of the river. They see it from the picturesque spot they have chosen for their discussion. Voskoboynikov is used to setting his watch by its passing; but this time, unaccountably, the train stops. "Strange," he says, "something is wrong. . . . Something has happened." The onlookers cannot know that what has actually happened is that a man has thrown himself off the train and that the emergency cord has been pulled by another passenger who has tried to prevent the suicide, nor that the man who has killed himself is Yura's father, that he was accompanied on his last journey by his lawyer Komarovsky, that the one who tried to stop him was the father of Misha Gordon, soon to become Yura's friend and schoolmate, and that, years later, the final comment on Yurii Zhivago will be the reading of his posthumously published poems by the middle-aged Nika Dudorov and Misha Gordon. Nor can they see the tragically impressive old woman who steps out of the train to view the dead body, she who is to become the guardian of Pasha Antipov, Lara's future husband. As in the candle episode, so now, men view uncomprehendingly the outward signs of fate. On a plane beyond their awareness, their lives are strangely knotted; and as they live, they proceed from crossroad to crossroad, making but half-willful choices, coming to milestones along the way, flares that light up for us, if not always for them, the inevitable but unpredictable march of events.

There is, for example, the moment when Tonya gives birth to Yura's son. The hour of delivery coincides with the acknowledgment of Zhivago's first, brilliant diagnosis and also with the news that he is to be called to the front. Here is another knot of unknown beginnings and ends: the beginning of a new life, the promise of a bright career, the end of peace—and, quite concealed from view, the start of passionate involvements, of crucial decisions, of the first unwilled and unwilling step in an extraordinary spiritual evolution. Past and future are enclosed in the immediate present, and Nature participates symbolically in the event. Tonya's labor is prolonged. During the three days she is in the hospital, a slanting rain keeps falling and the wind shakes an old vine, as if trying to uproot it:

The nasty weather continued the third day. . . . The rain came down in the most disconsolate way, without increasing or diminishing, despite the wildness of the wind which seemed to grow sharper because the rain that fell upon the earth was unresponsive to it. Gusts of wind tormented the tendrils of a wild grapevine which wreathed one of the terraces. As if wanting to uproot the whole plant, the wind tossed it, shook it in mid-air, and threw it down in disgust like a torn piece of clothing.

This tearing, tossing wind and slanting rain, like Zhivago's own anxiety and Tonya's unremitting suffering, are a contrast to an image that occurs to Yurii when, just after the child is born, he is allowed to peep into the delivery room through a slit in the door:

Tonya lay in the middle of the hospital room on a surgical cot with an adjustable plank. She lay rather high. . . .
Raised toward the ceiling higher than is usual with ordinary mortals, Tonya was sunk in the vapor of what she had suffered; she seemed to be misty from exhaustion. Tonya rose high in the hospital room, as in a harbor a bark might rise, when it has just arrived and been unloaded, a bark that plied the sea of death toward the continent of life, with new immigrant souls who came no one knew whence. She had just discharged one such soul and was now lying at anchor, resting in all the emptiness of her unburdened flanks. And with her, rested her strained and battered tackle and her casings, and her oblivion, her lost memory of where she had been recently, what she had traversed and how she came to port. And so, as no one knew the geography of the land under whose flag she had been moored, one did not know in what language to address her.

This timeless image of the boat at anchor, bringing new souls from unknown shores, with its Platonic, Virgilian, and Dantesque echoes, underscores the difference between the transient and the eternal, and strikes once more the major theme of *Doctor Zhivago,* which begins with death and ends with resurrection.

But now, like an echo in a more commonplace, though also mysterious realm, the harbor image is carried over to another woman. Directly after the birth of Yura's son, we are told about Lara's married life. She and Pasha Antipov have settled in a town on a large river. "She liked it in Yuriatin; it was her native city." After the unhappy uncertainties of her former life, this too is a haven, and because the town's name is a derivative of Zhivago's there is a suggestion of the spiritual harbor which, in future, she is to find in him. Here, too, is Lara's three-year-old Katenka, playing in the yard under an upturned boat, finding her own child's shelter beneath its roof. Yuriatin is, moreover, both a shipping town and a station of the Ural Railway, on which much momentous traveling is to take place; the symbol of the crossroads is unmistakable, and all these realistically plausible details are steeped, in themselves and in their juxtaposition, in the element of a mysterious Fate.

The most obvious coincidence in the book is an episode at the front, where several human beings whose lives have been, or are to be, interrelated are unexpectedly brought together, without any one of them knowing the identity of the others:

The dead, mutilated man was the reserve soldier Gimazedtin; the shouting officer in the wood was his son, the sublieutenant Galiulin; the nurse was Lara; Gordon and Zhivago were the witnesses. All of them were together, all side by side, and some did not recognize each other, others had never known each other; and the one remained forever unconfirmed, the other awaited discovery on the next occasion, at a new meeting.

But this episode differs from the others in the place it occupies in the narrative: it is a conclusion, not a beginning, and its mystery is self-enclosed. If it lacks the subtlety of the others, the explicit comment which accompanies it is a rare bit of explanation: its purpose is to underscore that sense of wonder out of which the whole is written.

Pasternak's habit of thought is not discursive; and his long narratives, held together by implicit similarities of episodes that are in themselves complete, have the elliptical continuity of modern verse, not the plain-spoken consecutiveness of the nineteenth-century novel. Only occasionally does he make use of explicit comparisons. Such a rare occasion is Yura's first impression of the October Revolution, of which he gets the news on a snowy street corner in Moscow:

Something similar [he thought] was taking place in the moral and the physical world, near and far, on earth and in the air. Somewhere, there sounded, like little islets, the last volleys of the broken resistance. Somewhere on the horizon leaped and burst the feeble glow of extinguished fires. And just such rings and funnels as these were chased and curled by the snow storm, steaming beneath Yurii Andreyevich's feet on the wet pavements and sidewalks.

This reminds one of Blok's first impression of the Revolution, and it is natural that Zhivago's should resemble that of his much admired poet; but here Fate weaves the moral and physical threads of his private fortunes into a more intricate pattern than the one of which he is aware. He happens to get the news at a crossroads already endowed with magical properties. "I know that place," he had previously said about it to a colleague, "unexpected things keep happening to me there: either I meet someone I haven't seen in twenty years, or I find something." Once he had helped a wounded stranger there, and this man later became his protector. Now, to see the newsprint better, he walks through the glass doors of a brightly lighted, five-story house, and there, in the lobby, encounters a youth who mistakes him, he thinks, for someone else:

Before him stood a youngster, about eighteen years of age, in a stiff reindeer jacket, with the fur outside, as they are worn in Siberia, and in a fur cap of the same kind. The boy's face was dark, with narrow Kirghiz eyes. There was something aristocratic in this face, that quick spark, that hidden fineness, which seems to have come from far away and is found in people of complex, mixed origin.

The boy stops, confused, as if he wanted to, but did not dare, speak; but discouraged from conversation by Yurii Andreyevich, who looks him coldly up and down, he leaves the building. On the way home, Yurii Andreyevich is lucky enough to get himself a piece of much-needed firewood, and this minor bit of good fortune is a presage of great beneficence to come. The fairy-tale quality of the whole episode is unmistakable, but only the most astute reader will straightway recognize the youth's identity, remembering a much earlier, and rather casual, mention of Zhivago's half-brother and of the house he lived in in Siberia, a photograph of which had filled Yura with superstitious discomfort, as if its five windows gazed ominously on him across the breadth of Russia.

In the next episode the identity is revealed, and again in a tangled skein of fateful circumstances. One winter night —it is not clear which of three successive, indistinguishable winters of want, cold, and anxiety it is—Zhivago is asked to attend a patient in a distant part of the city. He makes his way through deep snow on gloomy, deserted streets to a crowded tenement. The house turns out to be one which Lara used to visit as a girl, the one where Pasha had been brought up. Yurii had come upon Lara at the front, during the war, but had by this time, as he thought, put her out of his mind. After his call on the patient, he is escorted by Olya Demina, who had been Lara's girlhood friend, to a crossroads from which he will know how to find his way home:

And so they parted. The light of Demina's small lantern poked into some narrow stone steps, and ran ahead lighting up the soiled walls of a dirty stairway, but the doctor was left in darkness. To the right lay Sadovaya-Triumphalnaya, to the left Sadovaya-Karetnaya. In the black distance, on the black snow, these were no longer streets in the ordinary meaning of the word, but, as it were, two lanes cut through the thick taiga of far-stretching stone buildings, as in the impassable forests of the Urals or Siberia.

Olya Demina's little lantern, like Pasha's candle, lights up a bit of Zhivago's darkness, reaching prophetically into the future. The doctor had recognized his patient's case as typhus; it was not a nervous disorder, as her husband had supposed because the onset of the illness came just when an old, rundown grandfather clock had suddenly begun to strike. When Zhivago gets home, he learns that in his absence their broken alarm clock had started up of its own accord. "The hour of my typhus has struck," he remarks jokingly. He does catch typhus, though somewhat later; but meanwhile these wonderfully resuscitated clocks have another significance; they strike the hour of his revived interest in Lara; they are an accompaniment to the light which Olya Demina has thrown on his own situation at the crossroads of his fortunes. When he falls ill, he sees, in his delirium, how Tonya places "two Sadovayas on his writing table, Sadovaya-Karetnaya to the left, and to the right, Sadovaya-Triumphalnaya," and puts his bedside lamp near them. He himself is feverishly writing what he has always wanted, but never before been able, to write; and is now and then prevented from doing his work by a boy with narrow Kirghiz eyes and a reindeer jacket of the kind worn in the Urals or Siberia. It is clear to him that this boy is his death. But the boy is also helping him to write his poem. How, then, wonders the sick man, can he also be his death? "Can there be profit in death, can death be helpful?" The poem he is writing is called "Turmoil" and it has to do with the period between the Entombment and the Resurrection:

He had always wanted to write, how in the course of three days, the storm of the black, worm-ridden earth laid siege to and attacked the immortal embodiment of love, throwing itself on him with its clods and masses, exactly as the waves of the sea at full tide swoop down on the shore and bury it beneath them. How for three days the black storm of earth rages, advances and retreats.

And two rhymed lines pursued him. . . .

It is impossible to give an adequate translation of these two lines, because their meaning depends on associations suggested by the sound of syllables:

Rádi kosnútsya [literally, "glad to touch"]
Nádo prosnútsya ["one must wake up."]

The *a d* of *Radi* and *Nado* (glad and must) suggest other words to the delirious poet: "*ad* [hell], and *raspad* [dissolution], and *razlozhenie* [disintegration] and *smert'* [death]," the latter, of course, through an association not of sounds but ideas. "And yet," he thinks, "the spring, too, is glad to touch them, and the Magdalene, and life. And— one must awake. One must wake up and get up. One must be resurrected." Thus in the depths of delirium, through the confused symbols of transformed memories and perceptions, the major theme is once more adumbrated. The Sadovaya crossroads are recalled because of the emotions they had stirred, the boy with Kirghiz eyes has actually been visiting Zhivago's sick room, while the idea of death and resurrection is naturally induced by illness and the hope of recovery. The concept of the stormy three days' entombment as an attempt of earth to engulf immortal love could be an imaginative transmutation of Tonya's three-day confinement, as well as of the Gospel story, and the dual nature of death as both destructive and creative is a ruling idea of the novel.

Pasternak's crisscrossing lines of Fate are not the stock in trade of those eighteenth- and nineteenth-century novelists whose purpose was to astonish and amuse; they are exempla, rather, necessary demonstrations of an uncanny, but not unnatural world, a world of mystery, where man must wonder at how strange the evolution of events may be and at how illogically a moment may contain the past, how unpredictably the future. This is not the mystery of terror nor of thrills, but of a sense of the inscrutable, and of a reasoned conviction that to be honest man must stop short of ultimate conclusions, and that a poet can deal only with the particular, however spellbound he may be by generalities. All that is marvelous in the plot is the equivalent of such spellbound amazement. No explanation is attempted as to how or why the thread is knotted. Religious, political, philosophic discourses are peripheral to a prevailing sense of wonder; they elucidate beliefs, but do not reach out to the incomprehensible. Implicitly, the ultimate questions are there, but Pasternak, unlike Tolstoy, does not submit them to rational analysis. His conclusions are a sheaf of poems, and his answers—what answers there can be to the final *how* and *why*—are given in the structure of the story: the improbability of events and their summing up in poetry. Doctor Zhivago is a demonstration, or a drama, or a fable of Man, in which beliefs and ideas, like all the processes involved in the hero's development, have their being within one inclusive symbol, in the same way as the wanderings and journeys, the roads, streets, and railroad tracks wind and tangle within that vast enclosure, a relatively brief lifetime. The inclusive symbol is nothing less than the marvel of life itself in Pasternak's own, special view of it, as an endlessly reiterated challenge to death.

I I

His novel is the fullest and clearest affirmation of this concept of life, which evolved gradually in his mind. The best introduction to it is his first autobiography, *Safe Conduct*, a reticent, compressed sketch, published in 1931, which provides definitions, as it were, of the terms he uses. It is by no means a conventional self-portrait, and its silences are significant, for so strictly is it directed to the outcome, which is in essence aesthetic (the issue is the poet's knowledge of his function and his art), that it omits the kind of detail that is usually included in such histories, and results not so much in the story of a man, as in a little *ars poetica*—its three divisions representing three stages in the poet's progress: the arrival at the threshold of poetry, the discovery of poetry, and the portrait of the poet, who turns out to be not Pasternak himself, but Mayakovsky. Mayakovsky had begun his autobiography: "I am a poet. That is what makes me interesting," and had then listed those events in his life which had had a bearing on his work. But Pasternak says that he is not writing his biography at all, that he thinks "only heroes deserve a real biography"; what he does write is a definition of art in terms of his experience which, though entirely his own, is not at all exclusive. The end, like Zhivago's poems, gives meaning to all that precedes; and in the light of the goal toward which everything is pointed, chance meetings and casual occurrences take on magical significance, as they do in *Doctor Zhivago*. The book is dedicated "To the memory of R. M. Rilke," and there is a comment on this: "I do not present my reminiscences to the memory of Rilke. On the contrary, I myself received them as a present from him"; received them, that is, from the poet who had unwittingly and mysteriously come into his line of vision, had, all fortuitously, at a crossroads of devotion, fallen into his hands, had been, as it were, the recurrent sign of his destiny. This is the sense in which his memories had been *given* him by Rilke; if fate had contrived another ending, the reminiscences, too, would have been different and the autobiography inscribed to someone else.

The story begins with a train journey:

An express train was leaving Kursk station on a hot summer morning in the year 1900. Just before the train started someone in a black Tyrolean cape appeared in the window. A tall woman was with him. Probably she would be his mother or his elder sister. The two of them and my father discussed a subject to which we were all warmly devoted, but the woman exchanged occasional words with my mother in Russian, while the stranger spoke German only. Although I knew the language thoroughly I had never heard it spoken as he spoke it. And for this reason, there on a platform thronged with people, between two bells, this stranger struck me as a silhouette in the midst of bodies, a fiction in the mass of reality.

Presently the couple reappeared and talked of Tolstoy—to the boy "an endlessly important theme," which played "an obscure role" in his family and was "symbolised by the initials Count L.N."; the strangers, he gathered, were on their way to visit Sophia Andreyevna (that is, the Countess Tolstoy), but who they were was revealed to him only three or four years later, and by the merest accident. One memorable December twilight he was helping his mother tidy his father's bookshelves, "when suddenly from one particularly rollicking and disobedient stack fell a book in a faded grey binding. Absolutely by chance I did not squeeze it back, and picking it off the floor, afterwards took it to my room." After "a long time" he "grew to like this book, and soon another one too which came to join it and was inscribed to my father in the same handwriting," and still more time went by before he realized that this "Rainer Maria Rilke must be the same German whom we once left behind us on our journey a long time ago, in summer, on the whirling embankment of a forgotten forest halt." He ran to his father, "to check [his] surmise," and his father bore it out, wondering why it "should so excite" the boy. How could the father know what a sense of fatefulness was involved in this discovery! It was not only that the poems had come into his son's hands as accidentally as once upon a time their author had risen as "a fiction" before him, but that the hour at which the book fell to the floor was, in other ways, a crucial one in his history; but even the boy himself could not as yet be aware of this, and his own excitement was due in part to a premonition, a dim sense of what was to happen, as much as to knowledge of what had already happened.

On that day Scriabin, another friend of the family, came to say good-by on his way abroad. The boy was infatuated with him, as only a thirteen-year-old child can be infatuated:

This adoration struck me more cruelly and no less fantastically than a fever. On seeing him, I would turn pale, only to flush deeply immediately afterwards for this very pallor. If he spoke to me, my wits deserted me, and amid the general laughter I would hear myself answering something that was not to the point, but what exactly—I could never hear.

Now "good wishes re-echoed. Into the general heap of parting benedictions fell mine, like a clot of blood." Then, "the door banged, the key turned twice." His mother, at the piano, was trying out the études Scriabin had left, and Boris ran out "without a coat or hat . . . to make him come back or see him just once again." He did not catch up with him, and returned to help his mother with the bookshelves. Two passions had met in the trivial incident of the fallen book, the ruling one for music and the foreshadowed one for poetry, but this he was not to know for many years, not until after he had given up music for philosophy and philosophy, under the impact of love, for poetry.

After an absence of six years, the adored Scriabin, returning to Moscow, showered praises on Pasternak's compositions, telling him that "it was clumsy to speak of talent for music" with regard to them, when "something incomparably bigger" was involved. Why, then, after such encouragement, did Pasternak relinquish music? Because at the very moment of praise, his idol made light of a defect of which he was painfully conscious, his lack of "absolute pitch." Nor did it help him to discover that Scriabin himself was equally deprived, nor to hear him repeat the banal arguments: "What of Wagner? and Tschaikowsky? And hundreds of piano tuners who have it?" Such arguments could have no effect on one for whom music was not "a profession" but "a cult": a votary must be chosen, he may not impose himself on a divinity that rejects him. How great musicians could have come to terms with this insurmountable defect must remain a mystery. Pasternak retained his respect for Scriabin, but could not follow him:

Did the incident dethrone my god? No, never—it lifted him from his former height to yet another. Why did he deny me that most straightforward reply for which I so longed? That was his secret.

Why, that is, instead of talking about Wagner and Tschaikowsky and the "hundreds of piano tuners who have it," would he not admit: "Borya, why even I have not got it"? As he left, Pasternak ". . . did not know . . . how to thank him. . . . Something welled up in me. Something tore and sought freedom. Something wept and something exulted." "Something wept" for a great loss, and "something exulted" in freedom from falseness and the promise of a new devotion. Bringing the news of his success to his anxious parents, he "walked along the side streets and crossed the road more often than was necessary," not yet aware of what exactly had taken place:

Absolutely without my being conscious of it, the world which only the day before had seemed innate in me forever, was melting and breaking up inside me. I walked along gathering speed at every corner and I did not know that that night I was already breaking with music.

He did not drop music, and his friends and relatives thought that his career lay with it. For the rest, he wrote poems occasionally, but considered this "an unfortunate weakness," and with "wholehearted enthusiasm" studied philosophy at the University of Moscow, although the lectures were mostly boring, a "peculiar mixture of moribund metaphysics and cheerless enlightenment," the "obviousness" of which induced "attacks of chronic impatience. . . . The history of philosophy turned into belles-lettristic dogmatism and psychology appeared as breezy triflings in brochure style"; there was only one professor who could talk in such a way that "time did not take offense at him." Then, in the summer of 1912, he went to the University of Marburg, the seat, under the direction of Hermann Cohen, of Neo-Kantian Idealism. This summer, enchantingly re-created in *Safe Conduct*, was decisive.

The University of Marburg was not like Moscow:

It was independent, it uprooted everything from its rudiments and built on a clear space. It did not accept the lazy routines of all conceivable "isms," which always cling to their stock of omniscience at tenth hand, are always ignorant, and always for some reason or other afraid of a revision in the fresh air of age-old culture,

and Hermann Cohen was a great teacher. "*Il ne racontait pas l'histoire de la philosophie*," another of his students has said of him, "*il la vivait et forçait ses auditeurs à la vivre avec lui*." ("He did not relate the history of philosophy, he lived it and forced his listeners to live it with him.") To Pasternak his teaching was a revelation. He learned from him "how a great inner world is dramatised when it has been presented with a great man," how the history of mankind is the history of ideas conceived by individuals, how the thought of the past is alive in the continuity of its evolution, a philosophic concept as vital in the present as it had been at its inception. Many years later, after much had happened both to his world and to himself, and Hermann Cohen had long since died, Pasternak recalled

. . . how the crested old man in spectacles would lift his head and step back, as he held forth on the Greek conception of immortality, and how he would wave his hand in the direction of the Marburg fire-station in determining the shape of the Elysian Fields. . . . How on some other occasion, having already stealthily arrived at pre-Kantian metaphysics, he would bill and coo and flirt with it, then suddenly clearing his throat, would give it a terrible reprimand with citations from Hume. How when he had finished coughing and made a long pause, he would say, wearily and peaceably, *"Und nun, meine Herrn . . ."* And that would mean that the reprimand had been given to that century, the performance was over and one could move on to the subject of the course.

"With the delirious ambition of a novice," Pasternak wondered whether Cohen would ever notice him, ever invite him "to one of his Sunday dinners," for such an invitation was an accolade; it "raised a person in the esteem of the people there because it marked the beginning of a new philosophical career." And yet when the much-desired invitation was at last extended, Pasternak did not accept it, did not even acknowledge it.

This is what happened. In Moscow, to lighten his parents' financial burden, he had sometimes given private lessons, and from the age of fourteen had been in love with one of his pupils, "a beautiful and charming girl, perfectly brought up and spoiled from her very infancy by an old Frenchwoman who adored her." Now, with her younger sister, this enchanting girl stopped at Marburg on her way to Berlin. For Pasternak the three days he spent with them resembled his "usual way of living as little as holidays resemble ordinary days." He took them everywhere, talked "continuously, intoxicated with their laughter"; and on the morning of their departure, in a state of "terrible" nervousness, confronted the girl with the declaration that "it couldn't go on like this," and begged her to marry him. She refused. Their meeting was interrupted by men who came to fetch her trunk, he set himself to rights, accompanied the sisters to the station, and when the train was already pulling out, "just managed to grasp" that "the ability to say good-bye" had left him completely, that he "had said good-bye only to the younger sister," and so he "jumped at full speed onto the step of the carriage" and was dragged in by "an excited conductor." He had jumped on the moving train "simply to say good-bye" but now "forgot about it again" and remembered it only when "the roof of the Berlin platform was rushing upon [them] and snorting." The sisters assured him that they "had said good-bye and that [he] had merely not noticed it." They were to be met, he must not be seen with them, and at the station he "vanished in the crowd." It was a rainy night and there was no return train till morning. ". . . Without an overcoat, without luggage, without papers," he was turned away from lodging after lodging, and at last found a room of the kind "one would normally take only as a last resort." His face twitched and his eyes constantly filled with tears, because his "thirst for a last finally ravaging farewell remained unquenched. It was like the longing for a huge cadenza, which would shatter an ailing music to its roots so that it would all suddenly be transported far away at the descent of the final chord." Having been "denied this alleviation," he spent the night in his miserable room, sitting "sideways on a chair which stood by the window," his head resting on the little table that stood by the chair. Remembering this night eighteen years later, Pasternak writes:

Why do I describe my posture in such detail? Because I remained in it the whole night long. Occasionally, as though at the touch of something, I lifted my head and did something with the wall which drew away from me obliquely below its dark ceiling. I measured it as with a foot-rule from below with my unseeing intentness. Then my sobbing would start afresh. And again I would drop my head in my hands.

I have described the position of my body in such detail because this was its morning position on the bench of the flying train and was memorised for that reason. It was the posture of a person who had fallen away from something high which had long upheld him and long borne him onwards, until finally it let him fall and noisily speeding by above his head, vanished for ever behind a bend.

It was not the pain alone that made every detail of this occasion memorable; there was, emerging from it, an unexpected revitalizing force that picked him up from the place he had been dropped and carried him to what proved to be his ultimate destination. On the train back from Berlin, he had a vision of his disorderly room in Marburg, with the books he had spread all over the floor in preparation of a report in which, at Cohen's request, he was to develop certain arguments he had advanced in previous papers. Pasternak had given his landlady strict instructions not to "lay a hand on them," and the dust of many days had been settling in the room. Now, as the picture of his work flashed into his mind, lying "like a tree-fern which spreads its leafy coils" in the shape of those books with passages marked for quotation, he seemed to see his philosophic venture "in its entirety and also its probable fate." The morning train brought back to Marburg "a completely new person"; and now, when the landlady proudly delivered the Herr Professor's invitation to Sunday dinner, his only reply was to tidy up his room, "the equivalent to burning an uncopied manuscript."

Then I had a wash and went on to the balcony as I was drying myself. It was getting dark. Rubbing my neck on the towel, I gazed into the distance which joined Ockershausen and Marburg. I could no longer remember how I had looked in that direction

on the evening of my arrival. It was the end, the end! The end
of philosophy, that is, the end of whatever thought I had entertained about it.

He took another train—to Frankfort, where his father,
brother, and a cousin had arrived for a holiday. But he
"hardly noticed all this." He was "writing poetry. Day and
night . . . about the sea, about the dawn, about the southern rain, about the hard coal of the Harz." The emotion he
had experienced had brought him to himself, showed him
that his interest in philosophy had been poetic rather than
scholarly, that he had "turned to books . . . not from any
disinterested attraction to knowledge but for literary quotations." He was breaking with philosophy at the moment
of a coveted triumph, just as a few years earlier he had
abandoned music. And, basically, for the same reason. In
this case, too, his triumph was unjustifiable: he lacked "disinterested curiosity" just as he lacked absolute pitch; and
so, both philosophy and music had "fallen behind on the
deep horizon of remembrance," as he was sped on the
course of his legitimate, predestined sphere of action. It was
under the impact of two powerful emotions, the passions
of love and of philosophic speculation, that Pasternak was
impelled to his first serious poetic effort. And his first poems
are an expression of both. Every one of them is written
about something specific: a day, a place, an object, about
which emotions cluster, but this concrete center is only a
signpost to a larger theme.

I I I

There is, for example a little poem called "February." "One
must get ink and weep," it starts, "write sobbing about February." But is this really February—these rooks that, like
pears, drop into puddles, this cab that transports one

through the screech of wheels and the ringing of church bells to where the downpour is "louder than ink and tears"? It is rather a mood of desolation that happens to occur on a muddy winter's day, in which rain, ink, and tears are on the same plane of experience, all of them the stuff of an emotion which is conveyed in turbulent images, whereas the music of the lines is quiet, so that the poem is at once violent and subdued, in keeping with what it is actually saying, which is that when a poet creates, he stands at the still center of everything that roars, races, flies, rings, and screeches, while passion makes ink "loud" as rain and compels it to the spasmodic utterance of wind and sobs. February is only an excuse for this theme of poetic creation, a hint or token of it. Then there are "Venice" and "The Railway Station." Of these Pasternak wrote later that all he wanted of them was that the one should "contain the city of Venice" and the other "the Brest railway station," as he saw it, "far away, at the end of the tracks and platforms . . . all in clouds and smoke, a railway farewell horizon, behind which the trains were hidden, and which contained the history of relationships, meetings and partings, and the events before and after them." This, in effect, is what the poems are: the station of which he writes at a given moment becomes the microcosm of everything that has happened in it or ever will happen. And Venice, reflected in the canal— the gondolas, the sound of mandolins, and lingering above them in daylight, a mysterious cry he had heard in the night—Venice stands as the sign of a long history of art and crime; with its waves and gliding boats and the passing moment in which it is seen, it too is like the railway station with the trains that come and vanish, a place of endlessly unique and eternally repeated departures, meetings, and farewells. All of Pasternak's work seeks to re-create such particular instances as these in the way they occurred, unveiled by extraneous reflections and unadorned by rhetoric. But if they are vivid, it is that the feeling in them is not just the poet's as he confronts them, but all that his emotion leads him to perceive, around and back of them, all the his-

tory, the lives of others in the past and the future which a
fragment of life encloses, the "meetings and partings, and
the events before and after them."

Pasternak's perceptions were always too keen, his emotions too poignant, and his reason too active to permit his
doubting the reality either of objective fact or of subjective
experience. His own disillusionments were due to mistakes
of judgment, to revelations of error—Scriabin did not have
perfect pitch but would not admit it, the elder of the sisters
V. did not love him, his own interest in philosophy was not
genuine—the errors were his own, they did not involve confusion about reality as such. Moods and feelings, things that
could be touched and ideas that could not, were all real,
and poetry was generated by their impact. Were he writing
"an aesthetic of creativity," says Pasternak in *Safe Conduct,*
he would base it on two concepts, the "concept of power
and the concept of the symbol." By "power" he means "feeling," not the emotion of any one person at any given time,
but what one might call the *essence,* or *quiddity,* of feeling.
And "power" in this sense is the special province of art. For
example, to think that passion is the theme of *Romeo and
Juliet* or of *Tristan* is to underestimate them. "Their theme
is broader than that powerful theme. Their theme is the
theme of power itself." Art, born of this great theme, dictated by it, "cannot be directed at will," like "a telescope.
. . . Trained on reality, displaced by feeling, art is the
record of this displacement." It uses whatever objects will
serve it to express its theme. Any object will do. "Any one is
precious. Any one chosen at random serves as evidence of
the state which envelops the whole of transposed reality.
. . . Art is as realistic as activity and as symbolic as fact. It
is realistic inasmuch as it does not invent the metaphor, but
finds it in nature and reproduces it religiously." It is the
speech of feeling, and "the direct speech of feeling is allegorical and cannot be replaced by anything." Art is perception, and its function is to give a name to what would otherwise be nameless. The themes of other perceptions have
their names: number, meaning, idea. Power alone has none;
it receives it from art, which speaks of it in symbols:

. . . One cannot imagine power to oneself, the fact of power, power lingering only in the moment of its manifestation, except in the two-fold language of images, that is, the language of accompanying features.

But, in the artist's work, reality is "displaced by feeling." The poet, that is, aware of the imperfection of his understanding, of the difference between the nature of his knowledge and of a reality which cannot be fully known, takes account, like the scientist, of a margin of error and advances no claim to the absolute truth of the conclusions that his feelings and his world thrust upon him.

In the light of his theory, Pasternak's own poems can be explained as the "allegorical" speech of direct feeling, a language composed of the interchangeable images of a transposed reality through which alone "power" can be expressed. Take, for example, a poem called "Marburg," which re-creates the incident when his proposal was rejected. The minutely remembered details—the flagstones, the color of the street, the wind, the cobblestones, the lindens, "each of which lived accounting me nil, and rose in its parting significance," were, says the poet, all of them, "images," and "Martin Luther who had lived there, and the brothers Grimm, the clawlike roofs, the tombstones . . . they too were images." So, in the poems of Pasternak's alter ego, Yurii Zhivago, the candle and the star are images, symbols of illumination and rebirth, with all that made them symbols—events, thoughts, feelings both in history and in his own life—and back of them the "power" they represent. So also Venice, which Pasternak saw for the first time at the close of the Marburg summer, becomes, in *Safe Conduct*, a symbol of continuity and the unity of culture. From it the poet learns how the present confers eternity upon the past, a historical lesson that is not unlike the aesthetic one, for here too the present and the distant, the empirically and the imaginatively given, object and concept are united in the poet's vision. Previously, Pasternak had said that consciousness of death had shaped his understanding of history. He saw it as a relation between two necessities, of death and of life. Life was a "leap away" from the predetermined necessity of death to "possibility," an act of will toward uncertainty and mystery against the certitude of extinction. The instant of life could be understood only with reference to the larger context of death, just as appearances could be understood only with reference to a larger, transcendental reality. Symbolism is here given an added dimension, when life itself is seen as symbolic, a gesture in defiance of death.

In Pasternak's work, every sharp line, every bright color is etched on the indeterminate background of obscure Fate and certain death. The whole realm of perception has reference to another that cannot be perceived; and everything is the same, and everything unique in his universe of mirrors. That is why in his poems sense and thought are so closely intermingled, abstract concepts verified by sense perceptions, sense perceptions tested by abstract principles; and intangible states are so perfectly identified with what is seen and felt, that his images often seem to be neither metaphors, nor similes, nor symbols, except by implication, for nothing in them seems "to stand" for anything else, neither picture for mood, nor mood for picture, and it is as if, in a kind of extended synesthesia, emotions and perceptions—not just different kinds of perception—were fused and interchanged. A poem called "The Mirror," in which as in one of those luminous paintings of Pierre Bonnard, a room with its homely signs of domesticity blends with the green, airy world outside, is an image of this attitude. Here is a pier glass; in it a cup of cocoa evaporates, and a piece of tule is swaying. And down a straight path, the mirror runs forth to the swing in the garden, where pines have scented air with resin, where the small garden has lost its spectacles in the grass, where shadows read a book—and on, beyond the gate, into the darkness of the steppe. The enormous garden tosses in the mirror, but does not break the glass, as if colloid had been poured over everything so that the twig might not taste bitter and the lilac have no scent. Now the immortal world is mesmerized and minces, and only the wind can tie up whatever thrusts itself into life and breaks in prisms and wants to sparkle. In this "hypnotic homeland" the poet sees how the garden shakes its fist against the mirror, how it runs to the swing, how it catches, tags, and joggles, but does not break the glass. Here is Pasternak's view of what the soul and empiric reality make of each other. The mind, shaken but unbroken, runs out to meet the world, and, cold and smooth, holds the great tumultuous, sensuous life beyond it mesmerized in a reflected image. The poet knows what he himself can grasp, and what must be left to the wind.

The third part of *Safe Conduct* gathers up the argument in a portrait of Mayakovsky, who seems to be the very incarnation of poetry. Driven by his genius as a poem is driven by its theme, himself the subject of his art, the concealed direction of his inward self symbolized in acts and gestures which he had chosen as a shield and worn for protection, much as the images of a poem symbolize its theme, Mayakovsky, at the end, having thrown away the last shreds of pose, was reborn into a new adolescence, that period of life "when mountains are made of molehills, and poetry begins." In death "he was indignant, and he pouted." This is the final symbol: the poet as the ultimate rebel, whose life, having defied for a while the necessity of death, then turns against possibility, and "with that pedantry with which the will sometimes follows the direction of a realized necessity," gives, as it were, assistance to its own fate.

The book that is dedicated to Rilke ends with Mayakovsky. They stand at the starting point and the goal of that progress which brings the poet, at the last, to an awareness of the meaning of art, and in which others—Scriabin, the elder sister V., Hermann Cohen—have had their share. Each of the intervening, nonpoetic relationships was passionate and each was broken off in a way that involved pain, but each was also a step toward the marvellously fated end. The wonder of it was that, despite deflections, this progress had its secret continuity. It imposed a form on nearly all of Pasternak's narratives. His early stories are shaped, as Mr. Schimanski, the editor of the English translation, has noted, by "one single leitmotif . . . the problem of replac-

ing something that has been lost so as to restore the equilib-
rium that has been upset." In "Il Tratto di Apelle,"

a notebook has been lost; a life's purpose in the old actor's existence in "Letters from Tula"; a child in "Aerial Ways"; and the
innocence of childhood in the last story ["The Childhood of
Luvers"]. In every case the search is taken up to replace the
missing object. . . . And in three of the four short stories the
quest is crowned with fulfillment.

One might add to this astute analysis that in each case what
is found is augmented by the very loss; the loss is never absolute; it has its meaning; the search proceeds through error
and arrives at a truth larger than that originally conceived.
"Every love is a crossing into a new faith," says Pasternak
in *Safe Conduct,* and in his own progress from "faith to
faith," though much is suffered, there is no irretrievable
loss, but indeed, an enlargement, an unexpected gain: the
philosopher arises from the musician's dust, the poet from the
philosopher's, while music is retained in the shaping of poems, and philosophy in the theory that explains their genesis and, to a degree also, in their subject matter. The end is
a gratuitous, a superhuman gift, not the reward of effort or
of virtue, but something almost like compensation, which
seems to be inherent in existence; his poetic destiny is his
safe-conduct, the token of his citizenship wherever life may
take him, and the protection he requires.

I V

Pasternak writes of Nature, and his concentrated images
give a new intensity to the familiar. In "Spring," "the wood
is strangled in the noose of birdsong . . . like a buffalo in a
lasso; it moans in the net, as the organ's gladiator moans in
sonatas." Where but in the verse of the English Renaissance
does one find such copious piling up of images? Characteristically, Pasternak has here ascribed to Nature the emotion

it has aroused in himself. He feels overcome by the abundance of spring; it takes his breath away, but it is Nature he represents as stifled, and reversing the cliché that would have trees "alive" with birdsong, shows them limp and gasping. In the fullness of sticky, swelling April buds, of the overwhelming choruses of birds, he commands poetry to be a sponge, which he will leave on the wet plank of a green garden bench to soak up clouds and valleys and to expand in frills and furbelows, and at night he will squeeze it out onto his greedy paper. Thus is reality "displaced by emotion," the happy pain of abundance has been given a name and poetry assigned its duty. Or there is the first glimpse of dawn in the Urals. "Without midwife, in darkness, distractedly feeling her way through the night," the land "roars and falls as if dead, and blinded in torments, gives birth to the morning." So from the window of a rushing, noisy train, the sudden emergence from darkness into light, as the landscape falls away, might suggest a violent, agonized birth. Again a subjective experience is ascribed to the object, and in a monstrous image, the observer's sensations are united with the spectacle that provokes them. Or take a brief lyric in a light vein, called "The Storm Momentary Forever," in which the thunder, doffing his hat, takes a hundred blinding photographs as mementos; malicious glee pours on the roof in a coal-like shower; and the avalanche of consciousness begins to glisten, as if even the corners of reason, where it is already light as day, were now forever brightened. Pasternak does not write about, but within Nature; and the core of his work is the moment of intensity extended beyond itself in a prismatic universe of mirrored images and echoes.

The remarkable coincidences of *Doctor Zhivago* are part of this, and so also the infinite occasions, large and small, when the "inner" and the "outer" worlds, subject and object, the physical and the spiritual are brought together in mysterious correspondence. Such is the cow which Yurii Andreyevich, convalescing in a southern town during the war, watches one fine night as she is brought in from a distant village, tired, "yearning for the herd she has left," unwilling to take the food proffered her. He sees how she shakes her head angrily from side to side, and stretching out her neck, lows brokenly and pitifully, while back of the dark barns of Meliuzeievo, the stars shine and threads of unseen sympathy reach out from them to the cow, as if they were the cattleyards of other worlds, where there was pity for her.

Such is Lara's lighted candle, noticed by Zhivago on the frozen street, and such the Virgin Mary watched over by the Star of the Nativity. Such also is Lara's love of Zhivago as she thinks of it in her magnificent meditation by his coffin:

All of her was shaken by suppressed sobs. So long as she could, she struggled against them, but suddenly this would become too much for her; then her tears would flow and pour down her cheeks, her dress, her hands and the coffin on which she was leaning.

She said nothing, she was not thinking. Streams of thoughts, generalities, bits of knowledge coursed through her freely, like clouds over the sky, as in the times of their former conversations at night. This was as it used to be, and this it was that brought happiness and liberation: uncerebral, warm, mutually inspiring knowledge—instinctive, immediate.

It was such knowledge that filled her now, the dark, vague knowledge of death, preparation for it, absence of confusion in the face of it. Just as if she had already lived twenty times on earth, had lost Yurii Zhivago countless times, and had accumulated in this matter a whole experience of the heart, so that everything she felt and did by this coffin was appropriate and to the point.

Oh, what a love it had been, free, unheard of, incomparable! They thought, as others hum a tune.

They loved each other not of necessity, not "aflame with passion," as it is falsely expressed. They loved each other because all about them willed it so: the earth beneath them, the sky above their heads, the clouds and the trees. Their love was pleasing to those around them even more, perhaps, than to themselves; to strangers in the street, to vistas stretching before them in their walks, to the rooms they lived in and where they met.

Ah, it was this, this it was that was most important, that made them kin and united them! Never, never, even in moments of the most regal, most oblivious happiness were they abandoned by that which was loftiest and most absorbing: delight in the general sculpture of the earth, the sense of their own relationship to the whole picture, the feeling of belonging to the beauty of the entire spectacle, to the whole universe.

They breathed only in this community. And that was why the exaltation of the human being above the rest of nature, the fashionable ado about man and the idolizing of him did not attract them. The beginnings of a false social consciousness, transformed into politics, seemed to them a pitiful, homemade product, and remained ununderstandable.

And now she began to bid him farewell in the simple, ordinary words of a brisk, unconstrained conversation that shattered the frame of reality and made no sense, just as the choruses and monologues of tragedy make none, nor the speech of poetry, nor music and similar conventions, justified only by the convention of emotion.

The convention of the present instance, justifying the tension of her light, informal talk, was her tears, in which her ordinary, unceremonious words sank, bathed, and swam.

It seemed as if these tear-drenched words clung of themselves to her rapid, tender babbling, as wind rustles the silky, damp foliage, tangled by warm rain.

"So here we are together again, Yurotchka. How God has arranged for us to meet again! How terrible, just think! Oh, I can't! And, God! I keep bawling and bawling! Just think! Here again is something we know well, something of our own stock in trade. Your going is my end. Again something large, inevitable. The riddle of life, the riddle of death, the enchantment of genius, the enchantment of the naked, the revealed—that, if you please, we've understood. But petty, worldly squabbles, like the recarving of the earth, that, pardon us, that's not in our line.

"Farewell, my great and dear one, farewell my pride, farewell my swift, deep little stream. How I loved your day-long splashing, how I loved to plunge into your chilly waves.

"Do you remember, I said good-by to you there in the snows! How you deceived me! Would I have left without you? Oh, I know, I know, you forced yourself to do it for what you imagined was my good. And then everything was ruined! Heavens, what I went through then! What I endured! But you know nothing of this. Oh, what have I done, Yura, what have I done! I am such a criminal, you've no idea! But I am not guilty. I lay three months in hospital, one of them I was unconscious. Since then my life's been unbearable, Yura. Pity and suffering give my soul no peace.

But I am not telling you, not revealing the chief thing. I cannot speak of it, I haven't the strength. When I come to that point in my life, the hairs of my head stir in horror. And, do you know, I wouldn't even swear that I am altogether in my right mind. But you see, I have not taken to drink, as many do. I have not gone that way, because a drunken woman, that really is the end, it's quite impossible, isn't it."

And she talked on, and sobbed and tormented herself. Suddenly she raised her head and looked around. The room had long been full of people, of anxiousness, of movement. . . . She stepped down from the footstool and, swaying, left the coffin, passing the palm of her hand over her eyes as if squeezing out the remainder of her unwept tears to shake them out onto the floor.

Men came up to the coffin and raised it on three cloths. The funeral procession started.

Nowhere has Pasternak given a more touching and beautiful form to his semi-Christian, semipagan belief in the community of all creation, his metaphysical concern with the relation between feeling and being, subject and object, the "outside" and the "in." That a man's experience, however intimate, is meaningful, and indeed possible, only because it is part of an intricate and infinite pattern of human and transhuman relationships is the ground on which Pasternak always stood, the central point from which he viewed himself, others, and Nature, from which he commented on history, religion, society, and art.

As early as 1910, while he was still studying philosophy in Moscow, he read a paper to a literary society which he summarized in an autobiographic sketch written after *Doctor Zhivago*, called *I Remember:*

[It] was based on the idea that our perceptions are subjective, on the fact that the sounds and colors we perceive in nature correspond to something else, namely to the objective vibrations of the sound and light waves. In my paper I argued that this subjectivity was not the attribute of every human being, but was a generic and suprapersonal quality, that it was the subjectivity of the world of man and of humanity at large. I suggested in my paper that after his death every person leaves behind him a part of that undying, generic subjectivity which he possessed during his lifetime and with which he participated in the history of mankind's existence. The main object of my paper was to advance the theory that perhaps this pre-eminently subjective and universally human corner or separate part of the soul had since time immemorial been the sphere of action and the main subject of art. That, besides, though the artist was of course mortal like the rest of mankind, the joy of living experienced by him was immortal, and that other people a century later might through his works be able to experience something approaching the personal and vital form of his original sensations.

My paper was entitled "Symbolism and Immortality" because in it I affirmed the symbolic, conventional quiddity of every art in the general sense in which one can talk of the symbolism of algebra.

It is something like this that Yurii Zhivago says to the dying Anna Ivanovna, and something of this kind too that seems to him to be embodied in folk art, in the Russian folk song, for example, which, he thinks, is an attempt to do in words what people, of necessity, try to do in living:

The Russian folk song is like water in a dam. It seems to have stopped and to be motionless. But in its depths it flows unceasingly from sluice gates, and the stillness of its surface is deceptive. In all manner of ways, repetitions, parallelisms, it retards the course of its gradually evolving theme. All at once, at some given point it reveals itself and astounds us suddenly. It is an insane attempt to stop time by means of words.

Time does not stop, but words and actions give immortality to all that dies. Herein too lies the meaning of history and of Christianity as Pasternak understands them.

"One must be loyal to Christ [says Yurii Zhivago's uncle and guardian, the unfrocked priest Nikolay Nikolaevich, who becomes the strongest single influence in his nephew's intellectual development]. I'll explain in a moment. You do not understand [he is addressing his scientific and atheistic friend on that occasion when the five o'clock express stops unaccountably] that it's possible to be an atheist, possible not to know whether God does or does not exist, and at the same time to know that man lives not in nature but in history, which in the understanding of the present day is based on Christ, and that the Gospels are its foundation. And what is history? It is the explanation of the labor of centuries in accordance with a logical solution of death and its future conquest. It is for this that mathematical infinity and electromagnetic waves are discovered, for this that symphonies are written. To move forward in this direction is impossible without a certain inspiration. For these discoveries a spiritual equipment is required. The data for it are contained in the Gospels. Here they are. In the first place, love of one's neighbor, that highest form of living energy, overflowing the heart of man and demanding outlet and dispersion, and furthermore they are the chief components of contemporary man, without which he is himself impossible—and namely the idea of free individuality and the idea of life as sacrifice. Bear in mind that up till now this is extremely novel. Among the ancients there was no history in this sense. What they had was the sanguine beastliness of the cruel, plague-ravaged Caligulas, who never suspected how devoid of talent is every oppressor. What they had was the boastful dead eternity of bronze monuments and marble columns. Only after Christ did centuries and generations breathe freely. Only after Him did life in progeny begin, and man now dies not in the street and by a fence, but at home in history, in the heat of work dedicated to the conquest of death, dies, himself dedicated to this theme."

Nikolay Nikolaevich's ideas influence many people, and one day Dr. Zhivago hears them rephrased in the discourse of the strange, fanatical girl Simushka, as she talks to Lara:

"I would say that man is made up of two parts: God and Labor. The development of man's spirit breaks up, over an enormous extent, into separate pieces of work. They were accomplished by generations and followed one after the other. Such a piece of work was Egypt, such a one was Greece, such was the Biblical prophets' knowledge of God. Such, the last in time—and as yet unreplaced by anything else, the work accomplished in the inspiration of all that is contemporary—is Christianity."

And to explain the "full freshness, the unexpectedness, the novelty, the unprecedented view of life" introduced by Christianity, Simushka illustrates by a comparison between an Old Testament and a New Testament miracle: the Exodus and the Virgin birth. After the crossing of Israel, the sea once more becomes impassable; after she has given birth, Christ's mother still remains a virgin. "Both events are supernatural," both are acknowledged to be miraculous, but in one instance, the miracle takes place "by order of a nation's leader"; Moses waves his magic scepter and

". . . . the sea divides, permits a whole innumerable nation, a multitude of hundreds of thousands to cross it, and when the last one has passed over, closes up again and covers and drowns the pursuing Egyptians. The spectacle is in the spirit of antiquity; the elements obedient to a magician's voice; enormous, crowding multitudes, like Roman armies on the march, the people and the leader, things seen and heard, and deafening.

"In the other instance, a Maiden—a commonplace, to which the ancient world would have paid no attention—secretly and silently gives birth to an Infant, brings a being into the light of day, the miracle of life, the life of all, 'Life universal,' as He was later called. This birth is unlawful not only in the bookish sense, as extramarital. It contradicts the laws of nature. The Virgin gives birth not through the power of necessity, but miraculously through inspiration. It is that very inspiration on which the Gospel, by setting up the exceptional over against the commonplace, the festival over against ordinary days, wants to build life in opposition to enslavement.

"What an enormously significant change!

"Something in life has been displaced. Rome is finished, the power of numbers, the necessity, enforced by arms, to live as a whole, to live as an entire people. Leaders and peoples have receded into the past.

"Personality, the doctrine of freedom have come to take their place. The individual human life has become the tale of God, has filled the space of the universe with its significance."

Zhivago overhears this speech by chance. "Of course," he thinks, "all this is Uncle Kolya's. But how gifted she is, how clever!" And his own religious poems are a magnificent restatement and elaboration of what Simushka has said: all of them commonplace and magical, simple and mysterious, like "Star of the Nativity"; passionate, like the ardent monologues of the Magdalene, whose love of Christ gives her prophetic foresight of his doom, or like the lyrics about Christ himself, ordinarily human and supernaturally divine, accepting martyrdom in the name of "the terrible grandeur of the passing centuries," knowing of his resurrection and of himself as the judge of the years to come, when like logs or barges on a river, centuries will float up to him from "out the darkness"—they present the Christian myth, not in the modern fashion, by reworking it in terms of contemporary incidents, but by re-creating it dramatically, so that its relevance to modern times appears not as parody but as symbol.

In one instance, as Zhivago is writing his poems, we are given a detailed account of how, step by step, emotions and perceptions are transformed into images and endowed with the cadences most appropriate to them. The poem is called "Fairy Tale" and the images are borrowed from the medieval legend of St. George, who saves a maiden from the dragon to which, according to the custom of the land, she has been given in tribute. But the maiden is Lara; St. George, Zhivago ("Yurii" is a variant of "George"); the dragon is the wolves that have come into view on the horizon, themselves an omen of other dangers; and the weary, happy state of lethargy, the sleep that overcomes the heroine and hero and from which they cannot rouse themselves, is that of both the real and the legendary characters in the fitful oblivion of insecure bliss. But this does not mean that Zhivago is always St. George, always battling dragons and rescuing fair damsels of whom Lara is the ideal type. The figure fits the immediate occasion only; and if its implications stretch beyond itself, they are symbolic rather than allegorical, just as every man is himself and not the figure of a virtue or a vice, and an event in history has its specific character and function, although Zhivago may find himself in a situation that is like that of St. George, and the legend of St. George may typify chivalry, courage, love, or the perils of life.

Pasternak's religion is not a churchman's, his Christianity no more a convert's than his philosophy is a scholar's. What attracts him in Christianity is not its dogma but its myth, and the myth expresses what he values most: individuality, understanding of life in relation to death, belief in immortality. Within the symbol of the Christian myth, the wide-ranging episodes, opinions, and ideas of *Doctor Zhivago* are brought together. "Man lives not in nature but in history"; this cardinal truth, which, according to Nikolay Nikolaevich was first recognized by Christianity, does not contradict that pagan sense of man's unity with nature, that correspondence between creatures of earth and their universe—those stars responding to the cow, which both Lara and Zhivago understand—that love of theirs which is part of the impersonal world around them. There is no contradiction here, because the pantheistic, almost magical, communion is individual and momentary; it does not extend in time, nor account, as does the historic-Christian view, for the continuousness of events in the temporal process. Each moment is a microcosm: a man's whole life and the world he lives in are enclosed in it, but there is also a continuity of these in time and even beyond time in the transcendental sphere of principles, so that in a great imaginative jump life itself becomes a microcosm and a symbol; it contains the universe, both earth and heaven, the past, the present, and the future, and all the beliefs of men from paganism to Christianity, and affirms its "quiddity" as symbolic "in the sense in which algebra is a symbol."

From his earliest lyrics to *Doctor Zhivago* one can trace Pasternak's progressively deepening consciousness of relations: between the individual and his world, between brute fact and the historic process, between possibility and necessity. And there are two elements that may be said to characterize his work as a whole: the central roles assigned to consciousness and to the flash of intense perception. His poems record a series of such flashes, and nothing is profounder in his view of life than a sense of conscious personality. Not only people, but places, things, and events are personalities in his eyes, so much so that his poetry has a kind of anthropomorphism, which leads C. M. Bowra to write of his "near pantheism." It is, perhaps, the "pathetic fallacy" in the extreme, though with Pasternak it is neither fallacy nor pathetic, for actually it is an intellectual perception of similarities, not a Romantic identification with inanimate objects, but a Neo-Kantian respect for the nonself as the origin, or expression of the self. Each being achieves identity in relation to others, so that Pasternak might well say with Rimbaud: *"Je est un autre. . . . C'est faux de dire: Je pense. On devrait dire: on me pense."* ("I is another. . . . It is false to say: I think. One should say: I am thought.") The man, the event, the object are definable only in that which they are not: other men, other events, and ultimately a universal consciousness that transcends them all. The modern idea of the individual's, and especially of the artist's "alienation" is here curiously modified. *My Sister, Life* he called an early collection of his poems. And this title, with its implications of kinship and distance, of a difference between the individual and life, even his own, expresses that feeling of self-sufficient integrity which was exhibited to the admiration of the world not only in Pasternak's writing but in his conduct as well. A man is himself, he seemed to say, and life flows on beside him, close to him but distinct from him, the unique and lonely being who, nevertheless, is legion, to whom not only his own life but all life, and the universe, are kin.

V

I would never lift a finger to bring back from oblivion three fourths of what I have written [said Pasternak in *I Remember*]. Quite recently, I completed my chief and most important work, the only one I am not ashamed of and for which I can answer with the utmost confidence, a novel in prose with a supplement in verse, *Doctor Zhivago.*

If he permitted his old work to stand, it was, he wrote, that there were "often grains of truth, aptness, and acute observation in the mass of what [was] deplorable and annoying about those things" of his. And in the facsimile of a letter to an unnamed correspondent, written in English in October 1958 and reproduced in the same book, the condemnation is even more drastic:

I take the opportunity to repeat you, that except the "Dr. Zh." which you should read, all the rest of my verses and writings are devoid of any sense and importance. The most part of my mature years I gave off to Goethe, Shakespeare and other great voluminous translations.

The reasons for this severe judgment are doubtless that, in the first place, the early works, at a later stage of the poet's development, appeared to him to be artificial, "spoilt," as he said of *Safe Conduct,* "by unnecessary mannerisms, the common fault" of the years in which it was written, and secondly, that like the poems of Zhivago's youth, they were fragmentary, preparatory sketches for a large canvas. Pasternak always nurtured a desire for inclusiveness. Even his earliest lyrics enlarged private experience to universal meanings; and presently gigantic mass events, about which there is remarkably little in the autobiographies, laid siege to his consciousness and clamored to be expressed in poetry.

In January 1905, while Mayakovsky was taking part in the revolutionary riots in Kutaisi and Blok carried a red flag at the head of a procession in St. Petersburg and dreamed the dream that became *The Violet of Night,* fifteen-year-old Boris Pasternak was playing snowballs in the school yard of his *gymnasium* (or grammar school) in Moscow. Then one morning the "thunderous" news arrived that the patron of the school, the Grand Duke Sergey Alexandrovich, had been shot dead. It snowed hard that winter, and the boy "fell in love with storms." So he wrote twenty years later in a narrative poem, *The Year 1905.* But his "falling in love with storms" did not mean that he became a revolutionary. However much the events might appeal to his sense of humanity, they could not change his temperament, which, unlike Blok's, was not attracted to chaos, nor, like Mayakovsky's, in need of violence. That is why references to such events in *Safe Conduct* and *I Remember* are reduced to the bare, essential minimum: for a long while they could not touch him, could not lay hold of his imagination in the way music, philosophy, and poetry could hold it. Even before the momentous summer in Marburg, he was involved with advanced intellectual circles, "Serarda," "Centrifuge," the groups around the periodicals *Musaget* and *Apollon*, took part in their debates on art, wrote poetry, some of which was later, in 1914, published in a volume entitled *The Twin in Clouds*. He completed his university studies in 1913, and when war broke out was not accepted for military service because of a leg injury incurred in childhood—"I broke my leg, in one evening insuring my absence from two future wars," he says in *Safe Conduct*. He worked as a private tutor, translated a play by Kleist for the Moscow Kamerny Theater, was employed in the Urals in the management of a chemical factory; and the collection of poems he published in 1916 he called *Above the Barriers*. During the civil war he was a librarian in the Soviet Ministry of Education. His parents, Leonid Pasternak, a well-known impressionist painter, and Rosa Kaufman Pasternak, a gifted concert pianist, left Russia with their two daughters in 1921 not as political exiles but because Mrs. Pasternak required expert medical attention which she could get only abroad. They never returned, but they kept their Russian citizenship; and their sons, Boris and Alexander, remained in the U.S.S.R.

Living in the midst of social chaos, Boris nudged himself once in a while to look up from his books at what was going on around him. After the raging blizzard has covered everything with snow, he writes in a lyric called "About These Verses," he will suddenly remember, he thinks, that the sun is still there, and will see that, long since, while he was "smoking with Byron and drinking with Edgar Allan Poe, the light has grown quite different." Then, wrapped in a muffler, he will shout to youngsters through the opened transom, "What a century, my dears, we're having out of doors!" But it is not until 1923 that he writes a poem on a historical theme. This is "The Lofty Illness." "The moving rebus glimmers," the rebus, that is, of history, the days, months, years of comings and goings, of fires, explosions, rumors of surrender, belief and unbelief, and the birth of the

Trojan epos. Then Czarist Russia, in lines reminiscent of Blok's *Retribution,* is described with bitter wit: "Although on the surface everything seems the same, the sleep of earth is like convulsions, like death, like the quiet of graveyards," and there is talk—truth mixed with lies—in the tales of soldiers returning from war, and there is the reality of cold, disease, and lice. In the midst of all this misery and all these legends, the intellectual-idealist prints and writes placards about the joy of his own sunset.

> We were music in the ice—
> I speak of the whole class
> With which I had intended
> To go off stage, and shall go.

He will go off stage, but he will go off singing.

> I am ashamed and more ashamed each day
> That in this age of shadows
> A certain lofty illness
> Still bears the name of song.
>
> . . .
>
> With good intentions hell is paved
> And the opinion is now held
> That if with them one paves one's verses too
> All one's sins will be forgiven.

The poem concludes with a portrait of Lenin, perhaps the most condensed—it is just forty-three lines long—and certainly one of the most eloquent of all the admiring portraits that have been made of him. He is not mentioned by name, but one recognizes him by his gestures, the effect he has on others, and the role ascribed to him. Awaited, but not yet expected, he looms before he enters, and breaks in like a thunderclap; is greeted with roaring ovations; and speaks in words that are like a rapier thrust. He might be talking of mineral oil, or anything at all, he "rinsed his mouth with facts and knew that history shouted through them." He was on intimate terms only with history, and governed the land by the force of his thoughts. The last lines, which are about the nature of genius, are done in the meter of Pushkin's "The Prophet," where the Lord commands the poet to "sear the hearts of men"; here, in an implicit comparison, the political leader is equated with the poet in the power of genius which both possess.

"The Lofty Illness" was finished in 1923; it was followed by two historical poems, *The Year 1905* (1925-26) and *Lieutenant Schmidt* (1926-27). Obviously Pasternak was now finding symbols of "power" in recent Russian history, and these symbols, as always, occurred to him as brilliant fragments. *The Year 1905* is composed of seven individual poems, *Lieutenant Schmidt* of three parts, subdivided into separate incidents, so that these long narratives are actually collections of brief lyrics. Those of *The Year 1905* are, as it were, a pictorial history from January to December, dramatic scenes that include city, sea, and country, all classes of society, and the poet himself as he was at the time. The fifth episode, "Mutiny at Sea," about the battleship *Potemkin,* reminds one in its swift, concise episodes of Eisenstein's celebrated film. Out of it must have grown the poem about the hero of the occasion, Lieutenant Schmidt, whose letters Pasternak used in composing a work that is certainly one of the great poems of the century. Poignant, simple, eloquent, it has the fatefulness and the tragic heroism of antique drama; and the superb declaration of patriotism and stoic independence in Lieutenant Schmidt's parting words is what Pasternak himself might have been expected to utter in similar circumstances. But of the revolutions of 1917 and 1918 Pasternak did not write until *Doctor Zhivago,* and even that, he claimed, was not about the Revolution:

I have now come to the end of my autobiographical sketch [he concluded *I Remember*]. To continue it would be exceedingly difficult. To keep up the sequence of events I should have had to speak of years, circumstances, people, and destinies within the framework of the Revolution. Of a world of hitherto unknown aims and aspirations, problems and exploits, a new self-restraint, a new strictness—new trials with which this world confronts the human personality and man's honor, pride, and endurance.

This unique world, the like of which has never been known

before, has now receded into the faraway distance of memories and hangs suspended on the horizon like mountains seen from a plain or like a faraway big city against the smoky background of a red sunset.

One would have to write about it in a way to make the heart stop beating and the hair stand on end. To write about it in an ordinary and commonplace way, to write about it unemotionally, to write about it less colorfully than Gogol and Dostoevsky have depicted Petersburg, is not only senseless and useless; to write like that would be both dishonest and base.

We are far from that ideal.

And yes, he is right. *Doctor Zhivago* is not about the Revolution; it is about how and why poetry is written. The Revolution is but one of its many subjects. But if it does not "make the heart stop beating and the hair stand on end" —and I am not sure but that it does—it does, unquestionably, make the mind look deeper and the heart beat faster.

There is no more passionate voice in the history of Russian letters than Pasternak's, nor any more profoundly calm. His undemonstrative, exacting nature was not given to emotionalism; his passion was neither raw nor violent; his work, unlike Mayakovsky's loud outcry and splash of color, does not reproduce passion, but gives its essence; it is not turbulent but quiet with tragic wisdom, and it is moving as purity of tone and precision of line are moving. His sister, Mrs. Slater, who has done some admirable translations of his lyrics—the best, perhaps, in English—has left in a "Translator's Note," which prefaces her little book, *Poems by Boris Pasternak* (published by Peter Russell, Fairwarp, Sussex, 1959), a revealing glimpse of her brother as a young artist. She remembers, she writes, how as children, she and her sister were often kept awake and moved to tears by Boris' "improvisations on the piano," how he would moan "inarticulately" and hum as he "poured out his feelings into music," expressing his unhappiness, excitement, or inspiration in this medium rather than in words. Only later did he turn to poetry, but even then, "He never really abandoned music, he merely changed his instrument."

When he "changed his instrument," the words that held

his passion retained of music, not the song—his work is not "melodious"—but the structure of the musical line. It was something like this that Marina Tsvetaeva must have meant in her fine essay on Pasternak, "The Shower of Light," with the subtitle "The Poetry of Eternal Manliness." She had just read and reread *My Sister, Life*. A colossal stillness, she said, underlay the whole book, and quoting the lines, "Silence, you are the best that I have ever heard," remarked that Pasternak, "lived in words not like a tree in the evidence of foliage, but in its root—in mystery," and that "his book was as much a book of silence as of warbling." The quality of inward quietness that conveys not the storms but the stillness of passion Pasternak himself prized in Shakespeare's art: "The productions of *King Lear*," he said, "are always too noisy. . . . *Lear* is as quiet as *Romeo* and for the same reason." The reason is that these plays are about the *hidden* feeling of love: "the love of lovers . . . filial love, and more widely, the love of one's neighbor, the love of truth." In *Lear* "the only stormy thing . . . is the tempest at night, while the people, huddled in the tent and terrified, speak in whispers."

Passion alone gives art its theme, the theme of "power," and lyric intensity, as Poe declared, can be of only brief duration. This is the basis of Pasternak's own work and of his literary admirations. Blok, for example, who in his opinion "had everything that goes to make a great poet: fire, tenderness, emotion, his own image of the world, his own special gift for transforming everything he touched, and his own restrained, hidden, self-absorbed destiny," was most admirable in his "impetuosity, his roving intentness, the rapidity of his observations"; Tolstoy's supreme gift was "the faculty of seeing things in the detached finality of each separate moment, in sharp relief, as we see things only on rare occasions, in childhood, or on the crest of an all-embracing happiness, or in the triumph of a great spiritual victory." Blok's "adjectives without nouns, predicates without subjects, hide-and-seek, breathless agitation, nimbly darting little figures, abruptness," influenced his own poetry; some of his strongest effects are achieved through a rapid, disconnected heaping up of words, which are not so much symbols of events as signposts to them:

> Populists,
> Perovskaya,
> The first of March,
> Nihilists in jackets,
> Torture chambers,
> Students in pince-nez.
> > (*The Year 1905*)

> A cliff and storm, a cliff and cloak, and hat.
> A cliff and—Pushkin.
> > ("The Theme" from *Theme and Variations*)

> Stars raced. Washed in the sea were headlands.
> Salt was becoming blind. And tears were drying.
> Dark were bedrooms. Thoughts were racing,
> And the sphinx was harkening to Sahara.

> Candles swam. The blood of the Colossus
> Grew cold, it seemed, the lips aswim
> In desert's azure smile.
> The night was waning, as the tide receded.

> A light wind from Morocco touched the sea.
> A simoom blew. In deep snows snored Archangel.
> Candles swam. A rough draft of "The Prophet"
> Dried, and day broke on the Ganges.
> > ("Variation 3" from *Theme and Variations*)

This rapid passage from image to image, this swiftness and passion of utterance have led critics to call Pasternak's verse "breathless" and "disjointed." He was certainly the least rambling of poets, he wrote with telegraphic brevity, and he was always, even in his long prose epic, a lyric poet. The divisions of his narratives are like stanzas, and the prose he wrote was also poetry that only lacked rhyme and had a more fluid metrical structure.

Like Tolstoy he saw things "in the detached finality of each separate moment," but the effect he produced was very different, was indeed, the opposite of Tolstoy's celebrated *otstranenie*, "holding things off," or "making them strange," so that they were seen as if they had never been seen before and came to one as if to refresh the memory, to clear one's perceptions of the conventionalities that had obscured them, to make one see the world again as one had seen it once upon a time, in childhood. The effect of Pasternak's vision is to surprise one with its aptness and its novelty, not to remind one of something one has forgotten, but to rouse wonder at the justice of unprecedented comparisons. For Pasternak was a metaphysical poet, and the sensuous brief moment of existence was not for him what it was for Tolstoy, the end as well as the beginning of all that man can know. Tolstoy saw life as a succession of separate lives, each with its vital, unrepeatable experiences of sense and its moments of understanding; his man of wisdom was the creature of earth, who like General Kutuzov learned even military strategy from the ways of nature, waiting, as it were, in his war with Napoleon for the tree to ripen and the fruit to fall. But Pasternak's was a different idea that derived from a metaphysical assumption of a community, a universal consciousness, within which every individual receives his identity only as he is differentiated from "the other." Like John Donne, he too was "expert beyond experience." "Philosophizing" he did not like, had no sympathy with Tolstoy's "moralizing, levelling, and preaching," which lacked "the passion of creative contemplation" and belonged to an order of thought that was suspect, not only as being "inartistic" but as destructive of that individuality which art embodies and without which freedom is threatened and life loses value. Yet he respected the mind almost as much as Tolstoy despised it, did not revile it because of its limitations, and if his poetry began with a rejection of philosophy, if he was an apostate philosopher, his thought retained the interests of the discipline he had renounced. To Tolstoy all "self-conscious activity" was "stricken with barrenness"; only the unself-conscious "bore fruit"; and this conviction, demonstrated in the terrible lesson of Napoleon, the tragic attempts of Andrey Bolkonsky to understand the ununderstandable,

Karenin's pathetic intellectualism, and Tolstoy's own ardent, tortuous self-examination that brought him back to what his senses taught him before his mind took over, all this, by contrast with the intuitive wisdom of Platon Karataev and Natasha Rostov, proved history to be a lie, an intellectual distortion of the unfathomable events it sought to record, an abstraction that killed the living truth it attempted to immortalize. But to Pasternak it was precisely the mind's awareness that gave validity to what occurred. And if the unique moment contained both past and future, it was a crossroads in time, the truth of which was perceptible to the intellect rather than to the senses; history was the drama of man's thought, and like all man's endeavor, like life itself, an endlessly renewed attempt to arrest, deny, or conquer death, that inevitable death of which the human being was always conscious. Thence the great, hopeful gift of Christianity, which impelled men to live not in the moment only but "in time," "in progeny," and tragedy was given meaning, suffering alleviation, because the ultimate outcome was known to be benign. This optimism is not Tolstoy's pagan delight in the pleasure and mystery of succeeding generations, but a more Platonic joy in the immortality of understanding and of individual achievement. Zhivago, whose name connotes "living," survives not so much in his children—they are relatively unimportant in the story—as in his poems; it is by means of them that he is resurrected in the memory of those who read them.

Tolstoy's art is the art of process, of continuity; his novels do not end, they break off, and one knows that the story continues somewhere outside the pages of the book. Pasternak's is poetry of the epiphany; each self-enclosed mirror-like moment reflects the universe, and all of them build up to a great summation. In *Safe Conduct* there is the epiphany of his own realization of himself as poet; in *Doctor Zhivago*, the moment of triumph during the creative nights in Varykino; and every one of the poems Zhivago writes is, like Pasternak's own, also an epiphany. For years the heart wanders from faith to faith, and love to love—then in a flash reaches its goal; for years the matter of a poem accumulates, and in the end becomes manifest in a brief moment of intensity. Indeed, the whole of *Doctor Zhivago* is an epiphany, an *ars poetica* on a grander scale than *Safe Conduct*, the realization of all the scattered meanings, the "grains of truth" in everything that Pasternak had written before it. Tolstoy's epic ended in a backward glance, a disquisition that was meant to explain rationally the dramatic events of the story. Pasternak's ends with a gaze into the future, the summation of his hero's life, the mark of his immortality in the epiphany of his poems.

V I

To Marina Tsvetaeva, Pasternak himself was like an Arab and his mount: "alertness, attentiveness—and now, now —complete readiness for flight. . . . The impression that he was always listening to something, rapt intentness and, suddenly, a burst of speech . . . as if a crag had spoken, or an oak." His work is like that too: absorbed concentration, and then the leap, the gallop toward an unseen goal, with the rider always intense, alert, listening, noting everything on the way, the immense and the minute, the vast horizon and the fly or leaf. Pasternak seems bewitched by the marvelous manifestations of day-to-day living. His imagery captures the singularity of something seen or felt, but finds the "name by which it must be called" in an archetypal scheme beyond it. Nothing is "ennobled" in his poems, nor is anything degraded; and when the grand is equated with the little, this is done in all reverence and seriousness, not as with T. S. Eliot or Mayakovsky by way of parody, absurdity, or paradox. For example, in the title poem of a series called *Waves*, "All will be here," he writes, "what has been lived through and that by which I still do live; my yearnings and the stand I take, and what my waking eyes have seen. Before me are the waves of ocean," and these waves, which represent the whole of the poet's experience, are compared to waffles baked by the tide, and to cattle that have marked the shore with the hollow imprint of their hoofs. They are innumerable, and the sky that has driven them out to pasture has "lain down on his stomach by the hill." "Curled in trumpets over the breadth of my despair," they are the poet's deeds; "there is no sum to them, no count," and they come racing toward him, one on top of the other in endless change, and "by their changing all is covered, as the sea's song by the wave's foam." The lyrics that follow are a passionate enumeration of all that has engulfed his life: his wrestling with "living values," the parts of Russia in which he has been—the immense shore of Kobulet, "embracing, like a poet's work," that which in life is so widely separated that only two might see it at one time; night in Poti, and dawning in Batum. And there is also the yearning for home, for familiar Moscow, which he longs to put into words; and the mountains and forests of the Caucasus, and the passing of days, of years, of generations; and war, and "the immense beauty of Georgia," and the future of socialism and the future as such. All these come to the poet's consciousness in the eternal changefulness and sameness of waves: their billowing is the rhythm of emotion; their infinite aspects, the images they cast up.

Consistently does Pasternak admire what he calls "the modesty" of the particular, the given instance, the immediate perception. "The ordinary alone is fabulous when touched by the hand of genius," writes Zhivago in his diary, as he thinks lovingly of Pushkin and Chekhov with their "Russian childlikeness" and "shy unconcern" with "loud things" such as "the ultimate goals of humanity and their own salvation. . . . Such immodesties were not for them; their station was not high enough and they were too busy." Even Gogol, Dostoevsky, and Tolstoy were more pretentious: they

prepared themselves for death, sought meanings, drew up accounts, whereas these others were to the end absorbed in the current particularities of the artist's calling and their life passed in recording its passage, like another private particularity which was no one's concern, and now this particularity turns out to be everybody's business, like an apple that is plucked before it is ripe and reaches usefulness of itself, and fills itself more and more with sweetness and meaning.

This figure of the apple plucked before it is ripe seems to reply, whether intentionally or not, to Tolstoy's famous passage about Kutuzov's strategy:

He knew that an apple should not be plucked while it is green. It will fall of itself when ripe, but if picked unripe the apple is spoiled, the tree is harmed, and your teeth are set on edge.

Pasternak differs from the poets of both the Romantic and the Symbolist schools, although he does have something in common with both of them: with the Romantics, regard for emotional experience, with the Symbolists, a sense of eternal, intangible correspondences. But he is more objective than they. Steeped though he is in his own thoughts and feelings, bound for his subject matter to what he has himself lived through, it is not of himself he writes but of others, and he is, in this respect, more objective than many so-called "objective" novelists, not because his approach is "scientific," like Zola's or Leonov's, nor because, like Tolstoy, he is endowed with the gift of empathy, but rather through an aesthetic and metaphysical interest: a view of what art is, of what men are, and of what his own relation is to both. His creativeness was always accompanied by a critical scrutiny of the very process of creation. Poetry, he said, begins when mountains are made of molehills. Exaggeration, that is, is essential to the poetic process; distortion is involved in it, and precisely because he saw its role so clearly, he was always wary of distortion. His natural gift for feeling was accompanied by a well-cultivated habit of balanced and detached perception, which became second nature and made his work in essence, though not in its outward aspect, more like Pushkin's than any other poet's in the Russian language. It may lack Pushkin's chiseled quality and ebullience; it may be more sober in tone, more cerebral, but what it shares with Pushkin's is a broad, calm,

independent view of human destiny, through which the
deeply experienced event stands out in all its individuality,
because without being typical, it is seen in relation to the
general lot of men. Pasternak never thought of himself as
a being apart, having realized early in his career that he
could not be one of those artists who pride themselves on
their exceptional status. The kind of showy performance
which in contrast to medieval "Passion Plays, that needed
a Heaven if they were to be heard," always required "phi-
listinism" to be poetic, was foreign to him. "I shunned it
consciously . . . considering its brilliance unsuited to my
craft and feared any kind of poetizing which could place me
in a false and incongruous position." Like any Romantic,
that is, he saw the impulse to exaggerate as the necessary
beginning of art, but he could not assume the Romantic's
posture of self-admiring alienation. Just as Blok had found
to his surprise that his first poems had been written in the
Symbolist manner, so Pasternak discovered that, even before
his acquaintance with either the poet or his work, he had
begun to express himself in the manner of Mayakovsky.
When they first met, in 1913, so impressed was he by Mayakovsky, so inferior to him did he feel himself to be that, had
he been younger, he would have abandoned literature
altogether. "But my age was an obstacle. After all my meta-
morphoses, I could not decide to alter my course for the
fourth time." Instead, he determined to write in a way different from Mayakovsky's:

> The times, and everything which influenced us both, bound
> me to Mayakovsky. We possessed certain things in common. I
> took note of them. I understood that unless one did something
> with oneself, these would become more numerous later; that he
> must be preserved from their triteness. Unable to define this, I
> decided to renounce whatever it was which led me up to it. I
> abandoned the Romantic manner.

What he admired in Mayakovsky was the rebellious spirit,
the bold, independent inventiveness; but the friendship
which had begun with such overwhelming admiration that
he resolved to change his way of writing to safeguard the

originality of the man he regarded as the greater poet, turned to amazed incomprehension when Mayakovsky began to speak in the voice not of poetry but of propaganda:

> He read 150,000,000 to his own intimate circle. And for the first time I had nothing to say to him. Many years went by. We met in Russia and abroad, we tried to continue our intimacy, we tried to work together and I found myself understanding him less and less.

A respect for the organic, the necessity of a poet's immersing himself in his material and writing only as a result of being so steeped, was Pasternak's special quality, whether he was writing a poem or doing a translation. He was one of the great translators of the world, and his views about this craft apply to all his work. "A translation," he said, "must be produced by an author who has undergone the influence of the original long before his task begins. It must be a fruit of the original and its historic consequence." Like Blok, he was not content with surface aspects of reality; the world he wrote about had to become indistinguishable from himself before he could deal with it poetically. But Blok's world was the irrational experience of dreams and visions, the verbal equivalent of his emotions, a *music* that was the rhythm of feeling; Pasternak's, by contrast, is not the stuff of dreams but of cognitions and perceptions, and the subtle cadences of his verse are not an echo of his emotions. Their exquisite music has no reference beyond itself; it is the self-contained design of sound, formed with the assuredness of absolute pitch and expressing a devotion to art so complete that all life is seen through it. His theme of search is not, like Blok's, motivated by desire but by necessity: it is directed to the recovery of what has been lost, not to the discovery of a mystery that has never been known and of which there have been only hints and premonitions. The criterion which Blok never relinquished, even when under pressure of events he was forced to modify it, was accuracy to the private vision, the Romantic's view of the self as the court of last resort, the final point of reference. The perfection he sought was an archetypal form of which he could aspire to have no more than a glimpse; his whole experience was a search for it and his poetry is a record of this search. Pasternak's "perfection" is of a different kind, and even more exacting. A demand for "absolute pitch" sets standards beyond the self; it postulates an abstract and superhuman law as legislator in the realm of art, a rule of excellence not made by man, a gift of grace. Once a votary is chosen by his divinity, his devotion is complete. Such was Pasternak's devotion. It was through art alone that he perceived and understood. The aesthetic attitude was native to him. He knew it best and he lived by it; and his life and work, like those of Marcel Proust, were a dissertation on art.

VII

If the symbol of the Symbolists represents concealed reality, Pasternak's represents an instrument, the poet's mode of perception, which "displaces" reality. The "truth" which the poet expresses is the truth of experience as such, not of that which is experienced. Thence in Pasternak's paradoxical theory of art, the subjects of art are infinite but the theme of all of them is the same, the most subjective experience is also the most universal, the symbol represents not entity but process. Similarly the basic teachings of Christianity, "free individuality and life as sacrifice," are not ends in themselves but the "spiritual equipment" essential for attaining an end, for asserting life in the face of death. And although in his view these tenets, individuality, love, simplicity, are like those which Dostoevsky and Tolstoy also presented as essentially Christian, his emphasis is different from theirs. Christianity for him is not so much a rule of conduct as an explanation of the historic process of ideas. His ethics are explained by history and derive from metaphysics. Love does not necessarily involve humility, and individuality is a principle that transcends the human being. Nor is sacrifice extolled as voluntarily chosen; it is shown to be inevitable and necessary, mysteriously inherent in the process of historical development, something perhaps like the death of Virgil's Palinurus.

The sense of a transcendental reality with which his work, unlike Blok's, is imbued, is the reality not of private vision, but of logic. What he says about men, about history, about art is like the paintings of Cézanne, of which Rilke said that everything in them stood out in relief, their empty wine bottles and green apples "forced to be beautiful" against the deep blue paint with which the canvasses were uniformly covered before anything was drawn on them. Just so for Pasternak, the subject of a poem speaks in its immediacy of the general theme of power; the subject is the cage to which the universal theme is lured and where it is held, the microcosm that enspheres its essence and its possibilities, much as the individual contains others, and is himself only in others, as Pasternak is himself through Rilke, Scriabin, Mayakovsky, and as in "Childhood of Luvers" and "Letters from Tula," the "Stranger" makes the little girl and the old actor what they are. There is a sense here of human relationships that is not the usual sentimental one of "love" or "communion." It is reminiscent of an idea of Hermann Cohen, who through a logical analysis arrived at the conclusion that, as every sensation was accompanied by the sentiment proper to it, so the sentiment peculiar to art was "the love of Man," and called his treatise on aesthetics *Esthetik des reinen Gefühls, The Aesthetics of Sentiment*. The love he meant was neither an egotistic love, nor what is generally termed "altruism." "Love" in his sense was a consciousness that anteceded these derivative, personal emotions; it was cognition of "the other" as that which makes "the self," and without which art was impossible. It was the sentiment of "the love of man, the love of man's nature, of natural man and of man in nature, included in which was 'nature morte,' still life." It was this transcendental unity of man with man that interested Pasternak, not direct physical or emotional relationships but their essential humanity; and often in his work, as in "Il Tratto di Apelle" or "Aerial Ways," it is the most tenuous relationships that impose the strongest moral obligations, and what is not stated, but implied or pointed to, is the core of the story.

It was only by a special aptitude, Hermann Cohen held, that the mind was capable of drawing knowledge from that which was beyond it. Whereas thought could be concerned only with objects, in intuition the sharp distinction between subject and object was destroyed. Metaphysics must be based on philosophic faith, ethics on certitude in a moral scheme that transcended humanity and was rooted in an eternal Ideal of Reason. Moral actions were concrete manifestations, crystallizations of this Ideal. And just as in the realm of metaphysics, reality presented a constant problem for reason to solve, so "duty" was a search for truth, never attained but always approached in the historic process. History, to Cohen, united the various manifestations of this search, and was, therefore, the only means of understanding the close bond between the Ideal and its realization. That is why his presentation of the history of philosophy was so eloquent; and Pasternak, moved by this eloquence and finding the "transcendental method" of Kantian philosophy most congenial to his own way of thought, dwelt on the wisdom of intuition and rejected, as Cohen was inclined to do, the rigid classifications of all dogmatic systems; the densely intermingled images of his verse and the plots of his narratives, in which actual events appear as filaments of a metaphysical substance, seem to be intuitions of life's minutiae and particularities grasped in the grandeur of their transcendental meaning. Pasternak's conception of individuality goes farther than the customary idea that each human being is a special entity, different and separate from all others, capable of independent thought and experience, and to be respected for this independence. In his philosophy, this ethical belief and the view of its historic evolution from paganism to Christianity has its metaphysical, theological, and aesthetic counterparts: the principle of singularity, whereby each instance is differentiated from every other and from the sum total of the class to which it belongs; the idea of immortality as proof that the new is necessary; the view that the unique perception of the unique detail is, in

art, the starting point of creation. In each of these departments of thought, which together comprise all but the
scientific branch, a unity is achieved between the particular
and the typical, the single instance and general events, the
special occurrence and legend or history, just as integration
is constant between the limited and concrete world of individual experience and the limitless Nature in which it
occurs. Nor is science left out of Pasternak's inclusive
vision. It is not for nothing that his poet-hero is also a doctor;
his study of medicine leads him to reflect on the relation
between the body and the spirit of man, and here too a syn-
thesis is achieved: a Kantian reconciliation of empiricism
and idealism, while the specialty which Zhivago chooses,
the eye, is in keeping with his perceptions as poet—even,
perhaps, as seer.

There is mystery in this world of intricate correspondences, and it is this sense of mystery that makes Pasternak very different from Tolstoy and Dostoevsky, as well as
from the "scientific" and "sociological" writers of his day.
Unlike Tolstoy, it is the glory not of the commonplace, but
of the exceptional that he celebrates. The point of Simushka's example of the Virgin birth is that an ordinary person
is endowed with the gift of the extraordinary, of magical
performance and inexplicable experience. Pasternak's moments of illumination are not so much insights into the
possibility of Christlike virtue in simple people, as they are
for Dostoevsky and Tolstoy, as amazed realizations of how
constantly the improbable occurs in a familiar world. Both
Dostoevsky and Tolstoy were concerned with ultimate explanations, Pasternak, by contrast, with the impossibility of
these. "The wonder of it" is at the heart of his perceptions.
For him the principle of novelty defines the individual and
forms his experience, and it is this that gives a fairy-tale
quality to his work and makes of *Doctor Zhivago* a fable of
man rather than a history or a psychological study. With
the same feeling of wonder does Pasternak see events in his
own life, as when, for example, in *I Remember*, he writes of
his friend Paolo Yashvili:

He was always beset by the sort of surprises that one only reads about in novels. Chance played a prominent part in his life. He had a gift for it. He was lucky that way;

and when he speaks of his own good fortune in having such friends as Yashvili and Titian Tabidze, another Georgian poet:

It was at the height of the period when, according to Bely's witty definition, the triumph of materialism had abolished matter. There was nothing to eat; there was nothing to wear. There was nothing tangible around, only ideas. If we kept alive, it was thanks to our Tiflis friends, miracle workers who all the time managed to get something and bring something and provide us with advances from publishing houses for something we had no idea of.

No outlook on life could be further than this from the Soviet insistence on man's mastery of his fate and the importance of rule and dogma. This Lara and Zhivago both realize, and it is the lack of this realization that makes Pasha what he is and causes his tragedy—Pasha, whose face, even when from Antipov, the student and teacher and Lara's husband, he has been metamorphosed into Strelnikov, the rigid leader of a rebel band, still shows the qualities for which, says Lara, she always loved him:

The same handsome, honest, determined face, the most honest of all the faces I have ever seen. Not a trace of pretense, a manly character, a complete absence of pose.

Only one new trait appeared in it:

It was as if something abstract had entered that countenance and drained it of color. A living, human face became the embodiment, the principle, the image of an idea.

Pasha had become, as his mask-like face and newly assumed name indicated, an instrument of death, for, as Zhivago says, "Becoming typical is the end of man, his condemnation." The two attitudes are polarized in Lara's relations

with Zhivago and with Pasha, the men whose names symbolize what they are: on the one hand, life, on the other,
death; with Zhivago, whose life is suffering and thought
and passion, and whose death comes only when his heart
gives way, and with "Strelnikov," the Archer, or "Rastrel-
nikov," as he is sometimes called, the Executioner, who re-
places life with a rule for living and kills himself after killing
many others. As for Lara herself, she too is life, as much
as Zhivago. Zhivago is adaptable; his vitality and love of
life carry him through hardships. But Lara is the force of
life itself; strong, passionate, changeable and always the
same, she is like the waves of the sea, anarchic and elemental, or like the Revolution in its early stages; and she is
simple, unconsciously inspiring love and art, and misused,
as Nature is misused by the calculating and the selfish.
With her Zhivago feels no constraint, no smallness—as he
does, to a degree, with the more conventional Tonya—no
pettiness in either thought or feeling. With Lara, minor,
commonplace, day-to-day interests reflect the greatness of
the orbit within which they take place. And in his poems she
figures as the Magdalene, the Virgin, the Maiden saved
from the Dragon. She represents the lesson of Christianity
that "the individual human tale has become the tale of
God." Communism, by contrast, with its principle of col-
lectivity and its denial of the individual, is an even more
fundamental negation of Christianity than it professes itself
to be, for it does not realize, or refuses to recognize, that
what it negates is not just a cult but the nature of man and
the principle of life.

In its critical approach to men's beliefs and actions, Pasternak's novel continues the main tradition of Russian literature. But even more than Tolstoy's and Dostoevsky's
work it is shaped in opposition to its society. His great predecessors were provoked, each in his own way, to denounce
the implications of nineteenth-century science with its tendency to absolve the human being of responsibility for his
acts, Tolstoy taking his stand on the rationalistic ethics of
eighteenth-century thought, Dostoevsky on the theological
position of man's relation to his God. Their purpose was to

show the contradiction and the implicit hypocrisy of a society which, professing to be Christian, behaved in a way that reversed the tenets of Christianity; Pasternak's has been to re-examine the implications of Christianity itself in a society that is based on a rejection of it. And when, in his re-examination, he defines its central ideas as free individuality, he sees this as an echo, or another expression, of that which lies at the heart of all aspects of life: of history, ethics, metaphysics, and aesthetics, as well as of theology. Thereby his society stands condemned, not merely as a social experiment but as a system that attempts to destroy the spiritual life of man, to revoke his progress, and to return to the primitive barbarism of pre-Christian civilization. This is a much more radical criticism than that of any of his predecessors.

From the standpoint of Soviet officialdom, the violent resentment to his novel is entirely justifiable. But apart from immediate issues, above the barriers of political controversy, *Doctor Zhivago* must be acknowledged to be, in both form and substance, one of the most original works of modern times; rare in the depth and scope of its probing into the intellectual and moral assumptions on which society is built; complex and superbly integrated, even though, like *War and Peace,* it may, on a first reading, appear to be amorphous. Its integration is not the integration of allegory, a species of riddle with a hidden but specific solution that presupposes two distinct and separate realms of being, one of which is assumed to be capable of representing the other. Such mechanical ingenuities have no place in the intricate unity of Pasternak's conception. When he writes that "the direct speech of feeling is allegorical and cannot be replaced by anything," he means that emotion has no one recognizable aspect and must be expressed obliquely, but this does not mean that there is an absolute equivalent between what is said and what is meant, which the reader is invited to discover. No, Pasternak's world is complex and whole; much is mysterious in it, but nothing is "veiled." And Yurii Zhivago, during those few nights of gratuitously given happiness in Varykino, summing up his life in sparse, concentrated verse, can understand much, but not all, that he has lived through, interpret something and wonder at a good deal more, and must yet stay in the dark about the rest, the vast remainder which he may not even wonder at because he cannot know it at all. In this he is simply himself and "stands for" nothing other than himself, but there is no one who might not read in him something of his own condition and even that of every man.

CONCLUSION

"'Out to the street! It's shameful to stay at home!'" the revolutionists had shouted for fifty years, going from house to house and rapping on every door, wrote Gershensohn in *Vekhi* in 1909. "And each and every consciousness ran to the public square, limping, blind, armless; not one remained at home." For fifty years the Russian mind had grown "so used to stopping away from home that there was nothing left for it to do but to knock about in the public square, though it had no business there whatever." A guilty, vagrant conscience drove thought into the crowd, where it listened to what went on "from behind the backs of strangers, or didn't even listen at all." That the Russian intellectual lived *outside himself* was, said Gershensohn, the root of spiritual illness, the reason that nine-tenths of the Russian intelligentsia were neurasthenics: "restless," "misshapen" people, "either embittered or distressed," some kind of hidden dissatisfaction deforming them all. From the time of Peter the Great's reforms, "an individual's sense of will" and his consciousness had been torn apart, and this cleavage had become the norm in Russia, had been taken indeed as "the standard of holiness, as the only path to the soul's salvation," so that "a historian would not be wrong in studying the life of Russian society along two distinct lines: manners and customs, on the one hand, thought, on the other," for the two "have had almost nothing in common." All is "dirt, beggary, chaos" within, but "the master," the intellectual, is not "at home"; he is "busy elsewhere . . . among people . . . saving the masses," which is "easier and more interesting" than setting himself to rights. He has filled himself up with "all manner of truths, necessary and unnecessary," and it is no wonder that the history of Russian thought is divided "not into stages of internal development" but of domination by "one or another foreign doctrine: Schellingism, Hegelianism, Saint-Simonism, Fourierism, Positivism, Marxism, Nietzchianism, Neo-Kantianism, Mach, Avenarius, Anarchism—every stage has a foreign name." But the failure of the revolution of 1905, in Gershensohn's opinion, taught the intelligentsia a lesson. It liberated the mind from "the hypnosis of public opinion," the human personality suddenly "found itself free," and having recognized his errors, the intellectual would no longer be divided "between the *I* and the *we*"; thenceforth "every objective blessing would become for him a personal necessity."

These strictures, though not the optimistic conclusion, are borne out in the history of Russian literature, which even in its Golden Age was dominated by specifically humanitarian demands. At the end of the nineteenth century and the beginning of the twentieth, there was, it is true—with Symbolism in poetry and Formalism in criticism—a notable protest to the imposition on art of purely social criteria. "In essence, the Formalist method is simple," wrote Shklovsky. "It is a return to craftsmanship. Its most significant element is that it does not deny the ideational content of art, but considers this so-called 'content' as one of the manifestations of form." The superb studies which the Formalist school produced were at once meticulous and imaginative, their provocative new insights and theories rising out of minute examinations of literary texts. Gershensohn was not one of the Formalists; he thought himself a historian of literature rather than a critic, but his studies, which attempted to re-create living moments of the past, shared the Formalists' high respect for precision, for an approach to art that was scientific in its accurate investigation of data. In all kinds of ways, Russian literature at the turn of the century and down to the Bolshevik Revolution seemed bent on modifying the traditional emphasis on those "external" values which Gershensohn deplored, as well as the lax generalizations of Romanticism. It was this, no doubt, that had frightened Gorky when he wrote Chekhov: "Do you know what you are doing? You are killing Realism." And for his part, addressing himself not to the writers, but the vast illiterate population of Russia, and doing his best to arrest the new trend, he elaborated and propounded the theory of Socialist Realism. His followers, such as Leonov, and Sholokhov in part, have transformed what was formerly a demanding social interest into the law of Social Command, much more rigidly interpreted than the sense in which OPOYAZ had used it. What was formerly a habit of living on the street away from home, an inclination to vagrancy, has become a requirement. The vagrant conscience is now the hallmark of respectability. All three—that is, Gorky, the educator, Leonov, the imitator, and Sholokhov, the man of his own people—have so accustomed themselves to the public square that it seems natural to them to live there. Their consciences find themselves at home *outside themselves,* in crowded places. Blok, on the other hand, forces himself out, but does not venture far from home nor does he ever lose sight of it; Mayakovsky rages on the streets, calling to poets to join him, and dies for want of the private room he has willfully denied himself. Pasternak, the freest, wisest spirit of them all, is always at home, wherever he may be.

An ageless quarrel is involved in this debate between the public and the private voice, and it has become acute. With all their differences, writers of the nineteenth century were not such poles apart as those of the twentieth, not even Tolstoy and Dostoevsky. When Dostoevsky's Underground Man refused to accept "the wall" of mathematical law, arguing that if it suited him $2 \times 2 = 5$ would do as well as $2 \times 2 = 4$, he was insisting, in the teeth of science and all rational abstractions, on the individual's right to believe whatever it pleased him to believe; it was not to the mind he was objecting, but to the universal laws imposed by rational philosophy. But Tolstoy, in the days of *Childhood, Boyhood and Youth* and *War and Peace,* resenting the intrusion of analytic reason upon a world he wanted to grasp immediately, sensuously and concretely, denouncing therefore the very processes of rationality, advocated precisely that "empiric philosophy" by which, according to Santayana, "we feel dispossessed of our nature and cramped in our life." Nevertheless, for both Tolstoy and Dostoevsky, the impact of the world upon their senses and their minds was basic. Neither of them lived "outside himself," not even when in later years they engaged in didactic and journalistic work. Their public voice was the echo of their most intimate lives. They proclaimed to others the conclusions to which they had first arrived through the agonizing experience of their private selves.

But Socialist Realism is the aesthetics of the vagrant conscience, that well-meaning conscience of men of good will, so ubiquitous in the history of the Russian intelligentsia, whose desire to improve the human condition has, in the familiar pattern of modern times, run full circle from service to tyranny. The vagrant is now king; he rules in the square and persecutes those who stay at home. He has sycophants, of course, but he has critics also. And of these none has been more perceptive than Boris Pasternak, whose work is a detailed, comprehensive, and eloquent rebuttal of the official argument that has left no phase of it unanswered, just as his life and personality were embodiments of his independence and courage. Among his contemporaries, while Gorky lectured and Mayakovsky raged, while Blok wept, Leonov smiled, and Sholokhov gritted his teeth and clenched his fists, Pasternak listened and observed, and having pondered, explained what he saw in the unprejudiced, uncommitted voice of reason that reminded one of his great predecessors. Its timbre was neither Pushkin's, Dostoevsky's, Chekhov's, nor Tolstoy's, but like theirs it addressed itself to men with passion and authority, not from the public platform but from the home of its artistic conscience, where, schooled in the difficult task of perfect honesty and self-knowledge, it had grown accustomed to the most intransigent of all audiences, its own exacting self. That is why, although one of the most original writers of the twentieth century, and without question the most original in modern Russia, he is also the one who is closest to that main tradition of Russian literature, which is generally known as Russian Realism.

This realism has always been differentiated from that of the West in being less "descriptive" and more "philosophic," more "subjective" and "idealistic," which is another way of saying that, more than their European counterparts, its practitioners were involved in an interpretation of the reality they presented. And indeed, from the days of *Eugene Onegin*—that lyrical novel in which Pushkin dramatized his ethical convictions and his philosophy of art—Russian fiction, and even much of Russian poetry, steered a middle course between involvement and detachment. Taking its origin in European Romanticism, but always aware of vital differences between its own nation and those from which it borrowed, Russian literature was, almost from the first, essentially critical, analytically detached in weighing the values of East and West, but passionately earnest. Its special distinction came to be, therefore, a tendency to express actuality in terms of philosophical ideals. Theology, ethics, metaphysics were the backdrop that made Pushkin's, Tolstoy's or Dostoevsky's characters stand out in the relief of living creatures. They lived, these imaginary creations, in an atmosphere of infinitely varied experience; they made discoveries about humanity and nature, and dared to test the usually unquestioned, the almost axiomatic concepts of Western civilization. They were not flat, as characters are flat when they are merely described within a palpable, strictly "historic" setting, and only part of them is shown, because they are no more than looked upon and commented on; when their gestures, actions, and thoughts do not point to that boundless and timeless realm of being, where, as E. M. Forster puts it, "great chords begin to sound," so that they are capable of amusing, informing, satisfying curiosity, but not of quickening echoes from the past to ring out into the future. By the time of Chekhov and Gorky, the palpable setting had almost filled the writer's vision, blotting out philosophic questions and convictions. Chekhov complained that his work was fragmentary, that there was no single idea by which it might be held together, that unlike his predecessors, he was not able to call on men to follow him along the road of some great vision.

The changes in intellectual attitudes that were beginning to take place in Chekhov's day, and continued to the October Revolution, were as radical and disturbing as the upheavals of nineteenth-century thought. How radical and how disturbing is demonstrated in a brilliant little work that came into being quite accidentally in 1920. At that time Gershensohn, who eleven years earlier had edited *Vekhi*, found himself sharing a room in Moscow with the poet Vyacheslav Ivanov in a "Health House," or sanitarium, reserved by the Soviet government in those difficult years for writers and artists who were ailing, or merely needed a rest.

In their room, to the left of the door [wrote another poet, Vladislav Khodasevich, who shortly before their departure was in his turn admitted to the establishment], stood Gershensohn's bed, next to it, a small table. In the opposite corner, diagonally, near the window were Vyacheslav Ivanov's bed and table. In the corner of the ever restless Gershensohn reigned a neat orderliness: the bed well made, a few, carefully placed objects on the table. At the Hellenist Vyacheslav Ivanov's, everything was in a jumble:

piles of books, papers and cigarette butts beneath a layer of ashes and dust; under the books—a hat, on top of the books—a package of tobacco, ripped open.

Ivanov was translating Dante's *Purgatorio*. Every afternoon he would read to Gershensohn what he had done that morning, and Gershensohn, the original text in hand, would comment on his work. They fell into an argument about the meaning of culture, and finding that they expressed themselves best in writing, sent each other twelve letters across the room, which they later published as *A Correspondence Between Two Corners*.

Their discussion ranged over history, religion, metaphysics; and in all departments their views were irreconcilable, so divergent were the values and assumptions with which they started. The basic differences between them were the issues of individuality and generalization, concreteness and abstraction, the question as to which was the more valid source of knowledge: a man's immediate and wholly personal experience; or doctrine, which, according to Ivanov, was the embodied wisdom of the past. Ivanov was at home in speculative conflict and fond of intellectual skirmishing, but to Gershensohn these were burdensome, a mist of endlessly debated theories, in which all thoughts were echoes, all concepts derivative, any freshness of vision, feeling, or knowledge impossible; they blurred the senses, dulled the mind, constricted the individual. To Ivanov, on the other hand, individuality was not negated by the Absolute. God made His home in him, and was incomprehensible to his reason. God "has not only created me but is perpetually creating and will re-create me," he wrote. To which Gershensohn replied that he, too, knew "the individual to be the vessel of authentic reality," that he admired the skill and grace of Ivanov's speculative flights, but that he himself disliked soaring "mentally to metaphysical heights"—which was "a vain and hopeless business," an "oppressive" business, for these "transcendental speculations" were "invariably summed up" in logical systems, which weighed him down like heavy, stifling clothes. He wanted to cast them off and,

plunging into Lethe, forgetting "all religions and philosophic systems, all sciences, arts, poetry," to "step out naked
on the shore . . . remembering of the past one thing only:
how heavy and stifling had been those garments, and how
light it was without them." He could accept only what he
had himself "attained in living experience." The rest, the
accumulated, inherited knowledge of his ancestors, was
"general and alien . . . a dusty curtain between me and
my happiness, my pain, my every thought." What did he
himself really know, apart from what his forebears had told
him he could know? For a hundred years philosophy had
been dominated by the belief that man projected himself
upon his world, that he could know only himself. And now
that empiric reality was accepted again, still and all the
Kantian categories of time, space, causality remained "a
linear network on a map," inherent not in the world but
in man's consciousness, which imposed them on experience.
"The nightmare of illusion still envelops reason in the spi-
derweb of madness." Abstract reason tempted one with its
discoveries of objective truth, and this temptation was
"more coercive than coercion." And it was not metaphysics
alone, but "our entire culture," whose fine exhalations had
interpenetrated all existence, that had "corrupted, weak-
ened, deformed our spirit." The cultural heritage had entered into men; it weighed them down "with the weight of
sixty atmospheres"; only a genius could break through it.
"I do not know," he wrote, "but I believe that another
creativity is possible, and another culture, which does not
immure all knowledge within dogma, does not dehydrate
every blessing into a mummy and every value into a fetish."

To Ivanov, the student of history and the Symbolist poet,
mummies and fetishes still breathed the life of their original
creators; and Gershensohn, he said, was but another Faust
whom Mephistopheles could tempt with flowering meadows
and virgin copses, or another Rousseau yearning for primitivism. To himself, culture was not "a plain of ruins nor
a field sown with bones. It contained something truly sacred:
it was the memory not only of the fathers' earthly and outward visage, but also of the consecrations they achieved."

It was "a living, eternal memory," and it was not remembrance, but oblivion, that killed. "Let us believe in
the life of the spirit," he called to Gershensohn,

in sacredness and dedication . . . and let us go briskly forward,
without looking around or looking back. . . . One can be a
happy wanderer on earth, without leaving one's native city. . . .
And so, unconcerned and curious, let us, like strangers, walk past
the countless altars and idols of a monumental culture, some of
which lie in neglect and some are restored and newly adorned,
stopping when we will to sacrifice in forgotten places, where we
see unfading flowers, which, invisibly to men, have grown out
of some ancient tomb.

"You are a siren," Gershensohn wrote back. But he did
not trust the siren's song. He did not believe that memory
united the votary of truth with the "initiations" of the
fathers. Any creation lived only once, in its inception; after
that it was gone, metamorphosed into a general value and
used by the public for its own purposes. What had once
been a simple prayer later became Religion. "What used to
be the need of my heart [was later] declared to be my
sacred duty." The "full truth" of *Hamlet* or the Sistine
Madonna had "bloomed only once," in Shakespeare and
in Raphael. The original creation was indivisibly part of the
artist. Then it was placed upon a throne, on the stage, or in
a museum; it became an objective value, a despot, a fetish.
"Out of many *Hamlets* and Sistine Madonnas," the abstraction, Art, was made. And so it was with other generalities: Property, Morality, the Church, Religion, Nationality,
Culture. "Fleshless and invisible," these abstractions were
"something like legal personalities in the kingdom of values."
They lived on the concrete, they were vampires; and they
prevented Gershensohn, these fetishes and vampires, from
getting at the "full truth," at the initial creativeness, for
which he yearned.

Ivanov could not understand all this. To him all creations
were symbolic. Words were symbols of experience: "Inward
experience has a verbal expression; it seeks it, and longs for
it, because out of the heart's abundance do the lips speak

forth." He was "used to wandering in 'the forest of symbols' "; a word was symbolic, like "the kiss of love"; and a
cultural heritage was "a living treasure-house of gifts," a
source of endless veneration: of things and persons, of
man's creation and his labor, and of his "outraged dignity."
Gershensohn, he said, was arguing for the wrong kind of
simplification, not that of mathematics, which was a way of
reducing complexity to the greater perfection of unity (for
which the Russian word is *uprostit'*), but for the Rousseauistic or Tolstoyan simplification (*oprostit'sya*), which was a
return to primitivism. The savage took no delight in his
vapid freedom, neither did the man who "simplified" himself in the image not of God, but of the savage. Man must
become more and more clearly aware of himself as "forgotten and self-forgotten god." If one were to keep oneself
from being but "a gloomy guest" upon this earth, Ivanov
concluded, there was "one way only—a fiery death in the
spirit. *Dixi.*"

Gershensohn wrote the final letter, a conciliatory but
melancholy comparison of their differences. He did not believe Ivanov's assertion that culture would come full circle
to its primary sources, drawing us to them on a hidden current like those in the depths of oceans. Besides, there was a
contradiction in Ivanov's argument: either culture proceeded inevitably on its way in an elemental evolution, or
the individual must himself transcend it "in a fiery death of
the spirit." Yes, they differed deeply in their relations to
their world. Mine is "a dual life," wrote Gershensohn. From
childhood at home in Western culture, liking to discuss
cultural themes with friends and acquaintances, "really interested in these themes," and yet, "in the depths of consciousness," a "secret voice," repeating "ceaselessly, insistently: that is not it, not it." Something in him longed to
turn away from culture. He was bored, as if all that was
said and done around him were a "wrestling with phantoms,
a surging about in emptiness." And so he lived "like a
stranger who [had] become adjusted to a foreign land"; he
was fond of the foreigners he lived with and they were
fond of him; he worked "ardently for their well-being, was

pained by their pain, and glad of their gladness"; and yet he
knew himself to be a stranger, and yearned in secret for his
native land, for her "fields . . . her different spring, the
smell of her flowers and the speech of her women." Where
was this land? He did not know and would never know. "I
shall not see her, I shall die in an alien country." But in his
passionate longing he had "no need of railways and international politics"; and all arguments and debates "about
systems . . . about the transcendental and the imminent
God" seemed empty to him. But sometimes he had premonitions of his distant and unknowable homeland; "like a
wanderer in an alien country" who seems to glimpse his
home "in the colors of the sunset or the odor of a flower," he
sensed it

in fields and in woods, in the song of birds and in the peasant
walking behind his plow, in the eyes of children and sometimes
in their words, in a divinely kind smile, in the affection between
man and man, in sincere and unmarketable simplicity, in an occasional flaming word, and an unlooked for verse that cut the
darkness like a lightning flash, and in much, much else—especially
in suffering. . . .

You, my friend [he ended], are in your own country. Your heart
is here, where your home is also, your sky is above this earth.
Your soul is not divided, and this unity enchants me, because
whatever may be its origin, it is itself the color of that land, our
common, future native land. And that is why I think that in our
Father's home the same dwelling is prepared for both of us, although on earth we sit stubbornly each in his own corner and
quarrel about culture.

No philosophic labels can be adequate or appropriate to
this deeply personal and passionate debate, which is not
so much a discussion of opinions as a lyrical expression of
two very different minds and temperaments. To Vyacheslav
Ivanov, with his hieratic love of culture and his view that
objects and events were symbols of a universal and eternal
human spirit, it was impossible to understand Gershensohn's
desire for concreteness, his impatient longing for the fresh
and the immediate. They could only talk together, not an-

swer each other, much less persuade. Gershensohn, concerned with how beliefs are formed and with what he himself, in all honesty, can believe, raises the question as to
whether the deeply personal can ever be communicated
and whether other types of communication, those mental
exchanges that have no meaning to one's inmost self, have
any value at all. It was this question that was making itself
felt in Chekhov's day. However drastic Dostoevsky's argument had been, however convincing Tolstoy's anti-intel-
lectualism, their positions were not so extreme as those of
the next generation. For them, the problem of communi-
cability did not arise. Art was nothing if not communication; human beings were not irremediably cut off from one
another; the most intimate experience could, and should, be
made understandable to others. It was the artist's business
to make it understandable. But, on the other hand, the
artist's home was not the public square. His mind and conscience were legislators, not beggars seeking support beyond the limits of their own "back shop." By the end of the
nineteenth century, the mind's arena had, for many artists,
shifted from the public to the private sphere. Montaigne's
"arrière boutique" became an Ivory Tower; the artist who
immured himself in it looked down on the square, and the
square retaliated by charging him with inhumanity and by
accepting his alienation. Tolstoy, in *What Is Art?*, made
fun of him for being unintelligible, but denounced also
his antithesis, the sociable brother, who filled his work with
extraneous matter, which he thought "interesting."

In the Ivanov-Gershensohn debate it was, curiously
enough, the "difficult" poet who spoke for "humanity," and
the quite understandable historian who insisted on the exclusive validity of personal experience. But this strange
division of emphasis is not uncharacteristic of twentieth-
century thought, in which, among other drastic reversals,
philosophy sometimes tends to poetic concreteness, as in the
"nonsystem" of Existentialism, while the work of such poets
as T. S. Eliot and W. H. Auden is in large measure, like that
of Vyacheslav Ivanov, the poetry of abstract statement. Abstractions, of course, are not necessarily borrowed con-

structs of other minds, nor, conversely, does the graphic detail always derive from the perception of the senses. The personal may be coextensive with the Absolute, abstraction an immediate insight into the ineffable, and the concrete detail may be only an illustration of a universal Truth. That has been the experience and the method of Symbolist poets from Plato to Mallarmé. Among their contemporaries, Ivanov said in one of his letters, his own views would be termed "mysticism" and Gershensohn's "anarchic utopianism" and "cultural nihilism." To us they may appear as "conservatism" and "rebellion," or "traditionalism" and "revolutionism," or "humanism" and "individualism." But whatever the labels, the debate takes place on the stage of the personal and the rational, not in the arena of group action and social purpose—the last liberal debate in Russia on the theme of culture, in which the individual's demands for an unhampered spiritual life and the scholar's reverence for the past are voiced with the urgency of imminent loss. So, at any rate, they sound now—like the despairing cry of those who are about to drown. For now we know that in 1920, weighed down by heavier garments than those Gershensohn wanted to cast off, these values of reverence and self-assertion were on the point of being submerged in the doctrinaire sea of official systems and commands.

Gorky could have no sympathy with either Gershensohn's "anarchism" or Ivanov's abstractions, nor, indeed, with any kind of Absolute; what he meant by the "ideal" which he would give men, because they needed it, he said, was not the kind of metaphysical wholeness which Dostoevsky and Tolstoy projected in their Raskolnikovs and Myshkins, their Karamazovs, Bolkonskys and Bezuhkhovs, but a realizable possibility, a program of reform. Blok's vision was entirely his own, his paths were private; Mayakovsky had a nihilist's scorn of "ideals"; Sholokhov's and Leonov's views are an accepted dogma; and only Pasternak, from a broad intellectual perspective and a sympathetic meditation on man's fate, was able once again to make discoveries about humanity. It was only Pasternak who was able to achieve once more that passionate and wise detachment which had once been characteristic of Pushkin, a rare quality at all times, and never more so than in this century, when partisanship has become almost obligatory everywhere. In the U.S.S.R., with its assumption that a man must be either for or against the true faith, where he is held liable not only for what he says but even for what he does not say, where, that is, silence itself may be punishable, detachment must necessarily be almost nonexistent, and possible only to a genius, who must break through an even denser barrier than that of the ponderous cultural heritage of "sixty atmospheres" which weighed on Gershensohn.

Gershensohn, desiring above all the unambiguous security of immediate perception, was troubled by "the nightmare of illusion." And Chekhov, perhaps, was the last of the Russian artists who, finding illusion unavoidable, would have accepted Maupassant's opinion that Realists should call themselves Illusionists, since each of them could have no more than an illusion of the world, that "the writer has no other mission than to reproduce this illusion faithfully," and that "the great artists are those who impose their particular illusion upon humanity." Since then official proclamations have given clear and easy answers to the once unfathomable questions "What is real?" and "What is true?" By their decree illusion has become logically impossible to the right-minded, unthinkable to "engineers of souls." This assertiveness by fiat, characteristic of totalitarianism, is, of course, extreme; but a fondness for certitude is not new in Russia, whose authors, except for Chekhov, who had no answers, and Pushkin, who weighed them all, have never been distinguished by attitudes of doubt. In modern times, indeed, it is perhaps the quality of absolute conviction, both of dogmatic Communists and of those who answer them, that marks the central difference between Russian and Western literature, between, for example, the troubled questionings of Eugene O'Neill, seeking to explain the conscience of a guilt-ridden age, and the positiveness of Gorky, who levels accusations, but has neither sympathy with, nor interest in, the experience of guilt; or between the poetic certitudes of Pasternak and the analytic probings of Sartre. It is a basic difference. It is the very fabric of national predispositions; its roots lie at the heart of men's traditions and modes of thinking.

Consider Sartre's Roquentin, of *La Nausée*, whose excessive self-consciousness is comparable to that of Dostoevsky's Underground Man, and begins, like his, with an experience of anxiety which he does not understand. But Roquentin's anxiety, unlike the Underground Man's, is occasioned by his relations not to men but to things: to the pebble he holds in his hand and to his own image in the mirror, which shows him, not what Dostoevsky's hero sees, an unattractive, ugly man, but a thing, a disgusting lump of matter. Roquentin needs the security of his room, of the street he sees from his window—familiar things that set his mind at rest, whereas the Underground Man needs no such security, being more sure of himself: he defines himself by a comparison with others and finds that he is intellectually superior to them; he has a sense of superiority that compensates him for his feeling of disgust with himself. In his solitude, he is his own interlocutor, while Roquentin is disturbed because the absence of an audience robs him of the power to narrate. The effect of solitude on Roquentin is to set the world at a distance, to make him extraordinarily sensitive to the appearances of things, and when the objects he observes escape his grasp, like the piece of paper which he cannot manage to pick up, he is acutely distressed: his failure has shown him the limitations of his freedom, and he seeks out stones for comfort—*"Les pierres, c'est dur et ça ne bouge pas."* "What is real," thinks Roquentin, who is writing a biography, the facts or what he himself makes of the facts? Both these unhappy men are involved, that is, in metaphysical speculations, but even here the difference is that the Russian's have a social, the Frenchman's a physical and logical orientation. The Underground Man's introspection is ethical at bottom, and his freedom lies in the realm of the imagination and the will to believe. His fantastical daydreams have to do with his place among men, not objects; and what he questions is human justice and human values, not the reality of things.

These are fundamental distinctions that, broadly speaking, seem to be characteristic of Russian and Western thought, this primary concern, on the one hand, with what men are and how they deal with each other, and on the other, with transcendental problems which they must solve: on the one hand, with questions that are posed to be answered, on the other, with those that are asked just to be proved unanswerable; on the one hand, with solutions, on the other, with hypotheses; on the one hand, with the indubitable reality of lived experience, on the other, with the dubious conclusions of the mind. When Tolstoy ponders the truth of history, he hardly needs to put Roquentin's question as to the reality of facts and of what the mind makes of facts; he demonstrates what he *knows* to be true: that the fact is real, and history a lie. All that is human nauseates Roquentin. He wishes he were "bloodless, lymphless, fleshless"; all that happens seems meaningless to him. If only his own life could be the substance of a song! And as for life, a man tries to live it as if he were narrating, but he should choose: either to live or to narrate. Nothing is more foreign to the customary Russian way of thought, either in the past or the present, than this idea that life is self-dramatization, that nothing can happen except upon the stage. (The more extreme manifestations of the Symbolists, and Mayakovsky's life were tragic exceptions to this rule.) For Sartre as for O'Neill, though for different reasons, the lie is basic; living is lying. The Russians, filled with an unquestioning faith in "the brotherhood of man"—a faith that began with Orthodoxy, passed through Rousseauism, and arrived at Marxism—suspicious, not of the emotions but of the mind, have always fought the falsehood of dramatization. Tolstoy's battle with himself on these grounds is well known, and also his conclusion, that to narrate was not, necessarily, to misrepresent events, but to re-create and communicate the emotions involved in them. It is on the assumption that men live passionately, even in moments of dejection, that life in Russian literature is shown to be meaningful in every stage of its progress, not as with the Existentialists, only from the perspective of its end. So, for example, Dr. Zhivago's sense of fatefulness, of destinies implicit in small objects and commonplace incidents, is always attended by a feeling of the unpredictable and mysterious, never with the boredom of Roquentin's sense of *"déjà vu."* Roquentin's certainty about the future—*"Je vois l'avenir"*— which fills him with revulsion is due to emotional deadness and would be impossible to Tolstoy's, Dostoevsky's, or Pasternak's major characters. Even Pushkin's life-weary Onegin endures his emptiness emotionally, in malice, pride, and scorn; and though he ends, like Roquentin, by gaining what he has lacked, this gain is emotional, not intellectual: Onegin falls in love; Roquentin decides to write a book, which will embody his discovery that *being*, the world of logic and abstract forms, of "the pure and rigid lines" of melodies and circles, transcends the formless, massive, overabundant, oppressive order of *existences*.

Russian literature, traditionally concerned with great issues, with the crucial choices men make in life and their ways of meeting death, has seen these matters in the complex vision of a dual faith (that *dvoyeveriye* which such historians as T. G. Masaryk have traced to the source of Russian thought): on the one hand, a form of Christianity which emphasizes the absolute unity of the human situation, so that no man may with impunity hold himself apart from others, as Raskolnikov and Ivan Karamazov discovered at great cost; on the other, paganism, which has withstood religion and all philosophies, an innate love of life, a sense of community with Nature, a Karamazov passion for "the sticky leaves of spring," a Tolstoyan worship of "the natural," or Gershensohn's desire to throw off the cultural past and step out naked on the shore. To this attitude, intellectualism is irrelevant or inadequate. Since man is conscious of himself primarily as a feeling, not a thinking being, reason is variously discredited: as vain and egotistic by Tolstoy, as evil or useless, by Dostoevsky. To them, and to Turgenev also, the Existential Roquentin's disgust with life, to which the analytic habit of his mind has brought him, would in itself be proof of falseness. Life is a supreme value; nothing can be true that ends in hatred of it or that puts its essence in doubt. Skepticism and negation are evil, because humanity may not be constituted on a principle of self-doubt and self-destruction. If reason can lead to such conclusions, it contradicts the innate, irrational, indubitable experience of the senses and emotions, and is, therefore, false. It is precisely that "gluey" property of existence, as Iris Murdoch calls it, which nauseates Roquentin, that delights Tolstoy and Dostoevsky and their heroes; the sticky objects are ultimately real, and they are enchanting. To know them through the senses, unperverted by the artificialities of thought and habit, is to have true judgment, to be like Natasha Rostov, who in the wisdom of innocence can understand an operatic performance for what it really is, a vicious absurdity. Appearances, the world, that is, as it is apprehended by perceptions, are to Tolstoy a revelation of the real; to Dostoevsky they enter the material of dreams, which are more vivid than anything that can be seen or heard, or of arguments which are as agonized as nightmares and which show man what he is, better than even the most brilliant analytic reason; to Blok they are a gateway to the Beyond. To Pasternak, in a kind of Christian animism, "stubborn and irreducible fact" is not obdurate and inert, but as full of motion as the soul is of passion. To Gorky, Leonov and Sholokhov, the *cogito* of the philosophers does not exist at all. "I perceive" and "I think" are one and the same to them. They *know* what they perceive, and have no need to question the reality of their eminently useful vision. And since there is no discrepancy between what they see and what they accept as true, no questions as to reality, no conflict of duty and desire, no division between the citizen and the artist in them, they are, or at any rate they appear to be, happily integrated beings. They write for their world, and their world applauds them. They have not experienced alienation, and cannot sympathize with any Soviet man who feels estranged from his society, for if he does, it is his own fault, a proof of ill will, a crime against the state.

That "the mind is its own place" is an embarrassment to the Realist, who wants to be assured that his mind is at liberty to pass beyond itself into a realm of truth that has its own reality, that his ideas are not mere fantasies but perceptions of an empiric world. The triumph of the great realists is to persuade one that this is so, that their insights are discoveries about a place beyond their minds, of which everybody knows a little. But their insights are attended by a feeling of infinitude; their discoveries open doors and invite to further ventures. The wonderful concreteness of a Tolstoy, no less than the symbolist vision of a Blok, points to the invisible and is an intimation of limitless possibilities. The tendency of Soviet literature is, on principle, to limit this vision.

Several years ago, in a splendidly perceptive study of realism called *Mimesis*, Erich Auerbach noted some profound differences at the very source of Western literature. In Homer, he pointed out, there was no "perspective in time and place," all phenomena were "completely fixed in their spatial and temporal relations"; the past of Odysseus, for example, was lived on the same plane as the present. Events were immutable and real, whether experienced or remembered. Everything took place in the foreground, in the same bright, even light of knowledge; there was neither shading, flux, nor mystery—only enjoyment of the actual. But in the Old Testament, in the story of Abraham and Isaac for instance, the narrative "was not primarily oriented toward 'realism' but toward 'truth.' " Not a falsification of the real, it was an "inspired" version of the true; it had its shadows and complexities; it was mysterious and sacrosanct. Allowing for the enormous differences of widely separated epochs, something of the same distinction may be said to exist between Russian literature in the nineteenth century and that engendered by Socialist Realism in the U. S. S. R., for the latter, like the divinely dictated story of the Hebrews, is also oriented toward Truth. At any rate, the line between reality and truth is blurred in it and tends to be erased: what must be true is also seen to be real. But since Soviet Truth is humanly accessible, it does not tolerate the mysterious, the irrational, or the fateful; everything in its scheme is clearly explicable in terms of cause and effect. Yet this simplicity is not the lucid, plain eternity of Homeric legend. A kind of embryonic temporal concept, a kind of

rivalry with the past, lurks in the faith that a utopian classless society must, of historical necessity, come into being.
And looking on the past not with the prophet's, but the
reformer's eye, Socialist Realism attempts to create a new
legend of Man, the "axle of the world," and to rewrite or
parody the myths of a "mistaken" past. Gorky's "saintly"
Luke is a scoundrel; Mayakovsky's figure walking upon the
waters is the Most Ordinary Man; and everywhere the
solitary hero of Romanticism is banned. He is banned not
only because his rebellious position is no longer acceptable,
but because a man's inward life cannot now be comparable
in interest and importance to his social role. The unusual
personality, the dreamer of strange dreams, the bold philosopher are suspect. Gorky's heroes, Sholokhov's (except for
Gregory Melekhov), and Leonov's are ordinary men whose
greatness lies in "leadership." Unerringly do they understand the "people's needs," and these needs admit of no
variety, since, being elementary, they are perfectly homogeneous. They are exemplars of right thought and social
behavior; like their creators they make their home in public
squares.

Whatever happens to them, they are not tragic. Sholokhov's Razmëtnov and Nagul'nov wear the nimbus of saintly
martyrdom; their deaths are a pathetic waste, but they
themselves are replaceable, which is precisely what no
tragic hero can be. Tragedy is inadmissible to Socialist
Realism because "engineers of souls" must encourage men,
and also because to show their happy world in anything but
hopeful colors would be unrealistic, "contrary to fact," in
a favorite Soviet phrase. It is true, of course, that Russian
literature was always hopeful, that in the end everything
usually "came out all right" in Russian fiction, even in
Crime and Punishment and *War and Peace*. But if the
novel of "critical realism" was not ultimately tragic, its personages, nevertheless, were. The writer of the nineteenth
century, faced with revelations in science, society, and
philosophy that shook his faith in God and reason, was imbued with the sense of human beings tragically overwhelmed by nonhuman, insuperable, irrational forces. Ras-

kolnikov and Andrey Bolkonsky are tragic figures in spite of their stories' ending happily. Of Chekhov's plays, the question is still open: are they tragedies, as they are usually performed, or comedies, as Chekhov himself insisted that they were? To which the answer is, no doubt, that they are neither, since both comedy and tragedy imply a standard of philosophic certitude by which men's fortunes may be judged, whereas Chekhov held nothing certain and knew only sympathy for unfortunate individuals. All of this is different from Marxist optimism, with its dual view of historic inevitability on the one hand, and the "agency" of man on the other—a philosophy that, translated into literature, results in a kind of Morality play, in which every individual and each event has a role in the universal drama of Everyman, acted out on the unadorned stage of historic fact, without benefit of "aestheticism" or speculation.

G. K. Chesterton once remarked that Byron's gloominess was not to be interpreted as pessimism. "It was merely a recognition of the fact that one cannot write in white chalk except on a blackboard." The theory of Socialist Realism, one may say by way of comparison, enjoins writers to put white on white; thence the flat monotony of its eternally happy productions, and the sharp contrast etched on the prescribed white background by the great tragic figures of fine poets, Blok, Mayakovsky, Pasternak, whose work was neither white, nor black and white, but many-colored, and whose view of themselves as artists contradicted official expectations of them, for even Mayakovsky, however willing, could not tame his wild originality and leash it to a formula. These poets are heroic in a way that negates the concept of their society, to which "heroism" in the old sense has been leveled down to a philosophy of mass achievement, wherein all men are seen as being shaped in the same mold.

"Not only in this room, dear friend," wrote Gershensohn in one of his letters to Ivanov, "but in spirit, we are at the extremes of a diagonal from one another." And Ivanov developed the figure further. "My dear friend, we sojourn in a single cultural environment, just as we inhabit a single room, where each of us has his corner, but where there is but one large window and one door." The six writers who are the subject of this study, so unlike in temperament, upbringing, tastes, and interests, dissimilar, that is, in every respect but one, the accident of their inheritance, inhabit like Gershensohn and Ivanov the corners of a room, the chaotic age into which they were born. From out their window they gaze upon the vista of their literary tradition, and though there is but one door from which they can step out into it, they return with different impressions of it to the corners of their Hexagon at the ends of long diagonals, as long as the diagonal which separated Ivanov and Gershensohn, the great distances of spirit that seem to stretch beyond the temporal, confining boundaries of a historic moment. There is one conviction they all bring back from their wanderings, a love of their language, their land, and their people. They mean different things by "love," however. Gorky ridicules Blok's personification of the country: " 'Russia, my wife.' How do you like that?" he exclaims derisively in a letter. But Blok's feeling for his land was a lyric passion, expressed in descriptions that have never been excelled for grace and beauty. Gorky's, like Leonov's, is an enthusiastic but quite practical appraisal of the country's natural resources. Mayakovsky, with a habitual anthropomorphism, identifies himself with the land; and Sholokhov, like Blok, but not so tenderly, paints splendid, loving portraits of it. As great as any love is Pasternak's, but it is less narrow, experienced, like all his passions, within the framework of a sense of destiny. Love of the Russian people is for Gorky, Sholokhov, and Leonov a competitive, chauvinistic pride in the capacities of their countrymen; for Blok it is loyalty and an attempt to understand; for Mayakovsky a fantastic desire to "serve," a lie of love that led to martyrdom; for Pasternak, a humane sympathy for men caught in "the terrible days" of Russia and a clear-headed view of their mistakes.

If the invitation to the mind's adventures is rejected by the meliorist, to whose utilitarian outlook it is clearly suspect, if Gorky's legendary Danko, or the Satin of his *Lower Depths*, or the Kutuzov of *Klim Samghin* point nowhere beyond the necessity of respecting men as potentially happy workers and dignified citizens; if humanitarianism and common sense are man's ultimate attainments, and if Sholokhov and Leonov cut their poetic vision to fit these useful and sensible criteria—there are poets whose imaginations are not so manageable, as was the case with Mayakovsky, whose gift and nature were a denial of the doctrine he forced upon them and whose fulminations against ostensibly well defined, remediable evils were uttered in the tones of such despair as is usually called forth by terror of the inexplicable and malign.

Our six authors have taken account of Communist dogma each in his own way, and more freely than many less gifted men. Their work as a whole may be seen to exemplify successive stages in the possible reactions to Marxism, from Gorky's decision that it was the most humanitarian of all philosophies to Pasternak's condemnation of it as the least human. From the standpoint of art, their finest achievements either transcend official dogma or are irrelevant to it, or, like *Doctor Zhivago,* are a criticism of it. Gorky is at his best in portraits that belong in the tradition of his literary predecessors and have nothing to do with Marxist theory; Sholokhov's eminence is an ability to communicate the passion of a romantically independent spirit, and Mayakovsky's to paint his own tragic self. The wonder of Blok's poetry is its music and its private vision. Leonov's promise as an artist was early lost in subservience to prescribed ways of thought. And if Gorky is a bridge between the old world and the U.S.S.R., neither he nor his heirs, but Blok, Mayakovsky, and Pasternak are the true innovators in Russian literature and the inheritors of its Great Tradition: Blok of its lyricism, Mayakovsky of its revolutionary fervor, Pasternak, closest of all to Pushkin, to that poet's subtlety and wisdom, grandeur and simplicity.

Seldom, if ever, does the vagrant conscience find itself in art. And there is a mistaken greatness in the decision of such as Gorky to bring their work for judgment to an audience they mean to affect. The artist alone can judge himself, and his true audience comes after him. It is light-years away, as

Ossip Mandel'shtam (a fine, independent poet and critic, who perished, no one knows how, about 1945) once said in an essay called "About the Interlocutor." The poet, he said, does not address himself to anyone in particular; his words are like the drowned man's letter, sealed in a bottle and tossed into the sea; someone, someday, will find it by mere chance and read it.

Why not a living, concrete interlocutor, a "representative of the age" but a "friend in posterity"? I answer: an address to a concrete interlocutor makes a verse wingless, deprives it of air, of flight. A poem's air is unexpectedness. If we address ourselves to the known, we can say only what is already known. . . . Fear of the concrete interlocutor, of the "epoch's" listener . . . has constantly pursued poets in all ages. The more gifted the poet, the more acutely has he suffered from this fear. . . . Thence the proverbial enmity between the artist and society.

It is not the poet, but the literary man, who speaks to his contemporaries. His purpose is to educate. He must be "higher," "better" than society; he requires a pedestal. But "poetry is another matter. The poet is bound only to a providential interlocutor." Mandel'shtam's is a brilliant statement about the individuality of the poet's voice and the independence of his message, about the problematic audience for whom he writes, always implicit but unseen, about the tedium of having to address the actual and the known, about the difference between preaching and talking to an unknown friend beyond the grave.

But Russian poets have always been pressed to become "literary men." At the time of the meeting at Yalta, only Chekhov, of the three, had not yielded to this pressure. He never "addressed" his contemporaries, although all his work was a commentary on them. Tolstoy had by then effected the transformation; the great creator had made himself a preacher. Gorky alone had always been a literary man and never a poet. As for those who followed, Leonov may be said to be, like Gorky, a literary man by nature. The others are all "poets." But Sholokhov has sacrificed poetry to "literature"; Mayakovsky's desperate attempt to make "lit-

erature" of poetry was his doom; and only Blok and Pasternak, at tragic cost, were able to stand their ground against
those ceaseless assaults on poetry which are made by men
whom it makes uncomfortable, who find its unpredictable
ways disturbing, threatening, incomprehensible. Because of
them, the story of modern Russian literature is, perhaps
more acutely than that of any other place and time, the
story of an ominous conflict, as ominous as any that has
been or is being fought, in this warring century. Its issue is
nothing less than human creativity, and like all great battles it has been the occasion for sublimity as well as meanness—in Edmund Wilson's memorable phrase about *Doctor Zhivago,* for "great events in man's literary and moral
history."

INDEX

ABOUT THE AUTHOR

HELEN MUCHNIC'S life has been spent studying and teaching. She was born in Russia, came to
America as a child, attended grade schools and high
schools in Pittsburgh and Brooklyn, and received her
A.B. from Vassar, her Ph.D. from Bryn Mawr. In 1928
she studied at the School of Slavonic Studies of the
University of London with Sir Bernard Pares and D. S.
Mirsky. She has taught at Smith College since 1930,
first in the Department of English, then in the Department of Russian, which was formed in 1945. At Yale in
1943 she gave a course on Russian literature to students of the Army Specialized Training Program, and
at Harvard in 1948 she taught a course on Gogol and
Turgenev. She has published articles on Russian and
comparative literature; a monograph, *Dostoevsky's
English Reputation;* and a book of essays, *An Introduction to Russian Literature.*